Untangling the Income Tax

A Committee for Economic Development Publication

The Committee for Economic Development is an independent research and educational organization of two hundred business leaders and educators. CED is nonprofit, nonpartisan, and nonpolitical and is supported by contributions from business, foundations, and individuals. Its objective is to promote stable growth with rising living standards and increasing opportunities for all.

In issuing statements on national policy, CED often publishes background papers deemed worthy of wider circulation because of their contribution to the understanding of a public problem. This study has been approved for publication as a supplementary paper.

The contents of this volume have not been approved, disapproved, or acted upon by the Committee for Economic Development, the Board of Trustees, the Research and Policy Committee, the Research Advisory Board, the research staff, or any member or adviser of any board or committee, or any officer of CED.

UNTANGLING

the INCOME TAX

David F. Bradford

A Committee for Economic Development Publication

HARVARD UNIVERSITY PRESS
Cambridge, Massachusetts, and London, England

Copyright © 1986 by the President and Fellows of Harvard College
All rights reserved
Printed in the United States of America
10   9   8   7   6   5   4   3   2

Library of Congress Cataloging-in-Publication Data

Bradford, David F.
  Untangling the income tax.

  Bibliography: p.
  Includes index.
  1. Income tax — United States.   I. Title.
HJ4652.B67   1986   336.24′15′0973   85-27078
ISBN 0-674-93040-1 (alk. paper) (cloth)
ISBN 0-674-93041-X (paper)

Design by Gwen Frankfeldt

For Gundel, Theodore, and Lulu

Foreword

TAX POLICY and its impact on the American economy have long been among the central concerns of the Committee for Economic Development. In 1944, two years after CED's founding, the committee issued its first policy statement dealing with tax issues. Subsequently, as the absolute size of the federal government has burgeoned and its impact throughout the economy has escalated, CED trustees have repeatedly probed various areas of federal fiscal policy. In recent years the trustees have become concerned that the U.S. tax structure has grown so complicated and has so distorted the economy that it is a major handicap to U.S. economic performance. Increasingly, policy makers and the public are recognizing that healthy and equitable economic expansion in the future will require a much more disciplined and possibly a restructured tax system. But the very complexity of the tax system and its effects can frustrate its reform.

To help policy makers, the public, and ourselves wrestle with the basic issues in tax reform, CED turned to David Bradford, professor of economics and public affairs at Princeton University and director of tax research for the National Bureau of Economic Research. We commissioned Professor Bradford to prepare an analytical perspective on tax objectives, to synthesize the relevant research on various types of individual and corporate taxes, and to examine the consequences of some of the major options for reform.

Working closely with Dr. Bradford on this effort was a small design committee of CED trustees chaired by Dean P. Phypers, senior vice president of IBM Corporation. Assisted by several experts from business and research institutions, the design committee met frequently with Professor Bradford, commenting on the successive stages of his analysis. The result was this book, which provides an enlightening foundation for participation in today's complicated tax policy debates.

Untangling the Income Tax will be an invaluable resource for business executives, policy makers, tax experts, and citizens concerned with the economic and philosophical tenets of our current tax system and the options for major change. We are pleased to have played a role in its development and are grateful to the Alfred P. Sloan Foundation and the John M. Olin Foundation, whose generous and farsighted support helped to make the project possible.

Robert C. Holland, President
Committee for Economic Development

Acknowledgments

To QUOTE the words with which Henry Simons began his immensely influential book on personal income taxation, *Untangling the Income Tax* "perhaps combines strangely the characteristics of an academic treatise and a tract for the times." In early 1984 the Committee for Economic Development asked me to prepare a long paper on the principles of income tax reform. To be developed in consultation with a committee of CED trustees and expert advisers, the manuscript was intended to help CED and the general public sort out positions on the proposals for sweeping change in the income tax that were just beginning to emerge. The intent was to produce a manuscript rather quickly, in order to keep pace with the rapid political developments. But it proved beyond my power to say what I thought needed to be said either quickly or in the compass of a long paper. Instead, this not exactly short book resulted. Aimed at the student of taxation as well as the educated lay reader, it aspires to serve the functions of both treatise and tract.

Many people deserve thanks for their assistance in the preparation of *Untangling the Income Tax*. High on the list are officers of the Committee for Economic Development: Robert C. Holland, president; Sol Hurwitz, senior vice president; Frank W. Schiff, vice president and chief economist; and Claudia P. Feurey, vice president and director of information. All of them steadfastly encouraged me as the project evolved from its original conception. Equally supportive were Dean P. Phypers and the other members of the design committee of CED trustees. Working with them was, as they say, a privilege and a pleasure. I learned a great deal from all of them — and we had a marvelous time besides.

The advisers to the design committee included experts on taxation who were extremely helpful, and I should like to acknowledge particularly my former Treasury associate, Harvey Galper, along with Emil M. Sunley, James Hanson, and his Exxon colleague, Leslie Cookenboo, who provided detailed commentary on the early drafts. At a later stage Laurence J. Kotlikoff and Alvin C. Warren, Jr., read versions of the complete manuscript and gave me much useful advice.

Several people aided me with specific aspects of the book. A Princeton colleague, Pete Kyle, helped me see equivalences among apparently different tax systems that I think will surprise some readers. Seymour Fiekowsky and Jon Hakken of the U.S. Treasury Department clarified several issues related to tax expenditures. Princeton graduate students Andrew Lyon and Richard Rosen provided imaginative research assistance on issues of the lifetime burden of taxes and the quantitative importance of gifts and bequests, and Colby College student Kate Lucier helped pull the numbers together for the statistical appendix. Avinash Dixit and Jennifer Hochschild brought particularly amusing epigraphs to my attention. The book also benefited from the attention of two talented copy editors, Jacqueline Dormitzer and Patricia R. Murray.

No brief list can do justice to all those who have shared in a project such as this book: I hope the many unnamed here, including professional colleagues and several individuals at CED and at Harvard University Press, will not conclude that I am ungrateful. And of course no one cited should be blamed for errors or other shortcomings that remain in the finished work.

D.F.B.

Contents

Untangling the Income Tax

I can't make a damn thing out of this tax problem. I
listen to one side and they seem right, and then—God!
— I talk to the other side and they seem to be
right . . . I know somewhere there is a book that will
give me the truth, but I couldn't read the book. I know
somewhere there is an economist who knows the truth,
but I don't know where to find him and haven't the
sense to know him and trust him when I find him.
God! what a job.

Warren G. Harding conversation, 1922; reported in Joseph R.
Conlin, *The Morrow Book of Quotations in American History*

Introduction

1

We recommend the passage of . . . [the] income tax . . . in the confident belief that as soon as this tax and its administrative machinery become fairly understood by the people . . . [it] will meet with as much general satisfaction as any tax law . . . All good citizens, it is therefore believed, will willingly and cheerfully support and sustain this, the fairest and cheapest of all taxes.

Committee report on the Act of October 3, 1913 (establishing the income tax), U.S. House of Representatives

TAXES will always be with us. So, it appears, will income tax reform. The 1980s have been busy years for tax legislators. The decade began with a law with the grand title, the Economic Recovery Tax Act (ERTA) of 1981. This law was supposed to work miracles upon the American economy by cutting tax rates and introducing measures to encourage investment in the United States. Then in 1982 came the Tax Equity and Fiscal Responsibility Act (TEFRA), reversing some of the policies adopted in 1981 and claiming to improve the fairness of the income tax and to attack the growing deficit. In 1984 we had the Tax Reform Act (referred to as DEFRA, because it was one of two divisions in a law with the overall title of Deficit Reduction Act), an enormously complex piece of legislation, trying again to make the tax law fairer and to generate a little revenue to counter the huge deficits that appeared on the federal books after ERTA. And although as these words are being written the drafting ink is hardly dry on DEFRA, and implementing regulations for many of its provisions are months and years in the future, the Congress is once again grappling with an ambitious program of reform, probably the most ambitious ever.

Indeed, the 1980s have been good years for the income tax reform industry, but then, so were the 1970s. Remember the Tax Reduction and Reform Act of 1976 (known to cynics as the Lawyers and Accountants Relief Act), and after that President Jimmy Carter's efforts to fix a system he labeled a "disgrace to the human race"? Why is it so difficult for the country to settle on a stable system? An important part of the answer is the prevailing lack of understanding of the basic principles by which tax rules do their work. The object of this book is to remedy that situation, to assist readers to untangle the complicated system we call the federal income tax. Those who work through these pages will, I hope, come away better prepared to reach conclusions about tax policy based on sound logic and facts. They will, I hope, have a better sense of what questions can be answered with reasonable confidence and will recognize the rather large amount we do not know about the ultimate effects of tax alternatives. They will, I hope, have an improved appreciation for the forces that drive tax change. And maybe, understanding better how the rules work, they will even be able to save some money on their own taxes.

Myths, misunderstanding, and confusion abound when it comes to tax policy. Here are some examples:

· The mortgage interest deduction is widely perceived as the major subsidy to home ownership. Actually, the basic subsidy is the exemption from tax of the income that the homeowner realizes in the form of direct services from the home, such as shelter. By making this subsidy more widely available, the mortgage interest deduction probably makes the system fairer.

· Another controversial matter is the deductibility of state and local taxes from income subject to federal tax. It is easy to find individuals who will argue vociferously that this deduction is a regressive feature of the tax law because it can be claimed only by the well-to-do who itemize on their tax returns, with the largest benefits going to those with the highest income. On the other side are those who argue that the deduction is essential to preserve services, such as schooling and police protection and welfare, primarily benefiting the poor. To sort out this dispute requires the tools of the economic theory of tax and spending incidence.

· Most people think we have an income tax because we have a tax with that name. Actually, the so-called income tax is far from one based on the concept of income as understood by tax theory. Technically it is a mixture of a consumption-based system and an income-based system. The mixture is less effective than either purer approach would be.

· There are many myths about the relative merits of income and consumption taxes. It seems to be generally believed that a consumption tax would have to look like a retail sales tax, whereas there are actually many ways to tax on the basis of consumption, and some of those ways look like what we call an income tax. Consumption taxes are often thought to be regressive; in fact, they can be as progressive as one wants. Consumption taxes are supposed to be a good way to get at the underground economy; in fact, there is little basis for this belief. Consumption taxes are supposed to be good for U.S. exports; in fact, economics offers little support for this view.

· The corporation income tax is the subject of quite varied opinions. Some people think it is a tax on the well-to-do. Some people think it is like a flat tax on the sales of all corporations. Many — even *Wall Street Journal* reporters — appear to think it may not be paid by people at all but rather by a disembodied sector of the economy called "business." No economist would make the last mistake, and it is easy to show that the corporation tax is not the same as a sales tax. It is less easy to say with confidence who actually bears the burden of the tax.

· Some large and profitable corporations pay little or no income tax. Most people think this is a sign of the inequity of our income tax system. Actually it is, if anything, a sign of the inefficiency created by our income tax, and it may not even be bad. It has little, if anything, to do with the fairness of the way the system distributes tax burdens among people.

These are but a few instances that might be cited of the confusion about taxes that inhibits formulation of comprehensible and stable rules. Consider the following rather remarkable declaration, included in the report of the Senate Finance Committee on its work on the Tax Reform Act of 1984:

The committee believes that the current system of income taxation is unduly complex. The large number of tax preferences and special deductions, credits and exclusions increase compliance and administration costs, and undermine the taxpayers' confidence in the fairness of the Internal Revenue Code. Non-uniform taxation distorts individual and corporate economic decisions, thereby lowering economic efficiency. For these reasons it is desirable to study the effects of a more comprehensive tax base. Broadening the base also would allow a reduction in marginal rates, which would increase the incentive to work and invest. The committee believes that alternatives which increase the simplicity, efficiency and fairness of the tax system should be carefully studied.   (U.S. Senate, 1984, p. 931)

That no one seems to have detected the irony in this passage — an addendum to yet another another long and complicated revision of the income tax — is itself a commentary on the confusion about tax policy in the United States.

Certainly, as of 1985 the law is complex. The Internal Revenue Code fills hundreds of pages; the regulations required to implement the statute occupy several thick volumes. A torrent of rulings and other interpretations emerges from the tax law enforcement system but still lags behind the continually changing statute. At least three major publications compete for the business of tax advisers with *daily* reporting on tax developments. The Tax Reform Act of 1984, which gave rise to the Senate Finance Committee observations quoted above, was the third major attempt in four years to fine-tune the system; it was 590 pages long.

Complexity means different things to people in different economic circumstances. The "common man" may distrust the income tax system because it is so hard to understand, although he may not have much direct experience of its complications. For the proverbial ordinary citizen, direct compliance with the income tax law is fairly simple. Such a person, whose income is from wages or salary, with perhaps a few dollars of dividends or interest, does not itemize deductions and therefore can file a simple tax form (1040EZ or 1040A). Most tax is withheld at source. The common man needs no more to understand the complicated tax law than to understand the complicated laws regulating banks. However, just as stories about $500 hammers weaken public confidence in the nation's defense system, stories about millionaires' and multinational corporations' taking advantage of special provisions of the law to eliminate their tax liabilities undermine support for the tax system. Although the facts (or at least some of the facts) imply that the income tax remains quite progressive, the law's complexity makes it easy for the common man to believe that "other people," especially the rich, are not paying their fair share.

The "middle-class man" has to cope directly, either as an individual or as a member of a business firm, with the law's more arcane features. Rising real incomes and the bracket creep brought about by inflation through the 1970s and 1980s have pushed middle-income taxpayers into significantly higher marginal rate brackets. Consequently taxes have come to be a significant element in such choices as whether to install insulation, to renovate an old building, to hire a worker from the welfare roles, to purchase life insurance, to contribute to a religious or charitable organization, or to buy a house. In business and financial affairs, taxes are even more complicated and more important. Incorrectly structuring a corporate distribution or investment can have enormous consequences for tax liabilities. Tax considerations have much to do with the profitability of most merger and takeover transactions. Many have heard about, though few understand, tax shelters, safe-harbor leasing, unused tax-loss carry-forwards, zero-coupon bonds, and so on.

A kind of vicious circle has been at work, with complexity breeding more complexity. Special exemptions and credits give rise to complicated rules, and, because they imply that higher rates of tax must be employed, they create pressure for still other special exemptions and credits. Thus, at a low rate of tax it is not very important to a wage earner whether health benefits are included as part of income subject to tax. But at a high rate of tax the dollars at stake in the policy toward health benefits become significant. As tax rates rise, so does the potential payoff to efforts to obtain a favorable policy for any given interest group. Sometimes these quests are successful, at the cost of yet higher tax rates and a more complex law.

The Senate Finance Committee also noted the problems of inefficiency induced by badly designed tax rules. In 1985 the income-measurement rules do, indeed, suffer from inconsistency, by which I mean they prescribe very different tax consequences for transactions that are economically very similar. For example, in deriving the income of a business, it is necessary to subtract allowances for the depreciation of assets employed in the operation. These allowances are governed by statute. In the case of some assets, such as machinery used in manufacturing, the law provides for a write-off over a period considerably less than the actual span of time over which the machinery is used. In some cases, an investment tax credit — that is, a subsidy that can only be used to offset tax liability — is granted in addition. Other assets, such as inventories, receive no special preference. Furthermore, inflation grossly compounds measurement problems. For example, interest is partly compensation for the use of funds and partly a premium for the purchasing power lost to inflation by lenders (and gained by borrowers). But interest receipts are nonetheless taxed as income, and interest payments are fully deductible. Better known, and equally important, is the mismeasurement of capital gains and depreciation allowances in a time of inflation. (These problems are explained in detail in subsequent chapters.)

Although the corporation tax has diminished in importance as a source of revenue, it remains a source of distorting incentives, almost completely uncoordinated with the tax on individuals. The spread between the earnings before all taxes on a corporate investment and the yield after all taxes obtained by the provider of finance varies over an

enormous range. The consequences for the distribution of the tax burden are virtually unknown; we can be sure, though, that considerable
waste results from the effect of the tax on the allocation of investment
resources.

It is not only the separate corporation tax that distorts incentives. An
income tax inevitably changes (and usually diminishes) incentives to
work, to save, to take risks, and to seek technological innovation. Although it is unlikely that lowering all tax rates would increase the
revenue yield of the tax system, as the more extreme supply-side proponents have claimed, there is little doubt that making more consistent
the tax burden on productive activities of all kinds would result in
improved economic performance.

Although the situation may be getting worse, these problems are not
altogether new, and they have resisted correction for a long time. For all
its patchwork quality, the income tax system has not reached its present
condition entirely by accident. Tax law is based on statutes enacted by a
democratically elected Congress, not on commandments from a higher
authority. Because change in almost any provision of the law would
raise somebody's tax liability, essentially all provisions have some de-
fenders. The same polltakers who in 1985 record so much dissatisfaction
with the income tax, so much desire for simplification and lower rates,
also record the fierce reaction of people to any threat to "their" preferences, whether it is deductible mortgage interest or tax-free medical
insurance. Legislators, faced with a top-to-bottom reform proposal by
the Reagan administration, find among their constituents a generalized
desire for a simplified, lower-rate tax but little tolerance for the many
specific changes that would be required to attain those goals. The politicians fear that they would gain very little support from the many constituents for whom tax reform would not mean tax reduction.

Another impediment to change is the very pervasiveness of the effects
of tax rules on our lives. Major changes in the rules, even those designed
to maintain the existing degree of progressivity of the income tax, cause
redistributions of wealth in the course of transition. The fact that such
effects occur only once does not make losses any less painful to those
who suffer them or gains any less welcome to those who enjoy them.
This is why individual taxpayers and their representatives (for example,
the managers of firms) so energetically defend existing breaks and so
actively pursue new ones.

Finally, the American political process — perhaps any earthly political process — is biased against a simple tax system. Very simple rules
would not permit the sort of detailed economic management —

encouraging firms to increase outlays on research and development, for example — in which political leaders often engage. Moreover, to remain in office politicians are under constant pressure to deliver special provisions that advance the interests of their constituents and supporters. This often leads to narrow, special-interest laws that conflict with simplicity.

It is my thesis that the key to understanding the income tax, and to improving it, is a clear grasp of the meaning of income. No doubt the framers of the U.S. income tax themselves were unaware of how elusive and controversial the idea would prove to be when they wrote the lines quoted at the beginning of this chapter. There is nothing like money at stake to reveal the soft points of a definition. In fact, the concept of income is neither straightforward nor free of controversy. Furthermore, the dominant technical definition, referred to in this book as "accrual income," proved to be much more difficult to apply in designing practical, enforceable rules than was anticipated. For reasons that will be elaborated upon in due course, the practical income tax has had to employ income-measurement rules that diverge from the abstract principle in many ways.

What we call an income tax is a blend, or hybrid, of an accrual-income concept and a consumption concept. Under an accrual-income system all the accretions to wealth during a period — whether showing up in cash flow or simply in accruing growth in value (hence the name) — would be included in income subject to tax. In the actual system, some types of saving are actually deducted from current income, and both the saved amount and the return on it are subjected to tax only after a period of years. Contributions to pension plans are a good example. The returns on other forms of saving, such as capital gains, are subjected to tax at special rates, or are not taxed at all, as in the case of municipal bonds. Both sorts of rules — not including sums in taxable income until they are drawn on for consumption purposes or not taxing the return on amounts put aside — are more or less those that would be required to implement a tax based on the part of income that is consumed rather than saved.

Many analysts — I among them — have advocated that the tension in the existing income tax between accrual-income and consumption-type rules should be resolved by placing the system on a consistent consumption basis. For most people, however, the notion of "consumption tax" is equated with excise taxes on automobiles or jewelry, retail sales taxes, or a value-added tax. Depending on the technical details of their design, those taxes are, indeed, appropriately included in the list. The idea is much more general, though, extending to taxes that look in many ways like the individual income tax and having much the same potential for tailoring tax burdens to individual circumstances.

In the early part of this book I lay out as carefully as I can exactly how one might go about basing taxes on consistent notions of accrual income or consumption. Both strategies are, I think, possible ones to follow. But what quickly becomes clear is that accrual-income and consumed-income tax rules do not coexist comfortably in the definition of a single tax base. A hybrid income tax system of the sort we now have yields results that are inferior to those produced by either a rigorous adherence to accrual-income principles or a consistent application of consumption-type rules. To choose between the two strategic principles, or to mix them in a way that promises greater simplicity and stability than has been our recent experience, requires careful attention to basic principles.

The appendix at the back of the book contains, among other things, a description of how the changes made in the income tax over the last fifteen years or so, in response to the economic environment of inflation and slow productivity growth, gradually increased the hybrid character of the law. The general thrust of policy over the period was in the direction of alleviating the tax burden on undertaking real investment, through such devices as the Accelerated Cost Recovery System (ACRS) for depreciation, and on certain forms of saving, notably through the Individual Retirement Accounts (IRAs). As I shall explain, these changes can be characterized as movements toward a consumed-income system. But because the taxation of some saving and investment transactions — notably borrowing and lending at interest — was unchanged, the tension between income and accrual accounting rules was exacerbated. This created pressure for further revision. By 1985 a rather sweeping rewrite of the income tax became a serious possibility.

This discussion already allows me to provide a loose catalogue of the various tax plans that have been considered in recent years. Most of them have taken what I call the "traditional base-broadening" approach. Traditional base broadening is an expansion of the hybrid tax base and is typically slanted toward the accrual-income strategy. But it is usually not tightly related to a conceptual structure that would assure consistency and guide the implementing decisions that are the daily reality of the tax system. Its object is simple: by defining more transactions as included within the concept of income subject to tax, either more revenue can be raised at given rates or rates can be lower for a given level of revenue. The major tax laws of 1969 and 1976 can be placed in this category, as can President Carter's ill-fated 1978 proposal. Less comprehensive but in the same category are the Tax Equity and Fiscal Responsibility Act of 1982 and the Tax Reform Act of 1984, passed by Congress and signed by President Reagan in July 1984. The base-broadening tax bills of the recent past are sometimes described as taking a cats-and-dogs approach, picking out a few provisions of the tax system for change but not making wholesale revisions. Also in the hybrid category are most of the flat tax or so-called modified flat tax (in fact graduated rate) proposals that have been advanced, including the Fair Tax Act of Senator Bill Bradley and Congressman Richard Gephardt, and the Fair and Simple Tax Act introduced by Senator Robert Kasten and Congressman Jack Kemp.

The term "flat-rate tax" is generally taken to mean one that looks something like the existing individual income tax (that is, it does not look like a sales tax), except that the graduated-rate structure is replaced by a single percentage rate. However, the name is incomplete as a description of a program of reform. The critical characteristics of a tax system result from the combination of the definition of a base and the rate or rates of tax applied to the base to determine liability. For example, a flat-rate individual income tax could easily be achieved by substituting for the existing graduated-rate structure a single rate of roughly 19 percent applicable to taxable income as defined in present law. The resulting revenues would match those currently generated by the tax. Another possibility, a flat rate of about 15 percent applied to adjusted gross income on individual tax returns, would suffice to maintain the present revenue yield. (The figures refer to 1982 and represent the ratio of individual income tax before credits to taxable income and to adjusted gross income on individual tax returns, respectively. See U.S. Internal Revenue Service, 1984, table 1.)

Most flat-tax proposals consist of two steps. Step 1 is traditional base broadening; step 2 is replacing the graduated-rate structure with a single proportional rate. Later I shall take up the question of whether a proportional rate per se would substantially advance tax policy objectives.

Traditional tax reform has favored adherence to the accrual-income concept. Many examples could be cited. A proposal that strives rigorously for theoretical purity is described in the U.S. Treasury's *Blueprints for Basic Tax Reform*. (The original report is U.S. Treasury, 1977. A reedited version has been published as Bradford et al., 1984.) Called simply the Comprehensive Income Tax, it would, among other things, fully integrate corporate and individual taxes. The actual reform plan developed by the U.S. Treasury and made public as the Treasury's proposal in November 1984 represents as close an approximation as one is likely to see in practice to the systematic application of accrual-income principles. We shall take a closer look at it in Chapter 13.

The term "consumption taxes of the income type" refers in this book to proposals for taxes that look like income taxes but have the effect of exempting from taxation the return to saving. (Why these taxes are based on consumption will be clarified in the coming pages.) Although widely discussed in the literature and in tax policy circles, systematic proposals in this category have yet to make much headway in the political process. Examples are the *Blueprints* Cash-Flow Tax and the Cash-Flow Income Tax advanced by Henry Aaron and Harvey Galper (1985) of the Brookings Institution. A plan of quite different form, the Simple Flat Tax devised by Robert E. Hall and Alvin Rabushka (1983, 1985), also belongs in the category of consumption taxes of the income type (by virtue of its treatment of business investment). Traced by Hall and Rabushka to a suggestion by Nobel laureate Milton Friedman, the Simple Flat Tax has received considerable press attention primarily because of its flatness: the tax would be levied at a flat 19 percent on a very broad base above substantial personal allowances. However, at least as important and interesting is its simple and attractive accounting scheme, about which I shall have more to say.

The Simple Flat Tax is a close relative of a value-added tax (VAT), which is in turn a typical representative of the class of "uniform taxes," very broad-based taxes at a single rate, that is, truly flat taxes. The retail sales tax is the other major example. Normally, these taxes are of the consumption type in that they effectively exempt all interbusiness transactions, but they need not be. Although a textbook value-added tax is applied at a single rate, in most countries that use a value-added tax, different rates are applied to different classes of transactions.

In writing about income tax policy, I have had at the outset to deal with a dilemma. The ideas I hope to convey are not particularly time bound. I hope the book will be useful for many years. Yet the book would be dull indeed if these ideas were not related to concrete issues. Unfortunately, the income tax is constantly changing. Many of the rules currently in place may well have been replaced by others before the book is even off press. By using current tax law and currently discussed alternatives to it as my source of illustrations, I run the risk that readers will dismiss the ideas when the illustrations are no longer relevant. But in the interest of a more lively presentation, I have chosen to accept that risk. The reader is therefore urged to look for the general in the particular. Based on my reading of the history of the income tax, here and abroad, and on a certain amount of direct experience, I can offer reasonable assurance that most of the ideas discussed in this book will remain relevant, and most of the problems dealt with will remain with us long after the Hall-Rabushka plan or the Aaron-Galper plan or the Treasury's November 1984 plan have faded from memory.

TAX CONCEPTS I

Income, Consumption, and Wealth **2**

The income tax is not a tax upon income but a tax upon persons according to their respective incomes; and, subject to the requirement of adherence to simple, general rules, the objective of policy must be fairness among persons, not fairness among kinds of receipts (whatever that might be construed to mean).

Henry C. Simons, *Personal Income Taxation*

THE CONCEPT of *income* is obviously central to the discussion of income tax policy, yet advocates of income tax reform rarely attempt to state their objective with any precision. Interestingly, there is a considerable degree of consensus among tax scholars as to what the term "income" means.[1] That view of income takes as its starting point the idea that income is what is received in payment for services rendered. I am going to call this the "factor payment" view of income. Reflection on why a person who has more income than another should pay more in taxes suggests that the critical issue is not payments received, but what the individual can buy in the way of consumption or additions to wealth. The implied "uses" view of income as the basis for taxation is generally accepted.

Since what goes out (in expenditure on consumption and assets) must first come in, the two views of income are close relatives, and in some simple worlds they lead to exactly the same practical tax rules. In more complicated worlds, however, they may not. In this chapter I elaborate on the uses definition of income and explain how it relates to the factor payment view. I conclude with a quick scan of the existing income tax in relation to the various concepts discussed. Appendix 2–1 focuses on an often-controversial question, the place of gift and bequest transactions in defining income. All of this is a prelude to a closer look in subsequent

---

1. There is a large literature on the definition of income for tax purposes. An excellent overview is provided by Richard Goode (1977, pp. 1–30). I draw here heavily on a previous paper of mine on this subject (1983), which in turn draws on the treatment in *Blueprints*, chap. 2.

chapters at a whole series of issues in the design of taxes based on income and consumption.

The Definition of Income: Uses and Factor Payment Views

An income tax is a levy based on a particular aggregation of transactions according to a complicated set of rules laid down in statutes, regulations, rulings and court decisions, and the like. In one sense that set of rules *defines* income for tax purposes: income is what the law says it is. But those rules are motivated by some sort of ideal or target concept. Thus while a tax on income is really a complex set of taxes on particular transactions, such as the receipt of wages or interest, what makes that complex set of taxes halfway understandable is the underlying notion of a certain flow of purchasing power. Indeed, the key to making the income tax more understandable is bringing about greater consistency between the definition of income implicit in the law and a clear underlying idea.

Most discussions of tax policy build on what is called in the jargon the "Haig-Simons" definition of income, a label derived from the names of two influential writers on income taxation (Haig, 1921, and Simons, 1938). According to this definition, an individual's income is the sum of what he consumes during the year and the increase in his wealth.[2] This is the *uses* view of income that I have mentioned. Most people are at first puzzled by it. They not unreasonably think of income as something that comes in, such as wage or interest receipts. But the concept of income appropriate for tax purposes is supposed somehow to be related to the well-being of the person receiving it, and that depends on what the person obtains with purchasing power, not where he got it.

Information about sources of purchasing power is, however, essential in the practical accounting methods by which to measure the sum of consumption and the increase in wealth. Income accounting has to be based on transactions that we can observe — usually an exchange of something for money. Such transactions as the receipt of wage and interest payments form the basis for income accounting. Although the layman tends to identify these receipts with income, they are actually just the starting point for measuring income. Cash receipts as such do

---

2. I regret that the English language makes it necessary to choose between masculine and feminine pronouns; in most cases I have chosen to use the generic "he" and "his" as the least unsatisfactory option among stylistic possibilities.

not provide a good measure of a person's consumption or change in wealth. Consider, for example, the cash inflow that results when a person sells an asset such as a share of stock. A transaction of this sort is not necessarily associated with any change in the seller's position. One minute he has a stock of wealth that includes some shares with a certain money value. The next minute, after the sale, he has one less share of stock and more cash, but the money value of his wealth, including both shares and cash, has not changed at all. The sale of stock involves simply a reallocation of the individual's portfolio and provides no measure of an improvement in position. (Presumably both the buyer and the seller of stock prefer the postsale position to the presale position. Otherwise the transaction would not have taken place. However, there is no objective way to measure the improvement perceived by the two parties. The net improvement, or surplus, attributable to the transaction is not necessarily related to the value of the assets changing hands.)

A similar problem arises in ordinary business accounting. It is taken for granted that income is somehow to be defined *net* of the cost of obtaining it. But which outlays are to be subtracted from receipts during the year? A little thought on what it is that makes various cash inflows and outflows different from the receipt of salary leads one to look for a bottom line against which to judge the appropriate treatment of different transactions. We subtract the cost of materials and other inputs from receipts from sales because we want to know what is left over to spend. Ultimately our interest is in changes in a person's consumption or power to consume. It therefore follows that an individual has experienced income to the extent that he has either undertaken consumption or added to the stock of potential consumption we call his wealth.

According to the uses view, then, income is defined as the sum of consumption and the change in wealth during the year. An increase in wealth during the year is, furthermore, what we mean by saving during the year, so income is equivalently defined as the sum of consumption and saving. This will be a critically important point to keep in mind when we come to the question of taxing on the basis of consumption rather than income. The difference between a consumption-based tax and an income-based tax is entirely in the treatment of saving.

Two related aspects of this definition should be particularly stressed. First, in an accounting sense it is possible to start with a measure of income and reach a measure of consumption for purposes of taxation by *subtracting* amounts saved. If income is the sum of consumption and saving, then consumption is the difference between income and saving. Sometimes the saving is negative; that is, in some periods people draw on their savings. In such periods consumption will exceed income. The second point is that a tax based on consumption is in an important sense a tax on wealth: under a consumption approach, amounts withdrawn from past accumulation are subject to tax. This fact makes a consumption approach an attractive one from the point of view of taxing according to ability to pay. It also draws attention to the potential difficulty in making a transition from a tax based on income to one based on consumption, since there is a danger of unfairly subjecting individuals to a double tax on their past saving. But as we shall see, the difficulty of surmounting this problem is often exaggerated.

The uses view of income can be contrasted with the factor payment view. People typically think of income as what they are paid for rendering services — for example, wages earned for working, interest received for lending money, or profit made from producing a product for sale. In the economist's technical language, these are examples of factor payments; thus in the factor payment view, income is conceived of as the sum of wages, interest, and the like. The factor payment view is closely related to the uses view of income. Factor payments must be used for something. If the only sources of purchasing power were factor payments and the only uses of purchasing power were consumption or saving, then the factor payment view of income would be identical to the uses view. Whether either condition holds depends on how one defines factor payments, consumption, and saving.

But the practical policies that flow naturally from a factor payment view of income do differ from those that flow naturally from the uses view. Practical policies specify what is included in the receipts side of an income measure and what is to be deducted. Sources of purchasing power other than factor payments include transfers of various kinds, both private and public. Gifts, bequests, scholarships, Social Security, welfare benefits, and unemployment compensation are examples of sources of purchasing power that are, to one degree or another, distinct from payments for services rendered. They would arguably be excluded from a factor payment measure of income, and U.S. income tax practice has been to exclude some of them.

Deductions, too, are likely to differ between factor payment and uses views. We take it for granted that the costs of earning factor payments should be deducted from receipts (although there are difficult borderline cases). But the uses view implies that deductions should be allowed as well for uses of purchasing power that are neither consumption nor saving. State income taxes provide an example. While one can make a case for treating state income taxes as consumption, for example, many would regard it as stretching the concept. State income taxes, however, do not represent a cost of earning factor payments. State income taxes might thus seem more obviously deductible under a uses view than under a factor payment view of income.

The attraction of a uses view of income derives from its focus on what is left for the individual. In a sense it follows to its logical conclusion the netting out of expenses that is so obvious in the deduction of the cost of goods sold from sales receipts in determining the income of the owner of a retail store. The object is to obtain a measure of what is effectively available for the owner to spend on good things. A running theme of this book is that the test of a tax base is what it implies for the distribution of burdens among individuals, taking into account its effect on economic efficiency. Like most other commentators, I find the uses definition of income superior to the factor payments view for deciding how tax burdens should be distributed. I therefore take it as the basic notion of income throughout the book.

Jargon can be tiresome, but we need a label for this income concept to suggest that the term is being used in a technical, well-defined sense. The tax theorist's "Haig-Simons" is too academic. Because of the accounting ideal that is characteristic of the concept and also responsible for many of the problems it poses, I have instead chosen the term *accrual income* for purposes of this book.

The Concept of Consumption

Translating the concept of income as the sum of consumption and saving into practical rules requires attention to the definitions of the two components. While people probably share a rough idea of what constitutes consumption, as with income there are many gray areas in the definition. Like income, consumption is in the nature of a flow measured, for example, in dollars per year. And like income, it must, as a practical matter, be described in terms of transactions. Some transactions seem to fit naturally under the label of consumption. For example, we know we are enjoying consumption when we attend a movie or dine at a restaurant. But other activities are not so easily classified. Should we, for example, describe the purchase of medical treatment for a painful disease as consumption? What about the case, already mentioned, of taxes we are obliged to pay to our state governments?

The answers to these questions can be found not by referring to some abstract standard, but by referring to the function we want the aggregation of transactions called consumption to serve. For example, national-income accountants divide the expenditure of a country into three categories: investment, consumption, and government purchases of goods and services. Their object is to describe the overall composition of the nation's expenditure to assist in determining its level. The concept of consumption implicit in the definition of income to be taxed, as in the case of the definition of any tax base, has a quite different role to play: its purpose is to discriminate among taxpayers.

If an income base is defined as the sum of consumption and saving, an income tax will vary tax burdens positively with consumption, other things (including saving) being equal. This being so, the definition of consumption for purposes of taxation is inevitably an ethical and political matter. Medical expenses provide an example. For purposes of national-income accounting the services of physicians are regarded as part of national consumption. But when it comes to setting tax burdens, there is a reasonable argument that medical expenses serve to make up for unfortunate differences among taxpayers. Two taxpayers whose outlays would be the same except that one has larger medical bills than the other might reasonably be described as enjoying the same level of consumption. Thus one might want to exclude medical expenses from the transactions that make up a person's consumption.

That the definition of consumption is a matter of policy finds expression in hundreds of interpretations of the law by the tax authorities. Consider, for example, commutation expenses. The person who commutes to the city does so mainly because it is a necessary condition of employment; it is in an obvious sense a cost of earning income. On the other hand, how much commuting expense one has depends on where one chooses to live, and this is clearly a consumption choice. (Present tax policy is based on the second view: commuting expenses are not deductible.)

The preceding example well illustrates the basic approach employed to measure individual income for tax purposes: the use of subtraction. Individual income tax accounting works by keeping track of a person's receipts and then allowing various deductions. One way of interpreting many deductions is as allowances for outlays deemed not to constitute consumption or saving. Clear costs of earning income are obvious among these. But as the cases of medical expenses and state income tax payments show, there may be other outlays that are not considered consumption; deductions for them are also implied by the accrual-income concept.

The treatment of gifts and bequests in an income tax provides an interesting application of this idea. It often comes as a surprise that tax theorists are divided on whether money an individual gives away or bequeaths at death should be regarded as consumed by the giver. The usual intuitive argument is that it should not: an individual who gives money away transfers potential consumption to the recipient of the gift. This would imply that in determining income, the amount should be deducted from the donor's income and added to the donee's income.

The counterargument, that making a gift or bequest is a form of consumption, is based on the observation that the individual can choose between spending on consumption goods and services (as ordinarily conceived) or spending on a gift or bequest (see Simons, 1938, chap. 2). The choice is thus similar to any other decision about how to allocate purchasing power. If the individual favors a gift or bequest, it must be because a value is placed on the action at least equal to the value of the ordinary consumption that might alternatively have been chosen. In this view, although the recipient of a gift should include it in income, the donor should not deduct amounts given away.

Gifts and bequests also provide an instance in which the factor payments and uses views of income tend to lead to different results. Although it may be argued that the person who is good enough to accept a gift renders a service to the donor (so that a gift received can be regarded as factor payment), most people would probably regard this as considerably stretching matters. Therefore the factor payment view would ignore gift transactions, neither including amounts received in the income of the recipient nor allowing a deduction on the accounts of the donor.

As in the case of other decisions about what constitutes consumption, the preferred policy is to be sought not in abstract reasoning but in concrete comparisons of the effect on tax burdens and other characteristics of the tax system, when one definition or the other is used for tax purposes.

The Concept of Wealth

The concept of wealth also presents problems. In a general way, it refers to the total purchasing power a person commands at a given time. It is thus a *stock,* measured in dollars (with a date specified if the general price level is variable). Wealth thus contrasts with the flow character of income and consumption. The *change* in wealth during the year (or other accounting period), which enters the definition of income, is a flow, typically measured in dollars per year. For example, a savings account balance would normally be counted as part of wealth, because the owner of the account could withdraw the full amount at will and spend it on goods and services.

An asset consists essentially of a claim to future returns, that is, to future payments of money or future delivery of goods and services. Where the returns are in the form of goods and services, it is typically possible to place a money value on them. Thus the bank account asset gives its owner a claim to payment of the balance on demand. The owner of a bond has a claim on periodic interest payments plus repayment of the face amount at maturity. The owner of a share of stock has a claim on a proportionate share of dividends declared by the firm (plus certain rights upon dissolution of the firm). The owner of a pension has a claim against his employer or an insurance company to certain payments during retirement. The owner of a machine has a claim to its rental or to the value of the extra production it permits. The owner of a personal residence has a claim to the housing services provided by the residence.

Because the future services or payments that can be claimed by the owner of an asset are of potential value to others as well, an asset generally can be converted to some positive amount of current purchasing power. Conceptually, an individual's wealth is the maximum amount of present consumption he could finance currently by selling or otherwise committing all of his assets (withdrawing funds from a bank account is an example of "otherwise committing" an asset; a much more important example is borrowing against the security of an asset).

People rarely appreciate the degree to which wealth is a *psychological* phenomenon. The value of assets depends on what we believe is going to happen in the future. It is entirely possible that beliefs could change autonomously. For example, a spread of general pessimism might occur. As a consequence, a given physical collection of assets might fall in value and a loss in wealth occur, even though nothing has "really happened." Such wholesale shifts in value can be observed daily on stock markets. It cannot be emphasized enough that such changes in wealth are genuine and that a tax system based on the uses concept of income would recognize them.

Because wealth is a phenomenon of expectations and beliefs, it is also a function of information. One of the properties of information is that it need not be generally shared; it is, however, the generally shared part that determines the market values on which the uses definition of income depends. For example, if I am told on good authority that a meteor is going to fall on my house in one year, I will reevaluate the house. Perhaps, after a struggle with my conscience, I will put my house on the market without telling anyone about the meteor. I will then have suffered no loss in wealth because of the arrival of information about the meteor. When the meteor does land on the house, it will be an unpleasant surprise for the person who then owns the house, who will suffer a loss in wealth, that is, experience some negative income.

On the other hand, if the information about the meteor is revealed to everyone else at the same time that I learn about it, the market value of my house will fall to reflect the fact that in a year the house will be damaged or destroyed. I will then be the one to suffer the loss in wealth, to experience negative income. In a year, when the meteor hits, there will be no resulting decline in the value of my assets — that will have taken place in the past — no loss in wealth, no negative income.

Actually drawing the lines to produce a practical measure of wealth is difficult and inevitably somewhat arbitrary. Typically we do not even think about valuing the average person's most important asset, his "human capital," his earning power. It must be said, though, that if wealth is understood as the current purchasing power an individual can obtain by committing the future inflows from an asset (as by selling a share of stock or by pledging the profits of a business as collateral for a loan), the omission is sensible for most people. Anyone who has tried to borrow against future earning power will know that its current market value is quite limited.

Human capital is not alone in being difficult to value or, indeed, in having different values for different owners. In particular, an asset is often of much less value to others than to its current owner. For example, a house may be on the market for some time before it is sold, and the price at which the sale will take place is hard to predict. Furthermore, most houses are not on the market at all, for the simple reason that they are of much greater value to their current owners than to others. The built-in cold room of the neighborhood fish store is quite valuable to its owner; but it is of less value, or even of negative value, to another user of the same space, as would become clear should the proprietor of the fish store decide to sell his assets. The market value of an individual's claim to a pension, especially under a defined-benefit plan (under which retirement benefits depend on such things as earnings during the years immediately preceding retirement), is difficult to establish and no doubt quite limited, for much the same reason that one's human capital has limited current value to anyone else. (Frequently the value of a pension claim is intentionally reduced via limits in the extent to which it can be pledged as loan collateral.)

An individual's claim on a pension plan is one of many examples of claims on what might loosely be called "trusts." These are arrangements under which someone is committed to making payments to individuals under various contingencies. In the case of the pension, an insurance company may be committed to pay certain amounts to a person under the contingency that the person is retired. Another example that is important less for its quantitative significance than for its contribution to the complexity of the tax law is a legal trust in which assets are held for the benefit of a particular individual. The contingencies might be the earnings performance of a portfolio or the economic success of a business. The payments may depend on events relating to the beneficiaries, as when a trustee pays a young person's college bills. In view of the contingent nature of the claim of any given beneficiary, it may be very difficult to establish its contribution to his wealth. Elaborate rules have been devised to settle this matter by convention in the case of trusts that are part of the estates of wealthy people. Most of these rules are related to the taxation of gifts and bequests. An example is the convention that taxes generation-skipping trusts, whereby wealth is passed from a grandparent to grandchildren without having given rise to wealth in the hands of the children.

The most significant example of what I am calling trusts is the business corporation. The Federal Reserve Board estimated the total net worth of the United States at $11,376 billion as of the end of 1983. Of that total, a little over one-quarter ($3,259 billion) was estimated as the net worth of financial and nonfinancial corporations (Board of Governors of the Federal Reserve System, April 1984). The net worth of these corporations is, in turn, owned by the various claimants on corporations. Important among the claimants are stockholders, some of which, such as pension plans, are also trusts. Tracing through these linked claims to the individual owners and attributing an appropriate value to the claims present difficult accounting problems. Thus the apparently simple concept of wealth presents numerous challenges to policymakers who would base tax liabilities on it or its derivative, income.

Realization Income

Income tax practitioners are accustomed to thinking of income as a "realization" concept (see Simons, 1938, chap. 3). This refers to the procedure whereby the change in value of assets held over more than one period (which is an element of accrual income) is recognized on the books only when there is a transaction with respect to the asset. Present treatment of capital gains, which is based on a realization principle, provides an example. The change in value of a share of stock held throughout the year will not be counted in the stockholder's income for that year under the accounting practices followed in the U.S. income tax. In general, the changing value of the share will be taken into account only when it is sold or otherwise exchanged. Sale triggers a calculation of gain or loss that is counted as part of the income of the year in which the sale takes place. Income calculated in this way is sometimes referred to as realization income.

The need for a realization concept of income arises because of the difficulty of valuing assets on an annual basis. Rather than representing an independent definitional concept, realization income is a term describing the practice of income measurement. It is more reasonably described as the accountants' refuge from the requirement of excessive reliance on judgment than as a definition; and rather than offering insights into desirable tax structures, it draws attention to the limitation of the income concept as a guide to policy.

Illustrative Individual Income Accounts

To fix these ideas, especially the somewhat backward-sounding notion of income as, in effect, outlay, it will be helpful to work through an example of an individual's income accounts for a particular year.[3] As the purpose of the example is to illustrate concepts developed above, the details have been chosen for simplicity and clarity rather than for realism. Assume, then, that the individual—call him Peter—is a worker whose only sources of funds are wages and an accumulated savings account balance. The possible applications Peter can make of these funds may be divided into the purchase of goods and services for immediate use and additions to or subtractions from the accumulation of savings. Thus an account of the situation for the year might be the following:

Sources	Uses
Wages	Rent
Interest	Clothing
	Food
	Recreation
Balance in savings account at beginning of year	Balance in savings account at end of year

---

3. The material in this and the following sections draws heavily on U.S. Treasury Department (1977).

The two sides of this account must balance. Of the uses, the first four are generally lumped under the concept of consumption; the fifth constitutes the individual's net worth. Thus the accounts may be schematically written as:

Sources	*Uses*
Wages	Consumption
Interest	
Net worth at beginning of year	Net worth at end of year

The concept of income concerns the *addition,* or *accretion,* to sources and the application of that accretion during the year. This information can be found by subtracting the accumulated savings (net worth) at the beginning of the year from both sides, to give:

Additions to sources	*Uses of additions to sources*
Wages	Consumption
Interest	Saving (equals increase in net worth over the year; may be negative)

Accrual income is *defined* as the sum of consumption and the increase in net worth during the year. With this *uses* definition of income, Peter's situation may be represented by:

Additions to sources	*Uses of additions to sources*
Wages	Income
Interest	

This version of the accounts makes clear the way in which information about sources is used to determine the individual's income. To calculate income for the year, Peter would not need to add up the outlays for rent, clothing, food, and recreation and the increase in his savings account balance. Instead he would simply add together his wages and interest and take advantage of the accounting identity between this sum and income.

The classification of uses into consumption and increase in net worth is not sufficient, however, to accommodate distinctions commonly made by tax policy. Suppose, for example, that during the year Peter spends some money to rent tools required on the job. These outlays do not fit the category of consumption, nor do they represent an addition to net worth. It is helpful, therefore, to refine the accounts as follows:

Additions to sources	*Uses of additions to sources*
Wages	Consumption
Interest	Cost of earnings
	Certain other outlays
	Saving (increase in net worth)

The outlays to rent special tools needed on the job would reasonably fit the category "cost of earnings" in the new scheme. These outlays will be netted out in defining income. Note that, as emphasized earlier, the decision about which outlays to include in this category is a social or political one. Thus under existing tax rules the expense of purchasing specialized work clothes for the job is deductible, but commuting expenses are not. There is no unambiguous standard to which one can appeal to determine whether such outlays are consumption, and hence a part of income, or work expenses, and hence excluded from income.

Similarly, a judgment may be made that some outlays, while not costs of earning a living, are also not properly classified as consumption. The category "other outlays" is introduced to the accounts above for want of a better label for such transactions. For example, as discussed earlier, state income taxes would not be an application labeled "consumption," nor, clearly, do they reflect "increase in net worth." Thus, using the definition of income as the sum of consumption and saving, we now have:

Additions to sources	*Uses of additions to sources*
Earnings (wages + interest)	Income (consumption + saving)
	Cost of earnings
	Certain other outlays

As before, to *measure* income it is generally convenient to work from the left-hand, sources side of the accounting relationship. In this case,

Income = Earnings − Cost of earnings − Certain other outlays

In a similar way — and the fact is of great importance in implementing a tax based on individual consumption — consumption may be calculated by starting with sources data, including saving among the subtracted items:

Consumption
    = Earnings − Cost of earnings − Certain other outlays − Saving

Character of the Current U.S. Income Tax

While the present income tax system lacks a clear rationale, we can see in it elements of both income-base and consumption-base accounting. Thus, for example, the two items that represent the bulk of savings for most Americans, pensions and owned homes, are treated by the tax code in a way that is closer to the consumption model than to the income model. Retirement saving financed by employer contributions to pension plans (or made via Individual Retirement Account or Keogh Plan for the self-employed) is treated as it would be under a consumption tax. Additions to an employer-funded pension plan are not included in the tax base, but retirement benefits from those plans, which represent negative saving much like withdrawals from a bank account, are included. Contributions to Individual Retirement Accounts or Keogh Plans represent deductible saving, while subsequent benefits are treated as taxable dissaving.

If we were to design accounting rules to measure the accrual income attributable to an owner-occupied house, we would treat it like a business, in which the owner rents the house to himself. The result would be a certain amount of annual income. The amount would consist partly of consumption services provided to the occupant (these are the services that the renter buys with a monthly payment), and partly of the changing value of the house, viewed as an asset (accruing capital gain or loss). We might do something very similar to measure the flow of consumption from the house, first calculating the flow of annual income and then subtracting, as saving, any part of it due to an increase in the value of the house.

In actual practice nothing like either of these devices is employed in determining income subject to tax, and it may therefore be thought that owner-occupied housing represents a departure from both accrual-income and consumption approaches. The owner-occupied home is clearly not correctly dealt with as a matter of accrual-income accounting. Furthermore, its treatment seems exactly backward as a matter of consumption accounting, since no deduction is allowed for the purchase of the asset and no effort is made to measure and tax the returning flow of consumption services. In effect, the entire purchase price of the house is treated as consumption (since no deduction is allowed). Remarkably, however, this backward treatment — no deduction for an act of saving, but no inclusion of the subsequent dissaving — can be regarded as prepayment of tax on the consumption generated by the home. The resulting tax burden is equivalent to that which would result from actually measuring annual consumption services.

In addition to these examples of consumption-type base measurement rules under the existing income tax are others relating to specific assets, both financial (for example, the treatment of ordinary life insurance) and real (for example, the expensing of research and experimentation outlays). Moreover, numerous provisions of current law are designed to reduce the taxation of investment, and in effect are much like allowing immediate deduction. At the same time, of course, many rules in the existing system are those one would expect in an accrual-income tax. Perhaps most important is the taxation of interest receipts and the deduction of interest expenses. The coexistence of consumption-type and accrual-income-type rules gives the existing tax its hybrid character and accounts for many of its least satisfactory aspects.

The income concept implicit in current law has elements of both the factor payment and the uses concepts. The uses view of income seems to underlie several important deductions in the existing tax. Most obvious are the personal deductions for medical expenses, charitable contributions, and state and local taxes. While these deductions can be rationalized as (rather odd) matching grant subsidies to the activities in question, they can more naturally be explained as decisions about the consumption component of an accrual-income base. (My choice of terminology is a bit misleading in this instance. The factor payment view of income implies an accrual-type accounting just as much as does the Haig-Simons view of income as the sum of consumption and saving.) Yet many other provisions of the tax law seem explicable only on the basis of a factor payment view of income. The tax-free character of gratuitous transfers, such as gifts, inheritances, prizes (provided the recipients have not pursued them), and welfare benefits (including food stamps), as well as of the less gratuitous (because paid for with payroll taxes) transfers in the form of unemployment insurance benefits, and the partially tax-free character of the partially gratuitous (because partially paid for with payroll taxes) Social Security benefits, indicate that the income concept implicit in the law adopts to some degree the factor payment view.

With a bit of license the treatment of gifts and bequests under the current income tax rules can be interpreted as implementing a uses view of income in which these outlays are *not* regarded as a type of consumption. The uses view always calls in principle for inclusion of gifts and bequests received in the receipts part of the income calculation. If amounts given away are not regarded as consumption, a deduction would be allowed for them. However, not allowing a deduction while not requiring inclusion produces the same tax result as allowing a deduction and requiring inclusion if donor and donee are in the same tax bracket. Thus the present tax treatment has a certain equivalence with a uses approach that excludes gifts and bequests given from the donor's consumption. (There is, of course, in addition a specific tax on gifts and bequests that exceed certain amounts on a cumulated basis over the donor's lifetime.)

Appendix 2–1. Accounting for Gifts and Bequests

The illustrative income accounts presented in this chapter can be applied to the alternative treatments of gifts and bequests. Gifts and bequests received enter the accounts on the sources side, while gifts and bequests given represent uses of spending power. With these additions the accounts become:

Additions to sources	*Uses of additions to sources*
Wages	Consumption
Interest	Gifts and bequests given
Gifts and bequests received	Cost of earnings
	Certain other outlays
	Saving

Some argue that gifts and bequests given should be considered a form of consumption in defining income for tax purposes. Others contend that making a gift or bequest simply transfers the power to consume to others and should not be included in the income concept. We may give the label "bestowal-inclusive" to the consumption concept that treats amounts given away as consumed, and "bestowal-exclusive" to the concept that does not. (It is difficult to find terms for these consumption concepts that convey their respective contents. Readers of *Blueprints* will recognize them as "ability-to-pay" and "standard-of-living" consumption.) To each consumption concept corresponds an income concept, which can be derived from sources-side information as before. The two accounting equivalences for the consumption concept that includes gifts and bequests given are:

Bestowal-inclusive income
$$= \text{Earnings} + \text{Gifts and bequests received}$$
$$- \text{Cost of earnings} - \text{Certain other outlays}$$

Bestowal-inclusive consumption

= Earnings + Gifts and bequests received

− Cost of earnings − Certain other outlays − Saving

The difference between consumption and income is saving, or the increase in net worth, over the period. Thus, equivalently,

Bestowal-inclusive consumption

= Bestowal-inclusive income − Saving

The bestowal-exclusive consumption and income concepts, under which gifts given are not regarded as consumption, give rise to a deduction from the sources side:

Bestowal-exclusive income

= Bestowal-inclusive income − Gifts and bequests given

Bestowal-exclusive consumption

= Bestowal-exclusive income − Saving

Varying the treatment of gifts and bequests and of saving gives rise to four possible tax bases: bestowal-exclusive consumption and income, and bestowal-inclusive consumption and income. Going from income to consumption in either case means subtracting saving; going from bestowal inclusive to bestowal exclusive in either case means subtracting gifts and bequests given.

3 What Would a Genuine Income Tax Look Like?

A true accretion-type personal income tax would be free of many of the complexities and inequities of the existing tax. But a true accretion-type tax is hardly attainable in practice. Even a rough approximation of an accretion-type tax would require an utter transformation of the practical administration and computation of the tax from one depending mostly on cash transactions to one in which current, comprehensive property valuation would play a central role.

William D. Andrews, "A Consumption-Type or Cash Flow Personal Income Tax," in *Harvard Law Review,* 1974

APPARENTLY, translating the idea of income into tax practice has been the subject of controversy for a long time. In this chapter I propose to explore how the "uses" concept of income could be put into practice. To develop these ideas I shall describe how a tax might look that adheres rather rigorously to an accrual-income standard. The exercise also provides a convenient framework for analyzing many features of the existing income tax system, and it will help us assess the promise of various reforms.

An Illustrative Income Tax Plan

To describe an income tax, we need a form and a book of instructions. Table 3–1 provides the form for our accrual-income tax; the rest of the chapter constitutes the instructions — to be sure, instructions that go into more detail on alternatives and on philosophical problems than we are accustomed to find in the booklet accompanying Form 1040 of the U.S. individual income tax. The following commentary must, therefore, be read in conjunction with an effort to work through the form. To save space I shall consolidate discussion of obviously related inclusion and deduction items (R refers to receipts; D, to deductions; the tax base comprises total receipts less total deductions).

Table 3-1. Information on tax returns for an accrual-income tax[a]

Household receipts and deductions	Included on return?
Receipts	
R-1 Wages, salaries, tips, royalties, and so on, subject to tax[b]	Yes
R-2 Receipts of pensions, annuities, life insurance cash value, disability compensation, workmen's compensation, and sick pay[c]	Yes
R-3 Gifts, inheritances, trust distributions, and life insurance death benefits received	Yes
R-4 Interest received on financial assets, *adjusted for inflation*	Yes
R-5 Dividends received on corporate earnings	No[d]
R-6 Proceeds from the sale, exchange, or distribution of capital assets	Yes
R-7 Policyholder claim on earnings from life insurance, annuity, and pension plan reserves, *adjusted for inflation*	Yes
R-8 Increase in value of the claim on a trust beyond allocated share of amounts given or bequeathed to the trust, *adjusted for inflation*	Yes
R-9 Gross receipts from unincorporated business enterprises	Yes
R-10 Allocated share of *inflation-corrected* corporate earnings	Yes
R-11 Imputed service value attributable to owner-occupied housing and other household durables	Yes
Deductions	
D-1 Employee business expenses (including qualified travel expenses, union dues, tools, materials, and qualified educational expenses)	Yes
D-2 Contributions to qualified retirement plans	Yes
D-3 Gifts and bequests made to an identified taxpayer or trust with eligible beneficiary; net life insurance premiums (compare item R-3)	Yes
D-4 Interest paid on indebtedness (including interest on home mortgages and consumer loans), *adjusted for inflation*	Yes
D-5 Basis of assets sold, exchanged, or distributed (compare item R-6), *adjusted for inflation*	Yes[e]
D-6 Current expenses associated with unincorporated business enterprises, including contributions to employee pensions	Yes

Table 3-1 *(continued)*

	Household receipts and deductions	Included on return?
D-7	Capital outlays associated with unincorporated business enterprises	No
D-8	Depreciation allowances for current and past capital outlays associated with unincorporated business enterprises, *adjusted for inflation*	Yes
D-9	Special items as a matter of policy (for example, charitable contributions, medical expenses)	Yes

a. Accrual income is the concept labeled "Haig-Simons income" by tax theorists. It is the sum of consumption plus saving during the year. Because the table embodies some indirect techniques of income measurement (especially in connection with retirement accumulation), readers are advised to refer to the commentary in the text.

b. The definition of "wages subject to tax" could incorporate differential rules according to individual characteristics (for example, marital status might be used to mitigate the "marriage tax" problem). Under the illustrative treatment of pensions and the like (which involves an indirect approach to retirement income measurement), this item would *exclude* Social Security taxes attributable to retirement benefits and contributions to retirement plans. (See text.) R-1 would *include* employer-paid health and life insurance premiums and similar employee benefit outlays by firms.

c. This item would probably include Social Security benefits of all types. Pensions and annuities for which there has been no exclusion under R-1 or deduction under D-2 or D-3 would be excluded under R-2.

d. The exclusion of dividends is a corollary of the allocation of all corporate income to shareholders. Dividends result in a reduction in the basis of the shares for purposes of calculating gain from sale or exchange (capital gain).

e. The deduction of adjusted basis would have to be limited (as at present) in relation to sales proceeds in R-6. Unused deduction of net losses could be carried forward.

R-1 Wages, Salaries
D-1 Employee Business Expenses

For most people, earnings from providing labor services, usually in the form of employee compensation, constitute much the largest item on the sources side of the income calculation. (Some people obtain the return from labor services in the form of income from a professional practice or other unincorporated business.) The way employee compensation is currently treated in the income tax is, broadly speaking, what would be called for by accrual-income principles. The way present practice departs from strict adherence to accrual-income principles is suggested by the table's footnote to R-1. Employees are currently obliged to include a portion of the Social Security tax levied on wages, and they are allowed to exclude numerous employee benefits.

The treatment of Social Security in the illustrative plan actually represents a compromise with purity. Although the Social Security tax as such clearly represents a reduction in the wherewithal to consume or save, workers continually accrue valuable rights to retirement and other benefits. Thus the amount that a worker would have to put aside each year to purchase an insurance policy providing Social Security benefits is an increment to wealth that is omitted from the treatment of Social Security in the table. In many cases the omitted amount is significant.

Of more practical importance is the demand of a pure accrual-income tax to include the value of employee benefits of various kinds. Putting aside retirement schemes for the moment, we may distinguish statutorily sanctioned benefits, including employer-paid life and health insurance premiums and group legal services, and the many fringe benefits (increasingly also governed by statute) that create such controversy in tax administration. Many of these could easily be measured and included in employee compensation for tax purposes, but there will inevitably be difficult lines to draw concerning what is deductible for the employer and includable by the employee. Taxes of the income and the consumption types suffer equally from this unpleasant fact of life.

An employer's contribution to an employee's pension plan amounts to the payment of wages or salary in kind, in the form of an addition to the employee's wealth (the asset being the employee's claim on the pension plan). Strict income accounting would recognize this increase in wealth by including it in the sources side of the employee's reckoning. In subsequent years the increasing value of the pension claim over time (due to earnings on the funds set aside or to the approaching receipt of retirement benefits) would also be recognized as income. Yet the benefits that the employee ultimately draws from the pension plan would *not* be recognized as income, since they would represent the conversion of wealth to consumption. Retirement benefits would be treated just as withdrawals from a savings account are treated now. Present law follows a different course, allowing the exclusion of pension contributions and exempting accruing earnings from tax, but taxing all benefits as they are received.

In its suggested treatment of employer contributions to retirement plans (R-1), Table 3-1 presents a possible compromise with strict accrual-income accounting that is still consistent with the accrual-income approach. In accordance with good accrual-income principles, accruing pension earnings are subject to tax but, for simplicity, the treatment of contributions (by employer or employee) and benefits is the reverse. Contributions would be excluded from income, while benefits would be included. Rigorous adherence to accrual-income principles would require inclusion of contributions and exclusion of benefits. But since the two methods lead to exactly the same results if the employee is subject to tax at the same rate both at the time of contribution and at the time of receipt of benefits, the compromise is basically consistent with the accrual-income strategy.

The footnote to R–1 states that it would be permissible to vary the treatment of earnings according to the characteristics of the taxpaying unit. An instance in current law is the rule permitting a married couple to deduct from taxable income 10 percent of the earnings of the lower-earning spouse (up to a maximum exclusion of $3000). Such variation is in one sense inconsistent with the principle of taxing all income alike. It can, however, be reconciled with the accrual-income approach by regarding the information about sources of earnings as affecting the way accrual-income is to be taxed, much as it may be affected by information about the number of dependents in the taxpayer's family. Alternatively, special rules of this type may be regarded as the administration of an employment subsidy (a tax expenditure) through the income tax. As with many of today's tax expenditures, its objective is to offset an undesirable result of the basic taxing principle.

We take it for granted that an employer may deduct ordinary business expenses in arriving at a figure for business income. Such expenses might well include outlays for items such as tools used by mechanics or journals used by lawyers. In some cases, however, these outlays are made by the employee instead. The deductions for employee business expense is thus needed in the employee income calculation. Unfortunately, whether the deduction is taken by the employer or the employee, there are inevitably difficult lines to draw in deciding what constitutes an ordinary and necessary expense and what constitutes a consumption outlay. The notorious three-martini lunch is an example. There is no simple criterion that will ease identification of the expenses that should be deductible.

R–2 Receipt of Pensions
D–2 Contributions to Retirement Plans

Pensions and similar forms of deferred or contingent compensation are always a source of trouble for income measurement. The reason is that such payments involve a combination of compensation for services rendered and a return to savings. Wherever a return to savings needs to be measured, there will be a problem in an income tax.

Under current law employer contributions to pension plans that qualify by meeting certain requirements are deductible by the employer and not included in employee income. Earnings on pension fund reserves are not subject to tax. Upon retirement, the pension drawn by the employee is taxed in full as an income receipt. This accounting describes the classic method of implementing a consumption tax, but it is incorrect for a true income tax.

As indicated above in connection with the discussion of employer contributions to pensions, strict accrual-income tax treatment would oblige the employee to include the value of a pension contribution in current income and would then tax the earnings on the amount set aside. Benefits received at the time of retirement would be described as return of capital and would be no more subject to tax than would withdrawals from a savings account. The rules in Table 3–1 incorporate a twist on proper income accounting to achieve a roughly equivalent effect in a way more familiar to current taxpayers. The method would also have advantages in providing comparability between defined-contribution plans and the defined-benefit plans under which many employers operate.

As the footnote to R–2 indicates, Social Security benefits logically belong on the receipts side of the accrual-income calculation. But like the deduction for part of the earnings of the secondary worker in a married couple, the partial exclusion of Social Security benefits can be rationalized in an accrual-income framework as the incorporation of information considered relevant to determining the tax treatment of individuals of given income characteristics.

R – 3   Gifts, Inheritances Received
D – 3   Gifts, Bequests Given

Gifts and inheritances received belong on the receipts side of a proper accrual-income account. Later in the form (D–3) is an option to deduct gifts and bequests given. Allowance of a deduction would give the tax what has been labeled in the appendix to Chapter 2 a bestowal-exclusive character; not allowing a deduction leads to a bestowal-inclusive version of income. Present law does not allow a deduction for gifts or bequests given, but it also does not regard gifts and inheritances received as taxable. Income tax theorists typically regard exclusion of gifts or inheritances received from the income of the recipient as rather odd, although they disagree about the treatment of the donor. By contrast, my impression is that people who are not tax theorists regard the idea of including gifts and inheritances received in income as peculiar, if not revolutionary, and are unmoved by the argument that it is called for by income tax principles.

Currently, death benefits paid on a life insurance policy purchased by an individual are not taxed as income to the recipient. (Note that death benefits paid under a qualified retirement plan typically *are* taxed to the recipient, presumably in view of the fact that the policy has been purchased out of before-tax income.) Under accrual-income tax accounting, such benefits, like other transfers, would be taxed to the recipient. If a bestowal-exclusive approach is taken (as assumed in Table 3–1), the premium on life insurance that buys risk protection — as opposed to the increase in accruing value — would be deductible. A bestowal-inclusive approach would disallow the deduction and would, in addition, confront the question of whether the payoff on the policy should be taxed to the policyholder (in the final income tax settlement in the case of a policyholder who is also the insured).

R – 4   Interest Received
D – 4   Interest Paid

No doubt governors and mayors would notice immediately that our accrual-income tax rules provide no exemption for state and local bond interest; such an exemption is inconsistent with accrual-income principles. The law seems to have arrived at its present state somewhat by accident of constitutional interpretation. (The Constitution forbids the federal government from taxing the states.) Its effects on the income tax system are profound. Although typically criticized for treating differently individuals who ought to be treated the same, tax-exempt interest has its principal effect on the progressivity of the system.

Most people take for granted the inclusion of interest receipts in taxable income, and most people understand in a general way the rationale for deduction of interest payments. In fact, however, neither notion is straightforward. Taking it as our objective to measure accrual income, inclusion of the net interest received (that is, adding in interest received and subtracting interest paid) on the sources side of the accounts produces the correct result for an asset such as a savings account, in which the interest payment is exactly what is called for to maintain a constant asset value. A person whose only asset is a savings account and who is credited with $10 of interest during a year must either have gained $10 more in wealth by the end of the year (if the interest is left in the account) or have consumed $10. (Note that the reasoning breaks down if there is inflation during the year. I return to this problem later.)

More often, however, accruing liabilities and increases in value are not so conveniently identified. Even when a transaction is called an interest payment, as in the case of coupon payments on bonds, it is only by chance that the amount is precisely that required to maintain a constant market value for the asset, as anyone knows who has held long-term bonds during a time of changing interest rates. In many cases, such as installment purchases, there is wide discretion with regard to the labeling of payments. Unfortunately, the labeling makes a great deal of difference when borrower and lender are in different tax brackets. Rules must be continually adjusted to the ingenuity of taxpayers and to the complex realities of the highly varied forms of payment in order to achieve some consistency in taxation of interest, which presents a continuing enforcement and compliance problem.

The deduction of interest paid is simply the logical implication of the inclusion of interest received. It would seem odd, for example, not to allow a taxpayer to net interest payments against interest receipts. Limiting the deduction of interest payments would furthermore discriminate between a taxpayer who borrows from himself (by drawing on his savings, that is, by lending less) and one who borrows from someone else. Present law nevertheless incorporates restrictions on interest deductions. For example, the law disallows interest deductions for borrowing incurred to purchase or hold tax-exempt municipal bonds. The intent of the provision, which has been difficult to enforce because of lack of information about taxpayers' holdings of municipals, is to limit "tax arbitrage."

Arbitrage is the activity of buying something in one market and selling it in another market at a higher price. Someone who engages in a pure textbook case of arbitrage makes a profit apparently without doing anything. (Actually, the activity is often productive in improving the effectiveness of markets.) Borrowing at a low rate and lending at a high rate is an example; the thing being purchased is a flow of interest receipts on the funds loaned, and the thing being sold is a flow of interest payments on the borrowed money. The term "tax arbitrage" calls attention to instances in which the tax law affects the profitability of such transactions. Borrowing at deductible interest rates to purchase bonds on which the interest payments are untaxed is a good example. Indeed, if the tax rate were constant and the two interest rates were the same, this transaction would be in effect a "money machine." Every extra dollar borrowed in the taxable market and loaned in the tax-exempt market generates a payment from the government equal to the tax rate times the interest rate.

The forces that such opportunities create on competitive markets are very strong, a fact that is much exploited in the use of tax rules to influence saving and investment behavior. Restricting the deductibility of interest on borrowing to hold tax-exempts is designed to limit the extent of tax arbitrage to what a taxpayer can carry out with himself, by selling any taxable bonds in his portfolio and buying tax-exempts. There are enough such lenders to drive the actual yield on tax-exempts below that on taxable bonds. Thus there is an implicit tax on the tax-exempts. Though the differential has varied widely, a 30 percent implicit tax rate is representative. This puts a ceiling on the tax rate on the return from wealth, or at least it would if tax-exempt bonds were satisfactory as the only element of a portfolio. Any wealth holder in a higher bracket should prefer tax-exempts to taxable bonds. Salary receipts, however, may be subject to higher rates of tax, currently running up to 50 percent. If interest on borrowing to hold tax-exempt securities were allowed, we would expect high-bracket taxpayers to borrow with the left hand at deductible interest and to buy tax-exempts with the right hand. The result would be a clear profit until the interest deductions brought the individual's taxable income down to the 30 percent bracket.

Restrictions on the deduction of interest that relate to the purpose of borrowing must contend with the fungibility of money; that is, whatever the collateral pledged for borrowing, the money may be used for other purposes. The many homeowners who refrain from paying off their mortgages in order to invest the funds at higher return know this well. A second instance of a restriction on the interest deduction attempts to deal with the fungibility problem by casting a wide net. This is the limit on deducting so-called investment interest (interest incurred to buy and hold financial assets of all kinds). Such interest may be deducted only to the extent of the sum of a fixed amount (currently $10,000) and what is called net investment income (dividends, rents, royalties, net short-term gain from the sale of property). (Amounts disallowed may be carried over to future years.)

The justification for the investment interest restriction is really the same as that applied to state and local bonds. Present income measurement rules grossly understate the return from certain kinds of assets, much as they understate the return from municipals. Restricting borrowing to finance acquisition of such assets is designed to limit the lower effective tax rate to accumulated wealth and prevent it from spilling over to the earnings of executives and doctors through "tax shelters." Note, though, that like municipals, the assets in question bear an implicit tax in the form of low before-tax yields. Indeed, it is not clear that there is even much gain for a high-bracket taxpayer in holding the lightly taxed assets in preference to taxable ones.

It is sometimes suggested that the deduction of mortgage interest ought to be eliminated or capped. The underlying reasoning is much the same as in the two restrictions just discussed. The interest deduction itself is proper as an element of the income calculation. The problem is that the yield from the underlying asset, the owner-occupied house, is improperly measured and taxed. Limiting the interest deduction would be an indirect way of offsetting the undertaxation of the consumption services and wealth increase accruing to the homeowner. A drawback of this indirect approach is that it does not affect the tax advantage of home ownership obtained by those with sufficient accumulated wealth to buy for cash. The tax advantage is reduced only for those who must borrow to purchase the home. These considerations constitute a reasonable case in equity for permitting deduction of mortgage interest in the context of an income tax in which no attempt is made to tax income in the form of housing services and accruing capital gain obtained by owner-occupiers.

Sometimes loans are taken out to finance consumption — fly now, pay later. It is generally presumed that deduction of consumer interest is improper in an income tax. In fact, however, the interest paid on amounts borrowed to finance consumption should be deducted in calculating accrual income, that is, the sum of consumption and saving. The point may be understood by recognizing the equivalence between borrowing and reduced lending. No one would suggest that the interest foregone when someone reduces a savings account balance in order to finance greater current consumption should be taxed as though the interest had actually been received. For example, a person who borrowed $1000 last year to finance additional consumption must pay this year, say, $150 in interest to maintain the loan. If that person has no other transactions during the year (and thus no consumption), the payment must reflect a decrease in net worth (either through drawing on some asset or through additional borrowing) of $150. The deduction of $150 interest from zero receipts would give the correct measure of income for the year, namely, negative $150.

The usual argument for eliminating the deduction of consumer loan interest is based on the observation that the interest payment is not a cost of earning income. This argument is presumably grounded in the factor payment concept of income, which is a relative of the accrual-income concept but not identical to it. Even on the factor payment view, however, it is on shaky ground. Consider the case of a person who runs a grocery store and borrows money to support the carrying of inventory. The interest payments would be universally regarded as properly deducted in calculating the storekeeper's income, regardless of whether the store shows a profit, even though the purpose of the borrowing is to permit her to maintain her consumption.

The more persuasive argument for limiting the deduction of interest on consumer loans is the same as that for limiting the deduction of mortgage interest: typically the loans are used to finance the purchase of durable assets, the return on which is free of tax. In the mortgage case the durable asset is a house, which yields valuable housing services and substitutes for the payment of rent; in the consumer loan case the asset may be an automobile or a washing machine, for example. Limiting the deduction of consumer loan interest thus provides an indirect method of taxing the yield from consumer durables. The same counterargument as was mentioned in the case of mortgages, namely, that restricting the deduction of interest restricts the tax advantage to those with sufficient resources to pay in cash, applies here as well.

Table 3–1 calls for adjusting interest payments and receipts for inflation. It is difficult to overstate the corrosive effect of present rules for taxing interest in a time of inflation. To be fair, mismeasurement of interest income is only part of the problem created by inflation, but it is an important part. Here is how the mismeasurement arises: Interest rates tend to rise with inflation. In a time of inflation interest payments consist only partly of payment for a year's use of purchasing power. The rest is an "inflation premium," effectively a repayment of principal reflecting the erosion in value of any given dollar amount as inflation proceeds. The tax law, however, does not distinguish between the inflation premium and the real interest rate in allowing a deduction for interest payments and in taxing interest receipts. We would have no reason to expect a change in the attractiveness of borrowing and lending during a period of inflation in the absence of taxes. But under the present income tax rules, the effect of higher rates of inflation is to make debt more attractive as an asset for low-bracket taxpayers such as pension funds (which pay no tax) and less attractive as an asset (and therefore more attractive as a liability) for high-bracket taxpayers.

The strength of this effect is not widely understood, perhaps because the proverbial power of compounding is itself not widely appreciated. A decision to save can be thought of as a choice to purchase future consumption rather than current consumption. The amount one needs to put aside now to buy a dollar in the future is the buying price of that dollar. One shops for future dollars on the capital market, buying them by making a loan at interest (or acquiring some other asset). The more distant in the future is the dollar being purchased, the lower will be its current price. It is not unusual for a saver to be interested in claims on consumption thirty years hence. A thirty-five-year-old who is saving for retirement is in this position.

Table 3-2 demonstrates the effect of taxes on the price of consumption thirty years hence, with and without inflation. In the absence of inflation, the interest rate is assumed to be a modest 2 percent a year. A person who lends at 2 percent and accumulates the resulting return needs to put aside just $0.55 currently to obtain $1.00 thirty years from now, provided he is not taxed on the interest (see column 2). After paying tax on interest receipts, someone in the 50 percent bracket receives a net rate of return of 1 percent, so the price of thirty-years-hence dollars is somewhat higher, roughly $0.74.

If the amount one needs to lend at interest now to obtain delivery of a dollar in the future is the buying price of that dollar, the selling price is the amount one can borrow against a promise to pay a dollar in the future. Under the simplifying assumption that borrowing and lending rates are the same, the buying and selling prices will be the same. Table 3-2 tells us the price of a promise to deliver $1.00 thirty years from now.

Table 3-2. Effect of inflation on the price (via borrowing or lending) of a dollar of purchasing power thirty years hence

Individual tax rate (1)	No inflation or inflation plus inflation adjustment (2)	10% inflation with no inflation adjustment (3)
0%	$0.55	$0.55
10	0.59	0.79
20	0.62	1.13
30	0.66	1.62
40	0.70	2.34
50	0.74	3.40

Note: Entries show the present amount one would have to pay to purchase a claim on $1.00 (in present purchasing power) thirty years from now. The interest rate with no inflation is assumed to be 2 percent; with inflation at 10 percent, the interest rate is assumed to be 12 percent.

Inflation need not alter the buying and selling prices of real dollars (that is, dollars of constant purchasing power). If interest rates were to rise point for point with inflation, an inflation rate of 10 percent would lead to an interest rate of 12 percent.[1] Such a shift in the interest rate would keep the "real interest rate" (the rate earned in terms of real purchasing power) constant, at 2 percent in the absence of taxes. Furthermore, if individuals were taxed only on the 2 percent, with the extra 10 percent neither taxed to the recipient nor allowed as a deduction to the payer, the real rate of return after taxes would also be independent of the rate of inflation. The buying and selling prices of dollars would continue to be related to individual tax rates as before (column 2).

The picture is dramatically changed if the tax is levied on nominal, rather than real, interest. The calculations for the zero-bracket taxpayer are unchanged, of course: the real rates of return before and after taxes remain equal at 2 percent. However, for a taxpayer in the 50 percent bracket, the after-tax real rate of return drops from 1 percent to *negative* 4 percent (one-half times the before-tax return of 12 percent less the 10 percent rate of inflation). To obtain a dollar of present purchasing power thirty years hence would require the 50 percent taxpayer to put aside more than $1.00 now — $3.40 to be precise. The tax on the transaction has jumped from 35 percent ($0.74 less $0.55 divided by $0.55) to 618 percent ($3.40 less $0.55 divided by $0.55).

Remember, though, that the prices apply to buying *and* selling. The tax on buying acts as a subsidy to selling future dollars (that is, borrowing). Because there are assets on which the income measurement problems are different — on which the differential between before-tax and after-tax rates of return is less marked between high-bracket and low-bracket taxpayers — the high-bracket taxpayer will find it profitable to be a seller of future dollars (to be a borrower) in the market where the returns are labeled "interest." This is why it makes sense for doctors and lawyers to borrow money to buy apartment buildings.

In the case of an asset such as a savings account, it would be a relatively straightforward matter to adjust interest payments and receipts for purposes of income taxation. If the balance is the same at the beginning and end of the year, the real interest received by the account holder would be the nominal amount received (and withdrawn) less the decline in the purchasing power of the balance over the year (given by the

---

1. An adjustment of interest of 1 percentage point for each percentage point of inflation is less than would be predicted by economic theory in light of the taxation of interest, but it is more than seems to have been typically experienced. Compare Summers (1983).

inflation rate times the balance amount). That is, the rate of interest on which taxation is based would be the nominal rate less the rate of inflation.

When assets are more complicated in character (for example, in having a term structure of payments due), precise inflation adjustment is more difficult. This is in part attributable to the inherent weakness of cash interest payments as an element of income measurement. For example, a bond that called for annual payments of $50 per year for twenty years, with a repayment of $1000 in principal at the end, would sell at par ($1000) when the going interest rate is 5 percent. If the interest rate were to jump to 10 percent shortly after issue, the bond would fall in value immediately, to roughly half of par. Such a value change would not appear on the tax accounts of the holder unless the bond were sold. The interest payment of $50 in the first year, for instance, would represent the holder as having enjoyed an increase in wealth, whereas the actual situation is a large decrease.

The design of inflation adjustment to interest payments and receipts thus faces a problem of dealing with basic inadequacies in their use in income measurement even when there is no inflation. Partly for this reason, most commentators have concluded that correcting interest for inflation is more academic than practical (see, for example, Aaron, 1976; Shoven and Bulow, 1976; U.S. Treasury Department, 1977). The short political life of the inflation adjustment of interest contained in the U.S. Treasury's November 1984 reform proposal appears to confirm the traditional view. The Treasury plan may be illustrated as follows: Starting from the presumption that the rate of interest in the absence of inflation would be 6 percent and that the interest rate would increase point for point with increases in the inflation rate, in the absence of tax effects the typical savings account would yield 16 percent if there were 10 percent inflation during a year. Of the amount received in interest, only six-sixteenths would then represent real additional purchasing power; the remaining ten-sixteenths would be compensation for the inflationary erosion. Under the Treasury plan interest recipients would include in income subject to tax only six-sixteenths of interest receipts — the assumed real interest rate — and interest payers would deduct only six-sixteenths of interest paid. Generalizing, under the November 1984 proposal the Treasury would make a determination of the inflation that had taken place in a given year. Of the interest received in that year a fraction equal to six divided by the sum of six plus the rate of inflation (in percent) would be included in the recipients' income, and the same fraction would be allowed as a deduction to payers.

The Treasury plan was complex and flawed in various respects. As Table 3–2 indicates, however, some such correction of interest receipts (and payments) is essential for the workability of an accrual-income tax. If the adjustment is not made explicitly, strong pressures will be created to implement other approaches to dealing with the problem.

R–5 Dividends

Readers may be surprised that our plan does not call for taxation of dividends. Are not dividends income? In fact, dividends as such are not a good indicator of an individual's income. That is, it is unlikely that an individual who owned shares, had no other sources of funds, and consumed all dividends during the year would have the same wealth at the end as at the beginning of the year. A dividend amounts to a conversion of a part of an asset to cash, and it no more represents a good measure of income than does a withdrawal from a bank account.

The U.S. Treasury's *Blueprints* (1977) recommended the treatment of dividends shown in Table 3–1, in conjunction with a system of accounting for the value of shares by relating it to a measure of the corporation's income and with rules for taxing capital gains. In the suggested system, the tax consequence of receipt of a dividend is simply a reduction in the basis of the share (the concept of "basis" is discussed below), which is carried along for calculation of gain upon sale or exchange. Rules other than those proposed in Table 3–1 could certainly be imagined. But the adequacy of the present treatment of dividends as an approximation of proper income measurement cannot be assessed separately from a discussion of both the corporation tax and capital gains, topics taken up below.

R–6 Proceeds from the Sale of Capital Assets
D–5 Basis of Capital Assets Sold

Current law incorporates complicated rules regarding the inclusion in income of capital gains and the deduction of capital losses, defined as the difference between the proceeds (net of sale transaction costs) from the sale of an asset defined in the tax code as a "capital asset" and the "adjusted basis" of the asset. (In some circumstances, such as an exchange, an asset may be treated as though it had been sold, and the fair market value is substituted for sale proceeds.) An asset's basis is typically the acquisition price plus purchase transaction costs. Sometimes, however, basis is adjusted for events since acquisition, and so it is best to think of it as a kind of book value that is carried along with the asset.

One can hardly exaggerate the contribution to the complexity of the income tax of present rules for the taxation of capital gains. The reason is largely, though not entirely, the special treatment of capital gains on assets held for six months or more ("long-term" capital gains) and on assets held until a taxpayer's death. While gain from an asset held for less than six months is included in full, a deduction is allowed for a portion, currently 60 percent, of long-term capital gains, and income tax on gain from an asset held at the time of a taxpayer's death is forgiven (by the device of permitting an adjustment in the asset's basis to its then-current market value).[2] As a result, high-bracket taxpayers have a strong incentive to hold assets on which the yield will come in the form of long-term capital gain. (Note that by borrowing, taxpayers can take advantage of the write-up of basis at death even if they plan to leave no estate.)

More important for the complexity of the tax is the enormous value that high-bracket taxpayers realize by identifying income as long-term capital gain rather than as "ordinary income." Elaborate rules are required to impede taxpayers' natural inclination to organize their affairs so that virtually everything appears as long-term capital gain. For example, rules must define a capital asset and specify the time when its value is to be taken into income (referred to as a "recognition event"). In addition, the existing tax law designates certain forms of business income (for example, income from raising timber and certain other agricultural products) as long-term capital gain.

The special treatment of long-term gains is not the only reason capital gains are a source of complexity in the law. Normally the recognition event that triggers a tax liability is the "realization" of an asset's value through sale. Because the timing is under the individual's control, the sale can be arranged to take place in a period for which the marginal tax rate is relatively low (for example, in retirement) or in a year when other income receipts are low for some reason. (If the asset is held until death, the applicable tax rate is reduced to zero.)

Despite the mismeasurement of accrual income, one might argue that the ability of a taxpayer to locate income in periods of relatively low marginal rate is desirable as an averaging device. However, the option to decide when to realize gain or loss has other, more mischievous consequences. Even if the applicable tax rate does not change, the taxpayer

2. A full description of capital gains would include a discussion of the alternative minimum tax, as well as the odd feature that although 40 percent of net long-term capital gains is subject to tax, 50 percent of net long-term capital losses is allowed as a deduction (subject to fairly stringent limits on the total deduction allowed in a given year).

will benefit from postponement. Deferring payment is in effect an inter-est-free loan of the amount deferred. The limiting case of infinite post-ponement is equivalent to zero tax. Conversely, the value of the tax saving is increased by realizing losses immediately. In the absence of restrictive rules, taxpayers could actually wipe out virtually all income tax liability by a carefully constructed program of realizing losses imme-diately and holding gains until death (compare Stiglitz, 1983).

Elaborate rules to define and limit capital gains are thus inevitable in an income tax based on realization. The implications for complexity are significant. Many people seem to believe that the differential in rates between long-term and short-term gains is the only culprit responsible for this mischief. Taxing capital gains and other receipts at the same rate might ameliorate the problems (because it would reduce the finan-cial stakes), but it would not eliminate them, because it would not eliminate the need to identify capital gains.

The alternative to realization-based taxation of gains is annual mea-surement of the value of a taxpayer's assets and liabilities. Unfortu-nately, although more could no doubt be done along these lines than is at present attempted, annual appraisal would be costly and subject to substantial error. For that reason even plans that aim at a close approx-imation to accrual income (such as the Treasury's November 1984 plan) employ the realization method of taxing capital gains. The example in Table 3-1 also concedes defeat on this point, as summarized in items R-6 and D-5. As in the Treasury's 1984 plan, the gains calculated would, however, be subject to taxation in full, regardless of the length of time the asset was held. Losses would similarly be deducted in full, but a limit is required, along the lines of current rules restricting net capital losses to $3000, to prevent taxpayers from arranging to shelter all their income in capital losses.[3]

Realization accounting can be regarded as an attempt to approximate accrual taxation of the change in value of an asset held over the report-ing period. Presumably the more often the asset is subjected to tax, the better the approximation, and one possibility sometimes suggested would be obligatory appraisal of assets on a periodic basis. With the choice of a long enough period — say, every five years — the cost of implementation might be brought within acceptable bounds. An often-proposed version of the same technique would be to regard death as a recognition event. Among the possible alternative devices to deal with

---

3. As I state in the introduction to Bradford et al. (1984), I believe *Blueprints* errs seriously in imposing no limit on realization of capital losses in the Comprehensive Income Tax. The Treasury's November 1984 plan is silent on the point.

the problem of tax postponement that occurs under realization taxation of capital gains is to charge an extra tax as a proxy for interest on the postponed liability. (This was the approach suggested in the *Blueprints* Comprehensive Income Tax.) The Internal Revenue Service would publish a table of factors calculated by accountants so that the discounted present value of the tax would be about what would have obtained under annual accrual taxation. Gain or loss on an asset would be multiplied by a factor that depended on the holding period. Whatever the technical merits of the idea, it would certainly be a complicating element and seems destined to remain in the academic category.

Table 3–1 calls for correction of the basis of assets for change in the purchasing power of money during the holding period. Without such an adjustment, the measured gain or loss may bear no relation at all to the real gain or loss. If an asset is acquired for $100 and sold for $200 after the general price level has doubled, there will be a nominal capital gain of $100 when, in fact, the holder has had no gain at all in real purchasing power.

The widespread tendency, even in sophisticated financial reporting, to neglect the effect of inflation on financial data is amazing. For example, much attention is paid to stock market indices, and it is considered a major event when one reaches a "new high." But these indices are accounted for in current dollars; accounts kept in constant-purchasing-power dollars, presumably the units that investors should be interested in, may paint a very different picture. In the thirty years between 1953 and 1983, the price level much more than tripled; in the decade 1973–1983, the price level more than doubled.[4] The much-watched Dow-Jones Industrial Average, which represents a portfolio of high-quality stocks, increased from 276 in 1953 to 924 in 1973 to 1190 in 1983, an apparently impressive gain (U.S. Government, 1984a). But expressed in terms of 1983 purchasing power, the figures are 1012 for 1953, 1884 for 1973, and 1190 for 1983!

Under the circumstances, it would hardly be surprising if capital gains had been greatly overstated on tax returns in recent years. Indeed, we can be sure a large amount of capital gains reported on tax returns would have been recognized as losses if buying and selling prices had been stated in dollars of the same purchasing power. Using data from a

---

4. According to the *1984 Economic Report of the Council of Economic Advisors* (U.S. Government, 1984a) the gross national product (GNP) deflator grew from 57.92 in 1953 to 215.63 in 1983 (1972 = 100); by that measure, prices increased by a factor of 3.7 over the period. The deflator for 1973 was 105.75; prices thus increased by a factor of just over 2.0 in the decade.

sample of tax returns, Martin Feldstein and Joel Slemrod (1978) were able to compare real and nominal capital gains realized on common stock and reported by taxpayers for 1973. Although the transactions covered a period before the onset of the more dramatic inflation of recent years, their correction reduced the aggregate figure from a gain of $4.6 billion to a *loss* of $0.9 billion (in 1973 dollars).

Although it predated the onset of serious inflation, the exclusion of a substantial portion of long-term capital gains is sometimes rationalized as an inflation adjustment. However, partial exclusion effects an extremely crude correction. No exclusion (less than 100 percent) of the gain of $100 in the example with which I began this discussion would correct the mismeasurement. A reduced inclusion rate cannot change a recorded gain to a recorded loss. Nor can a reduced inclusion rate properly account for the very different relationship between nominal and real gains according to the length of the holding period.

Proper inflation adjustment would be conceptually fairly simple, although administratively unpleasant for the average taxpayer who had to deal with it. The object is to express all quantities in the tax return in dollars of current purchasing power. Correction of the measurement of capital gains calls for inflating the basis for the change in purchasing power from the date of acquisition to the date of recognition. The Internal Revenue Service would provide a table with inflation factors for each year in the past (perhaps for each month of the more recent past), and the taxpayer would simply multiply the basis by the appropriate factor in calculating gains. The Treasury's November 1984 plan incorporates essentially this procedure.

R-8 Increase in Value of Trusts

Entities in the nature of trusts, which hold assets on behalf of others, pose problems for income measurement (see Chapter 2). Item R-8 calls for the individual to record the accruing value of an interest in a trust. The point is somewhat academic, designed to remind readers that the income tax on trusts is a proxy for the tax on its beneficiaries.

R-9 *Gross Business Receipts*
D-6 *Current Business Expenses*
D-7 *Business Capital Expenses*
D-8 *Depreciation Allowances*

Measuring the effect of a business on an individual's income (consumption plus change in net worth) presents the toughest problems of all. An individual who owns a business may put into it time, ideas, and effort. He obtains a flow of cash and perhaps some goods and services in kind, and holds a continuing claim to the assets of the business, together with a continuing responsibility for its liabilities. Business assets are of many sorts, including both real and personal property. The going business itself is typically worth more than the sum of the market value of its components. This is true almost by definition of the valuation placed on the firm by its owner; otherwise, he would sell the bits and pieces.

Measuring the flow of cash from a business is in principle simple enough, whatever the practical problems of monitoring by the tax authorities may be. Measuring goods and services provided in kind — an office that doubles as a study, a business auto also used for private purposes, produce from the family farm used at the home table, and so on — is difficult and will always be a reason business income is more lightly taxed than cash compensation from employment. (Note that this does *not* necessarily mean that the owner of a business bears less of the tax burden than the wage earner. Competition tends to equalize *after-tax* rewards.) The problems of taxing payments in kind from a business are much the same as that of taxing employee business expenses. There is no perfect system.

Assessing the accruing changes in the value of the business to the individual, which is required for proper income taxation, is confined as a practical matter to applying accounting rules to the component pieces: structures, inventories, mortgages, receivables, and so on. The issues raised by attempts to account for borrowing and lending at interest, an important part of the accounting for a business, have already been discussed. Many problems are also raised by other aspects of accounting for financial transactions (installment purchases, leases of various kinds, and so on). However, this discussion will concentrate on accounting for "real assets": structures, equipment, and inventories.

In accounting for structures and equipment, businesses use depreciation allowances to reflect the accruing loss in value as the assets are used or as they simply age. Although they are described as cost-recovery rules, the function of depreciation allowances in income accounting is to track the declining market value of wealth. Because it is almost impossible to observe the value of such an asset as a component of a going business, and yet books must be kept without excessive reliance on hard-to-monitor judgments, accountants do in fact use a system of cost recovery with respect to "depreciable assets." That is, the purchase price or other measure of the acquisition cost of the asset is written off over a period of years.

Inflation wreaks havoc with accounts kept on this basis. But even with stable prices, the proper approach to writing off an asset's cost is inevitably controversial and complex. Some assets come in standard form (for example, a specific model of a tractor trailer). But most have a large element of uniqueness; and furthermore, the way an asset is used may greatly affect its productivity and therefore its value. Although recent research has improved the state of knowledge about depreciation, we have only a rough idea about actual "economic depreciation," that is, about the actual pattern of value decline.[5] Moreover, empirical analysis can at best tell us what pattern of depreciation held in the *past*. Unpredictable developments — a jump in the price of energy, a new technology — hamper projection from the past into the future.

Depreciation allowances have therefore been a source of great complexity for the taxpayer and tax collector and a subject of continuing political struggle. Our present Accelerated Cost Recovery System (ACRS) reflects an effort to cut through some of the complexity by aggregating assets into a small number of classes to which standardized "accelerated" depreciation allowances are applied. Although the system certainly reduces the number of lines that must be drawn and thereby serves simplicity, the crudeness of its approach to income measurement sets up incentives that misdirect investment.

There is a tradition (embodied in the tax code in provisions relating to so-called preference income) of regarding straight-line depreciation allowances (often derived from guidelines promulgated by the Treasury in 1942) as correct. (Under "straight-line" depreciation the same fraction of the value of an asset is written off in each year of its estimated "useful life.") Any pattern that results in cumulative cost write-offs being larger at each time point than would be implied by straight-line allowances is regarded as "accelerated." Although there is little doubt that ACRS allowances are, indeed, accelerated relative to the actual path of decline in the value of assets (if we neglect inflation), a degree of humility is in order about which scheme would best reflect the reality of changing asset values.

Inflation makes nonsense out of depreciation allowances that simply spread the historical cost of an asset over a predetermined time pattern

---

5. Research by Charles R. Hulton and Frank C. Wykoff suggests that depreciation of equipment follows a declining balance pattern that can be described as 1.65 times the straight-line rate over average lives. The corresponding declining balance rate for structures is 0.91 (Hulton and Wykoff, 1981, p. 94).

(see Aaron, 1976, and Shoven and Bulow, 1975). If an asset cost $100 when purchased, and a deduction of $20 would be appropriate to reflect depreciation during, say, the fifth year of the asset's use, the allowance should be $40 if the price level has doubled in the meantime. The overstatement of income due to historical cost accounting in a time of inflation is a very serious problem that requires correction through appropriate adjustments.

The accelerated depreciation provided by ACRS is sometimes justified as a response to inflation. But because it would call for a revision in the rules every time the rate of inflation changed, accelerated depreciation is distinctly second best as an inflation adjustment. The appropriate response to inflation is explicit correction of the measurements. Two basic methods have been suggested. The first would simply apply a multiplicative factor reflecting the rate of inflation to depreciation allowances designed to give good results in the absence of inflation. (Appropriate changes in the basis of assets would also be required.) This is the method adopted in the Treasury's November 1984 proposal. (Although the administration's May 1985 tax proposal differed from the November 1984 plan in recommending accelerated depreciation, it kept the inflation adjustment.) The second method, known in tax policy circles as the "Auerbach-Jorgenson method" in tribute to its designers (Auerbach and Jorgenson, 1980), would permit businesses to take a first-year allowance calculated to approximate the discounted present value of the allowances they would receive with correct depreciation deductions under stable prices. Placing the entire deduction in one period avoids the adding of apples and oranges that inflation would otherwise cause. This front-loading is generally regarded favorably by businesses, both because it renders predictable the tax consequences of making an investment and because it has a short-term positive effect on cash flows. The timing of the flow of tax payments makes the scheme less attractive to politicians, because the early deduction increases the measured deficit (even though the discounted value of tax payments is the same under both approaches).

Inflation also creates problems for the rules used by accountants to keep track of inventories in measuring income. As it happens, of the two basic inventory accounting methods one — last-in, first-out (LIFO) — provides a fair approximation to proper income measurement, as long as inventories do not change much. Curiously, in spite of the substantial tax advantages many firms still use the first-in, first-out (FIFO) method and therefore incur a tax burden that is significantly higher than necessary. (The LIFO and FIFO accounting rules are described in Chapter 6.)

Inventories are often overlooked in discussions of capital formation, and few seem to appreciate that inventories constitute nearly one-fourth of the reproducible assets of nonfinancial corporations in the United States (Board of Governors of the Federal Reserve System, April 1984). It is thus significant that present practices have the effect of subjecting investment in inventories to taxation at least at the level of statutory tax rates at a time when accelerated depreciation, investment credit, and the like do much to lighten the tax burden on other forms of capital.

R - 10   Allocated Share of Corporate Earnings

Determining the income of shareholders in corporations is an instance (quantitatively the most important one) of the general problem of taxing an individual's claim on trusts. Our plan attempts to solve the problem by "integration" of corporation and individual shareholder income accounts.

But for one class of corporations, those whose shares are actively traded on major exchanges, a much simpler method is available. The contribution of a share of General Motors to the income of a person who holds it over the tax year is readily observable; we can read in the *Wall Street Journal* the market value of the share on the first and last market days of the tax year. The difference is the bit of change in the shareholder's net worth that comes from holding the share. To this we simply add any dividend paid during the year. If income measured by this method differs from corporation income as measured by accountants, it is not because the market is wrong. There is no doubt that the market gives the true value of the corporation's income in the accrual-income sense (which *defines* income in terms of the market's valuation of assets and liabilities). Experts have occasionally advocated this approach to measuring shareholder income and favored replacement of the corporation income tax by an annual "marking to market" of share values.

There are problems, however, with using market values of shares to measure income. The shares of thousands of corporations are not actively traded on large markets. In addition, people do not appear to believe fully in market values. The market's valuation of the corporate sector in the aggregate, considering debt and equity claims together, varies greatly over time. Equity value, in particular, is highly variable, especially for individual firms but also for all corporations taken together. Income as measured by corporation accounting is much more stable, a fact that makes accounting income both more attractive to the tax collector and more plausible to individual shareholders.

These reasons suggest the approach, taken in Table 3–1, of using corporation accounting to produce a measure of income that would be allocated to individual shareholders as a sort of proxy for the true accrual-income measure. Because the plan taxes capital gains in full on realization, the corporation-level measure can be regarded as a way of capturing the accrual of income in the interval between the acquisition of stock and its disposal. Any error in the corporation accounting measure would be corrected on realization.

Much is made of the complexity of integrating corporation and shareholder accounts. Most of the complexity, however, has to do with managing the many deviations from proper income accounting in the existing system — tax-exempt interest, investment tax credit, accelerated depreciation, and all the other devices now decorating the code. Reasonably simple rules would suffice if a genuine income measure were employed at the level of the corporation (see Bradford et al., 1984, pp. 63–69).

All of this requires correct measurement of income at the corporate level, which means solving correctly all the problems enumerated above in measuring income (and many other problems as well).

The United States has a version of what is called in the jargon a "classical" corporation income tax. This means that, in theory at least, income is measured and taxed at the corporate level. Dividends paid out to shareholders are then taxed again as income at the individual level.[6] In most tax experts' view, the principal justification for the corporation income tax is that it substitutes for taxation of the individual shareholder's accruing wealth. Since the rules embodied in Table 3–1 purport to measure and tax that accruing wealth, no provision is made there for a separate tax on corporations.

Note, though, that there would be no *logical* inconsistency in retaining a corporation tax in the setting of proper taxation of individual income, and a continuing tax on corporations might well make sense as a compo-

---

6. Because income is so far from properly measured, the effective tax system is actually very different. The net effect of reducing the rate of corporation income tax to zero would probably be to *raise* the effective taxation of the return to capital employed in the corporate sector.

nent of a transition to a rationalized individual tax. Shareholder income would then be measured *net* of taxes paid by the corporation. But to avoid pernicious interactions with the personal tax, care would be required in the design of a corporate-level tax.

R – 11   Inputed Income from Durables

Item R – 11 expresses our plan's pious hope to tax the service value of consumer durables, including houses. It is in the ignoring of this service flow that the current system favors owner-occupied housing (relative to a strict accrual-income tax), rather than in its allowing a deduction for mortgage interest. Although the value of services of consumer durables can be rather easily captured under a consumption-type tax (see Chapters 4 and 5), generally this portion of a person's accrual income is omitted from income taxes.

D – 9   Itemized Deductions

Many people seem to believe that itemized deductions represent the main discrepancy between the actual income tax and one based on proper income measurement. In fact, this viewpoint has little merit. Whatever the defects of most of the allowances on Schedule A of Form 1040, clear violation of accrual-income principles is not among them. Remember that accrual income is the sum of consumption and the change in net worth during the year. In most instances itemized deductions can be understood as specifying the definition of consumption to be used for purposes of assigning tax burdens (see Andrews, 1972).

I have already mentioned the deductions for medical and dental expenses and for state and local taxes as examples. One may well argue that the deduction of medical expenses is an undesirable policy. (The effect of the deduction is to provide a rather peculiar health insurance program; if it were thought of in that way, policymakers might choose a different design.) However, it is not logically inconsistent with the concept of accrual income in the way that, for example, the realization basis for taxing capital gains is. Similarly, the policy value of the deduction for taxes is debatable. (It provides a cost-sharing program for local government, with the best terms to high-bracket itemizers.) But it does not conflict with the principle of accrual-income taxation.

Is a contribution to a church or hospital fund drive or university scholarship fund consumption? A reasonable case can be made that amounts given away are not consumed and therefore should be deducted in arriving at a measure of accrual income. As with the other itemized deductions, serious issues of policy are involved in determining the treatment of charitable contributions (for example, whether it is desirable that a deduction effectively provides a matching grant program, with the rate of matching higher for high-bracket than for low-bracket taxpayers). However, a charitable deduction is not logically in conflict with the basic theory of income taxation.

There is little quarrel that a casualty or theft loss represents a reduction in net worth and is in that sense an appropriate subtraction in the income calculation. The complaint about this deduction in the context of income measurement is that the assets in question are already outside the income accounts. Why bring them in just at this point?

We may sum up the key points of stress between theoretical purity and tax practice as follows. First, cash transactions form only the starting point for income measurement. Because, as the name suggests, the definition of accrual income embodies an accrual idea, namely, the change in wealth during the year, cash transactions in a given year are not sufficient to specify income. Even the treatment of interest payments and receipts is complicated as soon as one leaves the world of simple, constant rates of interest and no inflation.

Second, existing law deviates from accrual-income principles in a number of ways. Various forms of compensation for labor services are excluded from the base. Important among the exclusions are elements in the nature of consumption (such as use of the company car) as well as elements in the nature of saving (such as contributions to a pension plan). A similar remark applies to the return to the holding of assets. In some cases assets yield consumption services directly (as do owner-occupied homes); this consumption is not captured in the tax base. The law also makes little pretense of measuring accruing changes in the value of assets. Instead, rules of thumb are used in some cases (as in depreciation allowances), while in other cases realization accounting is used (as in capital gains).

Where the income measurement system fails to pick up an element of consumption, such as that of the homeowner-occupier or the employee who enjoys the tax-free use of a company gym, there is a degree of self-correction in the system. Owners will be inclined to consume only so much housing services; gymnasiums can substitute only so much for cash compensation. But the deviations relating to accruing wealth changes are inherently more mischievous. These deviations are particular sources of stress in an income tax, because taxpayers may be able to play off one tax treatment against another (for example, by deducting interest on a loan used to finance the purchase of an asset that is accruing long-term capital gains). Efforts to deal with such inconsistencies represent one of the most serious sources of complexity in the law.

Third, one of the most obvious inconsistencies of present law with the accrual-income ideal is the corporation income tax. If this tax is to be understood as a component of an income measurement system (rather than simply an ad hoc tax), it must be as an indirect substitute for measuring the accruing wealth changes of the corporations' owners. (The taxation of corporations will be considered in detail in Chapter 6.)

Finally, if achieving a reasonable approximation to accrual income is difficult in the context of an economy with stable prices, it is many times more difficult under inflationary conditions. Inflation completely upsets the normal treatment of interest, depreciation, and capital gains. The efforts to deal with these problems in the 1970–1981 period of high inflation lacked a clear connection to the underlying real objective of an income tax and seriously eroded the coherence of the tax rules.

Taxing Consumption:
Value-Added and Sales Taxes

The value added tax seems destined to remain among that honored list of ideas good enough never to be wholly forgotten, but not good enough ever to be adopted.

Henry Aaron, in Walker and Bloomfield, *New Directions in Federal Tax Policy for the 1980's*

TAXATION on the basis of consumption or expenditure has been considered, and sometimes used, in the United States and other countries. This chapter and the next describe rules that have the effect of taxing on the basis of consumption and explain how these possible tax systems differ. Although they lay out some of the policy issues involved in using one or the other approach, the main purpose of Chapters 4 and 5 is descriptive. Most of the discussion of matters such as equity, efficiency, and simplicity will receive fuller treatment later.

Altogether *six* approaches to consumption taxation are distinguished in this book: a value-added tax (VAT), a retail sales tax, a two-tiered cash-flow tax (modeled on the Hall-Rabushka Simple Flat Tax), a pure cash-flow tax (modeled on the Aaron-Galper plan), the *Blueprints* Cash-Flow Tax, and a phase-in of full use of consumption-type tax rules under the existing income tax. The first two approaches are taken up in this chapter. The last four constitute what are called in this book "consumption taxes of the income type" because of their similarity to the existing income tax. They are the subject of Chapter 5. It may seem excessive to enumerate six types of consumption-based taxes; however, they have many common elements, a fact that explains the considerable flexibility that is available for implementing a consumption strategy of taxation.

Primary emphasis here will be given to the VAT, commonly viewed as *the* consumption tax. The VAT implicitly or explicitly deals with almost all the issues that arise in any type of consumption-based tax, including many problems continually wrestled with in implementing the consumption aspects of an income tax (for example, the question of allowing a medical deduction or a deduction for commuting expenses). Discovering such problems in the VAT serves both to reduce the tendency to romanticize it as a panacea and to cast in a new light some of the policy choices confronted in broadening the base of the existing income tax. The fact that a VAT or similar consumption-type tax must deal with the conceptual matters of definition that have been raised so far is one of two broad themes running through this chapter. The other is the contrast between the accrual accounting concepts necessary to implement an income-type tax and the cash-flow accounting techniques appropriate for a consumption-type tax.

Value-Added Taxes

A consumption tax is identified in many people's minds with a value-added tax or its close relative, a retail sales tax. Both can be thought of as flat taxes on sales to households. How does a tax on sales to households relate to a tax on the consumption of households in the sense discussed in Chapter 2? The simple accounting framework presented there identified several categories of household outlays, including, in one version, "consumption," "gifts and bequests given," "cost of earnings," "certain other outlays," and "saving." Assuming that a decision has been made about which transactions constitute consumption for purposes of defining income subject to tax, we may ask whether outlays labeled "consumption" represent purchases from firms and, further, whether none of the other outlays represent purchases from firms. If so, then a tax on sales to households must be a tax on consumption in the same sense. If not, the tax on sales to households may still be a tax on consumption, but the notion of consumption must be a different one, and it will be of interest to inquire into the significance of those differences.

I have stressed that the difference between a tax on accrual income and a tax on consumption lies in the treatment of saving. Any tax that does not impose a burden on the return to saving — for example, a tax on chewing gum — may be classified as a consumption tax for some definition of consumption. However, it is not necessarily the case that a VAT imposes no burden on the return to saving. It will be easier to explain why after we have looked at some of the accounting details involved in the definition of value added.

The concept of value added describes the activities of firms. It is basically a simple idea: In producing, say, bitters, the Better Bitters Corporation purchases processed caraway seeds from the Cwality Caraway Company and fermented dandelion leaves from Dandy Dandelion, Inc. With any luck, the market value of Better's output of bitters will exceed that of the inputs obtained from Cwality and Dandy. The excess is the "value added" by Better.

Actually, in a tax context we typically measure not the value of the firm's output but the value of its *sales*. Additions and subtractions from the firm's inventory due to its own production are examples of differences between the value of output and the value of sales. Similarly, we measure not the value of inputs used but the *outlays* on inputs purchased from other firms. The accruing decline in value of productive equipment purchased in the past illustrates the distinction. The difference between recording the value of a firm's outputs and inputs and recording its sales and purchases may seem a minor technicality. It turns out, however, to be of fundamental importance. Because it determines whether the tax bears on the return to saving or not, we might say it makes all the difference between a tax based on consumption and a tax based on income. It also makes much of the difference between a simple tax and a complicated tax. A wider appreciation of the distinction between the two approaches would therefore advance the cause of clarity in the tax law.

Crucial Accounting Distinctions in VATs

Consider first the case in which we keep track of sales and purchases by firms. Purchases are understood as including all payments *to other firms* (not to employees) for business purposes, such as payments for currently used materials, additions to inventory, maintenance services, and capital equipment. On the other side of the ledger are included all receipts from the sale of products or services to firms or households. This method of describing the activities of a firm is an example of *cash-flow* accounting (as contrasted with accrual accounting).[1]

We can see that every interfirm transaction results in an addition to the calculated value added of the seller and a subtraction from the calculated value added of the buyer. If we add up all the bits of value

---

1. Once again there is a problem of terminology. Accountants are familiar with the concept of cash-basis accounting (contrasted with accrual accounting), under which firms may record some transactions on the basis of actual cash receipts and payments and others on the basis of accruals (such as accounts receivable). The important distinction in this book is between accounts that treat capital and current outlays and receipts differently and those (the cash-flow type) that do not.

added by the firms in the economy, we obtain the value of the aggregate net sales by firms to nonfirms. In a simple system in which all nonfirms are households, in which all household purchases constitute consumption, and in which no consumption is obtained other than by current purchases, it follows that the aggregate obtained by cash-flow value-added accounting is a measure of consumption. Exactly what sort of consumption concept is involved depends on the details of how we identify firms and exactly what transactions are counted (including perhaps some implicit transactions, as in the case of financial services paid for by consumers in the form of reduced interest earnings on bank deposits). In any event, a proportional tax levied on firms' cash-flow value added will be a form of tax on consumption. It is therefore called by tax theorists a VAT of the consumption type.

Now consider the implications of the cash-flow method of keeping track of a firm's activities in terms of its actual purchase outlays and sales receipts. If we really wanted to know how much value had been added by the firm, we could not be guided solely by such cash-flow data. The reason is simply that purchases are often directed to acquisition of assets, the value of which is not immediately used up in production. Similarly, sales often constitute liquidation of assets and do not signal creation of value. Furthermore, value may be created or lost by activities within the firm that have no counterpart in current sales or purchase transactions.

Some examples should make the distinctions clear:

1. The fish-store proprietor purchases a new cold room. Because the unit is of high quality, he expects it to last for many years. Under cash-flow accounting he deducts the full purchase price of the cold room from his receipts from sales. But this deduction is clearly too large if the object of the accounts is to measure the value of the firm's activities during the year, because most or all of the value of the cold room remains in place at the end of the year.

In future years the accounts will misstate the value generated by the store in the other direction by failing to recognize any change in the value of the cold room. Although durable, the cold room does not last forever; in a typical year there is a loss in value that is not reflected in any cash transaction. Furthermore, there is always the possibility that someone will want to turn the fish store into a bakery, at which point the cold room may be a positive nuisance.

If we want to keep track of the cold room's value, we cannot use cash-flow accounting but must try to follow the *accrual* of the loss in value of the cold room as it is used in the business. This would mean making a series of *depreciation* deductions over time rather than a deduction at the time of purchase of the cold room.

2. An oil company drills an exploratory well and makes a large payment to a drilling contractor. Under cash-flow accounting these outlays would be deducted immediately.[2] There are no immediate cash-flow consequences of success or failure of the venture (although there are large future cash-flow consequences).

Keeping track of the value generated by the exploration would imply a very different result. Suppose everything is going according to plan at the halfway point of the drilling, but the outcome is still as uncertain as at the beginning. Assuming the venture made sense in the first place, the oil company has at that point an asset (a half-completed well) worth at least as much as has been spent so far. No one's wealth has changed, and so there has been no income. Neither deduction nor inclusion is called for.

The possible situations on completion of the well range from disaster (a dry hole) to bonanza. If oil is found, no one knows exactly how much is there or what it will cost to extract it. Furthermore, even a dry hole may convey valuable information about other drilling opportunities for the company. The market will place a value on the complicated new asset that has been created by the drilling. That value will appear in the *change* in what people are willing to pay to own the company, and that is the wealth generated by the exploratory effort. Discovering the market's valuation is not simple (particularly because it may change from day to day), but it is not systematically related to current cash flow.

When, finally, the company starts pumping oil at the new well, there will be a positive cash flow from sales. Little or no income will be generated, however, because the main activity going on is the transferring of oil from inventory to consumption. Income accounting requires rules to impute a depletion offset to the marketed oil.

3. Anticipating a brisk demand for bitters in the spring, the Better Bitters Corporation steps up production in the fourth quarter. By the end of the calendar year, the company has a substantial stock of completed product that is certainly valuable (to judge from the insurance premiums it pays to cover the stored inventory).

2. Under U.S. tax law this outlay, called an intangible drilling expense, would be allowed as an immediate deduction; this is one of many instances in which U.S. income tax rules follow consumption tax principles.

No extra sales, however, have taken place. Therefore the valuable inventory is not recorded in the company's cash-flow value-added account. To account correctly for the value produced but invested in inventory instead of sold to consumers, a method of tracking the *accruing* change in inventory value would be required. Naturally the accounting rules would have to deal with such matters as physical deterioration and changes in market valuation of the items in stock, including changes that occur through general price inflation.

4. The opposite misstatement of value created or lost occurs in recording a sale out of inventory. The result is an addition to value added as calculated from cash flow, even though all that has happened is a transfer of existing goods. Both production of goods in process within the firm and capital construction projects using the firm's own resources represent value created and added to the economy's stock of wealth that is unnoticed by cash-flow value-added accounting.

5. The Better Bitters Corporation suffers a fire that destroys a fermenting tank used in the manufacture of bitters. There is no associated cash flow, so there is no entry in the cash-flow value-added calculation; but a loss in value has occurred. An accrual accounting system would enter a casualty loss deduction.

We can conclude that an accrual system of accounting will provide a measure of the sum of consumption and increase in wealth supported by the activity of a firm. An aggregation of value added defined in this way will give a measure of aggregate accrual income derived from the activities of the firms included. A tax based on value added in this sense is therefore a VAT of the income type.

As the preceding examples suggest, an accrual system of accounting is much more complicated than a cash-flow system. Actual cash transactions have no direct relationship to correct measurement of accruing value, even though they would be used as the basis for practical accounting (for example, the depreciation deductions to reflect the changing value of an item of equipment would typically be related to its acquisition cost). All the problems posed by such accounting systems are inevitably present in an income tax, whether it is a personal tax or the firm-oriented VAT of the income type. The identifying feature of the VAT of the consumption type is its (correct) use of cash accounting for interfirm transactions. The VATs common among industrial countries are of this type, and probably any VAT considered for the United States would be too.

Administration of a VAT

It is generally believed that a VAT is relatively easy to administer.[3] One reason is that it involves many fewer tax-filing units than a personal income tax does. A VAT is paid (not to be confused with "borne") by firms. Precisely what constitutes a firm for this purpose is to some degree a matter of policy. Clearly the concept reaches well beyond the corporation. All businesses (the term here extends to individual proprietorships, including professional practices) would normally be included. But individuals in their roles as employees or recipients of gifts and transfers would not file VAT returns, so the number of taxpayers would be far fewer than the number of income tax filers. (Those familiar with the income tax can think of the population of corporate taxpayers plus partnerships plus individual taxpayers who file Schedule C or Schedule F of Form 1040.)

There are two further, related reasons why a VAT *should* be simple to operate: cash-flow accounting and extensive use of linked tax accounts. Employing linked tax accounts is simply a method of cross-checking tax information provided by taxpayers. Already used to a limited degree in the United States, it provides one of the most obvious methods of improving compliance and simplifying enforcement. Because cash transactions provide the information directly needed, linked accounts are inherently better suited to a consumption-type tax than to an income-type tax. For example, if one firm sells a machine to another, under the consumption-type tax the sale will be included by the selling firm and the purchase deducted by the buyer. Under an income-type tax the sale may be offset by a charge against inventory on the account of the seller and deducted as depreciation over several years by the buyer.

The "invoice method" of administering a VAT provides a good illustration of linked tax accounts. Under this system, which is used in Europe, there is actually no calculation of a firm's value added. Instead, the tax is collected on the firm's gross receipts from sales, and a credit is allowed for taxes paid by suppliers as indicated on invoices. The firm claiming a credit for VAT levied against earlier production stages must possess the invoices from the selling firms recording the tax paid. The tax authorities therefore can, in principle, match expenses claimed by one firm against receipts reported and subjected to tax by other firms. Every selling firm knows that its invoices will be used to support a claim

3. This discussion relies particularly on the valuable set of studies of European VATs prepared for a Brookings Institution conference in October 1980 and published under the editorship of Henry J. Aaron (1981).

for credit by the buying firm, and therefore the seller has a strong incentive to report sales accurately.

A simplified description of the imposition of a 20 percent VAT on a loaf of bread sold at retail for $1.25, using the invoice method, may be helpful.

The first stage of production is the farm, where the farmer hires labor and also works himself to produce wheat. Assume the farm to be self-contained, using no purchased inputs. The farmer's sales are subject to the 20 percent VAT. Suppose wheat constitutes 20 percent of the cost of bread. Then $0.25 of the final value is accounted for by wheat, on which $0.05 has been paid in VAT by the farmer.

The next stage is a combined mill and bakery, where the $0.25 worth of wheat is assumed to be the only purchased input. The miller/baker hires labor and processes the wheat into bread, which he sells to the grocer for $0.75. He is liable for VAT on the *entire* $0.75; that is, he owes $0.15 in tax, but he is allowed a credit for the $0.05 shown on the invoice from the farmer. The miller/baker thus pays a net amount of $0.10, or exactly 20 percent of his value added of $0.50.

The grocer sells the loaf for $1.25. She is also liable for tax on the full sales price, so the sale implies a tax liability of $0.25. But as she has already claimed a credit for the $0.15 shown on the miller/baker's invoice, the net tax liability arising from the grocer's part of the transaction is just $0.10, or 20 percent of her value added of $0.50 ($1.25 − $0.75).

Note that the total net tax paid is $0.05 + $0.10 + $0.10 = $0.25, 20 percent of the total value added. (This is exactly what would have been collected from a retail sales tax levied on the grocer.)

As the example demonstrates, linked accounts provide some overlapping tax information. Unfortunately, the double coverage ends at the critical last stage, sales to households. Households obviously do not obtain a credit for previously paid taxes (or a deduction for purchases); therefore they do not report information to match final sales by firms. At that stage we are dependent, as always, on general honesty and the usual array of monitoring and auditing techniques. (Even here, though, the fact that it is cash flows that are needed, not hard-to-verify valuations, continues to facilitate enforcement.)

A much more serious source of difficulty in implementing existing VATs is the widespread practice of allowing special rates, exemptions, and the like. If, for example, policy calls for a low or zero rate of tax on the consumption of basic food items, rules are needed to distinguish basic from nonbasic foods, to allocate nonuniform taxes paid on inputs among various items of output, and so on. Complications mount quickly from the special provisions that can afflict a VAT as well as a personal income tax.

Consumption Covered by a VAT

The nature of the consumption covered by a VAT depends on the details of the rules defining who must file a return (in other words, the rules defining firms) and which sales are included. In addition, all actual systems make at least some use of multiple rates. A detailed discussion of the differences is beyond the scope of this book, but I will mention some of the major issues.

Owner-Occupied Houses and the "Prepayment Method" of Taxing Consumption. In explaining how the aggregation of cash-flow value added by firms constituted a measure of consumption, I sidestepped the interesting issue of household capital. Capital is generally thought of as consisting of equipment, structures, and perhaps inventories belonging to firms. But households are direct owners and users of a sizable share of the economy's total stock of capital. The capital so administered includes everything labeled "household durables," such as furniture, washing machines and other major appliances, and automobiles. Most important, it includes the huge stock of owner-occupied housing.

Application of cash-flow value-added accounting to the chain of producers (timber companies, nail makers, construction contractors, and so on) involved in the construction of a new house would imply taxing most of its price. The cash outlay of the person who purchases the house, however, is not a sensible measure of his consumption during the year in question. Rather, it is a form of saving on which he and successor owners earn a return in the form of housing services during the extended period of the house's use as a residence. An estimate of the value of those services in a given year is spoken of as the asset owner's "imputed consumption." In effect, the homeowner is treated as a firm in the business of selling housing services. The rent (net of operating costs) the homeowner-firm would obtain by letting the house on the market is the imputed consumption provided by the house. Under a VAT the firm would be allowed a deduction for the purchase of the house and would then be taxed on the rent receipts. In practice imputations of this sort are exactly what one wants to avoid. It is fortunate, then, that treating the full initial outlay as consumption for tax purposes comes very close to giving results identical with those from correctly estimating and taxing the housing service value.

Table 4–1 shows the equivalence from the investor's point of view of two apparently quite different tax treatments: deduction of the amount invested, followed by taxation of the return flow, and no deduction of the investment, with no taxation of the return flow. The table describes the case of an asset that in the absence of taxes yields a return flow of $1000 per year for each of five years, at which point it disappears (for example, a machine that wears out after five years). According to the data in the table, the market values such a return flow at $3300. Under the usual cash-flow accounting of a VAT (say, at a rate of 50 percent), the initial purchase would be deducted and therefore would require a net outlay of only $1650. The return flow of $1000 per year would then be subject to the 50 percent tax, netting the owner $500 per year. This sequence is shown in the third column of the table.

The second column shows that the identical result can be obtained by the investor if, instead, the return flow is not subject to tax and the initial purchase of the asset is not permitted as a deduction. The trick is to adjust the purchased amount of the asset. With a tax rate of 50 percent, buying a half-unit of the asset, with no deduction and no taxation of returns, gives the investor exactly the same result as buying one unit of the asset on a deductible basis with returns subject to a 50 percent tax.

Acquisition of an asset is deducted in the cash-flow method of calculating consumption for tax purposes; subsequent return from the asset

Table 4–1. Equivalence between tax prepayment and cash-flow asset accounting

Time (years)	Cash flow to purchaser	
	No tax[a]	50% tax on cash flow[b]
0	($1650)[c]	($3300 − $1650 tax saving) = ($1650)
1	500	1000 − 500 tax = 500
2	500	1000 − 500 tax = 500
3	500	1000 − 500 tax = 500
4	500	1000 − 500 tax = 500
5	500	1000 − 500 tax = 500

a. Purchaser buys a half-unit of the asset.
b. Purchaser buys one full unit of the asset.
c. Quantities in parentheses are net outlays.

is then taxed. The result is the same for the taxpayer, however, and therefore the equivalent burden is imposed, if no deduction is allowed for acquisition of the asset and none of the subsequent return is subject to tax. Because the effect is to move the actual payment of tax forward (by the foregone deduction), we call this approach the "tax-prepayment method" of implementing a consumption-based tax. The equivalence of the two approaches makes available a simple way to put home owner-ship and business investment on the same tax footing. The present treatment of homeowners under the income tax — namely, no deduction for the purchase of a home but also no attempt to tax the return flow in the form of housing services — provides consistent treatment of this form of investment with that of ordinary businesses that are taxed on the difference between their receipts from sales and their purchases from other firms. The homeowner's consumption is effectively taxed on a tax-prepayment basis.

Consistent treatment of business and household capital would be similarly simple in the context of a VAT that employs the invoice method, under which sellers (including sellers of rental housing ser-vices) charge VAT on sales and claim a rebate for taxes paid on inputs. If owner-occupiers are charged VAT on the purchase of a newly con-structed home but no attempt is made to levy VAT on the imputed service value of the home or on any subsequent resale of the property, the tax factor would be eliminated as the basis for the choice between owning and renting. This treatment would result in neutrality between investment in housing and other forms of productive capital and would include the value of housing services, whether from rented or owned dwellings, in the concept of consumption subject to tax.

Favored Forms of Consumption. Although it would be relatively easy to tax housing and business capital similarly under a VAT, it is generally expected that the present policy of favoring housing would be carried over to a VAT if it were adopted in the United States. The tax preference would presumably take the form of a low or zero rate of VAT on pur-chases of new homes and on real estate rentals. Educational institu-tions, hospitals, and the like might also receive favored treatment.

The coverage of the consumption concept implicit in a VAT is likely to be influenced by practical problems of measurement as well as by explicit policy choice. For example, small firms might be exempted from the tax. Note, though, that exempting a seller from tax is not the same as excluding the entire value of the consumption involved from tax, inas-much as the inputs used by exempt firms may have been subject to tax. To achieve the effect of relieving charitable activities from tax, the institutions involved may be made eligible for rebate of taxes invoiced on their purchases. The analogue in the income tax is a deduction for charitable contributions.

Other favored forms of consumption under current income tax practices include fringe benefits provided by firms, and these might well continue to receive favorable treatment under a VAT. For example, the firm might provide subsidized meals, athletic facilities, health care, free airline trips, and other valuable perquisites. In implementing a VAT, a decision must be made whether to permit a deduction for the costs of supporting these forms of employee compensation. (Under the invoice method, the practical issue would be whether to charge employees a VAT on such perquisites.) To the extent deduction is allowed, such fringe benefits are favored under a VAT just as they are under an income tax.

Equally important are the many ways, not normally identified as fringe benefits, in which employees and owners obtain consumption benefits directly from firms. The classic example is the hobby farm, operated for fun rather than profit; other examples are the doctor's private use of an automobile that is also required for her practice and the use of a minicomputer, nominally acquired for a small business, for the entertainment of the owner's children. The last two instances were the subject of restrictions written into the Tax Reform Act of 1984. Problems of this sort, so productive of complexity, are unfortunately not banished by choosing the VAT approach. We can get an idea of the breadth of the concept of consumption implicit in the typical system from the rule of thumb that the aggregate VAT base will be roughly one-half the aggregate annual consumption recorded in the national income and product accounts.

Imports and Exports. The European VATs are levied on a destination basis, in which exports are exempt and imports are subject to tax. The tax assessed on a sales transaction, for example, depends on the destination of the goods. This contrasts with a tax levied on an origin basis, in which the tax depends on where the goods were produced. Under an origin-basis VAT exports are subject to tax but imports are not. Similar distinctions are made for income taxes, with some countries taxing only income derived from domestic production (that is, they tax on an origin basis). A tax levied on the personal income (consumption plus change in net worth) of residents of a country, by contrast, is a destination-basis tax.

The U.S. income tax system is an amalgam. Individual residents, all U.S. citizens, and U.S. firms are taxed on all their income (that is, on the basis of the U.S. destination of the income), but U.S. citizens who are residents of foreign countries may exclude a substantial amount of foreign earnings from tax (origin basis). Foreign firms are taxed on their U.S. operations (origin basis). Within limits, income taxes paid to foreign governments give rise to a credit against U.S. tax liability, and an elaborate network of double-taxation treaties regulates the priority of claims by the different governments.

In theory an income tax can be structured on either an origin or a destination basis, but treaty restrictions constrain the rules the United States may apply. Under the General Agreement on Tariffs and Trade (GATT), a distinction is made between "indirect taxes," which may be rebated on exports and charged on imports, and "direct taxes," which may not. The distinction has no clear economic content, but the legal interpretation places what we usually call an income tax in the direct category and a VAT in the indirect category.

The fact that under U.S. treaty obligations a VAT may be rebated on exports is often cited as a major advantage. The view is based on the belief that a destination-based tax would enhance the international competitiveness of U.S. firms. Intuitively the point seems obvious. If a tax is rebated on sales to foreigners, U.S. goods will be cheaper to them, and more will be demanded. As so often happens, however, closer analysis casts doubt on the first impression, which neglects the adjustment of markets to different rules. (This subject is pursued further in Chapter 9.)

Gifts and Inheritances. The usual VAT does not treat a gift or bequest given as consumption; thus a VAT is normally levied on a bestowal-exclusive basis. To change the usual VAT to a tax on bestowal-inclusive consumption would require that givers and bequeathers file VAT returns, in effect treating the gift or bequest given like the sales receipts of a firm. The idea may seem preposterous, but it should be recognized as the same policy issue whether it is encountered in a VAT or in a personal consumption or income tax context.

VAT and the Underground Economy. It is widely believed that a VAT would be of great assistance in capturing revenue now lost to the underground economy. The argument is simply that those not reporting income to the tax authorities under the existing income tax would pay VAT on their purchases. Unfortunately, this reasoning neglects what it is that determines underground earnings in the first place.

Consider, for example, a carpenter who does not report his income. Suppose income-taxed carpenters earn $15 an hour and get to keep $10, whereas the tax evader charges $12 an hour on condition that his customers pay in cash. Now suppose we introduce a VAT and reduce the income tax. Our taxed carpenter now pays $4 an hour in income tax but also has to collect the VAT of, say, $1 an hour. The price of his service remains $15 an hour, and his take-home pay $10. The underground carpenter can stay in business at $12 an hour, now reporting his earnings neither to the income tax authorities nor to the VAT authorities.

In this description, the move to a new equilibrium following the partial shift from the income tax to a VAT does not involve a general price increase. Suppose, instead, that it does, and that the price of the taxed carpenter's services increases to $16 an hour, to cover the VAT. We would then expect the price of the underground carpenter's services to rise on the same basis. The result would be the same: the underground carpenter avoids both income and value-added taxes.

Retail Sales Taxes

Americans are familiar with retail sales taxes, which are levied by most states and many municipalities. Because the tax is paid by firms that sell to households, it is a form of consumption tax. As in the case of a VAT, the details of the definition of consumption depend on the exact specification of the transactions covered and the businesses obliged to file returns.

In the typical system, educational, charitable, medical, and government purchasers are exempt from tax, and no tax is levied on their sales. Often, particular goods and services, such as housing, certain foods, drugs, or clothing, are taxed at a zero rate. The purpose, of course, is to alleviate the burden of the poor or the sick, placing it instead on those for whom a heavier tax burden is regarded as appropriate. Although it need not be so, it is probably true that the coverage of the typical retail sales tax is narrower than that of the typical VAT. For example, professional services rendered to households are not commonly taxed. In principle, however, a VAT of the consumption type can be constructed to duplicate any retail sales tax, and vice versa.

The conceptual difference between the two forms of tax is in the collection method. A VAT is normally collected at each level of the production and distribution process, with each successive layer collecting its proportional share. The retail sales tax is collected only at the final stage, upon sale to households. It is commonly asserted that this difference makes the VAT easier to enforce, because it is believed that a final sale hidden from the retail sales tax collector escapes the entire tax, whereas the same sale hidden from the VAT collector escapes the tax on the last stage only. But this argument neglects the fact that under *both* systems the full rate is assessed at each stage, even though under the VAT the seller can credit taxes paid at earlier production levels. If the amount claimed as taxes paid on inputs is unchanged, hiding a sale leads to exactly the same revenue loss under either tax.

Hence the collection advantage of a VAT arises from the requirement that the final seller account for purchases from other firms. For example, under the invoice method taxes paid on purchases are claimed as a credit against VAT liability. A firm that failed to report any sales, yet regularly claimed credit for taxes on inputs, would presumably attract a prompt audit. No similar signal arises when the only tax is on gross final sales.

The earlier example of the taxation on a loaf of bread may be used to illustrate these points. First, however, we must deal with a technicality concerning the different ways a sales tax and a VAT are typically expressed. A sales tax of 5 percent implies that the cashier will add 5 percent to the marked price of an item; for example, we pay $1.05 for a $1.00 item. The *rate* of tax is expressed as a percentage of the value of the sale *exclusive* of the tax. By contrast, the rate of VAT is typically expressed on the value of a sale *inclusive* of the tax. If the customer pays $100.00, the tax collector gets $5.00 in a 5 percent VAT system (compared with $4.76 in a 5 percent sales tax). The sales tax rate is expressed on a "tax-exclusive basis," and the VAT is expressed on a "tax-inclusive basis." The difference is simply one of convention; the same effect can be achieved either way by appropriate adjustment of the applicable rate. But it is essential to know which basis is applied in a specific instance. For comparability to the VAT rate of 20 percent (tax-inclusive basis), assume that a sales tax rate of 25 percent (tax-exclusive basis) applies in the example. The loaf of bread sells for $1.25 after taxes in both cases.

The sales tax story is simpler than the VAT story. The retailer sells the bread at a pretax price of $1.00, which covers the wages and profits of all stages of production, and adds $0.25 in tax, which she sends to the tax collector. The consumer pays $1.25 for the loaf of bread. If the grocer hides the sale from the tax collector, she reduces her reported base by $1.00 and therefore saves $0.25. Referring to the VAT example, she would save the same $0.25 in tax in that system as well, provided the fact of hiding the sale does not diminish her ability to collect the rebate of $0.15 paid on purchases from suppliers.

We have noted that various options are available under a VAT to specify the concept of consumption. Some of those options, such as treating gifts and bequests as value added, admittedly seem a bit academic, but the immediate translation of the same issue to the personal tax sphere shows that to be a matter of custom rather than principle. What distinguishes a retail sales tax from a VAT in this connection is the generally accepted notion of the meaning of retail sales. Thus, because we do not normally think of a business as retailing fringe benefits to its employees, we are not likely to include fringes in the consumption concept implicit in a retail sales tax. This is even more obvious for gifts and bequests (although one could impose a separate tax on gifts and bequests to match a sales tax). Consumer durables are typically included in the base of a retail sales tax, but neither newly constructed housing nor housing rentals are. Exports are not regarded as retail sales and are therefore excluded from tax, whereas imports sold to households or incorporated in goods sold to households are included. A retail sales tax is therefore normally levied on a destination basis. None of these distinctive characteristics is inherent in a tax based on sales, but most of them are likely to be found in any system considered a retail sales tax.

Value-added and retail sales taxes have much in common. As far as the theory is concerned (neglecting enforcement issues), by adopting the appropriate definition of retail sales any value-added tax could be reproduced by a retail sales tax. Similarly, by adopting an appropriate definition of value added any retail sales tax could be exactly reproduced by a VAT. Both taxes are normally of the consumption type because they are levied, directly or indirectly, only on sales to households. More precisely, they are levied on sales to nonbusiness purchasers. This means that capital purchases by firms lead to taxation only when the productive capacity results in sales, and not as they generate stored-up value.

At a conceptual level, then, both tax types pose all of the design issues that were raised earlier with respect to the concept of consumption implicit in an income tax. And both types possess the very significant advantage that they can be appropriately administered with the use of cash-flow accounting methods. Although they are interchangeable in theory, in practice a VAT seems likely to be endowed with a broader base than a retail sales tax and to offer enforcement advantages through its system of linked accounts. Practice also suggests that a retail sales tax is less likely to employ the multiple rates of tax that are often used in VAT systems to promote distributive and other objectives and that greatly increase the cost of administration. Finally, a retail sales tax has the advantage of familiarity to taxpayers and of being easily understood.

Personal Consumption Taxes 5

No income tax is really just, from which savings are not exempted.

John Stuart Mill, *Principles of Political Economy*

AN ADVANTAGE of value-added and retail sales taxes is that administration can be concentrated on a relatively small number of taxpayers. Most individuals need have little or nothing to do with calculating or remitting taxes. At the same time, some latitude is available for varying the distribution of tax burdens through specification both of the details of the transactions subject to tax and of the filing unit. Basically, however, these taxes must be proportional to some measure of consumption. By contrast, a personal tax system — the existing income tax, for example — attempts to vary tax burdens in more complex ways in relation to differences among individuals. Most obviously, a personal tax is generally not *proportional* to a measure such as income or consumption. This chapter presents a review of four personal taxes based on consumption:

- A two-tiered cash-flow tax (modeled on the Hall-Rabushka Simple Flat Tax)

- A full-fledged cash-flow tax, in which all savings are deducted and all dissavings are included (the basic approach of the Aaron-Galper plan)

- The *Blueprints* Cash-Flow Tax, which employs a mixture of tax-prepayment and cash-flow accounting

- A phase-in of consumption-type tax rules under the existing income tax

Two-Tiered Cash-Flow Tax

The Simple Flat Tax, devised by Robert E. Hall and Alvin Rabushka (1983, 1985), is closely related to a cash-flow VAT. In fact, as we shall see, they are identical in all but one crucial respect. The quality of flatness seems to be principally responsible for the considerable journalistic attention paid to the Simple Flat Tax upon its introduction. It is called flat because it entails the application of a single rate of tax to the base defined by the combination of its two constituent taxes. Flatness so understood is regarded by some observers as extremely important and by others as inconsistent with a fair distribution of the tax burden. The Simple Flat Tax therefore has a controversial character that has unfortunately diverted attention from its innovations other than flatness.

The tax makes use of two postcard-sized forms, one filed by individuals and called an Individual Compensation Tax form and the other filed by businesses (whether corporate or not) and called a Business Tax form. The use of two tightly coordinated tax systems to achieve an integrated objective is a major strength of the Hall-Rabushka plan.

The base of the business tax is value added, calculated on a cash-flow basis, *less* payments to employees. That is, a firm records all receipts from sales and deducts all purchases from other firms, whether in the nature of current or capital expenditure (just as in the calculation of value added). In addition, the firm deducts payments to workers, whether for current, past, or future services. The tax due is equal to a flat percentage of the remainder, called taxable income. The base of the individual compensation tax is the sum of payments received by individuals in compensation for their services as workers (wages, salary, and pension benefits). Such compensation payments could be taxed according to a graduated schedule, much as under the existing income tax. The Hall-Rabushka plan, however, calls for an exemption consisting of a certain amount per tax return (differing for jointly filing married couples, single persons, and single heads of household) plus an amount per dependent. The amount left after subtracting the exemptions is called taxable compensation and is taxed at the same flat rate applied to taxable income under the business tax.

We can now easily see how the Simple Flat Tax is related to a VAT. The business tax is almost identical to a VAT; it differs only in allowing firms to deduct payments to workers. Under a VAT those payments would not be deductible by the firms and would therefore be subject to tax at the business level. But the sum included in the individual compensation tax is equal to the deduction allowed to firms. Thus, if individual compensation were subject to tax at the same rate as the taxable income of firms, the effect of the Hall-Rabushka system as a whole would be precisely identical to that of a VAT.[1] The Simple Flat Tax — business tax and compensation tax combined — differs in effect from a VAT only in the exemptions allowed to workers.

The close connection between the Simple Flat Tax and a VAT deserves emphasis as an aid to understanding both the character of the system and the nature of the transition that would be involved in substituting it for the existing income tax. The Simple Flat Tax is a tax system with enforcement and accounting characteristics that are virtually identical to those of a VAT, but with progressivity deriving from the exempt allowances under the individual compensation tax. If personal exemptions were omitted from the individual compensation tax, so that *all* income in the Hall-Rabushka sense were taxed at a single flat rate, the result would be indistinguishable from a tax levied on a broad-based cash-flow measure of value added by firms. Inasmuch as the two types of tax use the same accounting system (the only difference being that under the Simple Flat Tax, firms deduct payments to employees, with employees in turn reporting the earnings), they are technically identical. This means that the analysis of any issue, apart from one related to personal exemptions, that arises in the VAT context should be exactly the same for the Simple Flat Tax.

An example is the effectiveness of each tax system in dealing with the underground economy. An underground house painter would be obliged to report his sales on the business tax form and allowed to deduct his purchases of supplies. The same procedure would be involved in calculating value added. A difference would arise if the painter had an employee. The employee's wages would be deducted from the business tax component of the Simple Flat Tax but not from the value-added tax. However, the employee would be obliged to report the wages on the compensation tax form under the Simple Flat Tax, so the two systems would reach the same result; presumably, withholding would render the two systems virtually identical from an enforcement point of view.

Another example of the equivalence is the incidence of the Simple Flat Tax. We observe that under the Simple Flat Tax, individual employees are taxed only on earnings. We are therefore likely to conclude that recipients of transfers, such as retirees receiving Social Security

1. As in the income tax, the tax rate under the Simple Flat Tax is on a tax-inclusive basis. The flat rate of 19 percent in the Hall-Rabushka proposal thus corresponds to a sales tax rate of $19/(100 - 19) = 23.5$ percent expressed on a tax-exclusive basis.

payments, are free of tax under the Simple Flat Tax. Yet it is usually thought that a VAT has the property of imposing the same burdens on recipients of transfers and on wage earners. Because the two taxes are economically identical (apart from the personal exemptions provided under the Simple Flat Tax, which do not appear to affect the assumptions just mentioned), one or the other conclusion must be wrong. Which conclusion is correct will be part of the discussion in Chapter 13.

Treatment of Various Transactions

Tax policy may be varied along many dimensions by, in effect, changing the definition of consumption subject to tax. The Simple Flat Tax necessarily makes implicit or explicit choices about such policy alternatives as the following.

Exports and Imports. In its treatment of exports and imports, the Simple Flat Tax is levied on an origin basis. That is, value added abroad, whether by foreign-owned or United States-owned firms, is not included in the tax base. The value of exports as they cross the border is included in the receipts side of a firm's taxable income calculation, and the value of imports as they enter the United States is allowed as a deduction. This presents an interesting contrast to the usual VAT, which is on a destination basis. Typically a VAT exempts exports and taxes imports. The same policy could be implemented under the Simple Flat Tax by permitting firms to exclude sales abroad and disallowing deduction for imports under the business tax. (The possibility of implementing a two-tiered cash-flow tax on a destination basis is discussed below. The effect of the choice of policy on international competitiveness will be discussed further in Chapter 10).

Consumer Durables. It would be easy, from an administrative point of view, to subject owner-occupied housing and other consumer durables to the same tax as other forms of consumption. Hall and Rabushka describe the Simple Flat Tax as leaving the taxation of housing in the hands of state and local government, but a fairer description would be to say that housing is taxed like all other forms of consumption in the plan. That is, along with other firms, producers of new houses are subject to the Simple Flat Tax, and purchasers of houses for their own use are allowed no deduction. Firms or individuals who purchase housing for rent to others are taxed under the business tax. This makes the Simple Flat Tax rather broader than a typical VAT.

The same approach would apply to all other forms of consumer durables (assets that yield direct services to households). This is the tax-prepayment method of taxing consumption. If the tax rate applicable to the individual is constant over the relevant number of time periods, the tax-prepayment method provides for a tax *equivalent* to the taxation of the individual's consumption of housing services. The actual payment of tax is up front, however, in the form of a deduction foregone.

Itemized Deductions. The equivalent of the income tax's itemized deductions under a VAT is the exclusion of various preferred goods and services (medical care, for example) from the base. The Simple Flat Tax eschews itemized deductions of all types. Therefore in distributing tax burdens it makes no allowance for differences in medical expenses or charitable contributions, to mention two prominent examples. Deduction of mortgage interest would be inconsistent with the logic of the tax, which correspondingly excludes interest received from the individual compensation tax base. (Since interest is not deducted by the payer, it can be thought of as pretaxed.)

State and local taxes are not allowed as a deduction under *either* the business tax or the individual compensation tax. In effect, the Simple Flat Tax treats state and local taxes as payments for services received. For consistency with purchases from private businesses, these amounts should be subject to business taxation at the state and local government levels. Denying a deduction for taxes is thus a substitute for having governments file tax returns that treat tax revenues as sales receipts. The same procedure, providing firms no deduction for state and local taxes, could be followed in the case of a VAT. (The equivalent result is obtained under the invoice method by obliging state and local governments to pay VAT on their purchases, including the purchase of employee services.)

Gifts and Bequests. Inasmuch as gifts and bequests received are not included on the receipts side of either the business tax or the individual compensation tax, the Simple Flat Tax can be described as on a bestowal-exclusive basis (see the appendix to Chapter 2).

Services of Financial Intermediaries. A topic I have not yet raised in connection with either accrual-income or consumption taxes is how to tax the services of financial intermediaries, such as banks and insurance companies, consistently with other business activities. This poses a perennial challenge to tax design. The problem is that financial intermediaries provide some of their value to consumers in a sort of barter exchange. Thus, an individual may leave money on deposit with a bank at a low or zero interest rate, in return for which the bank provides checking services. A bank that had such accounts as its only business would have no revenue from sales in the usual sense. It would therefore show a loss on the business tax form (as in a conventional value-added calculation) to the extent of its expenses for the banking operations. In one of its few deviations from the line of simplicity, the Simple Flat Tax would oblige banks and other financial institutions to report as taxable receipts an amount imputed as the value of banking and similar services they perform but do not explicitly sell. A VAT could employ the same rules.

Fringe Benefits. The flat-rate character of the Simple Flat Tax is useful in taxing fringe benefits. The basic principle is that any deduction from business taxable income for compensation of employees should be reported on some employee's compensation tax return. Fringe benefits, which are noncash forms of employee compensation, involve outlays by the firm that are not reported by those who benefit from them. (The outlays by firms may include the costs of goods and services provided to employees at a discount, as in the case of low-price travel for airline company employees.) A possible substitute for requiring employees to report as compensation the value of fringe benefits they receive is to deny the firm a deduction for the cost of fringes. A common objection to this procedure is that the rate of tax thus imposed on the fringe (in the case of current corporate business, typically 46 percent) is higher than would be applied to the income of the true recipient. The present solution is often to allow the fringe to be tax free, but to surround it with exceedingly complicated restrictions.

Because the Simple Flat Tax applies the same rate of tax to firms and individuals, there would be no validity to the argument that denying a deduction is a poor substitute for requiring inclusion in the employees' compensation (assuming the employees have sufficient compensation —that is, more than the exempt amounts—to be in the positive tax range). Denying the deduction therefore provides a very simple mechanism for taxing fringe benefits, especially in cases where it is difficult or costly to identify the particular beneficiaries. (A VAT could employ the same rules.) There should be no illusion, however, that the Simple Flat Tax banishes the fringe-benefit problem altogether. What deduction should be denied, for example, to effect a tax on free standby passage to airline employees? To tax fringe benefits provided by tax-exempt institutions, such as local governments or universities, the Simple Flat Tax would require them to file a return and pay tax on the costs involved.

Alternative Two-Tiered Cash-Flow Tax Rules

The Simple Flat Tax is the prototype of a two-tiered cash-flow tax. It should be clear, however, that the same principle, essentially a variant on the cash-flow-type VAT, could be employed in ways that differ from its use by Hall and Rabushka. For example, the Simple Flat Tax is levied on an origin basis, whereas the typical VAT exempts exports and taxes imports. It would be possible to choose a destination basis for a two-tiered cash-flow tax. In that case sales to foreigners would be excluded from taxable income under the business tax, while imports would be disallowed as a deduction. (It is not obvious whether GATT restrictions would preclude implementing a two-tiered cash-flow tax on a destination basis. The issue turns on the definition of an indirect tax, which is not a clear economic category. It is possible that the business tax tier could qualify as an indirect tax, which could be rebated on exports and charged to imports under the GATT, but a large fraction of the Simple Flat Tax would be paid by employees on compensation. Note that, as in the case of a VAT, choosing a destination basis would require that imports be brought into the country by firms, not directly by consumers, or that direct imports by consumers be subject to tax at the border.)

One could include transfers such as Social Security or unemployment benefits in the individual tax base, in addition to compensation from employers. Similarly, it would be possible in principle to include gifts and bequests received. Each of these policy choices would affect the distribution of the tax burden.

Although the Simple Flat Tax rigorously resists the incursion of personal deductions into the individual tax, the structure is consistent with allowing them if it were desired. Certain deductions in the present tax system, especially interest payments, would be notably inconsistent with the underlying consumption orientation of the tax. Others, however, such as charitable contributions, medical expenses, or state and local taxes, are consistent with the approach. Of course, every deduction brings with it complexity and a higher rate of tax on the remaining base, together with its own particular pattern of distorting incentives.

Hall and Rabushka stress the importance of imposing a single flat rate of tax. It should be recognized, however, that the Simple Flat Tax is not a proportional tax. Although the proposed rate of 19 percent is applied to all taxable income of businesses,[2] the compensation of individuals is taxed according to a graduated schedule. That schedule is exceedingly simple: compensation below the specified personal allow-

---

2. A business for which allowable expenses exceed receipts from sales is not, however, sent a refund check. Instead, an unlimited loss carryover, with interest, is provided. Because losses carried on the books of an acquired business could be deducted from the business tax base of the acquiring business, the rules provided by the Simple Flat Tax come close to equivalence to refunding taxes on losses.

ances is taxed at a zero rate; compensation above the personal allowances is taxed at 19 percent, the same as business taxable income.

Certainly there are advantages in the use of a single rate of tax in this sense, but depending entirely on personal allowances to provide for progressivity is restrictive. The rate of 19 percent recommended in the Simple Flat Tax proposal would greatly ease the tax burden of the well-to-do, somewhat raise the burden on middle-income families, and lower taxes on the very poorest, who would fall below the exempt levels. A tax rate higher than 19 percent would shift the burden toward the well-to-do, but the corresponding increase in exempt allowances would have the effect of dropping from the tax rolls individuals now contributing to collective expenditure. Some might prefer more stages of rate graduation — two or three positive tax brackets, for example. Such graduation is consistent with the two-tiered cash-flow tax approach.[3]

A Full-Fledged Personal Cash-Flow Tax

An apparently quite different method of implementing a personal consumption tax makes no use at all of a company-level tax. Instead, a cash-flow accounting system is applied at the individual level. To contrast the pure form of this system with the *Blueprints* Cash-Flow Tax, I refer to it as a "full-fledged personal cash-flow tax."

The underlying idea is to measure individual consumption by subtracting savings from the individual's income. This involves essentially keeping track of cash intake from employment, transfers, and the like and adding in all cash returns from past savings and any dissaving (for example, selling stock). From this total are deducted outlays in any categories not regarded as consumption. Nonconsumption outlays might include medical expenses, for example, or state income taxes, depending on the concept of consumption chosen as a matter of policy. More important, outlays for the acquisition of assets — that is, savings — are subtracted from the tax base. This accounting system, particularly its treatment of savings, is called the "standard" method of implementing a personal consumption base.

---

3. Applying multiple rates in the compensation tax does weaken the clear argument for taxing fringe benefits at the level of the firm, as it no longer holds true that denying the firm a deduction is identical in effect to taxing the employee. However, the policy of taxing benefits at the firm level might still be attractive, even though it is not identical to taxing them at the employee level.

A classic proposal for a tax system based on consumption as measured by cash flow is that by the British economist Nicholas Kaldor (1955). The Meade Report (Institute for Fiscal Studies, 1978) includes a clear discussion of the approach, as does *Blueprints*. The most important single reference on the cash-flow approach in the U.S. context is the paper by William D. Andrews (1974). The Aaron and Galper (1984) proposal is an example of a full-fledged personal cash-flow tax.

Treatment of Various Transactions

Saving and Investment. The treatment of saving and investment is the critical feature that distinguishes the consumption from the accrual-income approach. A good example of cash-flow accounting is that currently applied to qualified employer-sponsored retirement plans, Individual Retirement Accounts (IRAs), and the like: all inflows are deducted, all outflows are included, and what happens inside the account has no tax consequences until it is reflected in distributions. Hence employer contributions to a pension plan have no immediate tax consequences for the employee. In effect, the employee receives compensation in the amount of the employer's contribution to the pension and then is allowed a deduction in the same amount. Employees are taxed on funds thus set aside only when they are drawn on in the form of pension benefits when received. The present treatment of IRAs is similar, in that the employee first includes compensation received and then takes a deduction for contributions to the retirement account. Taxes are paid only when funds are withdrawn in retirement.

Such cash-flow accounting is incorrect under an accrual-income tax, and in this instance results in a "preference," that is, a lighter tax burden than would normally apply. Accordingly, existing rules include a variety of limits as well as complicated nondiscrimination provisions intended to spread the use of the tax-favored retirement vehicles from high-salary, high-marginal-tax-rate employees to low-earning employees (who therefore presumably obtain more of their compensation in this form than they would otherwise prefer) and to prevent the use of sheltered retirement vehicles from serving nonretirement savings purposes. All such restrictions could be eliminated as wholly unnecessary under a strategy of basing taxes on consumption. Cash-flowing accounting of retirement saving is exactly what is called for. Indeed, by extending the treatment to all savings, cash-flow accounting provides a method of measuring individual consumption that can then be subject to taxation according to whatever rate schedule may seem appropriate.

Saving and dissaving transactions would be comprehensively defined under a full-fledged personal cash-flow tax. Cash-flow accounting would thus apply to purchases and sales of financial assets; to borrowing and repayment of loans; and to payment and receipt of interest, dividends, and the like. It would also apply to all direct business outlays and receipts. In particular, all outlays for equipment, structures, inventory, land, and so on would be deducted currently rather than capitalized. The proceeds from selling assets would be included in full.

A corporation would not be taxed as such in a classic personal-consumption tax. Instead, individuals would be allowed a deduction for purchase of equity shares. If the shares were purchased from another taxpayer, the seller would include the proceeds in the tax calculation, with no net change in the tax base. If an individual withdraws funds from a savings account to purchase newly issued shares, the reduction of the savings account gives rise to an increase in the cash-flow base, while the share purchase causes a balancing deduction. Retirement of equity shares by the corporation, like any other cash distribution to share-holders, would be reflected in an addition to the tax base, because the recipients would be obliged to include the amounts in their cash-flow accounts, but this would be balanced by the increase in the sellers' bank balances, which would be deducted from the base. (In a practical system, cash and bank deposits would probably receive special treatment that changes this result, as discussed below.)

Noncorporate forms of business — partnerships and proprietorships — would receive the same sort of treatment as that described for corporations. In the case of partnerships, each individual partner would be taxed on the basis of net cash flow. A net contribution during the year would be deducted from the partner's tax base, whereas any cash received would be included.

Fringe Benefits. As in all tax systems discussed in this study, payments in kind, including fringe benefits, present problems. For consistency, employees or employee-owners who receive benefits in the form of direct services (a company car, for example) ought to include the value of those benefits in their tax returns. Rules are therefore required to distinguish ordinary business outlays from those that, in effect, substitute for cash compensation of employees and to place a value on those direct benefits identified as such. No system has any magic solution to these administrative problems. Dealing with them, however, is more difficult under an individual cash-flow tax than under a system that includes a tax on business enterprises. In the latter case, denial of a deduction can be used as a substitute for inclusion of fringe benefits in the individual tax base. Under a full-fledged personal cash-flow tax it would be necessary to place a value on such fringe benefits as company-sponsored gymnasiums and add the amount to the individual employee's taxable cash flow. A possible approach would be to use a business withholding tax that could be levied on fringe benefits as well as on wages. The tax withheld on fringes not actually allocated to specific employees would then go unclaimed as credit against individual tax and would therefore be effectively taxed at the business level.

This device is, of course, only a help and not a full solution to the fringe-benefit problem. Furthermore, where a graduated-rate system is imposed at the employee level, the withholding mechanism runs into the difficulty of correlating the tax rate on fringes with that applicable to earnings.

Consumer Durables. I have discussed in the context of a VAT, and briefly again in connection with two-tiered cash-flow taxes, the problem of valuing the flow of services directly generated by individually owned assets, such as houses and automobiles. Providing a measure of consumption supported by these assets would involve treating the household as a business and allowing a deduction upon purchase, followed by inclusion of the imputed value of the return flow of services. An imputation of this sort is wholly impractical, however. Therefore actual personal cash-flow tax proposals typically provide for tax-prepayment treatment of consumer durables, including owner-occupied housing. This means no deduction for the purchase of the asset and no inclusion of any value of the return from the asset, whether in real services or in cash flow upon sale.

The tax-prepayment method may be expected to work well in a system with a constant tax rate, such as a VAT or the Simple Flat Tax. But as a way of dealing with isolated transactions in a full-fledged personal cash-flow system with graduated rates, the prepayment method encounters a problem of lumpiness. We can see this easily in the case of the typical individual who buys a house through a combination of accumulated savings and a mortgage loan. Both types of cash inflow (withdrawal of savings and proceeds of the loan) would be included in the cash-flow tax base and would typically result in an exceptionally large cash-flow tax base in the year of purchase. This would drive the individual into a high tax bracket, hardly an attractive consequence from any point of view. The opposite effect, an exceptionally low or negative tax base, would occur in the year of sale of a house, because the proceeds (in the form of either the settlement of the mortgage or cash) received for the equity interest would not be included in the base, but they would give rise to the deductible purchase of a financial asset or deductible absolution of a financial liability (the mortgage).

For example, a person buying a house for $100,000 might finance the acquisition with $35,000 of savings plus a mortgage loan of $65,000. The withdrawal of savings and the loan proceeds would add $100,000 to the person's tax base in the year; as the house-asset is on a tax-prepayment basis, the purchase payment is not deducted. When the house is later sold, say for $130,000, the process works in reverse. The sale proceeds, used to pay off any remaining mortgage and to add to the savings account balance, lead to a deduction totaling $130,000, but because the house is taxed on a prepayment basis, there is no offsetting taxable receipt.

Two methods are available to alleviate the tax consequences of applying graduated rates to such wide swings in the tax base. Some form of tax base averaging, along the lines employed in the existing system, may be introduced. Or special allowance may be provided for tax-prepaid treatment of mortgage borrowing (no inclusion of proceeds, no deduction for repayments of principal or interest). In addition, limited tax-prepaid savings might be allowed (for example, a special homeowner's saving plan, with no deduction for amounts put aside but no taxation of the returns or of any withdrawals from the plan).

Cash and Demand Deposits. Even a very comprehensive version of a full-fledged personal cash-flow tax is likely to add cash and demand deposits at banks to the list of assets to be accounted for on a tax-prepayment basis rather than a cash-flow basis. In the case of cash (coin and currency), the reason is partly practical. It would hardly be feasible for the individual taxpayer to record each addition to and subtraction from the stock of cash in the course of day-to-day transactions. Even a simple totting up of balances of cash at the beginning and end of the tax year may be impractical. Equally important, such accounting could obviously not be audited by the tax authorities.

Bank demand deposits could be monitored more easily. However, there is a functional reason for treating both cash and demand deposits on a prepayment basis. The reason is the same one that supports tax-prepayment accounting for consumer durables: in both instances there is a flow of services received by the individual that is not reflected in cash transactions. In the case of consumer durables, the services take such forms as housing (from the owner-occupied home) or transportation (from the automobile). In the case of cash or demand deposits, the service is liquidity, the advantage in convenience of money relative to other assets. This is the same problem discussed above in connection with the taxation of financial intermediaries under a two-tiered cash-flow tax. Just as in its application to household durables, the prepayment method provides a simple way to treat consistently these assets and those that generate a measurable cash return.

Exports and Imports. The consumption-type taxes considered to this point (the VAT, retail sales tax, and two-tiered cash-flow tax) have been amenable to either an origin or a destination treatment of international trade. However, a destination basis appears to be the natural approach to a graduated personal-consumption tax using cash-flow accounting. Conceptually, the tax would be levied on the consumption of a U.S. resident, regardless of the origins of the goods consumed; the location of production would play no role in determining tax liability. Because corporations are not separately taxed, their exports and imports have no immediate tax consequences; distributions would be taxed according to shareholder residence. Export sales and import outlays by individual proprietors would receive the same treatment as all other business sales and purchases: receipts are included, payments are deducted. (Whether receipts from sales abroad are taxed currently or on repatriation is of little consequence under cash-flow accounting.) Individuals buying imported goods for their own consumption would receive no deduction for the outlays, thereby paying tax on the imports.

Notice that including business receipts from exports in the tax base (and allowing deduction of business import purchases) expresses the destination principle of taxation in the context of a full-fledged personal cash-flow tax, whereas the corresponding rule in the VAT context is to exclude export sales and allow no deduction of import purchases. Because the tax is related to the circumstances of the individual consumer, it is not obvious what it would even mean to base it as well on the location of production.

Relation to a Value-Added Tax Base

The two-tiered cash-flow tax would be exactly equivalent to a cash-flow VAT if businesses and individual taxpayers were taxed at the same rate (and with no exemptions at the individual level). Is there a similar equivalence between a VAT and a full-fledged personal cash-flow tax at a uniform flat rate? The answer is yes, under certain conditions. It would take us too far afield to explore the equivalence in detail, but the basic outline may help in understanding both sorts of tax.

Imagine, then, the simplest economy, consisting of business corporations and households. The firms make payments to households in return for labor services, and households purchase consumption goods from the firms. In addition, the firms may buy from households or sell to them financial assets, such as bonds or stock (interest payments and dividends can be thought of as purchases of financial assets), and the households also may trade financial claims among themselves. Consider now the tax consequences of various transactions under a cash-flow VAT and under a full-fledged personal cash-flow tax. Financial transactions (borrowing and lending, payment of interest, purchase and sale of assets for cash) between households give rise to no change in the aggregate tax base under the VAT (because the firms are not involved at all) or under the full-fledged personal cash-flow tax (because for every deduction of an amount saved by one household there is an equivalent inclusion of an amount dissaved by another household). Financial transactions between firms (for example, payment of a dividend by one corporation to another) have no tax consequences under either system. A sale of goods by one firm to another also has no net tax consequences under either system. Under the VAT there is an inclusion in the base by the seller that is offset by a deduction on the part of the purchaser. The transaction does not register at all under the full-fledged personal cash-flow tax.

That leaves exchange of financial assets and of goods and services that cross the boundary between firms and households. Some of these transactions have net tax consequences, but in each case the results are the same under both systems. A sale of goods by a firm to a household produces an addition to the VAT base; because the household must draw on some savings (including cash and bank deposits in the set of assets counted as savings) to make the purchase, the transaction generates the same addition to the full-fledged personal cash-flow tax base. Payment of wages by the firm to the household triggers no tax under the VAT. Under a full-fledged personal cash-flow tax, the transaction by itself would add to the household's base, but since the payment would have to be in the form of a financial asset (for example, cash or a demand deposit), it would give rise to a simultaneous deduction for saving. Similarly, if a firm purchases a financial asset from a household, there is no VAT consequence, and the addition to the full-fledged personal cash-flow tax base of the household is offset by a simultaneous saving transaction.

That completes the catalogue of possibilities; in this simple economy the full-fledged personal cash-flow tax and VAT calculations lead to the same aggregate tax base. The same broad principles carry over to more complicated systems. Although a given VAT will have a different base in the aggregate from a given full-fledged personal cash-flow tax, one can generally construct consistent systems of the two types that will lead to the same result. The main reasons for differences in practical systems are likely to be differences in the underlying concept of consumption (for example, a full-fledged personal cash-flow tax might allow a deduction for state and local taxes that is not duplicated in a given VAT) and in the comprehensiveness of the definition of saving given the standard treatment (for example, cash would typically not be given standard treatment; the payment of wages by the firm would thus give rise to current tax liability under a full-fledged personal cash-flow tax and not under a VAT). The difference even here may be one of timing, not of tax burden in a discounted present-value sense. If the cash bears interest, as in a money-market fund, the tax not yet due under the VAT in the illustration will be paid with interest when the cash is ultimately used to purchase goods. It is perhaps sufficient for our purposes to note that in the aggregate (not accounting for the important differences in the rate structures) VAT and full-fledged personal cash-flow tax bases are very close relatives.

The Aaron-Galper Proposal

The proposal by Henry Aaron and Harvey Galper (1984, 1985) of the Brookings Institution belongs in the category of full-fledged personal cash-flow taxes. Three of the proposal's features illustrate well the significant choices to be made within a consumption framework. First, the Aaron-Galper plan would count noncharitable gifts and bequests as consumption by the donor. That is, recipients would add gifts and bequests received to the tax base; donors would not be allowed a deduction. Second, owner-occupied housing would be dealt with through the tax-prepayment method. That is, no deduction would be allowed for purchase of a house by an owner-occupier and no attempt would be made to impute and tax the resulting flow of housing services. Third, the proposal would retain a tax on corporations, also of the cash-flow type. The way this tax would work will be discussed in Chapter 6.

The *Blueprints* Cash-Flow Tax

If literal measurement of consumption according to the typical interpretation of the term is the objective, use of the tax-prepayment method of accounting for assets of any kind appears to be a defect in a cash-flow tax. The system labeled the "Cash-Flow Tax" in *Blueprints for Basic Tax Reform* turns the defect into a virtue. Like a full-fledged personal cash-flow tax, the *Blueprints* plan bases liabilities on information from individual tax returns only (that is, there is no separate tax on businesses) and levies tax according to a graduated schedule. It differs from a full-fledged personal cash-flow tax in giving individuals wide latitude to choose between standard and tax-prepayment treatment of savings.

The *Blueprints* Cash-Flow Tax can be thought of as a program to impose a lifetime tax based progressively on the individual's "lifetime wealth," defined as the amount of money an individual would need to fund his consumption for the rest of his life, that is, the amount of money he would need so that, taking into account both the principal and interest (but no other future sources of funds), he would be able to pay for all future consumption and have nothing left over. We can similarly conceive of a wealth-equivalent of taxes paid: the amount of money the individual would need to put aside to fund all future Cash-Flow Tax liabilities. The Cash-Flow Tax rules will have the effect of making the required tax fund larger, as a ratio to lifetime wealth, the larger is the consumption fund. The particular path of earnings or expenditure experienced by the taxpayer will not affect his tax burden. In technical language, the ratio of the present discounted value of the Cash-Flow Tax liabilities to the present discounted value of lifetime consumption is larger, the larger is the latter amount. (For readers not familiar with it, the concept of present discounted value is explained in Chapter 7.)

The *Blueprints* plan is also designed for ease of administration. One of the chief problems in implementing a cash-flow tax is monitoring the return on the savings that taxpayers have deducted in the past. Cash-flow features of the present tax system occur either in the context of a business activity (as when a business uses accelerated depreciation allowances) or with the collaboration of an intermediary (such as a pension trust) between individuals and their assets. The intermediary acts as a fiduciary on behalf of the individual and also serves a monitoring function in the tax system. These institutions ease the task of monitoring. Under a full-fledged personal cash-flow tax it would be necessary to monitor as well *all* dispositions of assets.

Arrangements such as IRAs, employer-sponsored pensions, and so on, all involving intermediaries such as pension trusts, are referred to as "qualified accounts" in the Cash-Flow Tax. The basic trick employed by the *Blueprints* plan is to generalize the notion of qualified accounts to permit any recognized fiduciary institution (subject to such rules for qualification as may be appropriate to guarantee integrity) to manage assets on behalf of individuals. For example, qualified accounts would be offered by banks and stockbrokers. Deductions for acquisitions of assets under the *Blueprints* Cash-Flow Tax would be limited to net cash flow into qualified accounts (or to a closely held business that is, a firm such as a proprietorship, over which the individual has significant control). Net withdrawals from qualified accounts would be included in the individual's tax base, along with any cash withdrawals from a closely held business. All other saving or investment transactions would be accounted for on a tax-prepayment basis.

The choice between tax-prepaid and qualified forms of saving and dissaving allows the taxpayer to smooth the tax liability over time, avoiding the need for averaging schemes that might otherwise be called for.

This averaging should not be thought of as a mere nicety; it is needed to avoid making the tax burden depend on the time path of earnings or expenditure. To give a simple example, suppose the tax is assessed at 10 percent on the first $20,000 of Cash-Flow Tax base and 30 percent on amounts in excess of $20,000, and the interest rate is 15 percent. Consider two individuals, each of whom earns $20,000 salary in each year of a two-year life. (The short life simplifies the example; the principle carries over to the general case.) The object of the system is to levy the same tax burden on the two individuals, regardless of how they choose to allocate their consumption between the first and second year.

Suppose one individual chooses to divide his consumption evenly between the two years, putting nothing into savings, making no deposit to a qualified account, and making no saving outside of a qualified account. Then his Cash-Flow Tax base will be $20,000 each year, and he will be able to consume $18,000 per year after paying Cash-Flow Tax. Suppose the other individual chooses to concentrate his consumption entirely in his second year. If he is obliged to save via qualified account, he will have a $20,000 deduction in the first year and owe no Cash-Flow Tax. In the second year his Cash-Flow Tax base will include his $20,000 in current earnings plus the $23,000 ($20,000 plus interest at 15 percent) he will withdraw from his qualified account, implying a tax liability of $8900 (10 percent of $20,000 plus 30 percent of $23,000). It is obvious that this tax burden is much greater than the $2000 in each of the two years paid by the first individual. In other words, the requirement that the individual save via qualified account in this case implies a large penalty on saving. But if the individual can save in unqualified form, under the illustrative circumstances he will find it in his interest to do so, taking no deduction in the first year (therefore paying $2000 in tax even though he has no consumption then) and paying $2000 in tax based only on his labor earnings in the second year.

The example can be elaborated in various ways, such as by including patterns of earnings that differ while patterns of consumption do not. As the reader can verify by working through some of these variations, if both qualified-account and ordinary savings vehicles (taxed on a tax-prepayment basis) are available, the taxpayer will find it in his interest to manage his saving so as to stay in the same tax bracket every year. Even though the actual pattern of earnings or consumption expenditure may vary, the individual will try to maintain a level of taxable cash flow that remains within a single tax bracket, which will depend on the general level of the individual's prosperity as measured by lifetime wealth. A well-to-do individual will find it in his interest to stay in a high bracket. Even though it would be possible to drop to a low tax bracket in a given year by making a large deposit to a qualified account, it will not be advantageous to do this because future withdrawals from the account will be all the more heavily taxed.

Allowing a choice between the two forms of saving also permits a system that is simpler and involves less day-to-day monitoring of the taxpayer's financial affairs than would be required by a full-fledged personal cash-flow tax. Institutions overseeing the qualified accounts would be obliged to report annual net inflows or outflows to the tax authorities and to the individual account holder, much as pension plans and IRA managers are required to do under the current income tax. The taxpayer's compliance problem is thereby greatly simplified. And since the monitoring institutions could be held under sanctions to perform their assignments conscientiously, the tax authority's enforcement problem would also be simplified.

The rules used to keep track of the savings given qualified-account treatment (to ensure that the returns are subject to tax) and isolate the saving undertaken on a tax-prepaid basis (so that the associated returns will not be subject to double taxation) may be summarized as follows:

All assets purchased for direct personal use (house, automobile, and so forth) must be treated on a tax-prepaid basis (no deduction). This treatment, which avoids the problem of measuring the returns from investment that take the form of direct services, is currently followed in the income tax. (Note that although tax-prepayment accounting gives a correct result in the consumption-based tax, it gives an *incorrect* result in an income tax.)

All assets purchased for use in closely held business enterprises must be given standard treatment (immediately expensed). In other words, individuals must keep track of their interest in unincorporated business enterprises, partnerships, and closely held corporations on a cash-flow accounting basis. All cash flows from the business to the individual are taxed, and all flows from the individual to the business are deducted.

Individuals may choose to purchase or sell financial assets via qualified accounts, monitored by a fiduciary institution such as a bank. Net deposits to a qualified account during the year (or other accounting period) are reported to the tax authorities and may be *deducted* from the depositor's tax base. Net withdrawals in an accounting period are similarly reported and must be added to the account holder's tax base. (This is exactly the way flows in and out of an IRA are handled now. The *Blueprints* Cash-Flow Tax would eliminate the various limits that now apply to such accounts.) Borrowing via a qualified account is permitted, in which case the proceeds of the loan are added to the tax base; repayments, whether labeled "interest" or "principal," are deducted. Nothing occurring inside the qualified account has immediate tax consequences — only deposits and withdrawals do. (Reminder: Employees are taxed on a cash-flow basis. Employer-provided pensions are taxed only on receipt of benefits.)

Transactions involving financial assets other than via a qualified account, including payment and receipt of interest, receipt of dividends, and asset purchases and sales, have no consequences for the tax base.

Under the *Blueprints* Cash-Flow Tax there is no separate tax on business firms, corporate or otherwise. Like the Aaron-Galper plan, however, the Cash-Flow Tax would be compatible with a separate tax on the cash flow of corporations (for example, along the lines of the business tax component of the Hall-Rabushka Simple Flat Tax). A separate tax of this sort could be useful in making a transition from the existing system to the Cash-Flow Tax.

Treatment of Various Transactions

Review of the treatment of selected transactions under the *Blueprints* Cash-Flow Tax illustrates again the possibilities compatible with the consumption strategy. Although the form of tax would easily permit itemized deductions, like the Simple Flat Tax the *Blueprints* Cash-Flow Tax recommends against most of them, interpreting them as favored forms of consumption. Thus no deductions are recommended for charitable contributions, medical expenses, or state and local taxes other than income taxes. *Blueprints* recommends the adoption of a residence basis for taxation, which translates into what I have called a destination principle. In the calculation of cash flow subject to tax, sales and outlays crossing the national boundary are treated like all other sales and outlays. Resident individuals would be liable to file and pay the Cash-Flow Tax.

Table 5–1 summarizes the treatments of a whole range of transactions under the *Blueprints* Cash-Flow Tax and places them in the context of the accrual-income tax discussion of Chapter 3. Differences between the two approaches have been indicated by a bullet on the left-hand side. While the two systems have much in common, most of the very serious problems associated with measuring accrual income, including inflation correction, are avoided under the Cash-Flow Tax. To give a rough idea of how the *Blueprints* Cash-Flow Tax compares with the existing income tax, Table 5–2 shows the rate structure that the U.S. Treasury estimated would have the same revenue yield as the combined corporation and individual income taxes in effect in 1976, with approximately the same distribution of tax burdens by consumption class (dollar figures have been inflated to 1984 levels). Because of changes since 1976, the corresponding table for 1984 tax law would show a lower rate in the top bracket and no doubt other differences in detail.

Phase-In of Consumption-Type Rules to the Existing Income Tax

Viewed as replacements for the existing income tax, all the plans discussed thus far have involved comprehensive reform. That is, they not only have the effect of implementing some variety of consumption-based tax, they also dramatically change the tax treatment of many transactions not centrally related to the income-consumption distinction. A less comprehensive reform program is outlined in the following six coordinated rule changes. Applied to both individual and corporation taxes, they would have the effect of converting existing law from a confused hybrid of income and consumption tax rules to a consistent consumption-type base.

1. Phase out present restrictions on deposits to and withdrawals from savings plans qualifying for tax-shelter treatment, such as employer-provided retirement programs, Keogh Plans, and IRAs.

Table 5-1. Information on tax returns for an accrual-income tax and the *Blueprints* Cash-Flow Tax[a]

Household receipts and deductions	Included on return?	
	Accrual-income tax	Cash-Flow Tax
Receipts		
R-1 Wages, salaries, tips, royalties, and so on, subject to tax[b]	Yes	Yes
R-2 Receipts of pensions, annuities, life insurance cash value, disability compensation, workmen's compensation, and sick pay[c]	Yes	Yes
R-3 Gifts, inheritances, trust distributions, and life insurance death benefits received[d]	Yes	Yes
• R-4 Interest received on financial assets, *adjusted for inflation*	Yes	No[e]
R-5 Dividends received on corporate earnings	No[f]	No[e,g]
• R-6 Proceeds from the sale, exchange, or distribution of capital assets	Yes	No[e,g]
• R-7 Policyholder claim on earnings from life insurance, annuity, and pension plan reserves, *adjusted for inflation*	Yes	No
• R-8 Increase in value of the claim on a trust beyond allocated share of amounts given or bequeathed to the trust, *adjusted for inflation*	Yes	No
R-9 Gross receipts from unincorporated business enterprises	Yes	Yes
• R-10 Allocated share of *inflation-corrected* corporate earnings	Yes	No
• R-11 Imputed service value attributable to owner-occupied housing and other household durables	Yes	No

Table 5–1 *(continued)*

		Included on return?	
Household receipts and deductions		Accrual-income tax	Cash-Flow Tax
• R–12	Withdrawals from qualified accounts (including withdrawal of borrowed funds)[h]	No	Yes
Deductions			
D–1	Employee business expenses (including qualified travel expenses, union dues, tools, materials, and qualified educational expenses)	Yes	Yes
D–2	Contributions to qualified retirement plans	Yes	Yes
D–3	Gifts and bequests made to an identified taxpayer or trust with eligible beneficiary; net life insurance premiums (compare item R–3)	Yes	Yes
• D–4	Interest paid on indebtedness (including interest on home mortgages and consumer loans), *adjusted for inflation*	Yes	No[i]
• D–5	Basis of assets sold, exchanged, or distributed (compare item R–6), *adjusted for inflation*	Yes[j]	No
D–6	Current expenses associated with unincorporated business enterprises, including contributions to employee pensions	Yes	Yes
• D–7	Capital outlays associated with unincorporated business enterprises	No	Yes
• D–8	Depreciation allowances for current and past capital outlays associated with unincorporated business enterprises, *adjusted for inflation*	Yes	No

Table 5-1 *(continued)*

	Included on return?	
Household receipts and deductions	Accrual-income tax	Cash-Flow Tax
D-9 Special items as a matter of policy (for example, charitable contributions, medical expenses)	Yes	Yes
• D-10 Deposits to qualified accounts (including repayment of borrowed funds)	No	Yes

a. Entries relating to accrual income duplicate those in Table 3-1. The Cash-Flow Tax description is based on the U.S. Treasury (1977) plan.

b. The definition of "wages subject to tax" could incorporate differential rules according to individual characteristics (for example, marital status might be used to mitigate the "marriage tax" problem). Under the illustrative treatment of pensions and the like (which involves an indirect approach to retirement income measurement), this item would *exclude* Social Security taxes attributable to retirement benefits and contributions to retirement plans. (See text.) R-1 would *include* employer-paid health and life insurance premiums and similar employee benefit outlays by firms.

c. This item would probably include Social Security benefits of all types. Pensions and annuities for which there has been no exclusion under R-1 or deduction under D-2 or D-3 would be excluded under R-2.

d. The present practice of excluding gifts and inheritances received from the tax base can be rationalized by the difficulty of measuring accruing wealth from anticipated inheritance. Corresponding to this treatment of gifts and bequests received would be the denial of a deduction to the giver, bequeather, or life insurer. The same procedures could be applied in the Cash-Flow Tax as well. An alternative under both approaches would be to require inclusion of gifts and bequests by the recipient and also to deny a deduction to the donor, leading to a bestowal-inclusive base.

e. Under the Cash-Flow Tax, a significant distinction is made between assets owned on a tax-prepaid basis, the return on which is excluded from the base, and assets owned via qualified accounts, the return on which is ultimately included in the base when withdrawn.

f. The exclusion of dividends is a corollary of the allocation of all corporate income to shareholders. Dividends result in a reduction in the basis of the shares for purposes of calculating gain from sale or exchange (capital gain).

g. Under the Cash-Flow Tax, qualified account treatment would be obligatory for closely held corporations. See R-12 and D-10.

h. "Qualified accounts," which are similar to IRAs in current U.S. income tax law, play a critical role in the Cash-Flow Tax. All inflows are deducted from the tax base, and all outflows are included. Nothing occurring inside the qualified account has direct tax consequences.

i. Borrowing via qualified account is included in the tax base, and *all* consequent return payments into the account, whether of principal or interest, are deducted. However, neither interest on nor repayment of borrowing outside a qualified account has tax consequences under the Cash-Flow Tax.

j. The deduction of adjusted basis would have to be limited (as at present) in relation to sales proceeds in R-6. Unused deduction of net losses could be carried forward.

2. Phase out taxation of interest receipts, dividends, and capital gains except as realized through withdrawals from tax-sheltered savings plans.

3. Accelerate depreciation deductions until full first-year write-off is the rule; similarly, move to immediate expensing of inventory purchases.

4. Allow borrowing from a tax-qualified plan, with the borrowed amounts immediately subject to tax, but all repayments (of principal or interest) fully deductible.

5. Phase out existing saving and investment incentives, such as the investment tax credit.

6. Phase out deductions for interest paid except in the case of borrowing from a tax-qualified plan.

As a sheer matter of administration, most of these changes would be quite within the bounds of modifications of the rules enacted in recent years. For example, moving to expensing of investment outlays would be a great simplification, in the same direction as and similar to the shift in 1981 from earlier depreciation systems to the Accelerated Cost Recovery System of the existing income tax. Expanding the use of qualified savings accounts along the lines of IRAs would be an evolutionary change. Eliminating the taxation of capital gains would effect an enormous simplification and would be in the same direction as the shift to 60

Table 5-2. *Blueprints* Cash-Flow Tax rate structure (basic exemption: $2882 per return plus $1505 for each taxpayer and dependent)

Cash-flow bracket ($)	Marginal tax rate (%)
Joint returns	
0- 9,784	10
9,784-56,443	28
Over 56,443	40
Single returns	
0- 6,020	10
6,020-56,443	26
Over 56,443	40

Source: U.S. Treasury Department (1977). Dollar amounts have been adjusted for inflation from 1976 to 1984.

percent exclusion of gains that was a part of the legislation in 1981. Present law allows a small exclusion of dividends from tax, and within recent experience an allowance has been available whereby dividends paid by public utilities could be deferred from tax if reinvested in utility stock.

In the list of six steps the most significant departure from present policy is the changed treatment of interest. Yet such a change is the most critical aspect of implementing a consumption strategy. Modifying the treatment of interest payments and receipts would bring about greater consistency in the taxation of savings and investment transactions even under the existing hybrid system. Consistent treatment under a rationalization of the hybrid system along consumption lines implies wholly eliminating the deduction of interest paid and inclusion of interest received. Of all the changes outlines, this is no doubt the one to which most objections would be raised and for which transitional rules would be seen as essential.

The six-step list indicates that, far from the wrenching change so often imagined, it would be comparatively simple to convert the existing tax system to a progressive consumption basis.

6 Taxing Corporations

The corporation income tax is one of the most fascinating species produced by the process of economic legislation around the world.

Arnold C. Harberger in Walker and Bloomfield, *New Directions in Federal Tax Policy for the 1980's*

FEW PIECES of the tax tangle pose a greater challenge in explaining tax policy to a general audience than does the corporation income tax. The corporation tax is variously viewed as a pernicious double tax on savings, a tax shelter for the small businessman, a critical instrument to preserve the progressivity of the individual tax, and a fundamentally just way to compel institutions that control a large share of the nation's wealth to contribute to the collective expense. After presenting an overview of the existing tax system, I try here to develop what may for some be a new slant on corporations and how tax rules affect them. Stressing the importance of coordinating the rules applicable to corporations with the individual tax rules, I shall analyze the two broad types of tax one might employ in systems rationalized along income or consumption tax lines. (A less technical discussion of the incidence of the corporation tax is provided in Chapter 7, which may be read independently of this chapter.)

The Existing Corporate Tax System

Everyone has heard that corporations are persons from a legal point of view. U.S. tax law, however, recognizes that it makes little sense to ignore the connections between corporations and their owners. Many features of the corporation income tax (such as the exclusion from a corporation's tax base of 85 percent of dividends received on shares it owns in other corporations) are designed to take account of the way the fictional corporation-person relates to real people. Present law allows two general approaches to the taxation of corporations. Corporations having no more than thirty-five shareholders may elect to be treated like partnerships for tax purposes. The various elements of the income calculation of a Sub-S corporation (so called because the applicable rules are set out in Subchapter S of the Internal Revenue Code) are passed through to the individual shareholder. These corporations can thus obtain the advantages of limited liability without any special tax consequences. There is little we need say about the taxation of such corporations that has not already been said in connection with the taxation of individual business income.

The bulk of corporate economic activity is carried on in corporations taxed under a variant of what is known as a "classical" corporation tax. Under a classical corporation tax, income is measured at the corporate level according to most of the same rules that apply to measuring individual income (including depreciation rules and the allowance of deductions for interest and state and local real estate and income taxes). No deductions are allowed for distributions to stockholders; and those distributions identified as dividends, or regarded by tax authorities as equivalent to dividends, are taxed as ordinary income at the shareholder level.[1]

We might note a few particular features of the U.S. classical corporate income tax. Corporations in sufficiently close ownership relation file a single aggregated tax return, in which dividend payments within the group are ignored in the calculation of taxable income. When the relationship among the corporations is less close, the law allows an exclusion of 85 percent of dividends received, thus reducing to minor dimensions the multiple taxation of dividends passing through more than one corporation. The taxation of both individuals and corporations is theoretically based on *worldwide* income; a credit is allowed for income taxes paid to foreign countries. In the case of income earned by foreign subsidiaries of U.S. corporations, U.S. tax is calculated (and foreign taxes credited) on the basis of dividends remitted to the parent company.

---

1. In general, a distribution of cash in proportion to ownership shares is regarded as a dividend to the extent of the larger of the corporation's current-year or accumulated earnings and profits. *Earnings and profits* are supposed to correspond to the notion of the surplus earned for stockholders, whereas *taxable income* departs from the measurement of surplus because of such devices as accelerated depreciation. But many of the criticisms we have directed to the measurement of income for tax purposes, especially in a time of inflation, apply equally to the definition of earnings and profits.

(Note the analogy with the treatment of dividends of individual shareholders in the personal income tax.)

Corporation income is subject to tax according to a graduated structure of rates. Currently a rate of 15 percent applies to the first $25,000 of taxable income, 18 percent to taxable income between $25,000 and $50,000, 30 percent to taxable income between $50,000 and $75,000, 40 percent to taxable income between $75,000 and $100,000, and 46 percent to taxable income in excess of $100,000. (Corporations with taxable income in excess of $1 million must pay an additional 5 percent tax on such excess, up to $20,250; the effect of this rule is to eliminate for large corporations the saving from the rates of tax below 46 percent applied to the first dollars of profits.) Losses in any year may be set off against income in earlier years (up to three years) or carried over, without interest, for up to fifteen years.

Important among the credits allowable against taxes is the investment tax credit, which applies at the same rates for corporations as for individuals: 10 percent for qualifying assets whose cost will be recovered over five years or more; 6 percent for property with a recovery period of three years, with a limit of $25,000 plus 85 percent of the excess of tax liability over $25,000. Since 1984, taxpayers have been obliged to reduce the basis used in calculating depreciation allowances by one-half of the investment credit; alternatively they may claim credits at rate of 8 percent and 4 percent for the two classes of assets, with no reduction in basis. For corporations paying a marginal rate of 46 percent, the 8 percent credit with no basis reduction is generally the more favorable option for five-year property; the credit of 6 percent coupled with a 3 percent basis reduction is more favorable for three-year property. Because giving up 3 percent of basis means losing roughly 1.3 percent of the tax saving from cost recovery allowances for a 46 percent taxpayer, current investment credit rates can be thought of as 8 percent and 4.7 percent in terms of the system in effect until 1984.

For large corporations that regularly have positive taxable income, the rate structure applied to taxable income is effectively flat, at 46 percent. But the graduated rates and the zero tax rate applied to losses become very important sources of differential tax treatment within the corporate sector as a whole, in view of the many smaller corporations, as well as large ones with highly fluctuating incomes. Long-term capital gains realized by a corporation are taxed at a flat 28 percent, with capital losses allowable only as an offset to capital gains realized within the previous three or following five years.

The Corporation as Financial Intermediary

A corporation is a creature of the law, a legal entity that is, indeed, recognized as a person in having the capacity to enter into contracts, sue and be sued, and so on. The key contribution of the legal system is to regard the corporation-person as distinct from the flesh-and-blood people who control it. The most important distinction is the limiting of the corporation's liability to its creditors (other than the liability for taxes) to the resources of the corporation itself. Although a variety of claimants, including creditors, employees (especially managers), and even customers, are likely to have some stake in the fortunes of a given corporation, most of the risk is borne by the owners of its common stock. Under normal circumstances, these shareholders, acting either directly or via elected officials, choose the management and expect it to act in their interests. (In the case of small corporations, often the managers are principal shareholders.)

Limited liability has proved to be an enormously productive device, primarily in permitting a separation of risk bearing and management (usually combined in the same people in a proprietorship or partnership). Related to this is the possibility for the ownership of business enterprises to change hands without affecting the ongoing business. Large-scale economic activities of many sorts could probably not be conducted on a free-enterprise basis without limited liability. Although one can argue that individuals ought naturally to expect the courts to uphold contracts freely executed with creditors on the basis of limited liability, it is sometimes suggested that corporations should pay taxes in return for the privilege of limited liability extended by the state. Whatever the merits of the case, it is hard to construct a connection between the benefits of limited liability and anything like the system of corporate income taxation in this or any other country. The sensible way to think about taxes on corporations, as about other taxes, is to look at who bears them and what their distorting effects are.

Any corporation is, in a sense, a financial intermediary. The usual sorts of financial intermediaries, which are called financial corporations, are firms such as banks, insurance companies, and mutual funds that operate by buying and managing certain financial assets, such as mortgages or personal loans, and repackaging them as assets that are bought by others in the form of demand deposits, life insurance policies, and so on. A successful financial intermediary is one that buys cheap and sells dear and that manages its assets and liabilities well. (When the buying and selling are of the same commodity — a foreign currency, for example — the process is called arbitrage.) Except that the assets acquired and managed by the corporation involve a much higher proportion of tangible property (buildings, machines, inventories, and the like), broadly speaking, much the same description applies to any business corporation. It buys some assets (buildings, advertising campaigns, inventories, research and development, and so on), sells others (bonds, new shares of stock), and manages the whole portfolio in the interests of its existing stockholders.

A closed-end mutual fund provides a good analogy to a typical nonfinancial corporation. A closed-end mutual fund is a corporation that owns and manages a portfolio of common stocks and other financial instruments, perhaps taking a negative position in some of them (for example, by borrowing). The fund-corporation is itself owned by shareholders, and its shares may be bought and sold. Note that because the shareholder has claim only to dividends and to such other distributions as the corporation may decide to make, owning shares in the fund is not exactly the same as owning the corresponding proportion of the fund's portfolio. There is no mechanical connection between the market value of the net assets held by the corporation and the value of its own shares in the market. (In this, the closed-end mutual fund differs from an open-end fund, in which stockholders have the right to redeem their shares for an amount equal to the corresponding fraction of the portfolio's current market value.) In the absence of taxes, however, there is a strong pressure bringing those two values into equality. The pressure is simply the possibility that if the shares fall below the value of the underlying net assets, individuals could buy a sufficient number of the corporation's shares to control its decisions and then distribute the corporation's net assets to themselves. But the tax treatment of dividends or other distributions may result in a systematic difference between the net value of the firm's assets and the value of its shares.

Viewing the corporation as a financial intermediary is often helpful in sorting out the effects of tax rules. Dividend taxation provides an example. Under present law, dividends received by a shareholder are treated as ordinary income and are therefore subject to tax at whatever that shareholder's marginal income tax rate may be. If the corporation took the *same* money that it would otherwise pay out in dividends and used it instead to purchase its own shares from the public, shareholders would have the *option* of receiving the same cash as they would have obtained with the dividend, but the distribution would be favorably treated because any tax liability would be the result of a capital gain, not ordinary income. Furthermore, the option itself is worth something, inasmuch as it permits the shareholder who does not want the cash distribution to postpone its receipt, achieving the effect of reinvesting the dividend in the company's shares, but without any current tax liability. In other words, the distribution is converted from ordinary income to accruing long-term capital gain (see Bradford, 1980b, pp. 50–58).

Variations on this theme include the purchase from the public of the shares of other corporations (not quite as effective because of the 85 percent, rather than 100 percent, dividend exclusion), takeover for cash of other corporations (just as effective), and liquidation of the corporation (in which case the distribution is treated as a repurchase of shares). (This discussion does not take into account the complicated rules of questionable effectiveness intended to inhibit these sorts of transactions.) The tax system thus exerts strong incentive effects on the corporation's financial choices.

Because the corporation has a choice about whether distributions will be taxed as dividends, the exact effects of the system are difficult to predict. Imagine the consequences of suddenly imposing on a closed-end mutual fund a 25 percent tax on all distributions, whether in liquidation or otherwise; think of it as a toll charge on passing the money out. Then a person who purchased the entire equity interest in the firm would be able to realize only 75 percent of its net asset position through distributions. We would expect such a tax to introduce a divergence of about 25 percent between the value of the fund's underlying assets and the price its shares would command in the market. The taxation of dividends is much like such a toll charge. Our financial intermediary model thus leads us to expect that if dividend payout is the main method of distribution (for whatever reason), the market will systematically value corporate shares below the value of the underlying assets (because the shareholder is subject to the dividend tax in getting the money out of the corporation). But if the possibility of avoiding the dividend tax through share repurchase and similar devices dominates, the market value should tend toward equality with that of the underlying net assets.

Analysts have given the name q to the ratio between the value of assets inside a corporation and the value of the shares representing ownership. (For discussion, see Auerbach, 1983b and c, and King, 1977.) The value of q is of considerable practical importance. A value of less than 1 would imply discouragement of equity finance (since selling a new share for $1 would add less than $1 to the market value of the firm's stock). The closed-end mutual fund analogy makes it clear that the present tax system tends to depress the value of q, although the availability of ways to avoid dividend taxes implies that the depressing effect is not certain.

The question of why firms pay dividends, in view of the large tax advantages of alternative forms of distribution, has long mystified analysts. The rational explanations (such as that dividends are a signal of financial strength) seem insufficient in view of many alternative ways to achieve the same end. Irrational explanations (such as that stockholders simply like dividends and do not care about the tax cost) seem, unfortunately, to hold the field at the moment. (For discussions and empirical studies see Black, 1976; Gordon and Bradford, 1980; Miller and Scholes, 1982; and Poterba and Summers, 1984.)

The view of the corporation as financial intermediary can give us some insight into the proposal advanced by William Andrews (American Law Institute, 1982, pp. 327–523) to move toward parallel treatment of equity and debt finance. Under the suggested rules, dividends on newly issued stock could be deducted from income subject to the corporation tax. At the same time, an excise tax would be instituted on all nondividend distributions (share repurchase or liquidation, for example). The result would be to reduce or even reverse (depending on the rate of the excise tax) the incentives to use nondividend forms of distribution as a way of avoiding tax, and to neutralize the choice between debt and equity as sources of new funds. An important and difficult question is what introducing the new rules would do to the value of existing shares. (This is an issue of what is called "transition incidence" in Chapter 7.) To the extent that existing shares already incorporate a discount for anticipated dividend taxes, the new rules should have little effect. If the market value of existing shares is based implicitly on the assumption that marginal distributions will be equivalent to share repurchase, the new rules could be predicted to depress share prices by roughly the percentage rate of excise tax.

As a third application of viewing the corporation as a closed-end mutual fund, consider the suggestion sometimes made that the tax on corporations be eliminated altogether, while individuals would continue to be taxed on interest, dividends, and capital gains as under the existing income tax. If applied only to mutual funds, these rules would create a strong incentive for individuals to hold their savings in the form of closed-end mutual fund shares, rather than owning the underlying securities directly, because the portion of the fund's return not distributed as dividends would tend to accrue as capital gains and losses, with all the implied advantages. The fund, in turn, acting in the interests of its shareholders, would have a strong incentive to postpone payment of dividends or, in fact, to avoid dividends altogether, making any distribution of cash take the form of repurchase of its own shares. The reasoning behind this conclusion, which is so transparent in the case of a closed-end mutual fund, applies just as well to corporations generally and illustrates the potential role of a corporation income tax in a system of individual income taxation in which it is impractical to measure accruing gains and losses.

Shortcomings of the Existing Corporate Income Tax

We may distinguish two sorts of problems in the existing corporate income tax system. Shortcomings of income measurement are much the same as those identified in the individual income tax (for example, inflation effects and realization accounting). Some of the inconsistencies in income measurement, however, are thrown into particular relief by the corporation tax. In this category are variations in effective tax rates among assets of different types and uses. As the instances just discussed suggest, some serious problems have to do specifically with the relation between the treatment of corporations and of individuals.

Effective Rates. The term "effective rate" is used in several ways in the discussion of tax policy. For example, the ratio of an individual's income tax liability to his income in a given year is often called the effective rate of income tax. The notion seems straightforward and can be helpful in summarizing the net effect of a complicated set of rules. It is, however, important to specify carefully what is meant in each case. For example, in referring to the individual income tax, is the income in the denominator correctly adjusted for inflation? What deductions have been considered appropriate in deriving the income measure used? Is accruing income from assets owned included? What about the service value of an owner-occupied house? Does the numerator take into account the future tax effects of current actions (for example, the future tax-increasing effect of a deposit in an IRA)? What about taxes implicitly paid, such as the differential between the yield on fully taxable and tax-exempt securities held? What about the burden of corporation and payroll taxes? Clearly, how such questions are answered will have a bearing on the interpretation of an effective tax rate figure.

Related to differences in definitions of effective rates are differences in the uses to which they may be put. We are most likely to use effective rates of personal income tax to assess the distribution of the tax burden. We may also be interested in describing the incentive effects of taxes, in which case what is called for is a measure of the *marginal* tax burden on some activity — the reward for working, for example, or for bearing risk. In this case, the data required are not measured taxes and incomes but calculated consequences of the extra taxes resulting from undertaking the activity in question. Thus the effective marginal rate of tax on labor would be found by working out the increase in a person's tax burden that would follow from earning an extra dollar of wages or salary.

In the case of corporations, the ratio of taxes paid by a corporation to a measure of its income in a given period may often provide dramatic material for the press or political speeches, but it is likely to be uninformative about the underlying issues. Because competition in the very active U.S. capital markets tends to bring about equality of the (risk-adjusted) rate of return after taxes by the holders of different assets, such a ratio tells us little about either the distribution of tax burdens or the incentive effects of the rules. For the incentive effects in particular, we need to employ forward-looking measures of *marginal* tax rates, because these determine the influence of the tax system on the allocation of investment.

The effective marginal tax rate on an investment activity is typically understood to be the ratio of the difference between the rate of return anticipated on a project before all taxes and subsidies and the rate of return received by the individual or institution providing the financing for the project after taxes and subsidies to the before-tax rate of return. This forward-looking concept is not necessarily reflected in the current flows of income and tax payments. We can, however, calculate the effective marginal tax rate on projects on the basis of existing and anticipated tax laws, and these calculations do tell us about the incentive effects of the law. (Effective marginal rates are themselves extremely sensitive to the particular assumptions made about such things as interest rates, before-tax rates of return, and the identities of the savers and investors. See Bradford and Fullerton, 1981; King and Fullerton, 1984; and Fullerton, 1984.)

Influence of Effective Rates on Various Investments. Although commentators often equate all business with corporate business, much business income is generated in noncorporate enterprises, and the rules for measuring business income are the same. We need not repeat here the discussion presented in Chapter 3 of the difficulty of measuring accrual income and the weaknesses of present income-measurement rules in this respect, particularly in times of inflation. But the problems of measuring the return to investment are particularly evident in the corporate tax context because a corporation consists essentially of a bundle of investment projects. The effect of existing rules is to provide very different incentives to undertake different sorts of investment — that is, very different effective rates of tax — according to the different characteristics of projects.

An extended example will illustrate some of the variations in the taxation of investment under existing rules. Consider the effect of taxes on an investment in a machine that declines in productivity at a rate of 13 percent per year (compare King and Fullerton, 1984, pp. 214–215), and on which the rate of return before all taxes is 10 percent in real terms. (The nominal rate of return is thus 10 percent plus the annual rate of inflation.) For purposes of the example, assume the corporation either can sell bonds to buy the machine or views retiring bonds as an alternative use of funds.[2] The influence of the tax rules on this particularly common tradeoff can be expressed by the difference between the rate of return on the machine and the maximum interest rate the company could afford to pay on bonds used to finance it, after taking into account all federal income tax provisions applicable at the corporate level. Here are the applicable provisions assumed:

- Corporate income tax rate   46%
- Investment tax credit   10
- Depreciation (on 95% of invested amount)
    First year   15%
    Second year   22
    Third year   21
    Fourth year   21
    Fifth year   21
- Deductible interest

It turns out that a corporation could afford to pay up to 17.4 percent interest on borrowing to finance the purchase of the machine, assuming there is no inflation.[3] (To keep matters simple, these calculations make no allowance for risk to either borrower or lender.) In the absence of taxes, or with a true accrual-income tax, an investor would just break even borrowing at 10 percent (the assumed before-tax rate of return on

2. It may be objected that often a smaller issue of debt, or retirement of existing debt, is not an alternative to the outlay on the project. Focusing on the tradeoff between debt and real investment, however, simplifies the analysis and captures the essential point. The tradeoff should be understood as just one of the margins strongly affected by tax considerations, although an extremely important one. Other tradeoffs could be dissected in a similar way.

3. These calculations are based on continuous compounding, with continuous taxation of receipts and deduction of interest but with ACRS depreciation deductions received at six, eighteen, thirty, forty-two, and fifty-four months. The investment tax credit is assumed to be received at the moment of investment.

the project); therefore the corporate tax structure effectively has provided a subsidy of 74 percent. That is, the effective tax rate is *negative* 74 percent, taking the corporate tax system by itself. Such a tax calculation is sometimes spoken of as *the* effective tax rate on a debt-financed investment. It is in this sense that the ACRS and investment tax credit provisions are sometimes described as more than eliminating the taxation of investment in equipment.

As far as the overall effects on distribution of the tax burden and on the incentives to save are concerned, it is important to note that this particular exercise, which focuses on the relative incentive for the company to purchase certain sorts of assets, stops at the corporate level and does not account for taxation at the level of the individual saver. The after-tax return to the lender depends on his tax circumstances. The investment would support a net return of 17.4 percent to a tax-exempt institution, such as a pension fund. For a lender in the same tax bracket as the corporation, the investment would support an after-tax return of 9.4 percent (compared with the 10 percent he would obtain if the investment were not taxable, and the 5.4 percent he would obtain if he were taxed on the full return). If we wish to describe the ACRS and ITC provisions as offsetting the income tax, the latter case is perhaps the more interesting one.

Now consider the effect of changing the inflation rate from 0 percent to 10 percent. This raises the anticipated cash return from the project and therefore the nominal interest that the corporation can afford to pay from 17.4 percent to 31.9 percent. Because the inflation premium in interest is deductible, the real return the company can afford to provide to a tax-exempt lender is now actually increased, to 21.9 percent (31.9 percent less 10 percent inflation). For a lender in the same tax bracket as the corporation, the investment would support a real after-tax return of 7.3 percent (54 percent of 32.0 percent, less 10 percent inflation).The reduction in after-tax return compared to the no-inflation case results from the reduced value of historical cost-depreciation allowances.

We can carry out the same exercise for a typical investment in a building, again assuming a 10 percent rate of return before taxes, with an assumed economic depreciation rate of 3 percent (compare King and Fullerton, 1984, pp. 214–215). The following tax rules currently apply:[4]

---

4. The example assumes the purchaser puts the building into service at midyear and holds it permanently. In fact, it may be highly advantageous to choose straight-line depreciation and sell the building for a capital gain after a few years, whereupon the depreciation deductions begin again. See Hendershott and Ling (1984).

- Corporate income tax rate   46%
- Investment tax credit[5]   0
- Depreciation (on 100% of invested amount)

First year	5%
Second year	9
Third year	8
Fourth year	8
Fifth year	7
Sixth year	6
Seventh year	6
Eighth through twelfth years	5
Thirteenth through eighteenth years	4
Nineteenth year	2

- Deductible interest

In this case, the corporation can afford to pay 12.6 percent in deductible interest in the absence of inflation, much lower than the 17.4 percent it could put up for an equipment purchase. With 10 percent inflation, the nominal interest it could support rises to 28.8 percent (compared with 31.9 percent for equipment).

A third broad category of business investment is inventories. When a corporation decides to hold an extra dollar's worth of inventories, it presumably expects to generate sufficient business to pay the carrying cost. To a first approximation, tax accounting for inventories correctly measures the return on this investment both in times of stable prices and, by virtue of last-in, first-out (LIFO) rules, in times of inflation. (Under LIFO rules, an item sold from inventory is taken to be the most recently produced, which therefore reflects the most recent cost-of-production experience. By contrast, under the alternative first-in, first-out [FIFO] accounting, the item sold is taken to be the oldest unit in stock; in a time of inflation, the cost of production will be artificially low.) The deductible interest the corporation could afford to pay to hold inventories with a real yield of 10 percent before taxes is therefore just 10 percent with no inflation and 28.5 percent with inflation at 10 percent per year. (In either case, a lender in the 46 percent bracket obtains a real return of 5.4 percent after taxes.)

---

5. Certain structures, such as a building that is an integral part of a manufacturing process, qualify for the investment tax credit.

A fourth major category of investment expenditure is for such intangible assets as good will (outlays for an advertising campaign, for example) and new ideas (research expenses). Quite apart from special provisions in the law to encourage the latter, these investment outlays are given the favorable treatment of immediate expensing. Expensing renders the effective tax rate zero on the cash flow related to an investment project; consequently, with no inflation a corporation could afford to pay up to 17.9 percent in deductible interest (54 percent of 17.9 percent is 10 percent) to finance a research project with a before-tax real return of 10 percent. At 10 percent inflation, the same project would justify paying up to 35.7 percent interest (54 percent of 35.7 percent is 20 percent, less 10 percent inflation equals 10 percent real interest cost).

It would be a mistake to conclude from these computations of effective tax rates that the corporate sector is somehow cheating the average taxpayer out of rightful revenues. The point is rather different: the corporation tax system, coupled with income-measurement rules that are poorly related to one another and to the existence of inflation, creates strong pressures on the composition of corporate investment, pressures that are quite sensitive to the rate of inflation.

Distortions of a different sort are produced when the graduated rate structure is applied to corporate income. The incentives bearing on a corporate decision are very different according to the current and potential future gain or loss positions of the company for income tax purposes.[6] For example, a corporation that had such large losses carried over from past tax years that it could anticipate many years with no tax liability is effectively exempt from the corporation tax. In evaluating the investments discussed earlier, that corporation could support interest payments of 10 percent in every case without inflation, and 20 percent with inflation at a 10 percent annual rate. These examples illustrate the sense in which increases in the rate of corporation tax act as an incentive to invest. The criteria for undertaking an investment are very different for a corporation effectively in a zero tax bracket than for a company dealing with a 46 percent tax rate at the margin; and, under the hybrid income-measurement rules, in many cases the taxable firm will regard as attractive investments ones that would not be interesting for the firm that is effectively tax exempt.

The analysis of cases in which the corporation currently has positive taxable income but expects to have tax losses for some period in the

---

6. See Auerbach (1982) and Warren and Auerbach (1982). The specific details of their discussions are already out of date, but the basic analysis remains relevant.

future, or is currently showing loss for tax purposes but expects to have positive taxable income in the future, is much more complicated. For example, a company not currently taxable can make no current use of accelerated depreciation deductions or investment credits. Although these items can be carried over for use in future tax returns, their value declines rapidly with the time until they can be used. For such a company, current deductions are of little value, while future receipts are fully taxable. The interest rate supportable by investments in such a case will be less than that for the nontaxed corporation.

Inconsistencies of this sort have no economic rationale, and economists have often argued for, in effect, refundable flat taxes at the corporate level. A rough substitute for refundability would be to permit corporations to sell depreciation allowances and unusable investment credits. Much the same function is potentially served by the practice of leasing, whereby the owner of the asset is fully taxable but the user is not. The controversial safe-harbor leasing provisions of the Economic Recovery Tax Act of 1981 represented an attempt to make the transfer of tax attributes easier, but the efficiency advantages of approximating uniform taxation of corporate investment were overwhelmed by the public-relations disadvantages of apparently profitable companies eliminating their tax liabilities by leasing property to less profitable companies.[7]

Distortion of Corporation Finance

The effects of taxation on the structure of corporation finance are the results of interactions between the individual and corporation tax systems. Commentators tend to emphasize the excessive incentive for corporations to use debt rather than equity finance because of the deductibility of interest. But the issue is somewhat less straightforward than is commonly supposed.

Imagine that for the ordinary saver just two types of assets are available: ordinary debt (including bank deposits) and equity (that is, ignore tax-exempt debt and directly owned business assets). Suppose, further, that the return on equity is entirely in the form of capital gains (no dividends), the realization of which can be postponed long enough to render negligible the tax at the individual level. Under these circumstances, a corporation that did nothing but sell equity and buy bonds, and that paid corporate tax on the interest it received on the bonds at 46

7. Warren and Auerbach (1982) argue that the safe-harbor leasing rules were, in any case, a poor substitute for a refundable flat tax.

percent, could provide a return in the form of capital gain to the holders of equity that equaled just 54 percent of the going rate of interest. (A corporation that tried to do exactly this would encounter obstacles in the existing tax rules, but the basic economic forces apply in more realistic cases as well.) For individuals in the 50 percent bracket, the corporation would be able to offer a slight advantage, whereas for low-bracket individual taxpayers, debt would be more attractive than equity.[8] The combination of individual and corporate tax rules has in this example the effect of influencing the corporation financial structure (the balance between debt and equity will depend on the relative amounts of wealth of high-bracket and low-bracket taxpayers), *and* an effect on the portfolios of the two types of taxpayers.

If we add to the picture the possibilities for individuals to have both high-bracket and low-bracket attributes (via pension funds, insurance policies, and so on), as well as direct investment in assets such as small businesses or real estate, tax-exempt bonds, and so on, the analysis will become very much more complicated. What will not go away, however, is the profound influence of the tax rules on the composition of wealth holdings in the United States. And as the simple example suggests, many of these effects are in no way directly desired as matters of public policy.

In concluding this overview of the distorting effects of the existing corporation income tax, let me point out that, although we tend to think of the corporation tax as adding a second level to the income tax, in some instances individuals may obtain tax *advantages* by operating businesses as corporations. (Remember that the limited liability advantage can be obtained with effectively no change from proprietorship treatment via the Sub-S option.) The advantages of incorporation should not be confused with the possibility generally available to small businesses of obtaining consumption services directly (use of the company car, for example). Such benefits, which may involve tax evasion, are equally available to proprietorships, partnerships, and Sub-S corporations. However, the regular corporate form does offer some legal fringe benefits (mainly company-paid medical bills). Furthermore, the separately

8. Merton Miller (1977) developed this proposition at length in his presidential address to the American Finance Association. See also Feldstein and Slemrod (1978). Gordon and Malkiel (1981) attempt to quantify the relative advantages of debt and equity financing. They conclude that the popular view of a bias toward debt remains true and that the cost imposed in the form of inefficient financial structure of corporations is significant.

taxed corporation may allow individuals to obtain their compensation in the form of corporate income in the low-bracket portion of the rate structure, subsequently realized as long-term capital gain. Whatever the direct distorting effects of such phenomena, they absorb considerable legal talent.

Corporate Taxation in the Context of a Personal Accrual-Income Tax

The corporate income tax as it now exists in the United States is only one of many possible variations. Even if we confined ourselves to the alternatives actually used in other countries, we would face a major project of description.[9] Instead, it will be more productive to focus on two broad strategies for dealing comprehensively with the problems enumerated above:

- Alternative ways of coordinating corporate and individual taxes in the context of a closer approximation to accrual-income taxation
- Alternative ways of coordinating corporate and individual taxes in the context of a shift to some form of consumption-type tax at the individual level.

I shall consider first the policies that comport well with accrual-income taxation at the individual level.

Corporate Tax with Full Integration

In Chapter 3 I discussed the problem of measuring an individual's income attributable to owning shares in a corporation. The most promising method available to deal with this problem appears to be imputation of a corporation's earnings to shareholders, the method referred to as "integration of individual and shareholder income accounts." Remember that the object of imputation is to measure the shareholder's accruing wealth change. The main difficulty created by corporations as such (beyond the various inevitable problems in measuring accruals) is dealing with retained earnings (profits earned in a year but not distributed to shareholders).

9. For an excellent overview of the tax systems used in four advanced industrial countries (Sweden, the United States, the United Kingdom, and West Germany), see King and Fullerton (1984).

Under the strong assumption that the income-measurement rules are otherwise well designed, a tax of just about *any* sort at the corporate level, whether on income or whatever, *could* be accommodated as far as the accounting is concerned. Such a tax would simply be treated as any other cost of the corporation and would result in a lower level of retained earnings imputed to shareholders. However, an extra tax on corporate income, along classical corporation tax lines, does not coordinate well because it imposes distortional costs with no obvious offsetting policy gains. We may distinguish two sorts of corporate taxes that *are* natural partners of the imputation of corporate income to shareholders: a tax on corporation income used as a withholding method, and a tax on corporate cash flow not integrated with shareholder taxes.

CORPORATE TAX AS A MECHANISM TO WITHHOLD SHAREHOLDER TAX

A flat-rate tax levied on corporate income, defined by using the same accrual accounting principles we have assumed apply at the individual level, would have certain advantages as a withholding mechanism. (The flat rate should be stressed because graduated rates at the corporate level, including a zero tax rate on losses, will inevitably be distorting. Refundability of the tax offset to losses is not critical, however, provided carry-forward with interest is allowed.)[10] In the context of full imputation of corporation income to shareholders, such a tax would logically be creditable to eligible shareholders.

Of course, if all shareholders are eligible, the withholding tax would not add real effects to the individual tax. But it would offer certain advantages. First, as with any withholding tax, it could improve and simplify compliance. Second, the possibility of denying or otherwise varying the credit would give the tax system the capability of differentiating the treatment of shareholders. Foreigners and tax-exempt institutions are often regarded as candidates for denial of credit for tax paid at the corporate level. (Note, though, that we would expect ineligible shareholders to choose some form other than corporate stock in which to keep their wealth.) Third, a corporate withholding tax might be easier to integrate with the existing system of crediting foreign taxes. Creditable foreign taxes would be used to fulfill withholding liabilities. (The

10. A neglected issue is what interest rate would be appropriate in such cases. In effect, the firm is lending the government money. From the firm's point of view the relevant rate is the opportunity cost of funds: what the firm has to pay to get the extra dollars from other sources. From a practical point of view it is more likely that some version of the government borrowing rate would be used.

alternative, in the absence of a corporate-level tax, would presumably be some sort of flow-through accounting to individual shareholders specifically with respect to creditable foreign taxes.) Fourth, a tax paid at the corporate level would probably fulfill the popular desire to tap corporate wealth, even though the real effect is the same as that of a tax paid directly by shareholders.

CORPORATE TAX AS A SUBSTITUTE FOR SHAREHOLDER TAX

A corporate tax could be used, in the context of an accrual-income tax at the individual level, as a complete substitute for shareholder-level taxation of retained earnings. This would typically be administered by allowing a deduction for dividends. Such a system subjects retained equity returns to taxation at the flat corporate rate, which may be higher or lower than the rate applying to shareholder income in other forms. Coordination with shareholder-level taxation would imply no taxation on capital gains accruing on corporate stock, inasmuch as such gains would correspond to post–corporate tax earnings. A further degree of integration could be obtained by treating dividends in the same way, taxing the earnings at the corporate level with no deduction for dividends, and dropping dividends out of the individual tax base. Again, the effect is to apply a flat tax to that portion of income, which may be higher or lower than the tax that would otherwise apply at the individual level.

The principle could be carried yet another step by reversing the treatment of interest payments: eliminating the deduction at the company level and ending the inclusion at the individual level. There would be enormous simplification advantages in such a step, which would render moot the intractable problem of correcting interest income for inflation, but which would come at the disadvantage of giving up graduation in the rate of tax applied to corporate-source income.

An Add-on Corporate Income Tax

Failing to impute the corporate-level income tax to shareholders *in the context of accrual taxation at the personal level* would result in the familiar "double taxation" of equity investment. The mutual fund analogy gives an immediate idea of the incentive effects. Because earnings accruing to the corporation are taxed more heavily than earnings on the same assets accruing directly to shareholders, corporations would have an incentive to shift corporation finance toward debt (with its deductible interest). But the point of corporations is that there are advantages to shareholders' owning assets indirectly; debt is not acceptable as the only source of finance. To the extent that this is so, the tax would penalize the use of capital in the corporate form of enterprise. The corporation as an institution would not disappear; it is, after all, a highly productive device. But the discouragement of this productive business form would impose an effective tax of only vaguely known character on workers, entrepreneurs, and wealth holders.

The fact that interest on borrowing is deductible from the corporation income tax base seems to put in the hands of corporations the possibility of avoiding a substantial part of the burden of the corporation tax. To what extent does deductible interest alleviate the double-taxation effect? The role of debt in determining the consequences of an add-on corporation income tax is rather critical and makes analysis of the effect of a tax on corporate income ambiguous. If corporations used only equity finance (no debt), a tax levied on the basis of accurately measured accrual income at both shareholder and company levels would look like the tax on corporate use of capital studied by Harberger (whose analysis is summarized in Chapter 7). However, because debt is available and interest is deductible, and because the corporate tax rate is roughly equal to the top individual tax rate, we would expect corporations to adopt a policy that approaches as closely as possible the exclusive use of debt finance (in which corporate income would be taxed only once, in the hands of interest recipients). If corporations could finance all new investment projects through additions to debt, there would actually be no extra tax imposed at the critical margin, even though tax might be collected on the basis of returns from better-than-marginal investments.

Because we do not now have a system based on consistently measured accrual income, at either the corporate or the individual level, we need to be somewhat careful in interpreting actual behavior. Statistics on flows of funds, however, are certainly in accord with the view that debt currently is not acceptable as the main source of incremental corporation finance. For various reasons, perhaps including the customs and expectations of savers, regardless of calculated tax advantages, corporations do use equity finance at the margin (principally via retained earnings), and it seems safe to predict that a tax on corporation accrual income would have substantial real effects (see Poterba and Summers, 1984).

Are the advantages worth the distortion? We know that all taxes have distorting effects. Might one want to use a double taxation of corporate income via a tax that is not creditable to shareholders, as a source of tax revenue? Harberger's analysis of the incidence of corporate taxation suggests a possible reason: a tax on the use of capital in the corporate sector (which a true accrual tax at the corporate level would be) will be converted into some combination of changes in the rewards to labor and capital generally. Indeed, the political appeal of double taxing corporate income seems to be largely the view that it is a tax on capital (although, to be sure, the shifting of the tax to all capital is not widely understood). A tax on corporations can be used to tax indirectly returns to saving or labor earnings, in addition to the other taxes imposed. But because so little is known about the incidence of such a tax, and because it implies significant distortion of production, it does not appear to be a very attractive policy instrument.

Corporate Cash-Flow Taxes

A cash-flow tax is sometimes mentioned as a possible corporate tax reform objective, particularly in the context of moves toward consumption-based personal taxation. Cash-flow taxes at the corporate level are in principle consistent with accrual-income taxes at the individual level *(including integration of corporation and individual income accounts),* in the sense that they would set up very different, and arguably minor, distorting forces when compared with a corporate-level accrual-income tax. It will assist our consideration of the merits of this approach to take up first corporation cash-flow taxes in their natural context of personal consumption taxation. I then return briefly to their possible place in an accrual-income system.

Corporate Cash-Flow Taxation in the Context of a Personal Consumption-Type Tax

Various possibilities exist for levying a cash-flow tax on corporations. Following the Meade Committee in the United Kingdom, I distinguish three basic types (see Institute for Fiscal Studies, 1978, chap. 12).

The most obvious, called by the Meade Committee the "R base" (*R* stands for "real"), would tax corporations on the difference between sales of goods and services and purchases of goods and services from other businesses and employees. There are three main differences between this base for taxation and the usual corporation income base:

· Outlays for buildings, equipment, inventories, and the like would be expensed rather than capitalized

- Purchases and sales would be accounted for on a cash, rather than an accrual, basis
- Financial flows, dividends, and interest received *or paid* would not enter the tax base[11]

We can see that the existing corporation income tax, including accelerated depreciation and the investment tax credit, has some of the character of a R-base cash-flow tax.

A second possibility, the "R + F base" ("real plus financial"), treats real purchases and sales of goods and services in the same way as in the R base but adds to the base all reductions of financial reserves, amounts borrowed, and interest received, and subtracts from the base additions to financial reserves, amounts loaned, and interest paid. The R + F base is the analogue at the corporate level of the full-fledged personal cash-flow tax. By virtue of its taxation of interest received and deduction of interest paid, the present corporation income tax has an element of R + F–base character. Minor details aside, under the accounting classification of a corporation's outlays and receipts into real and financial categories, a positive net total implies a cash flow to stockholders (whether in the form of dividends or of purchase of shares), whereas a negative net total implies a cash flow from stockholders (sale of equity interest by the corporation). Thus, for example, if a corporation has receipts of $100,000 from sales and operating and capital outlays (excluding interest) of $80,000, there is a surplus of $20,000 that must be used either to buy financial assets (perhaps by depositing the money in a money-market fund, paying interest, or retiring debt) or distributed to shareholders. By the balancing requirements of the accounts, there is no third possibility. Similarly, receipts from sales that fell short of operating and capital outlays would necessarily imply that the corporation had sold financial assets other than shares (borrowed) or sold shares.

The third type of corporate cash-flow tax base, the "S base" ("stock"), uses this equivalence between the R + F base and flows between stockholders and the corporation. The S base simply consists of all payments to stockholders, whether dividends or repurchase of shares, with no distinction made between liquidating and other distributions. (Purchase from the public of shares in other corporations would be treated as a taxable distribution.) Flows *from* stockholders to

---

11. As the Meade Report points out, the R-base tax might not be considered appropriate for financial institutions, which earn their surplus through buying and selling financial assets rather than real goods (Institute for Fiscal Studies, 1978, chap. 12).

the corporation (that is, sales of shares by the corporation) are deducted. An S-base corporation tax can be thought of as an excise tax on distributions to shareholders, with refundability in the case of negative distributions (issue of shares).

A tax levied at a constant flat rate on the R base makes the government a fully participating partner in all corporate real investment projects, that is, a partner whose interest is independent of how projects are financed. At a rate of 40 percent, for example, the government is a 40 percent partner, putting up 40 percent of the investment funds (via the deduction of outlays by corporations) and sharing in 40 percent of the return. Although a corporation's owners might not choose to let the government share with them on a project, there would seem to be little reason, apart from the matter of noncash entrepreneurial input, that the sharing arrangement would make an otherwise attractive project into an unattractive one.[12]

It is sometimes said that a tax on corporation income makes the government a partner in corporate enterprises. The critical difference between the partnership implied by taxation of income and the partnership implied by cash-flow taxation is that under a true accrual-income tax the government-partner provides none of the finance, only sharing the return. Under a cash-flow tax, the government-partner shares both outlays and receipts.

Much the same reasoning extends to the case of the R + F–base tax. In the case of the R + F base the project description includes a specification of any debt financing. Whereas the R-base tax has the effect of making the government share in the real consequences of the project, the R + F–base tax makes the government into a full-fledged shareholder, splitting the consequences of financial as well as real choices by the firm.

As has been pointed out, the accounting relationships imply that the S base (consisting of cash flows to shareholders) is essentially identical to the R + F base. But because the amounts received by shareholders are *net* of tax, it might be more natural to express an S-base tax in a tax-exclusive form. A 40 percent tax on before-tax distributions would be 66⅔ percent of the distribution actually reaching shareholders.

---

12. The reader may wonder about the limited time and talent of the manager or entrepreneur in all this. If a half-interest in the project takes the same amount of the manager's time as a full interest does, won't some projects no longer be attractive? Not if the value of the manager's time is correctly accounted for in the cash flow. Of course, compensation would be taxed as personal income, and that would inhibit the manager's efforts. But that is a separate matter from taxing the corporate cash flow.

Equivalence among Cash-Flow Taxes

There is an important equivalence among these three taxes (R base, R + F base, and S base): any cash flow that can be provided to shareholders under one form of the tax can also be provided under the other two. The choice among them can thus be made on the basis of familiarity, administrative convenience, fitness of transition effects, and so on. The example of a corporate project presented in Tables 6–1 through 6–3 may help clarify these points. Table 6–1 describes a corporate investment project requiring an outlay of $2.5 million in the initial period, an amount financed in part by borrowing $1.5 million (to be repaid in five equal installments) and in part by an equity contribution of $1 million. Think of the equity contribution either as consisting of retained earnings (in which case the corporation foregoes $1 million in distributions) or as a new equity issue. For our purposes it does not matter; but for concreteness, let us suppose that the equity contribution is a new equity issue. So that we can focus on the cash-flow taxes, it is assumed throughout the example that there are no other taxes.

The project does not pay off for five years. In the meantime, servicing the loan puts a further drain of $448,000 per year on stockholders. In the fifth year the project reaches fruition; the final loan installment is paid;

Table 6–1. Investment project cash-flow analysis (thousands of dollars)

Time (1)	Real asset (2)	Debt finance (3)	Equity finance (4)
0	−2500	1500	1000
1	0	−448	448
2	0	−448	448
3	0	−448	448
4	0	−448	448
5	6796	−448	−6348

Note: Entries show the cash flows of a corporation making an initial investment outlay of $2.5 million on a project that has its entire payback in a single year, five years from start-up. The yield on the project is 20 percent. (All calculations are based on continuous compounding.) It is financed in part by a constant-payment loan at 14 percent and in part by sales of equity interests to stockholders. The entire payback is shown as paid out to stockholders. (The income calculations for this table are presented in Table 6–4.)

Table 6–2. Effect of R-base cash-flow tax (thousands of dollars)

Time (1)	Real asset (2)	Tax (3)	Debt finance (4)	Equity finance (5)
0	−2500	1000[a]	900	600
1	0	0	−269	269
2	0	0	−269	269
3	0	0	−269	269
4	0	0	−269	269
5	6796	−2718[b]	−269	−3809

Note: Entries illustrate the calculation of a 40 percent R-base corporate cash-flow tax with respect to the project described in Table 6–1. The adjustment of financing implied by the tax payments has been divided between debt and equity in proportion to the original financing pattern. The cash flow to equity holders is 60 percent of what it was originally.

a. Equals 40 percent of $2.5 million, that is, 40 percent of the total real investment outlay.

b. Equals 40 percent of $6.796 million, that is, 40 percent of the total real return flow from the investment.

and the entire surplus, amounting to $6,348,000, is distributed to the shareholders. The project, together with its financing, looks attractive, and let us suppose the corporation would undertake it in the absence of cash-flow taxation.

Table 6–2 shows how an R-base cash-flow tax would affect the cash flows. Because the first real cash flow, to invest in the project, is negative, the government collects a negative tax at the outset; that is, the government provides a rebate of 40 percent of the project's cost. In other words, the tax rules allow immediate expensing of the investment by the firm.[13] This being so, less is required from the ordinary financing sources; in the example, the contributions by both creditors and stockholders have been reduced by 40 percent. In subsequent periods, the flows to creditors and stockholders, including the final payoff, are correspondingly reduced by 40 percent. The effect of the R-base tax is thus simply to reduce the scale of the project from the point of view of the stockholders; its other characteristics, such as riskiness or expected rate of return are unchanged.

13. It will simplify discussion to assume either that the tax is refundable or that the firm has other receipts against which to set the investment outlay. If the law does not provide for refundability, but instead provides for carryover with interest, the timing of flows is changed but the basic argument is essentially unaffected.

Table 6-3. Effect of R + F-base and S-base cash-flow taxes (thousands of dollars)

Time (1)	Real asset (2)	Tax (3)	Debt finance (4)	Equity finance (5)
0	−2500	400	1500	600
1	0	179	−448	269
2	0	179	−448	269
3	0	179	−448	269
4	0	179	−448	269
5	6796	−2539	−448	−3809

Note: Entries describe either an R + F-base corporate cash-flow tax or an S-base corporate cash-flow tax with respect to the project described in Table 6-1. The R + F base is equal to the receipts from the project less payments to creditors (so receipts from borrowing raise the tax due, and payments of principal or interest reduce it). The rate applied to the R + F base in the illustration is 40 percent. The S base is equal to the distribution to stockholders. A rate of 40 percent applied to the S base (66⅔ percent applied to the net-of-tax distribution) leads to the same tax liabilities as the rate of 40 percent applied to the R + F base. Debt financing has been maintained at the original level, so that the cash flow to shareholders is identical to that obtained under the R-base illustration in Table 6-2.

Because the R + F-type and S-type cash-flow bases are equivalent in effect, the two have been combined in Table 6-3. The R + F tax is 40 percent of the sum of the cash flow from the project and from creditors (with a refund if the sum is negative). The S tax, at 40 percent of the gross (66⅔ percent of the net) flow to shareholders, generates exactly the same liability. Now the government can be viewed in the position of a 40 percent shareholder, contributing to equity financing and sharing in equity payoff.

At the outset, then, the government provides a negative tax amounting to 40 percent of the $1 million in financing that is not raised in the form of debt. In subsequent periods the government contributes additional amounts as the debt is serviced (deductible under the R + F base or leading to reduced distributions under the S base). Finally, the government shares 40 percent of the payoff net of the final debt service. The ordinary shareholders obtain exactly the same cash flow in this case as they did under the R-base tax, that is, exactly 60 percent of the cash flow in and out that they obtained in the absence of the tax. If the original cash flow was attractive, it stands to reason the post-cash-flow-tax cash flow is also attractive.

Distortional Effects of a Corporate Cash-Flow Tax

A corporate cash-flow tax would involve little distortion, especially in comparison with the existing corporation income tax, for a very simple reason: the basic elements of an investment project are described by its cash flow. A "good" cash flow, characterizing a project the business will undertake, is typically one in which future positive flows are sufficiently large to compensate for the early negative flows associated with constructing a building, spending on an advertising campaign, and the like.[14] It is almost a matter of definition that if a cash flow is good, one-half of the same cash flow (half of all outlays and also half of all return receipts) is also good — not as good, but still good. Cutting all flows in half is like splitting a project with a partner who puts up half the money and takes half the return. If the project is attractive, so is half the project.

Although the distortion induced by a cash-flow tax should be minimal to the extent that a corporate investment project consists of nothing more than a cash flow, there are other margins of choice for which distortions would arise. For example, the argument above accepts the assumption often implicitly made that certain activities inherently require a corporate setting so that we can identify them as belonging in the corporate sector. In fact, however, there is often a choice of whether a project should be undertaken by a corporation or by a proprietorship or partnership (or Sub-S corporation). The reasoning also neglects the potentially important case in which part of the input to the corporate project is the time, energy, and ideas of an entrepreneur, who takes as a reward a share of the financial return.

According to our reasoning, a project that is barely worth undertaking in the absence of a cash-flow tax should continue to be barely worthwhile in the presence of the tax. The cash flow of stockholders keeps its character but is simply proportionately reduced. A project that is more than barely worth undertaking in the absence of the tax also continues to be worth undertaking with the tax, but some of the surplus from the project is transferred to the government-partner. By shifting the same project to a noncorporate institutional setting, the investors could cap-

14. Naturally, not all projects are of this character. Some may involve disinvestment — for example, selling a building (positive current cash flow) at the cost of foregoing the future rental receipts (negative future cash-flow consequences). Sometimes projects require early outlays, then yield positive cash flows for a while, then require terminal outlays. An investment in a strip mine, with an obligation to clean up the mess when the mineral deposit is exhausted, is an example.

ture more of the surplus for themselves. A corporate cash-flow tax thus would set up a disincentive to use the corporate form.

Often a new corporation is created when an entrepreneur or inventor cooperates with contributors of equity funds to undertake a project. In this case, a claim to some fractional share of the project is in effect compensation to the entrepreneur-stockholder, with the other stockholders contributing cash. In theory, the transaction could be recast, with the entrepreneur's contribution being valued at an appropriate cash equivalent to the actual cash contributions. Then the entire argument would proceed as before. The value of the entrepreneur's contribution would be deducted as an initial cash outlay, attracting the appropriate reduction in cash-flow-tax liability. In effect, the correct price is placed on the entrepreneur's services in the cash-flow analysis.

Whether such an evaluation is made explicit would perhaps depend on the details of taxation at the individual level (for example, whether such an accounting would increase the tax liability of the entrepreneur). If, as is likely, the entrepreneurial contribution is ignored, a cash-flow tax at the corporate level would be an additional tax on the reward to the entrepreneur and would therefore affect the application of entrepreneurial effort via the corporate form. Whether the result is to introduce a distortion or to correct an excessive incentive to incorporate is less clear.

Individuals' use of businesses to finance their consumption expenses is legal in the case of certain fringe benefits, just as it is with respect to employee compensation; but in other cases, illegal evasion is involved — for example, when a businessperson deducts the cost of maintaining an automobile for private use. However, it is easy to exaggerate the role of the separate tax on corporations in this practice. A corporation as such is no better than a proprietorship for purposes of tax evasion through illicit deductions. Indeed, the existing law may well put the corporation at a disadvantage in this respect because the marginal rate of tax is often lower than that applicable to the individual proprietor. But to the extent that a corporate cash-flow tax represents an addition to the tax otherwise triggered by a stockholder cash flow, it will present an additional temptation to use the corporation to fund owner-stockholder consumption.

Revenue from a Corporate Cash-Flow Tax

The subject of revenue from a corporate cash-flow tax may be separated into three parts. First is the revenue raised by a marginal project, a corporate investment that would be considered barely worthwhile in the absence of the corporate cash-flow tax. Second is the revenue from a better-than-marginal project, one that is clearly worthwhile in the absence of the tax. Third is the revenue from past decisions.

A corporate cash-flow tax would be expected to raise little revenue (in a present-value sense) at the margin. The basic reason is simple: because corporations will be able to generate a surplus from investments that yield more than the going rate of interest, they will tend to push investment to the point that equates the two sorts of yield. Equating the two yields means that the present value of the cash flow from marginal projects (adjusted for risk), discounted at the going rate of interest, will tend toward zero. But since the government revenue stream is simply proportional to the project cash flow (with another stream added that is proportional to the debt financing in the case of the R + F and S bases), the discounted flow of taxes will also tend toward zero.

Note that this contrasts with a tax on corporate accrual income. Application of accrual-income tax rules to a project that is barely worthwhile in the absence of taxation will produce positive tax revenue (in a present-value sense). For that reason, an accrual-income tax will have a disincentive effect that is absent from cash-flow taxes.

A cash-flow tax would discourage the use of the corporate form in the case of projects having a net positive value. Correspondingly, the tax would raise revenue (in a present-value sense) from better-than-marginal projects that continue to be pursued in the corporate sector. In evaluating the revenue potential, it is important not to be misled by the obvious point that only projects that are at least marginally valuable will be undertaken in the first place. Profitability is in part compensation for undertaking risk. If the government values risk in the same way that the market generally does, a positive revenue on average must also be viewed as bringing with it corresponding risk bearing by the government (that is, by the taxpayers collectively).[15]

Nevertheless, it seems a reasonable proposition that (a) there is only a limited degree to which projects can be shifted from corporate to non-corporate form and (b) that the U.S. economy does on average deliver a more-than-marginal positive surplus on corporate investment, even allowing for an appropriate degree of collective risk aversion. If so, receipts from a cash-flow tax will have positive expected present value even in a forward-looking sense.

15. An important question is whether the government should not be less averse to risk than is the market generally. For a discussion, see Lind et al. (1982).

Perhaps the most important function that might be served by a corporate cash-flow tax would be to raise revenue from decisions already made when the tax is introduced. A corporation's receipts at any time represent the positive part of the cash flow from past investments. These receipts would be entered on the plus side of the corporation's cash flow and would therefore generate revenue. We would expect to obtain positive revenue in this way even if all future investments were only marginal and therefore generated no net revenue (in a discounted-present-value sense).

A consumption-type tax at the individual level does not strictly call for any tax (other than for withholding purposes) at the corporate level. But among the transition effects of simply abolishing the corporation tax (assuming that were even feasible politically) would be windfall gains to stockholders, inasmuch as they had been *expecting* to pay a corporation tax on the return to investments made up to that point. A corporate cash-flow tax thus offers a way to rationalize the taxation of corporations while retaining the existing tax claim on them (a claim already discounted from the point of view of existing owners).

Because the idea of employing a cash-flow tax at the corporate level while maintaining an accrual-income tax at the personal level recurs frequently in policy discussions, let me close by commenting briefly on the compatibility of the two systems. Like any other tax at the corporate level, a cash-flow tax *could* be administered. But it would not avoid the problems of measuring corporation and individual income. A cash-flow tax, with its implied measurement rules, such as expensing of investment outlays, would be compatible as an *additional* tax at the corporate level. There is no escaping the measurement of accrual income if that is the desired tax base. Converting the existing corporation tax to a consistent cash-flow basis (it is now a hybrid between accrual-income and cash-flow taxes) would have much the same effect as eliminating the tax altogether as far as coordination with an accrual tax at the individual level is concerned. An add-on cash-flow tax at the corporate level could, however, be employed as a revenue-raising measure (at the expense of existing shareholders), and there may be other ways in which cash-flow tax devices could be used in the context of rationalizing the system.

Appendix 6–1. Accrual Income from an Investment Project

Table 6–4 shows, for reference, the path of accrual income associated with the illustrative project described in Table 6–1. Of particular interest is the recognition of the profit from the project (the excess of its return over the 14 percent interest assumed to prevail) at the beginning of its five-year life.

Table 6–4. Corporate accrual income corresponding to the investment project described in Table 6–1 (thousands of dollars)

	Time 0	Time 1	Time 2	Time 3	Time 4	Time 5
Assets						
Machine	3375	3882	4465	5136	5908	0
Liabilities						
Bond	1500	1278	1022	728	389	0
Net worth	1875	2604	3443	4408	5519	0
Income (change in net worth from previous period, less contributed capital)	875	282	391	517	662	829

Note: Balance sheet entries represent market values and assume that the market recognizes the true future return from the investment project as equivalent to a bond with the same payoff. Therefore the machine is shown as value at time 0 at the accrued present value of its future payoff. (Although this presentation accurately reflects the various balance sheet items, the reporting of true accrued values differs from actual practice, under which the initial outlay of $2.5 million would be capitalized and the asset carried on the books at that level until the final balance sheet. The picture shown is thus the idealized result of applying strict accrual principles.) Note that nominal values are used throughout; no account has been taken of possible inflation over the period.

ANALYSIS II

Who Bears the Tax Burden?　　　　　　　　　**7**

Anyone concerned with the wisdom of the corporation income tax must ask himself which *individuals* are richer and which are poorer by virtue of the imposition of the tax. Does the tax result in lower profits for shareholders, higher prices for consumers, lower wages for workers, lower salaries for executives, or lower prices paid to suppliers, or some combination of these? In the language of economics, what is the tax's incidence? Put this way the question may seem simple and straightforward, but this is a misleading impression.

William A. Klein, *Policy Analysis of the Federal Income Tax*

ONE OF THE most difficult problems in applied economics is identifying who bears the burden of taxes. Such analysis is difficult partly because the way in which taxes are borne depends on quantitative features of the economy about which we know very little. A tax on newly discovered oil, for example, affects prices throughout the economy, thereby imposing burdens in a variety of ways that may be hard to trace. Analysis is also difficult because the rules are complicated. Important tax changes are often effected through technical provisions, whose dollars-and-cents impact on individuals is hard to determine. Imagine trying to figure out the gainers and losers from a change in the complex rules relating to the treatment of losses carried on the tax accounts of a company that merges with another company. The challenge to analysis is to estimate the implications of tax changes for individuals and to describe the results in useful ways.

Nominal and Real Incidence

Keep in mind that taxes are borne by *people*. Too often one reads about tax changes as divided between "business" and "individuals," as though the taxes paid by businesses were not borne by people. All taxes ultimately translate into changes in individuals' purchasing power. Clearly, however, it is not only individuals who send tax checks to the Treasury.

Corporations and trusts, among others, also make payments. It is therefore necessary to distinguish between paying a tax and bearing the burden of a tax. We speak of the "nominal incidence" of a tax as the measured payments of tax by individuals or institutions. The "real incidence," or economic incidence, is the true burden, which can fall only on people.

For example, consider an excise tax on the sale of a commodity, such as telephone calls. Starting from a situation of no tax, introduction of an excise tax on telephone calls to be paid by the telephone company implies, in the first instance, a reduction of the company's profits and therefore a decline in the value of its shares. Here we would distinguish between the nominal incidence of the tax, which falls on the telephone company, and the real incidence, which falls on the company's stockholders.

The decline in the value of the company's stock would not be the end of the story about the tax burden. As far as the telephone company is concerned, the imposition of the tax is an event much like an increase in the cost of copper wire. The company will naturally take steps to offset that change, perhaps increasing the price of telephone calls. With higher prices for telephone calls, the number of calls made will decline. The company therefore will need fewer workers, fewer spools of copper wire, and so on. Slackening demand for workers means that some will be laid off who otherwise would not have been and that some will not be hired who otherwise would have been. There will be downward pressure on the wages of such workers. Similarly, slackened demand for other inputs will put downward pressure on their prices, and so the ripple effect will continue. Ultimately the tax burden is divided in some fashion among stockholders, workers, and consumers, with possible effects extending throughout the economy.

Payroll taxes provide another example in which the payments are made by firms but the burden, inevitably, falls on people. Social Security taxes illustrate the prevalence of confusion about incidence. Half of the Old Age, Survivors, Disability, and Health Insurance (OASDHI) Social Security "contribution" of workers is officially paid by firms; the rest is officially paid by the workers. Because the workers' share is normally withheld by the firm, the difference between the contribution of the firm and the contribution attributed to the workers, as actually perceived by workers, must be small. But politically it seems very important that the nominal incidence be shared by employers and employees. Economic analysis leads us to expect little or no difference between the effect of an employer tax and that of an employee tax.

Workers presumably base their employment decisions on what they get to keep, and employers base their hiring decisions on what they have to pay. The difference between the two is the amount of the payroll tax, regardless of its division between workers and firm.[1]

Analysts of tax burdens often treat the tax system as though its provisions had no effect other than to relieve individuals of some purchasing power. Tax policy choices are conceived of as alternative outcomes in a "zero-sum game" (a game in which one player's gain must be some other player's loss). But tax rules impose two sorts of burden. One is the transfer of purchasing power from the individual to the government; the other is the effective waste of purchasing power owing to the distorting effects arising from the effort to avoid tax. The latter burden, called by economists the "deadweight loss" due to the tax, represents a gain to no one — neither to other individuals nor to the government.

People are sometimes skeptical about the reality of deadweight loss. To understand that it can be a serious matter, consider the following extreme example. Imagine a tax of, say, $1 million per pack of cigarettes. Presumably, at rates so high very few packs of cigarettes would be purchased (certainly very few taxable transactions would occur). Most law-abiding citizens would pay no cigarette tax, because they would purchase no cigarettes. But they would not therefore avoid any burden from the tax. The smokers among them, at least, would be prepared to pay substantial sums to have the tax removed, even though, because they do not buy any cigarettes, the tax does not appear to cost them anything. The loss to them is every bit as real as a loss of money. For those smokers who are completely deterred from smoking, the tax has zero revenue cost but a high deadweight loss.

Few taxes are so extreme in their effects, but some taxes impose large deadweight losses in relation to the amounts collected. When we look at tables showing the taxes paid by individuals or families in different circumstances (different income brackets, for example), we are likely to see an imperfect picture of the distribution of tax burdens. In part, this is because such tables usually show the nominal rather than the real incidence of taxes; that is, they show who pays the bill rather than who

---

1. Because wage contracts do not adjust instantaneously, there are no doubt differences in the short run, depending on the sharing rule. But it is hard to see why there would be any difference in the long run if it were simply a question of who pays the bill. Actually, there is at least one noncosmetic consequence of the split into employer and employee payments: the latter are regarded as income to the employee and subject to income tax, whereas the former are not.

actually bears the burden. In part, it is because they show only the amounts received by the government, not the additional amount representing the wasteful distortion of individual choices. (Strictly speaking, the distortional effect of a given tax may be of positive value, because it may offset other distortions in the economy, such as those created by some other tax. On average, however, the distortional effects of taxes add a burden beyond the amount transferred to the government.)

Consider the employment choices of an individual in the 30 percent income tax bracket. Usually alternatives to the person's actual work will be available — more hours, perhaps, or more days of work per year, or a job with more responsibility but also greater worries. A firm might be willing to pay a person $500 to do some additional or more arduous task; that is, the extra value she would create by doing the task is $500. However, doing the task would also destroy value, since it would be costly to her in hours or worry or whatever. Reflecting this loss, she requires to be compensated with at least $400; otherwise she will be unwilling to do the extra work. The *net* value created by her doing the task would thus be $100. But because of the income tax, she would be able to keep only $350 of the $500 she would be paid ($500 less 30 percent of $500 in extra tax), so she does not take on the extra work. Because the tax distorts her choice, she loses an opportunity she would value at $100. But unlike the money she pays to the government, which she also loses, no one gains that $100. It is simply wasted, just as much as value is wasted when we throw surplus farm products into the sea.

An Important Example: Taxes on Corporations

Confusion between nominal and real incidence is particularly common in the case of the corporation income tax. There is no doubt that this tax is borne by persons, not by the institutions that file the tax returns and send in the checks. But there is doubt and controversy about how the corporation income tax affects the burdens on individuals in their roles as workers, consumers, savers, and so on. The problem of determining the true incidence of the corporation income tax is a classic in public finance. In a famous treatment of the problem, Arnold Harberger (1962) conceived of the tax as an extra levy on the use of capital (machines, buildings, inventories, and so on) in the corporate sector. His analysis of the tax has been so widely accepted that it can now be considered the traditional view.

As with an excise tax on telephone calls, a levy on an input to a single sector — in this case, capital services in the corporate sector — discourages the use of that input and leads to shifts in prices for inputs and outputs throughout the economy. (The price of capital services can be thought of as the interest rate a borrower must pay a lender for the use of the funds required to purchase and maintain a building, a machine, a bit of inventory, and the like.) Just as the process of adjustment of wages, prices, output, and employment generates the ultimate distribution of the burden of a tax on telephone calls, a similar process spreads the burden of a tax on corporate capital. The distribution after full adjustment of the economy has taken place will depend on the details of how demand for the outputs of the corporate sector varies with the prices of goods produced there and how the corporate and noncorporate sectors make use of the services of capital and labor.

Two things are clear in Harberger's characterization of the situation. First, no special burden can result for owners of capital employed in the corporate sector (corporate shareholders). Because resources are free to move between sectors, they must receive the same return in both. Economists use the term "shifting" to describe the difference between the nominal and the real incidence of a tax. In this instance, the tax on uses of capital in the corporate sector will certainly be shifted. The question is: onto whom? Second, the tax must be shifted to individuals in some combination of their roles as capitalists (owners of wealth) and workers. (Consumers as such can bear no special burden in the Harberger model, because he does not distinguish purchasers of corporate goods from purchasers of noncorporate goods.) That is, the tax will change both the after-tax return to savers and the wages received by workers. It is even possible that a tax on the use of capital in the corporate sector could raise the wages of workers (if lots of capital and not many workers are released by the tax-induced contraction of the corporate sector), in which case we would say capitalists (who might, of course, also be workers) bear more than 100 percent of the tax. Similarly, it is theoretically possible that capitalists could *gain* from the tax.

Harberger's famous conclusion, based on educated guesses about critical features of the production technology and demand behavior, was that the tax probably did not affect the wages of workers. The tax was thus probably borne entirely by individuals as owners of wealth and not as workers. The technique employed by Harberger involved describing mathematically the interrelationships of demand and supply throughout the economy, along with the ways in which inputs are combined by firms to produce goods and services.[2] Since the time of Harberger's first

2. The technique is referred to as "general equilibrium analysis," because of its attempt to encompass all the balancing relationships in the economy and thereby account for the full range of ripple effects of a policy change.

contributions, advances in computer technology have allowed other researchers to produce greatly refined versions of his analysis (see Ballard et al., 1985). More recent treatments have been able to distinguish many different industries, to allow for interindustry transactions, to recognize the existence of many other taxes, and to include individual workers/consumers of varying types. The primary inputs, however, have in most cases been held to two: capital and labor. These detailed models, increasingly comprehensive in coverage, have typically supported Harberger's original conclusion about the incidence of a tax on the use of capital by corporations.

I have been careful in this discussion to refer to a tax "on the use of capital by corporations," rather than to the corporation income tax. In recent years the view of the corporation income tax has been changing (see Bradford, 1980b). Although researchers are not challenging the correctness of the earlier work as to the effect of a tax on corporate capital, they have begun to question the adequacy of conceiving of the corporation income tax as a tax on corporate capital. They emphasize the importance of looking at the details of the tax as it affects various transactions, such as payment of dividends or undertaking an investment project. These details can be analyzed correctly only if the corporation income tax is seen as an element in the income tax system as a whole, that is, jointly with the personal income tax. Together, the two sets of rules determine how the corporation tax influences investment and financial decisions, employment practices, and so on.

This rethinking can be related to the view I have often encountered among businesspeople, that the corporation income tax amounts to a sales tax applied to corporations. To some extent this view is simply an expression of the point already emphasized here: taxes paid by corporations are borne not by institutions as such, nor by their stockholders as such, but by a wide class of individuals. The proceeds from a company's sales must cover taxes paid by the company, the cost of hired inputs (including labor and capital), and a residual profit or loss accruing to the owners of the company. In a competitive economy, owners will insist on receiving a competitive return, including compensation for bearing risk. (If they do not get it, they will change the firm's decisions.) Conversely, owners who regularly earn supernormal profits find them eroded by the entry of competitor firms. The tendency of the system is toward a situation in which owners who contribute capital to firms obtain a return equivalent to that of owners who hire out their capital — not more, not less. (*Equivalent* return is not necessarily the identical return. There are typically differences in risk.)

Thus taxes paid by corporations must ultimately be reflected in changes in prices paid by customers and received by suppliers (including suppliers of finance and of labor services). This is true whether the tax is a sales tax, a corporation income tax, or a payroll tax. Whether the tax that is labeled a corporation income tax is equivalent to a sales tax on corporations depends on the details. A cash-flow tax of the sort proposed by Henry Aaron and Harvey Galper would be based effectively on the difference between the sales and purchases of the corporate sector to and from the noncorporate economy. It would thus, indeed, have the character of a corporate sales tax. Yet a tax levied on the income of corporations, calculated according to accrual-income principles except with no deduction for interest paid (or taxation of interest received), would clearly be a double tax on corporate income and not equivalent to a sales tax. The effect of the existing system, as described in Chapter 6, with its deduction for corporate interest paid, its accelerated depreciation of investment, investment tax credit, inadequate inflation indexing, and so on, is, unfortunately, difficult to determine.

Estimates of the Distribution of Tax Burdens

Our concern is presumably with the real incidence of taxes, including any distortional effects; but because it is so difficult to determine the cost of distortions, we usually have to make do with estimates that simply allocate to individuals the total receipts of the government, and ignore the extra distortional cost. Figure 7–1 shows estimates prepared by Joseph Pechman of the way in which the burden of all U.S. taxes taken together — federal, state, and local — is distributed in the population. The two diagrams in Figure 7–1 correspond to two sets of assumptions about the way real incidence relates to nominal incidence. The top panel shows estimates under which certain taxes (mainly the corporation income tax and property taxes) are assumed wholly or predominantly to show up in a reduced rate of return to owners of wealth; the lower panel assumes that a substantial part of these taxes makes itself felt in higher prices of goods and housing relative to wages. In each panel data are displayed for 1966 and 1985. Under the less progressive assumptions, the data imply a lower average tax rate (tax burden divided by income) in the top decile, somewhat higher average tax rates through the middle of the distribution, and a significantly higher rate at the bottom.

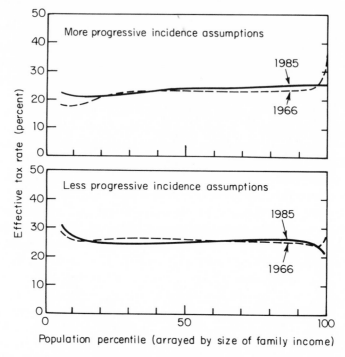

Figure 7–1. Incidence of federal, state, and local taxes, as a percentage of family income, 1966 and 1985. (From Pechman, 1985, p. 9.)

Among the more striking implications of the figures is that the tax system as a whole comes remarkably close to imposing a proportional tax on income. The proportionality results from the combination of a federal tax system under which burdens are estimated to increase more rapidly than income, and a state and local system under which they increase less rapidly than income. Also notable is the changing progressivity of the system; the decline in the importance of the corporation income tax, the increasing importance of the payroll tax, and the cuts in the highest marginal rates under the individual income tax are the main forces leading to the fall-off in the relative tax rate at the top of the income distribution between 1966 and 1985.

Statistical measures such as those summarized in Figure 7–1 give us a broad view of the shape of the tax system. It is important, though, not to attribute too much significance to particular features. As the differences between the top and bottom panels of Figure 7–1 suggest, conclusions about the distribution of tax burdens must be built upon a structure of assumptions about how the economy works. I have mentioned the matters of the incidence of property and corporation income taxes. Payroll taxes present another interesting case. Pechman's estimates refer to the tax side of the budget only. The combination of Social Security and unemployment insurance taxes paid by workers and the retirement and other benefits they accrue under present rules is quite progressive, but the tax taken by itself is regressive because it is a proportional levy on labor earnings up to a ceiling.

Even the individual income tax is certainly not borne exactly as might be thought from looking at nominal liabilities. For example, one effect of high tax rates on business executives is probably higher before-tax salaries than would obtain under a system of lower tax rates. The tax results in a greater dispersion of before-tax compensation and thus is to some degree shifted. Other, and probably more significant, shifting effects result from the way in which individual business activities are affected by the income tax. Finally, an extremely important set of tax effects neglected in the usual estimates of tax burdens is the complex of ways taxes influence the path of growth and development of the whole economy. The exercises with the corporation tax discussed earlier, for example, take as given the amount of capital to be allocated between corporate and noncorporate uses. Over the longer run, the tendency of taxes to discourage the advance of productivity and the rate of accumulation may dominate distributional effects as viewed at a given moment.

Distribution of the Federal Income Tax

Table 7–1, derived from data in *Blueprints for Basic Tax Reform,* represents one effort to describe the distribution of the federal income tax (individual and corporate combined). It presents estimates of the burden of these taxes (as usual, ignoring deadweight loss) on "taxpaying units" (meaning the units that would file tax returns with the Internal Revenue Service, which may be either single individuals or married couples) classified by a broad measure of income called "comprehensive income" (see U.S. Treasury Department, 1977, chap. 5). The entries in the table show the effective tax rates (the ratio of the aggregate estimated tax burden of the filing units in the group to the aggregate of their comprehensive income) estimated to apply within each income category. According to these estimates, the income tax system as a whole displayed a progressive incidence in 1976. The ratio of taxes to income increased from roughly zero at very low income levels to over 32 percent at the top of the scale. In line with Pechman's conclusions, displayed in

Table 7-1. Effective rates of combined
individual and corporation income tax

Comprehensive income class ($ thousands)[a]	Effective tax rate, 1976 law (%)
Less than 0	−0.6
0.9	1.7
9.2	6.4
18.3	9.9
26.4	12.7
35.5	15.4
53.9	19.8
88.2	25.2
175 or more	32.4

Source: Bradford et al. (1984, p. xv).
a. Dollar amounts are adjusted to 1984 purchasing-
power equivalents.

Figure 7-1, there is little doubt that the same exercise performed on
1984 figures would indicate a lower average tax rate at the top of the
distribution.

As in Pechman's work (Figure 7-1), Treasury analysts were obliged
to make assumptions about incidence in order to derive the data presented in Table 7-1. With respect to the corporation income tax, they
adopted Harberger's rough conclusion that the corporation tax leads to
a reduction in the rate of return received after taxes by wealth holders.
They then made an educated guess about the portion of each taxpaying
unit's income that could be described as a return to wealth and allocated
the corporation tax in simple proportion to that amount. Obviously
other assumptions would have led to different results.

Although Table 7-1 gives us helpful information, there is much we
would like to know that it does not reveal. For example, we may be
interested not simply in the tax burdens of taxpaying units as these
happen to be defined by current income tax law, but also in the burdens
of other groups. The burdens of different-sized families, of different age
groups, of people of different health status or labor force experience, or
of any other classification of people are likely to bear in important ways
on an assessment of the tax distribution. Furthermore, the table tells us
about averages. It gives us no estimate of the variation that exists within
each group. Finally, the table gives us a snapshot, a picture frozen in

time. The income of most individuals varies over their lifetime. Thus a given individual would show up in different classes at different times. We would like to know more about how the longer-term tax burden of individuals relates to their circumstances.

Ideally we would also like to analyze the burden of taxes on an individual in a more sophisticated way with respect to payments occurring at different times. Individuals live through many tax years and make many tax payments; in addition, many of our tax rules have effects that can be accounted for correctly only by recognizing their intertemporal character. To take a simple example, an individual who makes a deposit to an IRA experiences a reduction in current income tax payment by virtue of the deduction allowed. At the same time, the person becomes obligated to pay more in income tax at a future date, when making withdrawals from the IRA during retirement. Neither the tax payment at the time of making the deposit nor the tax payment at the time of the withdrawal adequately describes the individual's tax burden. The taxation of business income involves many features analogous to the IRA. Although we lack the capacity to describe effectively the influence of such rules on the distribution of burdens, we can try to avoid misinterpreting data based on current tax payments.

Tax Capitalization

A poorly understood aspect of the incidence of taxes is their capitalization into the prices of assets. The price an asset will command in the market is the "present discounted value" of the returns, net of expenses, that its owner can expect in the future. Future tax consequences of ownership therefore affect current values. The point is important, and the idea of discounting future cash flows is often misunderstood or ignored in tax policy discussions. Consider, as a specific instance, the bearing of real estate taxes on the market price of a rental property. The prospective owner of a building will consider the rent payments he may expect to receive from tenants, less any expenses, over the period of time he plans to continue as owner, plus the amount he is likely to obtain upon selling the property at the end of that period. If, at the asking price for the building, he can borrow the money to buy it, use the net cash flow in each period to amortize the loan (taking into account the proceeds of sale at the end), and have some positive amount left over, he clearly should strike the deal. (This exposition ignores matters of risk, which change the details but not the substance of the argument.) Furthermore, in setting a price at which he is willing to sell, the current owner has no reason to leave such a gap for profit, because an alternative to selling the building is to borrow against it the maximum amount that can be fully serviced, including repayment of the loan proceeds, by the cash flow from ownership.

The price of the building will thus tend to be bid up or down to the point at which it equals the loan that would be just barely retired by the stream of net cash returns over the period of ownership. That loan amount is the present discounted value of the net returns. Although the specifics of the calculation of the loan amount doubtless seem arcane to the average citizen, the general way in which it depends on the interest rate, the period of repayment, and the size of the periodic payment will surely be familiar.

The liability for periodic real estate tax payments is a negative element of the cash flow from owning a property. Naturally, just like periodic roof repairs, these tax payments will be taken into account when the asset's price is determined in the market. (The benefits that may be financed by taxes will also be reflected, positively, in a building's price.) As an important consequence, *changes* in the rules, such as an increase in the tax rate on the property (beyond what was expected in the past), that lead to a series of increases in future cash outflows give rise to a reduction in the price of the asset. The reduction will be the discounted present value of those new tax payments. The reflection of future tax liabilities in the present price of an asset is referred to as "tax capitalization."

Because of tax capitalization, the owner of the asset at the time of the unexpected change in the tax rate would bear the full burden of the whole stream of future payments. A purchaser who came along later would bear none of that burden because he would have obtained the property for an amount less than he would have had to pay before the tax increase. The exact amount less is equivalent (in present discounted value) to the extra future tax payments.

An understanding of the phenomenon of tax capitalization is important in connection with the incidence of changes in tax rules and with the interpretation of statistics on tax burdens. To take the latter point first, imagine a table showing the property tax payments of households in relation, say, to household earnings. Interpreting such data as describing the distribution of tax burdens may be highly misleading. The burden of the tax was imposed on the property owner at the time the tax was imposed. Often, the original and present households will be different, with the present owner bearing no tax burden at all. Tax capitalization can also have surprising consequences for efforts that might arise to ease burdens of past taxes. For example, changes in the property tax affect the current owner, who may not have borne any of the existing burden. If the owner of the property at the time the tax was imposed (on whom the entire burden was placed at that time) has in the meantime sold it, obviously no change in taxation of the property can affect him at all.

Transition Incidence

The effect of a change in the tax law on the value of property is not an oddity. Changes in tax law almost always give rise to burden effects associated with the long-term nature of some commitments (as an owner of property has a long-term commitment to pay the real estate taxes). Obvious instances in tax policy discussions are homeowner dependence on the income tax deduction of mortgage interest and real estate taxes and the dependence of holders of municipal debt on continuation of the exemption of state and local bond interest from tax. Another important example is the tax treatment of retirement benefits. Individuals who are now accumulating their retirement benefits in tax-sheltered form (as in an employer-sponsored pension plan) enjoy a windfall gain if marginal tax rates are reduced; those accumulating on a "defined-contribution" basis (under which the amount contributed is specified but the amount received in benefits depends on the earnings experience of the funds put aside) will also be affected by asset-value changes brought about by tax law shifts.

When the tax law change affects individuals differentially on the basis of past commitments, we may distinguish "transition incidence" effects from ongoing incidence effects. Sometimes, where tax capitalization in current property values is complete, transition incidence is all there is. Indeed, transition incidence effects may be dominant even when current property value (as the term is usually understood) is not affected. For example, imagine that anyone who can learn to be a carpenter can also learn to be a plumber, and vice versa, and that the learning process itself is similar in time and other costs. Under these circumstances we would expect carpenters and plumbers to earn about the same amount, after allowing for the cost of tools and so forth and after all taxes. Now, suppose the tax rules were changed to eliminate the carpenters' income tax deduction for tools. Then already-trained carpenters would, in effect, suffer a wealth loss, because their after-tax earnings would be reduced. However, the loss would not show up in property value changes because we do not have a market for human capital in the form of acquired skills embodied in an individual.

Notice that under our assumptions, the tax burden borne by *future* carpenters would be no different from that borne by plumbers. That is because individuals coming along who could learn either trade would all choose to become plumbers until, finally, the wages of the two kinds of worker adjusted to restore the original situation of indifference. In the new situation, carpenters would be more heavily taxed than in the old situation in the sense that the tax rules would be less favorable to carpentry. But the individuals involved would bear the same burden as plumbers, as evidenced by the fact that they are indifferent between entering one trade or the other. Notice, too, that typically *both* future carpenters and future plumbers would be affected by the change in rules applying to carpenters because the wages of plumbers would be affected (probably driven down, as more people entered the trade). The carpenters in the trade at the time of the rule change would eventually be restored to equivalence with plumbers in the forward-looking sense, but they would have suffered a loss in the transition.

Tax law changes always have transition incidence effects. Often, indeed, the transition effects provide the principal political motivation for rule changes. In the example just considered, the rule change in question was eliminating a deduction for carpenters' tools. Once the rule had been in place for a sufficiently long time, there would be no differential tax burden between plumbers and carpenters. There would nevertheless be a strong incentive for carpenters to lobby for allowance of the deduction, because they would be able to reap a gain from the tax saving during the period it takes for the wages of carpenters to fall relative to the wages of plumbers.

Economists often adopt the working assumption that competitive entry into various lines of business will eliminate any systematic opportunity for better-than-normal profits. Under this assumption, there is little or no *long-term* advantage to those engaged in a particular business from a tax rule that treats investment in their industry more favorably than investment in other industries. A favorable tax rule will only encourage entry into the business, leaving unchanged the position after taxes of those already involved. But there may be a major *short-term* advantage accruing to those in the business at the time of the change, since they will earn extra profits during the period of transition. (In a well-functioning capital market, the short-term advantage will be reflected in an increase in the market value of the business.)

Consider, for example, rules designed to make investment in rental housing more attractive, by allowing the investor to take depreciation earlier than would be the case for investment in an industrial structure. Individuals and firms in the business of building rental housing would have an incentive to lobby for the institution of such deductions. They would gain from the extra demand for rental structures, because it takes time for firms not yet engaged in the business to enter. But because the rental housing-construction business is not highly specialized, we would expect the after-tax profitability of rental housing construction in the long run to be independent of the tax rules that apply.

In some instances prices may take a long time to adjust to the point that people in the favored line of business gain no advantage from rules favorable to them. The adjustment may even never go that far. The critical issue is the degree of specialization of the resources involved in the production process. There are only so many potential baseball superstars in the population, so that rules that favor baseball superstars would no doubt have a permanent favorable effect on those individuals happily endowed with the right combination of athletic aptitudes. But economists are fond of pointing out how resourceful the market system can be in creating substitutes for products that increase in price, a process that tends to erode the advantage that particular individuals gain from favorable changes, whether due to tax legislation or other causes.

Transition effects arise wherever long-term commitments are involved. Investment decisions of all kinds lead to such commitments. These need not be incorporated in durable physical assets. Intangible assets such as reputation may also be involved. (The value of the reputation of a construction contractor will be adversely affected if a change in the tax law leads to a reduction in demand for housing.) Equally common are commitments to careers and programs of education, the value of which may be sharply changed by changes in the tax law — a humble example, the recent change in the rules taxing as income scholarships traditionally received on a tax-exempt basis by professors from their employers. Transition incidence effects represent an important fact of life about changes in tax (or spending) policy. Often, the transition incidence of a change is unrelated to the announced purposes of the change and is in that sense both unintentional and undesired. These effects therefore bear on what one regards as fair and politically feasible. Although tax policy cannot be the prisoner of its own past, it can be designed with a view to minimizing the redistributive effects (losses *and* gains) that are not themselves the object of policy.

8 Who Ought to Bear the Tax Burden?

For too long this country has been taxing people on their ability to pay, rather than who they are. Take, for instance, tall people. They have advantages money can't buy. Tall men get all the girls (get all the women just does not sound the same), see better at movies, block the view of people behind them, are better suited for most sports and command respect from people who, like the Pentagon, confuse size with authority.

Slim people should also be taxed. I am not referring here to people who diet or exercise to stay slim. I am talking about people who do nothing, eat anything they want, and don't gain a pound. No tax can be too exorbitant for these people. In fact, there should be a surcharge for every time they look up from something like a banana split and say, "I don't know why it is. I just can't gain weight." Tax 'em!

Richard Cohen, *Washington Post,* March 19, 1984

MAKING the tax system fairer would probably be rated by many as the most important objective of tax policy. But identifying an improvement in tax equity is difficult because there is no single measure of fairness. At bottom, an individual value judgment is involved, and it is not realistic to hope for complete consensus on a particular standard. But there is room for reasoned argument on the subject. In this chapter I explore some of the arguments concerning the fairness of the distribution of tax burdens, with particular attention to the thought that Richard Cohen has it about right: tax burdens should be related to the quality of individuals' opportunities. Those with better opportunities than others should be expected to bear relatively more of the tax burden. If this premise is accepted, then attention can focus on defining what is meant by "better opportunities" and on determining the degree of differentiation the tax system should undertake.

Taxes are borne by *people.* It follows that such issues as the distribution of liabilities between individual and corporate taxpayers, or among different types of corporation, are not in themselves matters of equity. Whether General Motors pays more in taxes than Ford Motors raises issues of equity only insofar as some people (stockholders or employees of the two companies or of other companies, for example, or perhaps *potential* stockholders or employees) are affected. Any notion that there is such a thing as a fair share of taxes to be paid by some class of taxpayers is to be understood only as it relates to burdens falling on individuals.

The hard equity issues arise only when interests collide. In cases in which the distorting effect of taxes is large, it may be possible to change the rules so that everyone is better off. Some have argued, for example, that lowering the tax rate applied to realized capital gains will increase the revenue obtained by the government. If this relationship holds, then such a change must make some better off and no one worse off. More commonly, though, the less cheerful situation prevails in which gains to some must come at the cost of losses to others. An equity judgment is required to determine when such a policy change represents an improvement.

Equity concerns choices. The objects of choice that interest us here are tax rules. Available alternatives include the range between income-type and consumption-type rules; they include as well such details as deductions for medical expenses or charitable contributions; and, of course, they include the possible schedules of rates and exemptions that might apply to any given tax base. Underlying these choices among policies, however, are tradeoffs among more fundamental concerns — such matters as the procedural fairness of the rules and the degree to which they interfere with individual privacy, and especially the distribution of burdens among people.

Traditional Equity Concepts

The problem of sharing financial burdens does not arise only in the context of government. Many groups, ranging from families to social clubs to religious organizations, face a similar problem. Because of the ease of exit from most nongovernment organizations, the range of policies available to them is much more limited than that available to governments. But generally there is some flexibility, and the choice of sharing arrangements has equity aspects. In some instances, such as a club organized to provide a collective facility (a swimming club, for example), it is taken for granted that contributions will be related to the services members receive. In other settings payments reflect differences in individuals' situations, independently of the services they receive. For example, the brothers and sisters in a family may agree to contribute differentially to the support of aged parents, with the well-to-do doctor chipping in more than the poorly paid teacher. Similarly, burdens of supporting churches or universities are usually shared in some sort of accordance with the differing means of their supporters. The relation of burden to means may be informally determined by the individuals' sense of what is appropriate, or it may be more formally determined, as in the practice of tithing.

In the jargon of tax theory, these two broad approaches to burden sharing are referred to, respectively, as the "benefit" and "ability-to-pay" principles. Benefit taxes are supposed to impose burdens that are in some way commensurate with services received, by analogy with the price paid for a good in the market. Ability-to-pay taxes are supposed to be related to the individual's capacity to contribute to the collective good. I use the term here in an extended sense, to apply to taxes that aim to relate burdens to some notion of an individual's appropriate share of the burden, whether or not that share is determined by capacity in any simple sense (such as funds in the bank). The boundary between benefit principle and ability-to-pay principle is not clear-cut. We are likely, for example, to feel that well-to-do people should pay more in taxes than poor people both because it accords with our sense of justice and because we believe that well-to-do people typically derive more benefit than poor people do from services such as national defense. The concepts of benefit and ability to pay are sufficiently meaningful, however, to allow for a rough division of functions.

Some federal taxes are motivated by the benefit principle. This applies clearly to taxes identified as user charges and to excise taxes such as those on highway fuels (earmarked for the Highway Trust Fund). It applies as well, in some degree, to Social Security and unemployment taxes (more formally, the Federal Insurance Contributions Act [FICA] and Federal Unemployment Tax Act [FUTA] taxes). Social Security retirement and other benefits received are related to taxes paid because the same earnings base ("covered earnings") is used in the benefit and tax formulas. Similarly, unemployment benefits are related to the worker's history of employment subject to the tax, and the amount of the tax is related to the employer's history of layoffs. Many expenditure programs provide benefits that are related to the means of the recipient. Thus the formula determining Social Security retirement benefits replaces a higher fraction of the earnings of a low-wage worker than of a high-wage worker; welfare and food stamp benefits are tied to the income and wealth of recipients. Often benefits are related to the means of beneficiaries, not as a matter of policy, but as a matter of social circumstances. For example, aid to higher education tends to benefit higher-income families. On the revenue side of the federal budget, the income tax on individuals and corporations provides the primary instrument relating the distribution of burdens to ability to pay (with some role played as well by the estate and gift tax).

Horizontal Equity

The notion of ability to pay involves a ranking of individuals: those with more of it should bear a greater burden than those with less of it. To say that two people have the same ability to pay is to say that they are similarly situated as far as determining their appropriate tax burdens is concerned. The principle of "horizontal equity" prescribes equal tax burdens for those who have equal ability to pay. In discussions of tax policy this principle is commonly reinterpreted as prescribing that those with equal incomes should bear equal taxes. The assumption (often unstated) is that the equality of the commentator's concept of income appropriately specifies the conditions under which two people should be equally burdened. The requirement of horizontal equity gives little guidance to tax policy precisely because it does not address the key issue of defining those conditions.

Horizontal equity may even be a poor guide to policy, as a grim example suggests: Two men are crossing the desert on a camel. They have enough water to keep just two of the three of them alive for the full crossing, which cannot be completed on (human) foot. Following the prescription of horizontal equity would require each man to sacrifice the same amount of water to keep the camel going. The result would be that only the camel survives the trip. Of course, if the set of available policies is expanded to include the possibility of flipping a coin, the criterion of horizontal equity in the sense of equal expected burden could be satisfied. Probably the two men would choose flipping the coin over alternative policies. The example illustrates the distinction sometimes made between *ex ante* and *ex post* equity.[1] (Appendix 8–1 provides a brief discussion of these ideas.)

Vertical Equity

Once people have been classified by the principle of horizontal equity into groups of individuals considered to have equal circumstances, the

---

1. The example is adapted from one in Joseph Stiglitz's forthcoming textbook on public economics.

principle of "vertical equity" prescribes that those with the better circumstances should bear more of the tax burden. Obviously, as a guide to policy vertical equity depends as much as horizontal equity does on the specific criteria for deciding when two individuals have equal circumstances. To these criteria must be added a judgment about which circumstances are better and which worse, and, further, the degree to which burdens should differ in the different circumstances.

A vertical equity judgment is involved in determining how progressive the tax system should be. Note that progressivity as such is not a principle of equity. It is simply a technical characteristic of a relationship between the tax burdens and some specific, quantitative measure of individuals' means. Although there is no universally accepted definition, typically a tax system is said to be progressive if the ratio of tax burden to income increases with increasing income. For such a measure to tell us something about the equity characteristics of a tax system, the concept of income used to classify individuals must express an acceptable view of their appropriate tax burden.

People often equate progressivity with a system of graduated tax rates. But graduated rates are not necessary for progressivity (they are not, strictly speaking, sufficient either). For example, a flat tax on income above an exempt amount would produce tax liabilities that are a larger fraction of income for high- than for low-income individuals. Progressivity with respect to one base, such as income, can also be obtained through taxes that are proportional to another base. For example, because household expenditures on food represent a smaller fraction of the budgets of the well-to-do than of the poor, a proportional VAT that exempts food will be (slightly) progressive with respect to income.

Another common view is that a proportional tax system offers a kind of natural zero in the range of policies, a condition under which "all dollars are taxed alike." This reflects confusion about the nature of tax burdens (they are borne by people, not dollars) and attributes a kind of absolute quality to the measurement of the base that has no logical foundation. No theoretical case can be made on distributional grounds for or against proportional taxation of any particular base. Indeed, if there is a natural zero, it would seem more likely to be equal per capita sharing of collective burdens rather than sharing on the basis of proportionality to some often-unspecified aggregation of transactions.

It is tempting to argue that having twice as much income makes one twice as well off, and therefore at least twice as able to bear taxes. But such a view really expresses no more than that the observer believes it.

Note, in particular, that to make the assertion meaningful requires that the details of the definition of income be specified (for example, whether income is to be understood as amounts in excess of some minimum standard of living). Furthermore, if more income is better, we could equally identify increases in a person's means by the square of income, or its square root. Taxes proportional to such measures would be different from taxes proportional to income itself, yet apparently equally justified. The justification of proportionality, as reflected in policies such as value-added taxes or flat taxes, is to be found in administrative convenience, not in any theoretical virtue as a sharing principle.

The Utilitarian View

Discussions of distribution frequently assume that everyone is basically identical (ignoring conditions such as age, sex, health status, attitudes toward work, and the like). Equally important, to make the analysis tractable, what is to be distributed is usually taken to be a substance that, like cake, is easily measured and predetermined in total quantity. The idea that taxes should be progressive derives from the notion that taking a bit of cake away from someone who has lots and giving it to someone who has very little should be regarded as a social improvement. Sometimes this idea is clothed in the technical garments of utilitarianism. Individuals are viewed as producing well-being, or "utility," from cake (income). The extra utility generated by adding a bit of cake to an individual's consumption is asserted to be smaller the larger is the individual's amount to begin with. (This is called the principle of declining marginal utility. It is often considered justified by introspection, but it is better thought of as a description of a typical view of one person about the distribution of cake among *other* people.) Provided the policy has no effect on the amount of cake available to distribute, the sum of utility in the population will be largest when the cake is equally distributed. Translated into tax policy, this would imply taxing 100 percent of amounts above the group average and providing grants to make up any shortfall of an individual's pretax share from the group average.

Such abstract principles should be regarded not as externally imposed criteria for policy but as ways of describing commonly held values about the effects of policy. Economics has long since recognized that there is no observable quantity called utility. Indeed, the only meaning one could give to the idea in this context would be as a measure to reflect the particular distributional views of the observer. If I say the extra utility Jane gets from an extra dollar exceeds the extra utility Dick gets from an extra dollar, I am saying nothing more than that I would regard the result of giving an extra dollar to Jane as better than that of giving an extra dollar to Dick.

Equity, Opportunities, and Choices

A helpful way to think about issues of fairness is to ask how one would like to divide burdens among individuals or groups that differ according to some single specified characteristic (such as age, marital status, or family size) but are alike in all other respects that one might regard as relevant (salary level, health status). Such comparisons help sharpen the intuitive judgments about fairness on which the matter must ultimately rest. Here are two examples of comparisons we might make in attempting to classify individuals by appropriate tax burdens:

1. Two individuals are alike in most respects, but one has the rare mental and physical characteristics of a professional football quarterback, which enable him to command a higher wage than the other.

2. Two individuals are similar except that one is endowed with entrepreneurial skills and the ability to create new products demanded by consumers; the other has no such gifts.

These two examples have in common a difference in the opportunities available to two individuals. In each case it is fairly clear who has the better opportunities. If taxes are to be levied in accordance with means, in each case it would be appropriate for the one with the better opportunities to bear the heavier burden.

Notice that nothing is said about the choices the pairs of individuals actually make from among the available opportunities. It might be that the nonathlete works very hard at a menial job and manages to earn more than the athlete, who chooses to work only on Saturday afternoons. If the athlete has the option of doing the same thing as the nonathlete but in addition has the opportunity to earn a high reward as a quarterback, the fact that he chooses to use the better opportunity in part to enjoy more leisure does not alter the conclusion that his opportunities are better or the theoretical case for assigning him the larger burden.

Of course, if we cannot observe opportunities directly, the case may be just that — theoretical. Typically what we can observe is the result of both an individual's opportunities and the choices made from them, as they lead to some measurable level of earnings; we may have no alternative but to use earnings, this imperfect signal of the underlying conditions, as the basis for taxation. There are instances of taxes that attempt a more direct measure of opportunities: the "faculty taxes" employed in colonial times were based on a person's profession rather than earnings. Even that measure incorporates some elements of choice as well as of opportunity, since two individuals equally capable of becoming, say, doctors could still choose different professions. Taxes based on the market value of property, rather than on the return received by owners of the property, also attempt to measure opportunities separately from choices. A tax based on an individual's wage *rate* rather than earnings would be another example. But for the most part taxes rely on something like income, a product of opportunities and effort, thereby making use of imperfect measures of opportunities.

The next three examples elaborate on another aspect of tax base measures: the different uses that individuals make of the same opportunities.

1. Two individuals differ only in their taste for consumption goods; otherwise, their circumstances are the same. One prefers to spend more on clothing, less on food; the other likes high-quality food but does not care so much about clothing.

2. Two individuals have the same wage rate and in all other respects are in similar circumstances. However, one prefers to work long hours in order to purchase more goods; the other prefers less work and therefore accepts having fewer goods.

3. Now suppose we do not know whether the difference in work effort of the two individuals in example 2 is a matter of preference. All we know is that they have the same wage rate and in all other observable respects are in the same circumstances. But one works more hours than the other.

That the two individuals in example 1 deserve to bear the same taxes probably seems obvious. We are not likely to regard the difference in taste as relevant to the sharing of tax burdens. Example 2 is essentially the same, except that the choice is not between food and clothing but between leisure and goods. There is no obvious reason for the conclusion — the two should bear the same taxes — to be any different, although it is clear that earnings (the product of wages and effort) may be the only *practical* measure of opportunity. Example 3 introduces the question of whether it matters if the difference in effort is a matter of choice, a matter of habit, or is perhaps imposed by some external compulsion (such as need to support a relative) that we cannot observe. Given knowledge of their wage rates, does knowledge of the individuals' hours of work convey extra information about their circumstances that is relevant to the judgment of appropriate tax burdens? If not, then — although practical difficulties may preclude it — tax burdens should *ideally* be dependent on wage rate and independent of hours of work.

The last example prompts once again the observation that earnings are an imperfect measure of ability to pay. It would be attractive on equity grounds to have a measure less dependent on taste and effort and better related to opportunities. But we cannot obtain the necessary information. The interplay of values and information requirements is a major element in the choice of tax policy. What one might like to have is a tax based on an individual's potential earnings: the individual's tax would then be unrelated to his choice of what to do. Unfortunately, potential earnings, or more generally the quality of a person's opportunities, cannot be observed directly.

We could imagine using a questionnaire about sources of funds, or mental and physical aptitude tests, to elicit information about opportunities. But, quite apart from the administrative, political, and technical problems such procedures would present, they suffer from the inevitable problem of incentives. Because a piece of information is known to be used for determining tax liability, the respondent has an incentive to dissemble (for example, to pretend to have less than the actual level of ability). The questionnaire we now use to determine ability to pay is called Form 1040, and it clearly suffers from this problem. Respondents dissemble in that context both by hiding information in the literal sense (not reporting income) and by actually changing their behavior (for example, working less). The problem of tax design is to find rules that serve as well as possible, taking into account the incentives the rules will inevitably create.

To explore the equity aspects of the use of accrual income or consumption as the basis for assigning tax burdens, let us take a look at the way income-type and consumption-type taxes treat different individuals as their opportunities differ.

Equity Problems Common to Income-Type and Consumption-Type Taxes

Labor Market Opportunities

Although the rate structures might differ, both types of tax have the property of increasing individual tax burdens with increases in labor earnings. Whether the base is personal income or consumption, or one of the versions of a uniform income or consumption tax, much the largest part amounts directly or indirectly to a tax on the reward for individual effort.

Most people probably take for granted that it is appropriate for taxes to increase at least in proportion with such earnings. Considering the matter carefully, however, it is unfortunate as a matter of equity that the tax system cannot discriminate between those whose earnings are high because the market values highly their particular talents and those whose earnings are high because they put in a great deal of effort. Similarly, it is regrettable that the tax system cannot avoid reducing the burden on the individual who elects a low-paying but pleasant occupation over a high-paying but arduous one. In such instances the tax system is reflecting differences in taste rather than differences in opportunities. (Keep in mind, though, the example of the plumbers and carpenters in Chapter 7; if many people are equivalently qualified for two occupations, the rewards *after taxes* in both will tend to equality, regardless of the tax rules applied. Only the tax collected, not the effective burden, will differ.)

Gifts and Bequests

Although there is no apparent political interest in changing current tax policy regarding gifts and bequests, many experts most interested in fundamental tax reform view the issue as central. Opinions seem to divide sharply: some feel that gift giving in general, and the inclination of parents to accumulate wealth for the security and well-being of their children in particular, should be encouraged (after all, both donor and recipient derive value from the transaction); others see inheritance as an undesirable phenomenon, providing the fortunate recipients an unfair advantage.

Existing federal tax policy can be described as expressing the former view toward even relatively large gifts and bequests, and the latter view toward very large gifts and bequests. Receipt of gifts or bequests is excluded from the income tax base of the donee. The estate and gift tax (which is wholly separate from the income tax) bears only on substantial transfers. When and if the 1981 amendments to the estate and gift tax are fully phased in, estates of up to $600,000 will be free of tax. Estates of any size passing to a spouse are currently free of tax. However, a tax of 37 percent applies to transfers above the exempt amount, with graduated rates reaching 50 percent for transfers exceeding $2,500,000.[2]

In the appendix to Chapter 2 I described two broad approaches to these transactions that might be taken under either an income-type or a consumption-type tax. In calculating the personal version of either base, the logical procedure would be to include amounts received on the sources side of the calculation. The different possibilities are on the uses side, with those who regard amounts given or bequeathed as consumed arguing that no deduction should be allowed for these uses of spending power, and those who regard the transaction as transferring consumption to others arguing that such amounts should be deducted from the base of the donor. (Reminder: The existing income tax allows the donor no deduction but does not include gifts or bequests in the base of the recipient. Large transfers are also affected by the estate and gift tax.) One cannot decide in the abstract between these two approaches to gifts and bequests. They must be considered as they would affect the distribution of burdens.

Many would argue that society should try to ensure that individuals start at the same place in life's race, and therefore if two individuals are otherwise similar in every way (same salary, family responsibilities, health status, and so on), the one who receives a gift ought to bear the greater tax burden. This would suggest including gifts and bequests received on the sources side of the income or consumption calculation (or imposing a tax on accessions, related to the circumstances of the recipient). Of the reform programs mentioned in Chapter 1, only the Aaron-Galper plan takes this approach. On the other hand, it can also be argued that a person who gives purchasing power away ought to be taxed the same as someone who did not have the purchasing power to begin with. To implement this approach, a deduction would be allowed for gifts or bequests given. Apart from the instance of charitable gifts,

2. The rules provide for a consolidated treatment of the estate and gifts during the decedent's lifetime. The exemption is implemented by means of a credit against tax of $192,800, starting in 1987, and phased in over the years after 1981. The credit is scheduled to be $155,800 in 1986, implying an exempt amount $500,000. In the case of decedents dying in 1986 or 1987, a top rate of 53 percent applies to estates between $2,500,000 and $3,000,000, and a rate of 55 percent to estates over $3,000,000.

none of the programs under active discussion adopts this policy. (The *Blueprints* Cash-Flow Tax includes gifts and bequests in the base of the recipient and allows deduction by the donor.)

These views of policy toward gifts and bequests focus on just one side or the other of the transaction. But the burden of taxes on transfers is shared between donor and donee. Therefore, to analyze policy toward gifts and bequests in terms of comparisons across individuals, we need to bring at least two *pairs* of individuals into the picture. Consider, then, the comparison between two mother-and-daughter pairs, Jane and Janet Jones, and Susan and Susanna Smith. Both pairs are similarly endowed with individual earning power and are otherwise apparently equally situated. Jane, however, chooses to pass some of her purchasing power along to Janet, whereas Susan does not do the same for Susanna. The question is whether that difference should affect the combined tax burdens of the two pairs. If gifts and bequests are included in the base of the recipient and a deduction is allowed for the donor, or if they are ignored (neither deducted nor included, as under the present income tax), the combined tax base of the donor and recipient is unaffected by the size of the transfer. Including the amount in the base of the recipient while allowing the donor no deduction would result in a relatively greater burden on otherwise similar pairs of individuals between whom gifts are passed.

The same sort of comparison may be put another way. Consider two dynasties, identically endowed in the form of earning power of their successive generations. In one dynasty each generation consumes what it earns. In the other each generation gives away some of what it earns to individuals outside the family. Does one want the second to bear a heavier tax burden than the first? Suppose a generation of one dynasty chooses to pass some of its earnings forward to future members. Is there a basis for assessing it with a heavier tax?

Other issues related to gifts and bequests concern such matters as the line between charitable and other transfers, and the way to treat a succession of bequests (for example, from husband to wife to new husband to new wife) and the differential importance of bequests under different circumstances (the life insurance proceeds replacing the earnings of the parent who dies in midlife leaving young children, compared with the transfer from aged parents to somewhat less aged offspring). There are, in addition, very considerable problems of measurement. An example is the matter of comparing the college education provided by one family to its children with the gift of money in equivalent value provided by another family. Another example is the problem of identifying what is transferred to whom, as in the case of a gift from one person to a trust in which another person has a contingent interest (that is, a claim on payments that are contingent upon specified events or conditions). Practical issues such as these involve equity aspects.

Most of these arguments tend, on both equity and practicality grounds, to favor a policy roughly like the current one of subjecting only the donor or the recipient of a gift or bequest to tax under the mass tax (that is, the income tax), with perhaps a special tax on very large transfers. (The latter is also supported by the argument that large concentrations of wealth endanger the functioning of democracy. This argument is rarely, if ever, supported with quantitative reasoning. Nor is it clear that the problem is controllable at all through taxes. But if so, one would expect it to be an issue only in the case of very large accumulations.)

In spite of the strong opinions on whether or not to tax inheritances, surprisingly little information is available about the role of gifts and bequests in determining the lifetime resources available to individuals in the United States. In Appendix 8–2 I have attempted some "back-of-the-envelope" calculations regarding bequests. The figures suggest that bequests are often important, although not typically very large relative to lifetime earnings. I know of no way to translate the figures into clear conclusions about policy, but to me they suggest that whether inheritances are included or not in income subject to tax is of some significance, but not enough to dominate the choice of income tax policy.

Other Aspects of the Definition of Consumption

Gifts and bequests represent only one of many issues in the definition of consumption for the purpose of distributing tax burdens. Existing itemized deductions provide many similar instances. For example, although the charitable deduction can be (and usually is) analyzed in simple incentive terms, it has some of the same equity dimension involved in the treatment of transfers between private individuals. Existing practice with respect to gifts and bequests can be interpreted as a backward way of taxing the amount involved "only once." Instead of inclusion by the recipient and deduction by the donor, we have no deduction and no inclusion. By analogy with the mother-daughter example cited earlier, if the desired policy toward charitable gifts, based on equity considerations, is that they should not be counted as consumption by either donor or donee, then deduction by the donor is called for.

A more obvious instance in which a comparison of opportunities is helpful in thinking about policy is the deduction for medical expenses, which might be viewed as the money necessary to compensate for the worsening of opportunities occasioned by bad health. Of two otherwise identical individuals, the one who has a broken leg ought arguably to bear the lesser tax burden. The availability of insurance, however, affects the reasoning in such cases. If the two individuals had equal opportunity to purchase insurance against broken legs, one might feel differently about the basis in equity for differentiating the tax burdens. (A rule permitting deduction of the purchase of medical insurance and of uninsured medical expenses and providing for inclusion in income of any insurance proceeds — roughly speaking, current policy — would in effect ignore differences in outcomes among insured individuals and share the risk with the uninsured. For more on the subject of risk, see Appendix 8–1.)

The Unit of Taxation: Individual or Family?

Another equity issue that cuts across the income-consumption policy choice is the way tax burdens ought to be related to family circumstances. Although discussion of incidence is usually couched in terms of individuals, many individuals live mostly in a family context. It is hard to imagine sorting out the consumption of parents and children or of husbands and wives. Here again, comparisons of circumstances involve groups rather than individuals.

Two questions of practical importance arise in this connection: what is the appropriate treatment of a married couple (putting to one side how one identifies marital status), compared with two otherwise similar individuals who are not married, and how should tax burdens vary among families with different numbers of children? I take up the former question in Chapter 12, in connection with the simplification potential of single filing under the income tax. On the latter question there seems to be little doubt that family size counts (since the available consumption total is divided among more individuals); but there is less consensus about whether a family's burden should be reduced further by the addition of a child as the income level of the family increases. Under a system of graduated rates, allowing a deduction from the income calculation for each additional family member has the effect of giving a larger tax reduction to higher-income families. This is sometimes mistakenly interpreted as reducing the progressivity of the tax. Progressivity can be adjusted by adjusting the rates. The issue here is how burdens should vary by family size at each level of income. A practice of dividing the family's total income among its members, a procedure with some intuitive appeal as a basis for thinking about burden sharing, would undoubtedly result in a larger allowance for high-income families than does the per-person exemption. (An interesting question, which I shall not pursue here, is how the reasoning is affected by the recognition that tax burdens are actually spread over the lifetime of individuals as they pass through various stages, from child to earner to retiree.)

Equity Aspects of the Choice between Income and Consumption Bases

The choice between accrual-income and consumption bases is often argued in equity terms. The most common argument is simply that high-income people save more than low-income people; therefore a consumption-based tax must be less progressive than an income-based tax. This argument overlooks the fact that even if the premise is valid, the conclusion does not follow. If high-income people systematically save more than low-income people, and if liabilities progressively related to income set the standard for sharing burdens, a given degree of progressivity with respect to income could also be attained with respect to consumption by altering the applicable rates. The equity issues raised by the consumption-income choice are thus not those of progressivity. They concern the different ways the two types of tax differentiate among individuals of different characteristics. These differences can, in turn, be usefully divided into ongoing properties of the two approaches and properties of a transition from the current system to either one.

Ongoing Properties of Accrual-Income and Consumption Bases

The ongoing difference between the accrual-income and consumption approaches to taxation lies in the treatment of saving (see Chapters 2 and 3). If a single rate applies over time, a consumption-type tax is neutral with respect to an individual's choice (via saving) between consuming currently and consuming in the future. The neutrality derives from the fact that a change in this choice will not affect the present discounted value of taxes paid. By contrast, under an accrual-income approach the present discounted value of taxes increases with an increase in savings.

We can place this difference in the context of one of the comparisons made above — the comparison between the two individuals with the same means but with differences in taste for spending, one favoring food, the other clothing. Financial markets extend the range of commodities we can buy from, for example, clothing and food to clothing *today,* clothing *next year,* food *today,* food *next year,* and so on. Just as one can choose various ways to divide expenditure between clothing and food, one can choose various amounts of clothing today, clothing a year from now, food today, and food a year from now. The usual way to buy the commodity "food next year" is to put some money aside (as in a money market fund) and then withdraw the balance in a year and take it to the food store. The result is the same as if one had simply paid the original amount to a "food-next-year" store, taking delivery of the food a year hence. (If the ordinary price of food stays the same in the two years, a dollar in the first year will buy more food next year than food today because of the interest earned on the money put aside.) Choosing to spend more on food next year and less on food today is the same kind of choice as that between food today and clothing today. Taxing on the basis of accrual-income results in a discrimination based on this taste factor (because it would tax the interest element in the price of food next year), whereas a savings-neutral tax scheme such as can be achieved under a consumption-type approach does not.

We have already noted the unfortunate necessity of using tax rules that discriminate among individuals of the same endowment of talents and skills according to their taste for hard work or long hours. Discrimination on the basis of inclination to save (at *each* level of basic endowment) is another unfortunate characteristic of an accrual-income tax, but this discrimination can be practically avoided under consumption approaches. It is sometimes said that discrimination against individuals who save is appropriate because the tax system does not capture the benefits people obtain from having wealth even if they do not spend it. This has always seemed to me to focus too narrowly on the reasons people may alter the timing of their spending. Among the reasons for postponing consumption is any advantage that might accrue from having unspent purchasing power available in the interim (such as a feeling of security against unexpected expenditures). These reasons apply to the one who saves as well as to the one who does not save. It is not clear, however, why such reasons for saving should lead us to want to penalize it as an equity matter, any more than some particular motivation for favoring food relative to clothing should alter the presumption of not discriminating among individuals on that basis.

Table 8-1. Effective tax rate on future
consumption implied by income tax

Individual income tax rate (%)	Date of consumption (years)			
	1	10	20	30
	Effective tax rate (%)			
0	0.0	0.0	0.0	0.0
25	1.2	12.7	27.1	43.2
50	2.4	27.2	61.9	106.0

Note: Calculations assume tax is based on real
interest rate of 5 percent per year.

The view of savings as the purchase of future consumption brings out
a rather odd characteristic of an income tax. Table 3-2 showed how the
current price at which one can buy future dollars is determined by the
amount one must set aside now to accumulate (at compound interest) to
a dollar at a specified time in the future — in that context, thirty years.
Our concern was with the way inflation interacted with the taxation of
interest to produce very high tax rates on the purchase of such dollars.
Table 8-1 draws attention to the varying effects of an accrual-income
tax on the purchase of dollars at different times in the future. For
purposes of illustration, the table assumes that the relevant interest rate
is 5 percent and that there is no inflation. In the absence of income
taxation, with that interest rate it costs (in the form of money put aside
to accumulate with annual compounding) about 95 cents to purchase a
one-year-in-the-future dollar, 61 cents for a ten-years-in-the-future
dollar, 38 cents for a twenty-years-in-the-future dollar, and 23 cents for
a thirty-years-in-the-future dollar. A tax on consumption leaves these
relative prices unchanged; it simply introduces a uniform wedge between the receipt of wages, transfers, and so on, and consumption at any
time. These prices are also obviously unchanged by introducing a tax on
interest at a zero rate. But an income tax at a 25 percent rate has the
effect of making future consumption more expensive, with the price
increasing, not by a uniform percentage, but by a percentage that increases with time. Table 8-1 translates the effect into an excise tax
(beyond the tax on current consumption implied by an income tax) on
the commodities "x-years-in-the-future dollars." For the case of a 25
percent income tax, the excise tax ranges in value in the table from 1.2

percent on the purchase of a one-year-in-the-future dollar to 43.2 percent for a thirty-years-in-the-future dollar. At a 50 percent tax rate the corresponding range is from 2.4 percent to 106.0 percent. If we were to find a similarly erratic pattern of excise taxes applied for different people to different commodities in the supermarket, we would doubtlessly be surprised and demand that the system be rationalized. But when the commodities being purchased are dollars' worth of consumption in the future, the peculiar structure of implied taxes on different goods goes unremarked.

Another comparison might be made between two individuals whose circumstances differ in a particular way. One has relatively high wage earnings early in life but low earnings later in life; the other has low earnings early and high earnings late. Through saving by the first individual in early life, and through borrowing by the second individual early in life, they can achieve the identical pattern of consumption over time. One might reasonably say the two individuals are equally well endowed. A savings-neutral tax will also place the same burden of taxes on these two individuals (in present discounted value terms), whereas an accrual-income tax will tax the early-earning individual more heavily.

This argument may be related to the wealth-as-special-source-of-utility argument. Although from the construction of the example just given we know that the two individuals are equally well endowed, the early-earning saver would be observed to have more wealth than the late-earning borrower. Under our assumptions, however, they have exactly the same opportunities; practical methods of measuring wealth fail to register the higher earnings in later life anticipated by the second individual.

It may be objected that these two individuals are not in fact equally well off; it is preferable to have the earnings early in life. This objection really expresses the inadequacy of the assumption made in the example that the two have the same consumption opportunities by virtue of their ability to borrow and lend in the capital market. Actually, transaction costs may result in a higher interest rate paid on borrowing than is received on lending. Furthermore, because anticipated earnings make poor loan collateral, the late earner may not be able to borrow as much at any rate as his counterpart has available early in life. In this circumstance, individuals with different earnings profiles necessarily have different possibilities for consumption over their lifetimes. The comparison of the two equally well endowed individuals becomes more complicated, because it is not obvious what constitutes "equal." Is the combination of $50,000 in earnings in early life and no earnings in later life better or worse than $10,000 in early life and $50,000 in later life? Given the opportunity to choose (and told of the capital market opportunities), different individuals will choose differently, according to their tastes. If we have identified two individuals as having equal endowments, however, then a savings-neutral tax will have the property of reducing proportionately the set of alternative consumption profiles of both individuals proportionately, whereas an income tax will twist the alternatives in such a way as to benefit, relatively, borrowers over lenders. Good? Bad? Indifferent? I do not see any basis for preferring the income tax result.

Transition Problems

Transition to either an accrual-income or a consumption base from the existing system poses equity problems. Transition to a consumption-type base is often stressed in policy discussion, and it is often claimed that the problem is insuperable (for example, see U.S Treasury Department, 1984, vol. 1, p. 31). The argument usually assumes that the starting point is a pure accrual-income tax, and the transition is to a tax that is based on literally measured current consumption (as opposed to a tax that is savings-neutral but based on a combination of tax-prepayment and standard consumption rules). Then those who have large accumulations will be subject to a second tax by the change in rules, since they will now have to pay taxes on savings that they had expected to consume without further tax. At the same time, those with large accumulations will be able to earn a higher rate of return than before the change, because the consumption-type rules equalize the before-tax and after-tax rates of return. (This argument assumes that any downward pressure on the rate of return accompanying the change is insufficient to outweigh the saving in tax on the return at its previous level.) The transition is thus both too hard on past accumulations and not hard enough.

A more careful statement of the problem would identify it not so much in terms of past accumulation as in terms of plans for future accumulation. Those who plan to consume a great deal currently, whether out of past saving or out of borrowing against the future, will experience an increase in tax burdens. They will pay an extra tax on past accumulations if they have saved in the past, or on borrowing (because the proceeds are subject to tax) if they have not. Those who plan to postpone consumption for a long time, whether out of past saving or out of current and planned future saving, will experience a decrease in tax burdens. Stated in this way, the basic problem is that the change in rules will shift the incidence of the tax system from one that discriminates against those who postpone consumption to one that does not. It is true that there is no way to square the circle — to discriminate against neither. If one had concluded that to discriminate on the basis of saving behavior was unfair, it would seem odd to continue the policy because it was unfair not to maintain the favorable treatment of those who had benefited from the discrimination, or because it was unfair to give more favorable treatment to those who had been discriminated against in the past.

The problem of designing a transition to a savings-neutral system from the current one (which is, of course, not at all a pure accrual-income system) is that of finding forward-looking rules that make current decisions between present and future consumption free of tax consequences, while mitigating new burdens on those who have accumulated in the past and who want to consume currently. As the discussion in Chapter 13 will suggest, some ways of moving to a consumption-type tax base give rise to transition effects that seem well within the bounds of such effects associated with tax law changes in the past.

Appendix 8–1. *Ex Ante* and *Ex Post* Equity

A somewhat controversial question is whether the practical measure of ability to pay assigned to an individual who is exposed to risk should be based only on *ex ante* information (facts that can be ascertained before the risk is resolved), or whether *ex post* information (facts based on the outcome) is needed. If two individuals have the same prospects, by the standard of opportunities they should bear the same tax burden. But suppose those identical prospects are risky, and one individual is fortunate and reaps a rich reward, whereas the other is unfortunate and loses everything. Does it not violate our sense of fairness that the lucky person should bear no heavier tax burden than the unlucky one?

The discussion of this subject tends to confuse two issues: first, the basis upon which we wish to discriminate among individuals for the equitable sharing of tax burdens, and second, the possibility for improving upon the sharing of risk effected through markets. We can see this confusion by considering the case of individuals who clearly *choose* to bear risk by accepting gambles.

Taxes and Pure Gambles

A good example of a pure gamble is a lottery. Two individuals may share the same risky situation by virtue of having purchased lottery tickets with the same probability of payoff. There is less difference here than meets the eye between a tax on opportunity (which ignores the winnings and losses) and a tax on outcomes (which taxes winnings and allows deduction of losses). The tax based on outcomes simply changes the effective terms of the lottery. The players might differ in their valuation of the change in terms and in that sense bear different burdens,[3] but there is no reason to think that the difference would be related to who wins and who loses.

Suppose, for example, the ticket costs $1 and pays either $50 or nothing. A tax on outcomes might assess the loser nothing and the winner $25. That changes the terms from "$1 gets you $50" to "$1 gets you $25." Neither gambler will like the new terms as much as the old. They will no doubt differ in their preference between the new terms and, say, the alternative of a sales tax of $0.50 per ticket (the opportunity standard). But any difference in evaluation has to do only with their attitudes toward risk (their taste, in other words) and has no connection with the outcome of the lottery. The argument that taste should be irrelevant to the tax burden seems to have as much intuitive appeal in this context as in other choice contexts.

When the situation is one of proportional taxation of what we might call "reproducible risk taking" (as in financial markets, where one can buy as many shares of stock as one wants), there is really no difference between *ex ante* and *ex post* taxation. In the example above, *ex ante* taxation might involve a tax of $0.50 per $1.00 lottery ticket, with no tax consequences based on the outcome, whereas *ex post* taxation bases no tax consequence on purchase of the ticket but taxes the outcome at 33 percent. With *ex ante* taxation, the risk taker must give up $1.50 to buy a chance of getting $50.00 if the investment pays off or nothing if it does not. With *ex post* taxation, the same outlay buys $1\frac{1}{2}$ units of the same gamble. If it pays off, the investor gets $50 after paying a tax of $25 on the total winnings of $75; if it does not, the investor gets nothing. For the investor/gambler the two results are not merely similar; they are identical. There is nothing to dispute, as far as tax burdens are concerned.

---

3. The difference in valuation of the change in terms is the same as the difference in effective burden placed on two people by a tax on chocolate ice cream. The vanilla lover will not notice any burden; the chocolate lover will. In the case of a tax based on the outcome of a risky situation, the effective burden will depend on the individuals' tastes for bearing risk.

(There is a difference from the point of view of *other* taxpayers, who share the risk with the gambler in the case of *ex post* taxation and do not in the case of *ex ante* taxation.)

Endowment Risk

The argument is different in the case of individuals who have endowment risk — two similarly situated farmers, for example, running the risk of bad weather. Although they might have chosen the farming business in the same sense that the gamblers chose to purchase lottery tickets, we think of the farmers as having less freedom to alter their risk circumstances. The reason is the limited market for reallocating risk through insurance.

If insurance markets were perfect, the two farmers would have to be thought of in exactly the same way as the two gamblers. A farmer who did not want to bear the risk of bad weather would simply insure against it. His payoff would then be secure against weather risk, which would have been shifted to the insurers.

But insurance markets are far from complete, and the tax system provides one way of compensating. An *ex post* tax system has the effect of shifting risk from the individual farmer to taxpayers as a whole. The advantage of the approach is a matter of efficiency, however, not of equity. Both farmers bear an *ex ante* tax burden in either case. We need only ask whether the farmers would be prepared to pay some amount *ex ante* to be relieved of paying taxes on an *ex post* basis. Clearly they would.

Another aspect of the choice between *ex ante* and *ex post* tax rules involves how we *know* how good an individual's opportunities are. Sometimes the best way of knowing is to observe the outcomes actually obtained. In the case of different labor market opportunities, this may mean measuring earnings; in the case of risky enterprises, it may mean observing the *ex post* rewards. The practical measurement problem, however, should not be confused with the underlying equity objective.

Appendix 8–2. The Distribution of Estates and Inheritances

This appendix compiles information about the size distribution of gifts and estates in the United States.[4] The object is to estimate their likely importance as forms of wealth for recipients.

4. I should like to thank Richard Rosen of Princeton University for extensive assistance in the preparation of this appendix.

Most of the data on estates used here come from Bentz (1984), who presents information from federal estate tax returns on estates of more than $300,000 filed in 1983. Other major studies have relied on probate records filed in a particular area. Menchik's (1980a,b) work concerns estates of over $40,000 recorded in Connecticut in the 1930s and 1940s. Smith's (1975) data are on the estates of white males recorded in Washington, D.C., in 1967. The calculations here assume that the populations in these studies are representative of the population as a whole. Table 8–2 presents an estimate, pieced together from the cited studies, of the breakdown of estates by size in 1983. Roughly 1 percent of estates left in 1983 exceeded the $600,000 level projected as the exempt amount under the federal estate tax; 99.9 percent of estates amounted to less than $2,500,000. Only a small fraction of estates exceeded the market value of a modest house.

Although tax return data provide a reasonable basis for judging the size of estates, they do not indicate how estates are distributed among heirs. Estates are often parceled out to more than one person or institution. Family members usually inherit the largest share of an estate. Charitable contributions also make up a significant fraction of many estates. The importance of the inheritance to a recipient will depend on the recipient's financial situation, the share of the estate received, and at what point in life the inheritance is received. The evidence indicates

Table 8–2. Size distribution of estates, 1983

Estate size ($)	Percentage of estates smaller
2,750	50
24,400	62.5
63,250	75
175,500	87.5
250,000	95
300,000	97
500,000	98.7
1,000,000	99.6
2,500,000	99.9
5,000,000	99.97
10,000,000	99.99

Source: Calculations based on Smith (1975), Menchik (1980a,b), and Bentz (1984).

Table 8-3. Charitable contributions by estates, 1983

Estate size ($)	Percentage with charitable deduction	Mean charitable deduction ($)	Percentage of class midpoint
3,000,000 plus	15	256,000	—
300,000–500,000	14	65,000	16
500,000–1,000,000	16	115,000	15
1,000,000–2,500,000	21	252,000	14
2,500,000–5,000,000	29	563,000	15
5,000,000–10,000,000	41	1,442,000	19
10,000,000 plus	49	9,114,000	—

Source: Calculations based on Bentz (1984).

that a married decedent leaves most of the estate to the surviving spouse. The marital deduction accounted for 70 percent of the total tax deductions from estates of over $300,000 in 1983 (53 percent of the returns, accounting for 57 percent of the gross value of estates, were filed for married decedents). Further, 79 percent of the estates claiming the marriage deduction paid no tax. (The rules allowed an unlimited deduction of bequests to a surviving spouse for decedents who died after January 1, 1983; before that date the deduction was limited to $250,000. The Bentz [1984] sample includes estates involving deaths in both periods.) Of particular interest for us is the fact that children of decedents also receive a significant share of estates. Empirical studies to determine the nature of the division of estates when there is more than one child suggest that, although primogeniture and other forms of unequal sharing occur, equal sharing is common. Most of the children in the sample studied by Menchik (1980a,b) received their inheritances when they were in their late thirties or forties.

The distributional consequences of inheritance are affected by charitable bequests. Table 8-3 provides summary data for the 1983 returns studied by Bentz. About 5 percent of the gross value of these large estates was given to charity in 1983. Charitable contributions were far from uniform in the sample, however. Only 16 percent of the estate tax returns showed a deduction for charitable contributions, which averaged 32 percent of the estate. The proportion of returns showing a charitable deduction was markedly greater for the very largest estates;

Table 8–4. Simulated size distribution of inheritances, 1983

Size of inheritance ($)	Percentage inheriting more
70,000	9.23
180,000	2.51
250,000	1.13
300,000	0.95
500,000	0.34
1,000,000	0.11
2,500,000	0.03
5,000,000	0.01
10,000,000	0.00

Source: My own calculations (see text).
Note: Assumed distribution of heirs per estate: 1, 15.7%; 2, 49.8%; 3, 23.3%; 4, 11.1%.

but the fraction contributed by estates that showed any deduction appears to have been rather similar among estates of different sizes.

Lacking direct evidence, we can use the data in Tables 8–2 and 8–3 to simulate the size distribution of inheritances under assumptions about numbers of heirs and the division of the estate among them. Table 8–4

Table 8–5. Lifetime income valued at age forty by income ranking, 1982

Percentile	Males ($)	Females ($)	Households ($)
25	418,000	67,000	571,000
50	762,800	274,000	999,000
75	1,155,000	565,000	1,515,000
90	1,675,000	864,000	2,140,000
95	2,198,000	1,070,000	2,653,000

Source: Simulated lifetime profiles constructed by interpolating total money income for 1982 from Current Population Reports, series P–60, no. 142, discounted to age forty at 3 percent.
Note: The age of a household is that of its head. Persons or households with no income are included in the figures. Employment (income) from ages 21 to 70 is assumed, with total money income always having the same ranking. Linear interpolation within age brackets used where necessary.

describes a typical simulation. It makes the following assumptions: All estates within a given range have the same value (the mean). All estates are divided equally among the children of widowed decedents, with a decedent having no children giving the entire estate to one person. The distribution of the number of heirs is assumed to be the same for all estate size ranges and is based on lifetime expected births for white wives 18 to 34 years old in 1975 (*Statistical Abstract of the United States, 1984*, p. 68). The data from Table 8–3 have been used to simulate charitable contributions.

The significance of inherited wealth is presumably related to its magnitude relative to the other resources available to individuals. Table 8–5 shows, for purposes of rough comparison, calculations of the wealth equivalent to lifetime-earnings profiles in the population as of 1982. The table displays the discounted value of the lifetime income experience of individuals or households who, at each age, are at the indicated position in the income distribution.

No pretense is made that these data convey an accurate picture of the distribution of lifetime wealth; this would require attention to matters such as household formation and dissolution. However, placing side by side the distributions of inheritances (see Table 8–4) and discounted-income streams, we obtain a rough idea of the potential significance of inheritance. For example, if a male with the 90th-percentile position in the discounted-income ranking received at age 40 the 90th-percentile inheritance, the effect would be to increase his lifetime wealth by about 4.2 percent; at the 95th-percentile position (by interpolation), 3.6 percent.

9 Tax Distortions

Every tax ought to be so contrived as both to take out and to keep out of the pockets of the people as little as possible, over and above what it brings into the public treasury of the state.

Adam Smith, *Wealth of Nations*

TAXES change incentives. Sometimes that is desirable, as when the tax system is used to discourage the use of a polluting substance. But more typically, taxes give rise to undesirable distortions of market incentives, discouraging activities such as working and saving. This chapter is concerned with the distortions.

Economists use the term "efficiency" to describe the effectiveness of an economy's use of resources to serve the objectives of its members. Technically, resource allocation is said to be efficient when there is no available way to make one person in the economy better off without making someone else worse off. It seems obvious that efficiency is a good thing, but it is a limited objective. We are not often presented with opportunities to choose a policy that would make everyone better off. Indeed, we probably never encounter precisely such a condition. Most feasible policy changes create some losers. (Thus, in a narrow technical sense, most existing policies are probably efficient: no alternative is available that makes everybody better off.) When policies are changed, evidently those making the decision regard the gains to the gainers as overwhelming the losses to the losers.

Policy choice is often informed by primitive and inaccurate assessments of costs and benefits. In evaluating tax policy, for example, people tend to equate costs with tax liabilities. But nominal liabilities may be worthless as a measure of the burden placed on particular taxpayers. Furthermore, the real burden of taxes exceeds the aggregation of tax liabilities, because it includes both purchasing power transferred to the government (the tax liabilities) and the cost of distortions.

Taxes generate waste in a number of ways. Perhaps most apparent to the layperson are the costs incurred by individuals and firms in complying with the law, including the time of paid tax-return preparers and the record keeping and other preparation activities of taxpayers (see Slemrod and Sorum, 1984). Probably more significant are the talents devoted to structuring taxpayers' affairs to take full advantage of any opportunity to reduce their tax liabilities. The existence of a tax shelter "industry" is testimony to the magnitude of the resources devoted to tax planning. These costs can be reduced by the use of simple, consistent rules. Cash-flow accounting, for example, is simpler for the taxpayer than accrual accounting. The existing tendency to use a hybrid of income-type and consumption-type tax rules has placed a premium on expert tax planning.

Substantial resources are also spent on influencing the tax law itself. A variety of actors, ranging from individual firms and industry organizations to labor unions to charitable groups, devote their efforts to promoting rules favorable to their interests. The incentive to incur costs in such activities, as in others, is related to the potential reward. In extreme cases the resources directed toward influencing the law could be comparable in magnitude to the gain actually at stake. Consider, for example, the calculations of an industry group, interested in some favorable tax rule, about how much to spend on a lobbying campaign. Presumably they ought to be willing to spend any amount up to the full gain expected, rather than not obtain the desired result. Of course, what they would actually spend would depend on their perception of the likelihood of success, but the amount could be large in relation to the potential payoff. Unlike costs incurred to produce a good for sale, these expenditures are wasteful, since they are directed mainly at the distribution of benefits. They are thus likely to reduce the size of the pie.

Costs of this sort are referred to in the economics literature as "directly unproductive" or "rent-seeking" expenditures (see Bhagwati, 1971, and Kreuger, 1974). They are to some degree the necessary cost of political life. Certain tax policy choices, however, may help to diminish them. Most obviously, a system with low rates reduces the payoff to obtaining favorable tax treatment of some particular transaction. Thus the advantage of tax-free status for a fringe benefit when the marginal tax rate on salary payments is 50 percent is double that when the rate is 25 percent. A strong tradition of adhering to a very broad base for an income tax would also reduce the incentives to engage in costly efforts to influence the law. The same reasoning supports the use of more than one form of tax. Even when the combined effect on some margin of activity is the same as that implied by a single tax (for example, a 10 percent payroll tax and 10 percent income tax would have the same effect on work incentives as a 20 percent payroll tax or income tax alone), the political incentives may be quite different.

It is often pointed out that the U.S income tax is less progressive in effect than the statutory graduated rates would suggest. Manipulating the exclusions and deductions from the tax base is a standard approach to modifying the distribution of income tax burdens. Changes in the nominal rate structure have been less frequent. In some ways this is surprising. Consideration of the problem of picking a rate structure as an outright political game would lead one to expect continually shifting coalitions. It is always possible to find a majority coalition of individuals in one or more marginal rate brackets who would gain by the imposition of higher rates on those outside the coalition, and therefore instability and wasteful political competition seem all too likely. Perhaps the relative absence of this form of political activity is explained by the heterogeneous (in income bracket terms) character of political jurisdictions. But political struggle over the rate structure might become more common if the character of the base were less subject to modification. In that case, reducing the number of degrees of freedom (for example, by limiting the number of allowable brackets to one, as in the Hall-Rabushka Simple Flat Tax, or to three, as in the typical modified flat-tax proposal) might be a stabilizing policy choice.

Arguments that political choice will inevitably lead to an excessive use of government to distribute economic resources have persuaded some commentators that taxes ought to be narrow based. This concern is most often heard in connection with the possibility of introducing a VAT. The fear is that having a tax that causes relatively little distortion of economic decisions will simply induce the legislature to expand the size of the government sector (see Brennan and Buchanan, 1980, and Buchanan, 1983). The tax policy implication of this view is ambiguous. On the one hand, by placing reliance on a very narrow base — for example, by a constitutional provision limiting taxes to excises on some select group of commodities — the total size of the governmental sector would indeed be restricted. On the other hand, the distortion of production and exchange decisions would be correspondingly larger. Direct limitation of the size of government expenditures would be a less wasteful approach than imposing an inefficient tax structure.

Distortions of Production and Exchange

Distortions in production and exchange arise in a market economy from differences between buying and selling prices or between buying prices and production costs. For example, a tax on labor earnings puts a wedge between what a firm has to pay for the services of an employee and the amount actually received by the employee. Employers may be willing to pay employees $10 per hour to do some job, a wage the employees would be willing to accept. But if a 30 percent tax on wages puts a $3-per-hour wedge between the hourly cost to the employer and the wage received by the worker, the employees might prefer to take some extra time off, and the job may go undone. Because of the tax, employers and employees make their decisions on the basis of different signals about the economy, and some potential value (the difference between the value of what would have been produced and the value of the extra leisure taken by the workers) is lost. The tax on wages inhibits an exchange between employer and employee that both would find advantageous and thereby upsets the remarkable capacity of a competitive economy to seek out and exploit potential gains through production and exchange.

Types of Distortion

Economists distinguish three types of distortion, or wedges, created by taxes in a competitive system: consumer-consumer, consumer-producer, and producer-producer.

Differences in taxes on savings provide an example of "consumer-consumer distortions." Suppose that savings are in interest-bearing bonds and that the going yield is 10 percent. An individual subject to a 50 percent tax on the return on savings obtains an after-tax yield of 5 percent. If he puts aside $1.00 extra now, he can add an extra $3.38 to his retirement consumption twenty-five years from now (after taking into account the effect of annual compounding). Presumably he will adjust his saving up or down to the point at which the benefit of an extra $3.38 in retirement barely compensates for giving up $1.00 extra now. For an individual subject to a lower tax on the return on savings, say 15 percent, the terms are more favorable. He obtains an after-tax yield of 8.5 percent, so by putting aside $1.00 now, he can add $7.69 to his retirement consumption. He will adjust his saving until he regards an extra $7.69 in retirement as equivalent to $1.00 extra now.

We see that because of the tax, the tradeoff between current and retirement consumption will differ for the two individuals. If they could, they would engage in exchange. The high-bracket saver would be willing to give the low-bracket taxpayer $1 currently in return for, say, $5 in retirement. The low-bracket taxpayer would gladly give up $5 in retirement for the extra $1 currently. Both would regard themselves as better off, and no one would be harmed. But because of the tax this potential gain goes unrealized.

A tax may also create a wedge between the price paid by consumers and that received by producers, thereby creating a "consumer-producer distortion." The employee-employer distortion created by a tax on earnings is an example (where the employee is regarded as a consumer of goods and nonmarket uses of time). Whereas consumer-consumer wedges result in failure to exploit the gains from trade between individuals, consumer-producer wedges result in failure to exploit the gains from trade between individuals and the production process. If a person can produce $100 worth of goods by working an extra day (and would willingly make that trade of leisure time for goods if it were offered) but does not do so because the tax results in his keeping only $50, a valuable production opportunity goes unused.

When tax rules make the costs of production different for different firms, or when they lead a given firm to use inputs in a way that does not generate as much output as possible, "producer-producer distortions" occur. Such distortions are common in the existing income tax system. For example, the cost of using certain kinds of equipment may be very different for a corporation showing a current loss on its tax books from the cost for one with positive taxable income. The firm with positive income can take advantage of accelerated depreciation deductions and investment tax credits, whereas the firm with no current income may not be able to do so. One of the virtues of a competitive economy is its automatic tendency to seek out the least costly organization of production, considering both the internal operation of firms and the division of activities between firms. Producer-producer distortions interfere with this tendency and are therefore wasteful.

Neutrality

The "neutrality" of a tax system refers to its freedom from distorting effects in the marketplace. A completely neutral system would create no wedges between prices paid and prices received or between prices and costs. It would therefore induce no distortions. The critical question is whether a tax system interferes with production and exchange alternatives, such as those between leisure and employment or between using long-lived and short-lived equipment, in such a way that individual choices are based not on the actual tradeoffs available, but on different apparent opportunities. Most taxes are distorting because people are guided by the after-tax consequences of their actions, whereas it is the before-tax consequences that express the costs and benefits to the economy as a whole. To be completely free of distorting effects, a tax system would have to assign liabilities in a way that did not depend on individuals' actions at all; that is, the liabilities would have to be based on characteristics that individuals could not change, such as eye color, age, and sex.

As the examples suggest, it is hard to think of characteristics that are not in any way alterable in response to tax incentives. Surgical techniques might be used to alter eye color or sex. Age might seem hard to change, but birth records can be forged. Existence as such is usually taken by economists as an immutable condition, and the uniform lump-sum tax (a flat amount on each individual) is normally taken as the standard for neutrality in economic theory. To the extent that tax liabilities depend on matters over which individuals or firms have discretion, taxes do distort choices. Clearly all practical taxes involve distortions; the problem is to design tax rules with an eye to moderating the costs.

Instead of overall neutrality, it is more useful to analyze the neutrality of a tax system with respect to specified activities or transactions. For example, a flat-rate consumption tax system would be "neutral with respect to" saving. This means that the tradeoff between present and future consumption is the same for all individuals (no consumer-consumer wedge) and the same for all individuals as available tradeoff through investment (no consumer-producer wedge). It may seem evident that the neutrality of a tax system with respect to a given transaction or activity is desirable. Neutrality in one dimension, however, usually implies nonneutrality in another. For example, a flat tax on consumption, which is neutral with respect to saving, is not neutral with respect to the choice between market employment and nonmarket employment, because the tax puts a wedge between what firms can produce through application of labor services and what the laborers get to consume from their wages. Tax policy thus cannot eliminate distorting effects; it must balance among them.

Policy Guidelines

In view of the complexity of possible interactions between distortions, it is difficult to state policy principles that will be valid in all circumstances. But taking account of the following observations is likely to lead to better decisions on average than would result from ignoring the problem:

Except as a way to distribute one-time benefits and costs upon their introduction, producer-producer distortions rarely serve the interests of tax policy. The corporate tax system, in particular, induces many serious producer-producer distortions. Few are really required for reasons of facilitating tax administration, and few serve such tax policy objectives as favorably influencing the distribution of tax burdens among individuals. Usually the announced objectives of rule changes involving producer-producer distortions can be better served with less wasteful rules. (To be sure, announced objectives are not always the politically motivating force.)

Distortions of production and exchange depend on the net effect of all tax systems bearing on a particular activity. For example, the combination of a 10 percent value-added tax and a 15 percent income tax will have the same distorting effect on labor supply as a 25 percent income tax alone.

Distortions depend on taxes *at the margin.* The average or effective income tax rate on an individual indicates the revenue consequences of the tax. The distortion results from changes in behavior, and these are governed by the *extra* tax that will be caused by a decision to work a bit *more,* save a bit *more,* and so on. In a progressive income tax, the marginal tax rate is higher than the average rate, so average rates understate distorting effects.

Distortions from tax wedges tend to be largest for activities that are most responsive to prices and smallest for activities that are least responsive. The distortion is related to the degree of behavior change induced by a tax. For example, if, as many believe, the labor supply of husbands is relatively insensitive to earnings rates but that of wives is very sensitive, the distorting effect of taxes on earnings will be smaller for male household heads than for their spouses. Existing rules giving tax relief to a second-earner spouse are based partly on this reasoning.

Distortions tend to increase more than proportionately with the tax rate. The rule of thumb is that the revenue from a tax increases in proportion with the rate, but the distortional cost increases with the square of the rate. Doubling a rate thus quadruples the waste. For example, a 40 percent income tax rate induces sixteen times the cost in distortion of a 10 percent tax. The primary effect of low-rate taxes is to raise revenue; with high rates, distortion can impose a significant additional burden.

A low-rate, broad-base tax is likely to impose less cost in the form of distortions than a high-rate, narrow-base tax, even when the tax is effectively borne by the same individuals.

A full analysis of distortions would, unfortunately, oblige me to add numerous qualifications to these observations. For example, even if everyone had the same inclination to make charitable contributions and there was no policy reason to encourage contributions, eliminating the charitable deduction and lowering the income tax rate *might* not decrease costs due to distortion. If households *always* made contributions in direct proportion to existing taxable income, the new and old rules would be identical in effect, even though they looked different. It is even conceivable that eliminating the charitable deduction and lowering the tax rate (still assuming there was no policy reason to encourage charitable contributions) would increase distortions. Suppose that people tend to choose between donating money and donating time. If it became less attractive to donate money, people might accept less (taxed) market employment and spend more time in volunteer activities. The result could be a greater deadweight loss than under the original high-rate, narrow-base income tax.

As a matter of theory, to make full use of our knowledge about the behavioral effects of taxes would imply a complex structure of taxes on different activities, incorporating all available information about the effects of the taxes on distribution and resource use. But practical policy formation will no doubt be better served by general attention to the rough guidelines I have suggested. The Meade Committee in Britain made this point eloquently as follows:

To base a tax structure on the principle of considering each rate of tax on each specific type of transaction separately is to invite distortions through the influence of pressure groups of particular interests, each obtaining some specific exemption or other advantage until the whole structure becomes a shambles of irrational special provisions. A complex system which was devised and administered by a committee of wise philosopher kings, advised by a group of omniscient economists and subject to no democratic pressures from well organized special interests, might be preferable to any one more simple system which was debarred from making many specific and detailed provisions and exceptions which would in fact be improvements. But the latter would also be debarred from making many undesirable special provisions, and in the world as it is the acceptance of a simple system based on one or two easily understood, clear rules (provided, of course, that they were well chosen rules) would almost certainly be preferable. There will, of course, inevitably be some special exceptions and exemptions; but it is desirable to start from some simple, reasonable, clearly understood general set of rules, from which only a limited number of very special exceptions are permitted.   (Institute for Fiscal Studies, 1978, p. 44)

Major Issues in the Incentive Effects of Taxes

A review of the way existing taxes affect some major margins of choice will also provide an opportunity to comment on the way distortions would be changed under a comprehensive application of either accrual-income or consumption tax strategies.

Work Choices and the Terms of Employment

The Influence of Taxes on Labor Supply. Empirical research makes clear the need to distinguish among different types of workers in analyzing the effect of taxes on labor supply. Husbands, wives, and female heads of households (to cite one such classification) display different degrees of responsiveness to the rewards of employment in the labor market. Early research results led most analysts to conclude that the labor supply of husbands is rather insensitive to the rate of pay, whereas that of wives is quite sensitive. These findings comport with the traditional view of the breadwinner husband having little choice but to work full time and of the wife having a comparative advantage in nonmarket employment, including child rearing, and having greater discretion with regard to market employment.[1]

More recent studies, using new data sources and improved estimating techniques, support the relatively greater sensitivity of wives' market employment to the wage rate; but they find that husbands are also significantly responsive. For example, Hausman (1981) concludes that the taxes on labor supply implied by the combination of federal and state income and payroll taxes, together with the taxes implicit in certain transfer programs, result in husbands working about 8 percent less

---

1. It seems likely that the difference in work behavior between husbands and wives is more properly understood as a difference between a family's primary and secondary labor market participants. As far as I know, no study has yet attempted to distinguish on the basis of primary and secondary status, rather than of sex.

than they would if the same revenues were collected in a fashion neutral with respect to labor supply.

The effects of taxes on the well-being of individuals, however, are not measured simply by their influence on labor supplied or commodities demanded. Because more labor supplied to the market involves giving up nonmarket uses of time and effort, it is not unambiguously desirable. Conversely, because of offsetting incentive effects (the lower effective rate of pay makes extra work less attractive, tending to reduce amount supplied, but the reduced income makes it necessary to work more to maintain a given consumption standard), a tax on wages might have no effect on labor supply, yet still impose a large distortional cost (because the worker would like to work more at the wage the employer is willing to pay). Hausman concludes that the deadweight loss of existing taxes on labor supply amounts to nearly 30 percent of the revenue collected.

Hausman's estimate of a 30 percent deadweight loss represents an average of a much higher figure for individuals in the high tax brackets and a much smaller figure for those in the low brackets. The average also takes into account individuals of different sex and family-status characteristics. Because of their greater responsiveness to wage rates, females experience greater deadweight loss at every tax-rate level. Because the losses in the high brackets are so much larger than those in the low brackets, the replacement of the existing tax system with a flat-rate income tax (with prescribed exempt amounts for each individual and for families) would substantially reduce the distortional costs.

This example brings out well the difficulty of drawing tax policy conclusions from efficiency analysis. It is no doubt true that the waste induced by taxes could be greatly reduced through lowering the top rates and making up the difference by raising the low rates. The problem is that this would also produce a shift in the tax burden (consisting of the sum of purchasing power transferred to the government and the deadweight loss) from high-bracket to low-bracket taxpayers (unless the immediate effects were ultimately offset by sufficiently large favorable effects on economic growth, wage rates, and so on). Whether such a shift is desirable is a value judgment outside of economics. What we clearly should take away from the analysis, however, is an awareness that the burdens imposed by high rates are much larger than simply the revenue raised.

Although I have been discussing the effects of taxes on labor supply as though the latter could be fairly easily measured, say by hours worked per month or years worked during an individual's lifetime, the application of human effort is actually a much more complex phenomenon.

People can choose not only how many hours to work but also how intensively to work, how risky an occupation to accept, how much training to undertake, how much of a sacrifice of pleasant environment to accept, and so on. Taxes affect all these choices and invariably introduce a waste-causing wedge between the tradeoffs from the viewpoint of employers and the tradeoffs from the viewpoint of workers.

To take but one example, for all the glamour associated with being a senior executive of a corporation, the climb to the top typically involves years of hard work. Many who would like to attain a high position in a firm do not make it. Yet companies depend on individuals' willingness to make the effort, and so the prize for attaining high position must be large. From the viewpoint of the employee, the relevant reward is what can be kept after taxes. High tax rates mean that the pay differential upon promotion must be higher before taxes than it would otherwise be or that the incentive effects of given differentials are dampened. The influence of the tax is thus partly to change the ways employees use their talents and partly to change the ways employers organize themselves. (Note that the tax tends to increase the observed inequality of before-tax compensation among employees of different ranks.)

Accrual-income and consumption-type taxes are broadly similar in the distortion of labor supply choices they imply. Accrual-income, personal-consumption, and value-added taxes all give rise to a wedge between the reward to the person providing labor services and the cost to the buyer. Differences among alternatives are partly matters of degree, relating to the rate of tax applied. But the fact that the extra current consumption a worker can obtain by working a bit more is higher under one set of rules than under another (that is, that the effective marginal tax on the tradeoff between labor and current consumption is lower) does not conclusively establish that there is less waste due to distortion of labor supply. We noted a hypothetical example above, in which lower rates under an accrual-income tax obtained by restricting the deduction for charitable contributions could conceivably increase waste. This illustrates that what we may call an income or consumption tax is really a bundle of taxes on separate activities. In the example, the reduced rate of tax on labor earnings, combined with no deduction for charitable contributions, makes it possible to obtain a larger quantity of groceries for a given amount of extra work for pay, but a smaller amount of charitable contributions. (Thus, if the tax rate drops from 50 percent to 25 percent, an extra dollar earned will permit the worker to buy $0.75 worth of groceries instead of $0.50 worth, or $0.75 worth of charity instead of $1.00 worth.) The example shows that the combination of effective price changes *may* have effects that either increase or decrease the overall waste due to the tax.

A more important context in which such interactions occur bears on the comparison between income and consumption rules. To raise a given amount of revenue it may be necessary to use a higher rate of tax under a consumption tax than under an income tax. (Whether this is so in practice will depend in part on whether the transition effects a one-time wealth tax. See Auerbach and Kotlikoff, forthcoming.) Commentators often conclude that the labor market distortion must therefore be greater under the consumption approach. However, their reasoning focuses only on the worker's tradeoff between current effort and current consumption, which is less favorable under the consumption tax if it involves a higher rate. When account is taken of the more favorable tradeoff between current effort and *future* consumption, the conclusion becomes ambiguous. The correct result about the relative distortional costs of consumption-type and accrual-income taxes, including their effects on labor supply, cannot be established on the basis of abstract principles. It requires empirical study. Although refined empirical analysis can help to improve the measurement of waste due to taxes, however, in setting policy we would do well to keep in mind the advice of the Meade Committee, quoted earlier.

The Influence of Taxes on Compensation. There is another important way that tax rules enter the relationship between employer and employee: taxes affect the form in which compensation is paid. Particularly for those in high tax brackets, tax-free fringe benefits are worth relatively more than cash. More precisely, the willingness to accept a given fringe benefit rather than cash increases with the employee's tax bracket. Here the distortion is primarily in the consumption pattern of employees — more of the favored forms, such as fancy office decor or business lunches, and less of other forms than in the absence of the tax discrimination.

It is commonly thought that tax-favored fringe benefits give rise to a horizontal equity problem. It is not fair that executives can enjoy lavish business lunches without paying tax on their consumption value or that airline flight attendants have the possibility of reduced fares when apparently similar individuals in other jobs must pay taxes on all their compensation. But this view neglects the way the compensation of employees is determined in a market economy. After all, even if they do not adjust from moment to moment, wages and salaries are not what they are by chance. Employers try to pay as little as they can to attract and hold employees with the desired qualifications, and employees seek out employers who offer the best combination of monetary and non-monetary compensation. Occupations involving substantial amounts of tax-free compensation will thus tend to have a lower level of taxable compensation than they otherwise would. The employee who gets the tax advantage pays for it with reduced taxable compensation. The problem with untaxed fringe benefits is thus mainly one of efficiency (too much is spent on fringes relative to other things), not equity.

If there is an equity issue raised by tax-free benefits, it is related much more to the progressivity of the system than to its horizontal equity (like treatment of likes). Given a graduated structure of rates, expansion of legally allowed tax-free fringes typically reduces the effective progressivity of the tax system because these forms of compensation will tend to be concentrated among the more highly paid employees, such as executives and workers in high-wage industrial occupations. There is an obvious economic reason for this. The bias toward tax-free consumption is directly related to the rate of tax that applies. Employers get little extra power to attract low-wage workers by offering to pay them in the form of untaxed fringes because the same outlay will buy those workers cash compensation that is in any case lightly taxed. For low-bracket workers, the effective discount on fringes is small, and they would rather have the flexibility to choose how to use their money.

There is no systematic difference between income and consumption approaches as far as the taxation of most fringes — apart from retirement programs — is concerned. The typical VAT, for example, would allow the employer to deduct (or claim credit for the VAT paid on purchases of) inputs involved in the production of such employee amenities as free stand-by passage on airlines. However, other fringes, such as legal advice or medical care, might not be allowed as deductions. The appropriate treatment of pensions and other retirement benefits is, however, very different under income and consumption approaches. Proper accrual-income taxation would include employer contributions to retirement plans as well as the accruing increase in value of pension assets in the employee's income (similarly, the accruing value of pension rights under defined-benefit plans would be recognized as employee income). Hybrid taxes generally exclude such forms of compensation, at least up to allowable limits. Exclusion of both contributions and accruing increase in the value of retirement benefits until withdrawn is exactly what is called for under the consumption approach. Thus treatment constituting a special exception to the rule under one system, resulting in a distortion, is the prescribed norm under the other.

Size and Composition of the National Wealth

The classic debate concerning saving and investing is between advocates of accrual-income and consumption-based taxes. Equity issues tend to dominate that discussion. But the presumption has commonly been that the consumption approach is preferable as far as the efficiency of resource use is concerned. Indeed, it was thought that the crucial argument for taxing on the basis of consumption rather than income was that the former would encourage savings. The reason is that a consumption tax is neutral with respect to savings; that is, savers receive the full return on consumption foregone, whereas under an income tax they receive only the return after tax.[2] A number of studies (some motivated by an interest in evaluating the tax policy alternatives) have attempted to determine the responsiveness of savings to the rate of return (see Summers, 1984). Although it is fair to say that the findings support the likelihood that savings respond positively to an increase in the return on savings, the research has been marked by technical controversy and has not produced the same degree of consensus as have the studies of labor supply.

It is perhaps fortunate, therefore, that a closer look at the efficiency issue leads to the conclusion that the relative deadweight loss burden of income-based and consumption-based taxes depends not on the responsiveness of savings to the rate of return but on an even more elusive aspect of behavior.[3] We need not dwell on the technical details, except to point out that the critical issue determining the relative efficiency loss of raising revenue via a consumption rather than an income tax is the responsiveness of *labor supply* early in life to the rate of return on savings (as it influences the price of retirement consumption). The deadweight-loss-minimizing policy is as likely to call for a subsidy to as a tax on saving and investing. To date, there is no reliable empirical information on this behavioral response. (The analysis provides a good example of the dangers of focusing too much attention on the neutrality of the tax system with respect to some particular margin of choice, to the neglect of others. There are always tradeoffs.)

2. The statement assumes that the same rate of tax applies to consumption at different times, a condition that may not hold in the case of some forms of consumption taxes (such as the full-fledged cash-flow tax with graduated rates). See Chapter 2.

3. Remember that in the efficiency analysis, savings as such are not regarded as having particular value. Just as labor market employment must be balanced against its cost in foregone alternative uses of time, savings must be evaluated against the cost of foregone current consumption. For discussions, see Bradford (1980b) and King (1980).

In the choice between income and consumption tax bases, as in the case of using efficiency analysis to determine the desired degree of progressivity of a tax on earnings, the point is not to determine policy but to inform policymakers of the true burdens involved, including deadweight losses. Many who advocate adoption of a consumption approach do so primarily on the basis of equity (that the tax system should not discriminate among individuals on the basis of their taste for or against saving) and ease of administration (cash-flow versus accrual accounting). Were information to become available which demonstrated that one or the other base imposed a greater deadweight loss, policymakers would still have to worry about whether the necessary burdens, including efficiency costs, were fairly distributed and whether the resulting tax system could be administered by ordinary mortals.

The Existing Tax Treatment of Saving and Investment. For all that political and philosophical passions are aroused by the debate between income and consumption taxers, the single most important characteristic of the existing tax system is not heavy or light taxation of saving and investment but *inconsistent* treatment of these transactions. When one looks into the details of saving and investing, one sees an extraordinarily complicated set of tax wedges.

To illustrate with a fairly simple example of a savings choice, consider a taxpayer in the 50 percent marginal rate bracket with $1000 to invest for his retirement in twenty-five years. If he puts his money into a bond fund yielding, say, 15 percent and withdraws enough each year to pay the income tax due on his interest, at the end of twenty-five years his $1000 will have grown to $6521. Suppose instead he can find an asset with the same rate of return but for which the yield comes in the form of capital gain. The situation is economically equivalent to the one first described. But he will pay no tax at all until the end of twenty-five years, at which point the gain is realized to finance retirement consumption. After paying tax at long-term capital gains rates, in the second case he will have $34,217 instead of $6521. Even without the favorable tax treatment of long-term relative to short-term gains, the advantage of deferral would mean the second approach would yield $21,761 instead of $6521.

To carry the example a step further, suppose the taxpayer elected to borrow $1000 (at 15 percent) to add to his own $1000, so he could purchase more of the capital gain asset. Now he would have interest deductions each year. To make the comparison easier, suppose he borrows enough extra each year to pay the interest net of the annual tax savings, with all the debt to be repaid at the twenty-five-year point.

Once again, in the absence of taxes his real situation would be the same as in the previous examples: he sets aside $1000 of his own money in the first year, reaping any return twenty-five years later. But now, the combination of the favorable treatment of long-term capital gains, the deferral of tax on accruing gains, and the deduction of interest provide him with $61,913 instead of $6521. (This example is particularly interesting, as it shows how the tax system may even improve the yield on the savings of the higher-bracket taxpayer. In this instance, the proceeds after twenty-five years exceed the $42,521 of lending for twenty-five years at 15 percent with no taxes at all. Other features may improve the yield on the savings of low-bracket taxpayers.) Finally, note that even without the favorable long-term capital gains rate, the investor would have $37,001 under the scheme with borrowing.

These illustrations of inconsistencies in existing income tax law could easily be extended to investment choices and multiplied repeatedly. The consequence is complexity in the rules and inefficiency in resource use. Inconsistencies are particularly troublesome in the case of saving and investment transactions, because of the absence or weakness of natural limits to their exploitation. I alluded above to inconsistencies in the treatment of economically equivalent forms of employee compensation, cash versus fringe benefits. The effects of those inconsistencies tend to be self-limiting, because of the bounded interest of individual workers in the tax-favored goods or services. There is just so much traveling the airline employee can do, even though the fare is tax free. The inconsistencies with respect to savings or investment transactions are more mischievous. To exploit them, the taxpayer does not have to change his occupation or lifestyle, just his portfolio; and in many cases the natural limits are very wide on the profit to be made from arbitrage involving different tax treatment. Because of this, unless the inconsistencies are dealt with explicitly, the tax law must include complex provisions setting limits to tax arbitrage.

Retirement savings plans provide a simple example. If there were no limit on the amount an individual could deposit in an IRA, it would be possible to borrow at deductible interest and accumulate funds in the IRA tax free. The potential gain over many years is very large indeed, even despite the natural limit that would apply here, in the form of the reduced taxable income (and therefore lower marginal tax rate) that would result from large interest deductions in the initial phase, and the increased taxable income (and therefore higher marginal tax rate) that would apply in the draw-down phase. Various rules have therefore been introduced to limit this arbitrage, most obviously the ceiling on annual

additions to an IRA and the limitation on the allowable interest deduction when it is not matched by cash receipts. Such rules add complexity
to the law and limit the incentive effects that devices such as IRAs are
designed to produce.

Refining the Concepts of Saving and Investment. To address the effect
of taxes on the nation's wealth, it will be helpful to extend the earlier
discussion of saving and investing in Chapter 2. As noted there, saving is
the activity of adding to one's stock of wealth. Because a person's wealth
is a measure of the amount of consumption he could finance now by
selling off assets (including the indirect form of selling that occurs when
an asset is committed as security for a loan), saving involves foregoing
current consumption. A given individual's stock of wealth will include
claims he may have on other individuals. For example, if I have loaned
some money to a friend, my wealth includes the value of my claim to
repayment by my friend. Corresponding to this positive item on my
balance sheet is a negative item, the liability to repay the loan, on my
friend's balance sheet. If we calculate the aggregate wealth of individuals in the group consisting of all U.S. citizens, such offsetting assets
and liabilities will cancel each other. The net figure for the value of U.S.
citizens' wealth can be classified under the labels of "claims on nature"
and "claims on others."

Under claims on nature are included the stock of real things we
usually refer to as capital, including land, machines, buildings, and
inventories. Claims on nature also include all kinds of less tangible
instruments with which we wrest from the environment a future flow of
value, such as technical know-how (sometimes embodied in patents),
marketing potential (sometimes incorporated in trademarks), and
works of popular and fine arts and literature. Certain claims on nature
are often excluded from statistical data on national wealth. An important example is the potential future value embodied in accumulated
knowledge and skills (human capital). The future flow of services implicit in government facilities and infrastructure is also rarely captured in the aggregation of individual wealth because there is no practical way to allocate the claims to individuals. We may thus distinguish
private wealth (which does or would show up on individual balance
sheets) and public wealth (which does not).

The category of claims on others may be subdivided into claims on
foreign individuals and institutions and claims on ourselves that do not
net out when we aggregate (I shall explain). The idea of claims on
foreigners (loans to foreign individuals, for example) needs little explanation. Since one sometimes gets the opposite impression, it bears em-

phasis that from the point of view of U.S. citizens as a group, claims on foreigners are neither superior nor inferior to claims on the real stuff we usually call capital as far as generating future consumption is concerned.

The idea of claims on ourselves that do not net out is less obvious but may be illustrated simply by the example of federal debt. When the federal government issues a bond and sells it for $1000 to a U.S. citizen, that citizen's balance sheet shows an additional asset valued at $1000. By our usual way of keeping books, however, there is no offsetting liability on anyone else's balance sheet. The effect is thus to increase aggregate measured wealth without any genuine increase in future consumption having been created. Of course, there is a liability out there in the form of an increased requirement for future taxes to be levied on some unspecified citizens, but it does not show up on the books. Whether individuals in the aggregate recognize this liability and adjust their demand to hold wealth upward accordingly is the essence of the question whether government debt crowds out private capital.

A working definition of national private wealth (excluding human capital) is the sum of:

· Domestically owned domestically located capital

· Domestically owned capital located in other countries

· Net financial claims on foreigners

· Domestically owned U.S. government debt

Economists have a specialized definition for the term "investment": the activity of adding to a stock of capital. The notion of capital involved may be more or less broad (for example, including or excluding the skills embodied in individuals). Accumulation of claims on foreign individuals and institutions may be included (for example, in the national-income accounting concept of gross national investment), but adding to the stock of publicly held government debt is not normally included. A further distinction is made between domestic and foreign investment. A number of policies have been adopted to promote additions to the stock of capital goods (machines, structures, inventories) physically located in the United States. (I shall discuss the wisdom of such policies in Chapter 10.) This domestic investment need not be financed by the savings of U.S. citizens; we have recently observed a huge increase in the extent of the financing of domestic investment by foreigners. Such financing may be effected either by foreign nationals' putting real capital (such as machines or buildings) in place in the United States or by foreigners' lending money to U.S. nationals to enable them to hold real capital located here.

Three aspects of the savings and investment process should be stressed:

Wealth includes much more than the stock of business fixed investment shown in the national income accounts. Business inventories, all kinds of consumer durables (including owner-occupied homes), and household inventories constitute huge stocks of potential future services, as does the accumulation of knowledge and skills in the population. Discussion of tax policy regarding accumulation often ignores these other forms of wealth.

Taxation affects the savings and investment process in two ways. First, budget deficits have a *wealth effect,* in that they generate a flow of additions to the supply of private wealth that must be held by someone. (Deficits may also affect the demand side, the stock of private wealth that people wish to hold.) Second, taxes affect the return that can be earned by sacrificing current consumption or by investing in particular assets and thus, through a *price effect,* alter the desired amount and composition of private wealth.

The influence of taxes on domestic capital must be balanced by an offsetting effect either on the stock of wealth in other forms (foreign capital, net financial claims on foreigners, or some form of domestic capital that does not "count") or *somebody's* stock of savings. There is a tight connection, indeed a definitional one, between a change in the world's stock of capital and an increment to savings.

The Influence of Taxes on Capital Stock and Method of Finance. The existing tax system generates a hodgepodge of incentive effects on the composition of the economy's capital stock and its method of finance. Unfortunately, it is difficult to separate the analysis of the composition effects from the financing effects. The critical issue is the size of the wedge inserted by taxes between the rate of return actually earned on an investment and the rate of return received by the saver who, directly or indirectly, finances that investment. In the existing system that wedge will vary according to the method used to finance the purchase of a real asset. To take one problem at a time, however, let us consider the makeup of the real capital stock as chosen by a taxpayer for whom the alternatives are lending (or borrowing) at a given interest rate in the financial market and purchase or sale of business assets.

In an ideal accrual-income tax, for example, the wedge would be just equal to the saver's marginal rate times the before-tax return. In a flat-rate consumption tax, that wedge would be zero. In the actual tax system, the wedge depends in a complicated way on the method by which the taxpayer is allowed to write off the cost of assets (for example, by depreciation allowances); on any applicable special subsidies (such as the investment tax credit); and on the rate of inflation (depreciation allowances, for example, are based on the acquisition cost of assets but the return comes later in inflated dollars). The rules in the United States, much like those in other advanced industrial economies, provide for very different treatment for different kinds of assets. Whereas under accrual-income accounting the annual write-off would depend in a regular way on the durability of an asset, under ACRS, assets are grouped into a small number of discrete classes for purposes of determining depreciation allowances — most personal property is classified as three-year or five-year property, and most real estate is classified as eighteen-year property. Complex rules provide an investment credit for certain assets. The net effect is substantial and variable deviation between the treatment called for by accrual-income measurement and that actually allowed by the tax law, resulting in quite varied wedges between the before-tax and after-tax returns received by investors in assets of different types. More than one commentator has pointed out that the U.S. government is, in effect, operating an extensive economic planning system, or industrial policy, through the tax law (see, for example, Dixit, 1984, and Henderson, 1984).

Why does variation in wedges matter? Consider a very simple tax system in which there is a proportional income tax at 25 percent and production takes place in individual proprietorships. (This eliminates the need to take the double taxation of corporate income into account.) The proprietor of a business that purchases an asset, such as a building or machine, would account for its cost by taking a series of depreciation deductions. If the deductions are correct, the tax on business income will have the effect of taxing the yield on investment in the asset at 25 percent. If the yield before taxes is 10 percent, the proprietor will get to keep 7.5 percent after taxes.

In this situation, the firm will undertake investment projects that yield at least 10 percent and reject projects that yield less (before taxes). The tendency will thus be toward a situation where the *marginal* investment of any type yields 10 percent. This equality of marginal yields before taxes is exactly what we would want as a matter of economic policy. The before-tax yield, sometimes referred to as the "social" yield, expresses the total return on the investment, independently of the division of that return between the firm and the government. If equality of before-tax yields did not hold — for example, if some investments undertaken were to yield 5 percent while some unexploited opportunities would yield 15 percent — it would be possible to reduce the low-yielding investment by $1.00, shift the $1.00 to the high-yielding investment, and thereby obtain for society as a whole a greater output of $0.10 a year forever. By shifting more than $1.00, more pure surplus could be generated.

In our illustrative economic system the efficient outcome — equal before-tax yields on all asset types — resulted from consistently applied accrual-income measurement rules. Now suppose that for some class of asset, such as equipment, the tax law is changed to allow immediate expensing of investment instead of the schedule of depreciation allowances over time. As we know, immediate expensing has the effect of exempting an asset's yield from income tax. The wedge on the yield from the favored asset is no longer at a rate of 25 percent; instead the rate is 0 percent. By buying a machine, the proprietor now obtains a rate of return of 10 percent instead of 7.5 percent.

The story is clearly not over, however. The proprietor could make more money after taxes by reducing other investments and increasing investment in equipment. This will be profitable so long as the yields after taxes are different. For example, the profit opportunities would be exhausted when investment in equipment has been carried so far that the yield from another dollar's worth is 7.5 percent before taxes while the pretax yield on the other assets remains 10 percent. At that point, the allocation of investment generates the most value possible from the private, after-tax point of view of the proprietor but *not,* as we have seen, from the point of view of the economy as a whole. There is a waste of potential value. That is why variation in wedges is bad.

The extent of the waste depends on how much of an adjustment in the amount of the favored asset used in production is required to drive down the return on investing in it. If, for example, there is really no way the proprietor can productively use more of the favored asset, there will be no distortional cost at all. As in the case of the other distortions we have examined, the more room there is in the economy to substitute one thing for another (in production or consumption), the more costly will be the distortions induced by tax wedges.

The Influence of Taxes on Domestic and Foreign Investment. A further important slice across the allocation of wealth is that between domestic and foreign investment. At least four separate issues, all important, have the domestic-foreign label. One set of questions concerns the physical location of productive capital, whether in the United States or in other countries: where is capital located? A second set of questions concerns the amount of national saving relative to the amount of domestic investment: who owns the capital? A third set of questions concerns the country of domicile of the company that directly controls the productive assets: whose companies manage the capital? And yet a fourth, and quite different, set of questions concerns the influence of taxes on the extent of international trade in goods and services. These are complicated subjects, deserving extended treatment on their own, and I can offer here only very brief comments (I shall postpone discussion of the effect of taxes on the extent of trade to Chapter 14, where, in the context of discussing adoption of a VAT, I point out how little reason there is to expect the choice of income tax policy to make much difference apart from any consequence it may have for budget deficits.)

In a survey of the international tax policy scene as of 1985, an eminent practitioner of international tax law commented that "U.S. international tax policy, and the Internal Revenue Code rules in this area, probably involve the greatest degree of complexity of any area of the tax laws. . . . The last two revenue acts [TEFRA of 1982 and DRA of 1984] have contributed to this condition, which is reaching alarming dimensions. . . . The most recent changes did not raise fundamental issues, other than the issue of whether the sheer complexity and weight of the many provisions in the foreign area is now approaching a situation where neither taxpayers will be able to comply nor the [Internal Revenue] Service to implement this huge morass" (Ross, 1985, pp. 702, 706).

With these words of warning from an expert, I shall venture cautiously into the international tax terrain. Yet there is little doubt about either the importance of international capital markets to the U.S. economy or the salience of international tax considerations in the policy discussion. Probably no opinion is more frequently voiced by businesspeople than that the U.S. tax system puts them at a disadvantage in international competition.

In identifying some of the main issues, I shall start with the basic economics of the situation, focusing on a tax on the income of U.S. firms. If international capital flows consist simply of borrowing and lending at interest (so the only real capital acquired by U.S. taxpayers is domestic), the analysis of the U.S. investment decision and its tax consequences is much the same as in the closed-economy case. From the standpoint of the U.S. economy, lending to foreigners is just like acquiring a domestic machine. An efficiency issue is raised if U.S. tax laws make it attractive to acquire machines on which the before-tax yield falls short of the worldwide interest rate. An example would be the application of consumption-type rules to U.S. investment while fully taxing interest receipts (and allowing a full deduction of interest payments). Such rules could be described as subsidizing domestic investment.

Debt flows are not the only way in which U.S. residents acquire an interest in foreign assets; U.S. taxpayers may acquire equity interests in foreign firms, and U.S. firms may also invest directly in business assets located in other countries. These possibilities bring with them most of the hard issues of international taxation. In the case of directly owned assets, the new issue is whether the U.S. rules for calculating income should differ from those applicable to assets located at home. Under current law, capital located abroad does not qualify for the investment tax credit or ACRS. A second issue, the "foreign tax credit," concerns the treatment of taxes paid to foreign governments. U.S. practice is to permit a U.S. taxpayer to credit against U.S. income tax liability income taxes paid to foreign governments (up to the amounts that would have been payable on the same income in the United States). The possibility of ownership of equity interests in foreign firms brings with it another major international tax issue, the matter of "deferral" of tax on the earnings of a "controlled foreign corporation," a special case of the general problem of integration of corporation and shareholder income accounts. U.S. law taxes a parent company on the dividends received from a subsidiary corporation located in a foreign country, rather than on the currently accruing income of that subsidiary. A somewhat less important issue that arises in connection with both debt and equity flows is whether interest or dividend payments to foreigners should be subject to "withholding tax" by the United States.[4] Currently the United States imposes withholding taxes on a variety of payments to foreigners. Typically the level of these taxes is regulated by bilateral treaties with other governments. A significant change in policy was the

---

4. The term "withholding" has a special meaning in the international context. Unlike taxes withheld on wages, for example, a withholding tax on interest paid to foreigners is not merely precollection of income tax due. It is itself the tax due; that is, it is a separate tax.

phase-out, incorporated in the Deficit Reduction Act of 1984, of the withholding tax of 30 percent applicable to earnings on foreign "portfolio" investment.

Each of these tax institutions influences the distribution of activity among firms of different tax domicile, the allocation of capital among nations, and the methods by which it is financed. Evaluating their effects is made doubly difficult by the fact that the rules are themselves bargaining counters in a system of agreements among national governments. I can do no more here than identify certain major efficiency issues.

One issue is the efficiency of the allocation of the world's stock of capital. If capital is internationally mobile, imposing a heavier tax in one country than in another will result in an inefficient allocation, in the sense that there would be a potential gain to the world as a whole from shifting capital from the low-tax to the high-tax country. Although the criterion has been important in policy debate, it is not at all clear why efficiency in this sense should carry a great deal of weight in the writing of U.S. tax rules, since it says nothing about who gains and who loses from divergence from world efficiency. One might expect the main question to be whether U.S. taxpayers as a class could be made better off by changes in the rules. Such a purely nationalistic viewpoint would cast doubt on the system of crediting taxes paid to foreign governments, since it is the return net of foreign taxes that is available to the combination of U.S. taxpayers and the U.S. government.

Finally there is the question whether the United States gains by treating domestic investment differently from accumulation of either financial claims on foreigners or productive assets located abroad. Economically speaking, the two types of claim are equivalent to the claims on nature in the form of domestic investment. Thus there is an efficiency case to be made for working toward a uniform approach to the domestic taxation of all three forms of wealth.

Philosophically, both the pure accrual-income and consumption-type tax strategies are nationalistic in the sense described above. The notion that taxes should be based on either the consumption or the sum of consumption and increase in wealth (accrual income) focuses on the *individual*. Sources of income are irrelevant in this approach.

Portfolio Choice

The rules applicable to a taxpayer-corporation that buys an asset are only part of the story about the wedge between saver and total return on investment. (I should emphasize that the rules in question also apply to individual taxpayers. All too often, one encounters the view that "business" is synonymous with "corporation.") The tax burden also depends on how the investment is financed — through borrowing, issue of equity, or retained earnings. In addition, the saving may be held on behalf of individuals by an intermediary such as a pension fund or life insurance company. The way these institutional arrangements affect the tax wedge depends, in turn, on the inflation rate and on how the rate of interest responds to the inflation rate.[5] A true income tax would not influence the financial structure of corporations. The actual tax system, including its separate taxes on corporations and individuals, creates strong incentives affecting such corporate decisions as the division between debt and equity finance, the payout of dividends, and the details of transactions to create, merge, and liquidate firms.

It is widely known that the tax laws affect a corporation's choice between debt and equity finance. Because interest payments are deductible in calculating income subject to tax but dividends are not, there is an incentive to use debt finance.[6] Because debt finance brings with it certain costs, including the risk of bankruptcy, the resulting distortion of financial structure imposes deadweight loss on the economy.

The argument that an increase in the leverage of the corporate sector (that is, the extent to which corporate investment is financed by debt rather than equity) imposes extra costs on the economy is actually rather less straightforward than is usually supposed. Although there is no doubt that the tax system strongly influences the financial structure of the corporate sector, there is room for disagreement about whether it matters much. From the point of view of the economy as a whole, bankruptcy as such is not necessarily a bad thing. Presumably, the reason for the bankruptcy — a bad crop, for example — is a bad thing, but the bankruptcy itself primarily affects those who bear that loss. It simply results in a shift of ownership of a corporation from its shareholders to its debtors, a matter foreseen among the various risks by all

---

5. The study by King and Fullerton (1984), which focused on the taxation of income from corporate capital in the United States, the Federal Republic of Germany, Sweden, and the United Kingdom, revealed a remarkable variation in the tax wedges on investment projects, depending on type of asset, industrial sector, financing arrangements, intermediary institutions, the level of interest rates, and the rate of inflation.

6. Actually, the matter is more complicated than this suggests. One must also consider the taxation of the returns on debt and equity at the individual level. Remember that the returns on equity need not come in the form of dividends but may be taken in the form of more lightly taxed capital gains.

sides in the market for debt and equity. The argument that "excessive" leverage is bad depends on the extra costs imposed by such ownership shifts, such as litigation and perverse incentives on managers (for example, the incentive to undertake excessively risky investment as a gamble to avoid possible loss of control).

Researchers have come to different conclusions about these extra costs. Merton Miller (1977) has argued that the cost imposed by the influence of taxes on financial structure is minor. But Roger Gordon and Burton Malkiel (1981) estimated that the extra costs due to increased bankruptcy risk induced by the corporation income tax amounted to 10 percent of corporation tax revenues in 1975. All three analysts would agree that the financial structure of the economy is profoundly affected by tax rules and that tax lawmakers inadequately appreciate the subtle ways in which risks may be transferred in financial markets.

The Influence of Inflation and Taxes on Financial Decisions. Because income-measurement rules are inadequately indexed for inflation, the interaction of inflation and taxes has a powerful effect on the financial choices of individuals and firms. The recent period of high inflation provided an interesting testimony to the influence of tax rules on financial decisions. Because the U.S. income-measurement rules do not make any allowance for price-level changes, inflation strongly influences the relative attractiveness of different financial instruments to taxpayers in different circumstances. Particularly important is the failure of the tax law to distinguish between the inflation premium and the real interest rate in allowing a deduction for interest payments and in taxing interest receipts. (The November 1984 Treasury reform proposal included an inflation adjustment in the taxation of interest.) Because different sorts of mismeasurement apply to the income taxation of other assets, such as common stock or direct ownership of an apartment building, the effect of inflation is to make debt increasingly attractive as an asset for low-bracket taxpayers, such as pension funds (which pay no tax), and as a liability for high-bracket taxpayers, such as corporations. It is therefore not surprising that between 1965 and 1983 the ratio of interest payments to the total income of corporations increased from 8.6 to 31.7 percent. The financial shift, incidentally, had much to do with the decline in corporation income tax liability from 38.1 to 26.6 percent of the sum of corporation income and interest.[7]

7. The figures, derived from the *Economic Report of the President* for 1985, refer to domestic profits, before interest and taxes, of nonfinancial corporations in the national income and product accounts.

The Influence of Taxes on Corporate Distributions. The tax law also creates incentives influencing the way corporations distribute funds to shareholders. Indeed, as pointed out in Chapter 6, one of the mysteries of tax analysis is why, in spite of significant extra tax costs and with better methods available for getting money out of "corporate solution," stockholders seem to want corporations to pay dividends at all. Most people believe that there is a certain incentive for corporations to retain earnings (rather than pay them out) because the stockholders thereby obtain their returns in the form of an increase in share value rather than a taxable dividend. If realized through sale of some part of the stockholders' shares, an increase in share value will be taxed to individuals as capital gains, which usually means at a lower rate than dividends. Furthermore, the stockholder who does not wish to receive cash can postpone realization indefinitely. The postponement is itself of value and results in avoiding income tax altogether if the asset is held in a stockholder's estate at the time of death.

The argument as thus normally laid out is incomplete, however, because it fails to explain why $1 of earnings retained in the corporation should result in an increase the value of the company's stock by $1. Furthermore, it clearly implies that companies will *eventually* have to pay dividends. (Otherwise why would anyone hold the stock?) The two issues are related. The market ought to value $1 of retained earnings at $1 if the $1 can be withdrawn by the owners of the firm. But if the owners must pay a dividend tax in order to get the $1 out of the corporation, the market should value the extra $1 inside the corporation at less than $1.

We do not really know how the market regards an extra $1 of retained earnings, because there are so few opportunities to observe an otherwise unanticipated increment to the money in a corporation's bank account (for one attempt to find out, see Gordon and Bradford, 1980). But we do know that there are ways to get money out of corporations without incurring the penalty of the high tax on dividends. The basic technique is for the corporation to repurchase its own shares. This transaction transfers money from inside the corporation into the hands of those shareholders who choose to sell. They may incur a capital gains tax (if they are taxable); but for individual shareholders, the tax will certainly be less than would result from a dividend. A closely related technique is to purchase the shares of another company from public shareholders for cash. The argument is somewhat involved, and all that need be said here is that one way to carry out this transaction is to merge with another corporation.

Many corporations have clearly learned that repurchase of shares and related transactions have advantages over dividends. But evidently many shareholders value dividends over other methods of receiving funds; thus every year a large volume of dividends is paid out and subjected to substantial double taxation in shareholder income tax returns. In short, we can calculate the large incentive effects of the tax system on the distribution practices of corporations, and we can see that these effects are real. But we do not have a full understanding of the way tax rules affect corporate behavior.

Policy Alternatives and Portfolio Distortions. Because of the difficulty of implementing full accrual-income accounting, some degree of distortion of the corporate financial structure is almost inevitable if accrual income is to be the guiding tax principle. By making better use of what we know about the functioning of capital markets, however, we could do much better, even while staying within an accrual-income framework. The basic strategy called for is to seek the closest reasonable approximation to accrual accounting, the major elements being depreciation allowances (keyed to economic lives and indexed for inflation), capital gains (indexed for inflation, perhaps taxed as though realized upon transfer of assets by gift or bequest), and interest (payment and receipt adjusted for inflation). These components could be combined to reduce the waste now associated with inconsistent treatment of different assets, a form of waste that buys little in the way of benefits to particular classes of taxpayers (unlike, for example, the waste associated with graduated tax rates, which buys a distribution of tax burdens in favor of the poorly endowed).

The waste associated with distortion between corporate and noncorporate investment, and with distortion of corporate financial decisions (including much of the waste associated with tax-motivated merger and acquisition activity) would be only partially relieved by available techniques for more consistent accrual-income accounting. The inefficiency associated with a classical corporation tax, with its distinction between interest and dividends as methods of distributing the payoff from investment in the corporate sector, is most naturally addressed through the available methods of integrating corporation and shareholder accounts. (See Chapter 6.)

The accrual-income strategy necessarily brings with it the waste associated with the double-taxation of saving. (Remember that, since not all waste can be avoided, the best policy from the point of view of efficient resource use might well include a tax burden on saving.) Practical income-type rules will also inevitably leave a distortion between business capital and household capital, including owner-occupied houses. Consumption-type taxes, using cash-flow accounting, more or less automatically provide neutrality in these two dimensions, as well as among different types of assets, forms of financing, and institutional vehicles for saving. It would be possible to pursue various mixtures of consumption- and accrual-income-tax strategies without generating the degree of distortion I have described, but only by carefully coordinated rules. We shall look again at this possibility in Chapter 10.

The Influence of Taxes on Individual Assets. The tax system has a strong influence on the form in which individuals hold their savings. For the most part, the effects of tax rules on the composition of individual savings are not the object of policy, but simply its side effect. Among the features of the system with portfolio effects are the different tax treatments of debt, equity, and real business assets. The tax rules applied to financial intermediaries, such as insurance companies and pension funds, also affect the pattern of assets held by households. In addition, taxes affect the incentives to acquire household durables, including owner-occupied housing, and to build up human capital.

The Tax Shelter Problem. The "tax shelter" problem is an example of a portfolio bias — attributable to inconsistent treatment of different assets — induced by the tax system. Actually, in spite of much discussion and the common use of the term "abusive tax shelter," I am not aware of a generally agreed-upon definition of a tax shelter. The well-known characteristic of a shelter is that it reduces an individual's current income tax liability. The consequences for future tax liability, critical to determining the overall effect, vary greatly among different techniques.

A simple example of a tax shelter is an IRA. A deposit reduces current tax liability at the price of an increase in future liability when the funds are withdrawn. The reason there is a "problem" is that the combination of reduced current liability and increased future liability amounts to less, in discounted present value, than would apply if income were currently measured and taxed. The essential reason is that the IRA is accounted for on a consumption tax basis. Because the rules permit borrowing to make a deposit to an IRA, it is possible for an individual to obtain the advantages of tax deferral without actually sacrificing current consumption. For example, a person in the 50 percent bracket, who earns a 10 percent return on an IRA, saves $1000 in current taxes by making a $2000 deposit. He will be able to maintain current consumption by borrowing the second $1000. Suppose that he can borrow at 10 percent as well and that he closes his IRA after one year. At that point there will be a $2200 withdrawal, netting $1100 after tax on the withdrawal, and he will owe the bank $1100 on the loan. But of the amount paid to the bank, $100 is deductible as interest, so there is a net surplus of $50 on the whole transaction.

This set of matched transactions is a good example of tax arbitrage. If there were no limits on deposits to an IRA, and if the tax rates were unaffected, this individual could make an unlimited amount of money just by increasing the scale of the operation (for example, by putting $1 billion into the IRA and borrowing $500 million). But there *are* limits on deposits to an IRA — although there are no similar limits on investment in, say, planting trees. Furthermore, under the present tax rules an investment in timber is treated even better than an IRA in that the withdrawal of funds when the timber is mature is subject to taxation as long-term capital gains. Nevertheless, the basic arbitrage potential is much the same. By borrowing, an individual can obtain the current tax write-off of expenses without actually sacrificing current consumption. The deductibility of interest payments against ordinary income means that there would still be the potential for surplus *if* timber investment generated the same yield before taxes as is charged on the loan.

There's the rub. The asset acquired is not essentially identical to the funds borrowed (by contrast, one could actually borrow from one's own IRA, resulting in literal identity between the IRA's asset and the individual's liability). If enough individuals want to invest in timber, the yield on timber will be driven down; we would predict (and it seems to be true) that the after-tax rewards to an investor in timber would be about the same as those to an investor in assets that do not receive the favorable treatment. But the observed effect on individual portfolios (physicians owning pieces of oil wells and the like) will persist even though no one actually gains an after-tax advantage on the margin.

The observed fact of individuals' reducing their current tax liability by such transactions is, not surprisingly, offensive to the untrained observer. Consequently, complicated rules are drawn to limit the extent to which an individual can participate. It is doubtful that such rules are necessary from the point of view of the substance of the matter as opposed to the appearance. There is a question, however, about whether doctors and dentists (or other high-earning individuals) are well placed to evaluate the sorts of investments providing tax shelter, and there is certainly social waste involved in the maldistribution of risk bearing, the talent devoted to the design and marketing of the schemes, and the temptation to fraud in their complexity.

The Influence of Taxes on Financial Intermediaries. The rules relating to retirement savings and life insurance provide instances of taxes affecting the intermediaries that hold savings. By applying cash-flow accounting to retirement saving plans administered by duly recognized firms, the tax system induces a concentration of individual savings in the hands of these institutions, savings that might be held in other ways in the absence of the tax rules. The much greater flexibility to choose the type of asset the intermediary will hold on the saver's behalf that has been introduced to the system in recent years has no doubt greatly reduced the cost of this distortion.

At present, the income tax treats the accruing value of a whole life insurance policy very much as it does a short-term capital gains asset. No deduction is allowed for the purchase of an ordinary policy by an individual, but tax on the growing cash value is deferred until the policy-holder realizes it, typically in the form of an annuity. At that time, there is a recovery of basis (like the deduction for the cost of an asset in calculating capital gain), subtracted from the amounts received, with the remainder taxed as ordinary income. If, however, the value of the policy is realized only by the beneficiaries because of the death of the insured, no income tax is due. (This corresponds to the write-up of basis at death in the case of capital gains.) Much like an IRA, then, life insurance presents opportunities for tax arbitrage that have not been overlooked in practice. Complex rules must be drawn to keep the arbitrage within bounds because, as in the case of an IRA, there is no natural limit. The result is unnecessary costs devoted to designing, selling, and administering insurance policies to accomplish tax reduction.

It should not be necessary at this point to elaborate upon the steps that might be undertaken to bring about consistent treatment of these saving and investment transactions through rigorous application of accrual-income or consumption tax principles. But the desire to influence saving and investment is very strong, even among those who advocate an accrual-income standard. It is almost unheard of, for example, for a tax proposal to advocate any fundamental change in the special rules typically applied to particular forms of retirement saving. The Comprehensive Income Tax plan described in *Blueprints* is an exception, but it was never actually embodied in a legislative proposal. The Treasury's November 1984 plan is representative, in providing for consumption-tax rules (much like those of existing law) for employer-sponsored retirement plans and for IRAs up to specified limits on the annual net contribution. I shall have more to say on this subject in Chapter 10.

The Influence of Taxes on Investment in Human Capital. For many individuals the stock of potential future earnings embodied in themselves as workers dwarfs other forms of wealth they may acquire. Many activities serve to enhance this stock of human capital. Obvious among them are schooling at all levels. Also important are accumulated experience in the job market. Even the activity of meeting new people may enhance an individual's earning power. The tax system affects the payoff to alternative forms of investment in human capital, much as it affects investment in tangible forms.

For analytical purposes we can view a decision to undertake a course of education as a simple investment matter. By incurring certain current expenses, including expenses in the form of earnings foregone because of the time devoted to study, the individual obtains a flow of extra earnings in future years. Unless the tax system results in the government's sharing equally in the cost and the return, it will affect the profitability of such investments. Suppose that by spending $1000 on a training course I can obtain extra earnings amounting to $1150 a year hence. (Most educational investments, of course, involve much longer payoff periods, but the one-year example simplifies the calculations without affecting the basic point.) In the absence of taxes, I should be interested in undertaking the training if the rate of interest is 15 percent or less, because I could borrow or draw on savings to cover the cost and still come out ahead. An income tax of the usual sort will change the attractiveness of the opportunity, and to a much greater degree than in the case of an ordinary investment. Thus if the figures referred to an ordinary investment of $1000, an income tax at a rate of 30 percent would reduce the payoff to $1105 ($1150 less 30 percent of the income of $150). In the human capital case, the usual income tax will take 30 percent of the entire return flow of $1150, leaving me as an investor-student with $805 ($1150 less 30 percent of $1150, which will appear as labor earnings on my tax return) to show a year from now in return for my current outlay of $1000.

The case of an educational investment financed by foregoing earnings provides an interesting contrast. Suppose, in the example, the $1000 cost of the training takes the form of reduced earnings in my current job. In that case, because the lower current earnings imply $300 less in income tax (continuing the assumption of a 30 percent tax rate), the government becomes a partner in my investment. The cash flow is thus changed from a current outlay of $1000 and year-hence payback of $1150 to a current after-tax outlay of $700 and year-hence after-tax payback of $805. The rate of return is the same with and without the tax. If the income tax has the effect of reducing the after-tax rate of interest, it actually encourages human-capital formation in this instance.

One sometimes encounters the view that a shift toward a consumption-type from an accrual-income tax would bring with it a new urgency to deal with the bias against human capital investment described in the first case above. Whether outlays for education ought to be classified as consumption or investment appears a particularly obvious question if the tax is to be based on consumption. However, the issue is present in both systems. Education as an investment would be recognized by a deduction under the standard consumption approach, but it would be recognized by depreciation allowances under an accrual-income approach. In neither case would the outlay be properly ignored altogether. Substituting a consumption-type tax for the accrual-income tax in the examples worked out above would change the description of the taxation of interest, but not that of the tax treatment of the human capital investment. Under both systems there is a potentially serious bias against human capital formation.

Public policy toward education clearly encompasses a far broader range of instruments than tax policy alone. I cannot answer here the question whether the many subsidies to education are too much or too little to offset the disadvantages created by the tax system. All I can reasonably do is note the real possibility that the tax system, either the actual existing one or any likely alternative, creates harmful disincentives to undertake investment in productivity-enhancing learning.

The Influence of Taxes on Acquisition of Household Durables. The last major element of individual portfolios to be considered here is household durables, including owner-occupied houses. Because the income tax at least partially taxes the return on other forms of savings, individuals have an incentive to acquire assets that yield their services directly and are not subject to income taxation. Houses (principal residences and vacation homes) are the most important, but not the only, example. Automobiles, jewelry, art works, and pleasure boats are others. Even such convenience appliances as refrigerators and washing machines become relatively more attractive as a result of the failure of the income tax to measure the return from owning them.

The effective exemption from tax of the yield on household durables that characterizes the existing income tax is most likely to hold in any alternative income tax. Although it is theoretically possible to develop a system of imputing income to the owner of a house or other piece of household capital, there seems little prospect that this would be carried out. By contrast, the natural accounting associated with consumption-type taxes puts household durables on the same footing as other forms of saving and investment and therefore provides neutrality among the different types of capital. Economists typically regard the flow of services from houses as neither inherently better nor worse than the flow of value from other capital, and they therefore regard as desirable neutrality between the two classes of assets. But many people clearly believe owner-occupied housing has virtue beyond the flow of value it directly delivers, and therefore they do not advocate this form of neutrality.

The Marginal Cost of Public Funds

Taxes affect choices at a great many margins, as is evident from the discussion in this chapter. How important are the distortions? The question can be answered in many ways. I shall discuss some of these in connection with the options for reforms addressed in Chapters 13 and 14, where the emphasis is on the question of how much deadweight loss can be saved through changes in the income tax. Two recent studies have attempted to place bounds on the cost of tax distortion by asking a different question: how much does it cost to raise an additional dollar for the public sector?

Charles Stuart (1984) estimated the extra cost due to distortions of labor supply from a proportional increase in all U.S. taxes (including state and local) that was sufficient to raise an extra dollar of revenue. His "benchmark case" estimate for 1981 was just under 25 cents. Of course, varying assumptions about such features of the economy as the responsiveness of the labor supply to the wage rate would lead to variations in Stuart's figure. The second study, by Charles L. Ballard, John B. Shoven, and John Whalley (1985), placed the extra deadweight loss per dollar of extra revenue from a proportional expansion of all taxes in the range of 17 to 65 cents.

Such estimates require heroic assumptions indeed. The issue, however, is important. These figures suggest a significant allowance for the deadweight loss that should be added to the straight dollar figure in evaluating public expenditures.

10 Saving and Investment Incentives

Neither a borrower nor a lender be . . .

Shakespeare, *Hamlet*

IF SHAKESPEARE were working on the final draft of *Hamlet* now, he would have to change the famous advice that Polonius gives to his son, Laertes, to something like the following: "Should you find yourself in a high tax bracket, look that you borrow to the hilt. Put your money in apartment buildings, or maybe shopping centers with rapid depreciation. Neglect not to seek out capital gain–producing assets, but beware of recapture. All this counsel mark with special force if inflation there be. Should perchance the turning wheel of fickle fortune land you in a low tax bracket, avoid real assets altogether; sell them short if you can and lend your money at interest. This above all: make not a move without consulting your tax adviser."

Over the years the treatment of saving and investment in U.S. income tax law has become extremely complicated. The difference in tax consequences is often enormous between the most favorable and least favorable forms of transactions that have essentially the same economic effect, which is why it may indeed pay to keep in touch with a skilled tax adviser. A good deal of this complexity arises from inherent problems in measuring income. But many of the problems are attributable to muddled efforts to use the tax system to encourage saving and investment.

There is a certain irony about the existence of saving and investment incentives in the context of an income tax, inasmuch as the principal reason for believing that special incentives for these activities are needed is the tax itself. The rules that we think of under this heading are largely aimed not at mitigating some inherent defect in the economy but at offsetting a problem created by the tax system in the first place: namely, the disincentive effect of income taxes on saving and investing. This schizophrenia reflects a serious lack of understanding about how tax rules bearing on saving and investment transactions really work. For example, I often encounter businesspeople who argue that it would be a great improvement in income tax policy if firms were allowed to write off their investment outlays immediately instead of being obliged to capitalize these expenditures and take a series of depreciation allowances over a period of years. Advocates of such a policy rarely recognize the need for a coordinated set of rules on financial transactions to go along with their preferred approach to investment. They are usually appalled at the suggestion that, if investment outlays are expensed, problems will result unless the deduction for interest is also eliminated.

My object here is to explain how one can determine what is necessary to construct rules that are consistent and to point out some problems that can occur when rules are inconsistent. In the process I am going to ask the reader to work through some moderately difficult but fascinating economic analysis.

Major Saving and Investment Incentives in the Income Tax

The term "saving incentive" usually refers to rules designed to encourage individuals to forego consumption to add to their stock of private wealth. In practice, incentives usually focus on particular forms of wealth (thus human capital is often neglected), sometimes with surprising results. We know that in the absence of international capital flows and government deficits a saving incentive would also be an investment incentive: since saving must equal investment, one cannot encourage one without encouraging the other. But net government saving creates a difference between increments to private wealth and additions to the world's capital stock. Furthermore, international capital flows create a difference between U.S. saving (public plus private) and domestic investment, that is, additions to the stock of capital located in the United States.

The term "investment incentive" typically refers to rules intended to encourage domestic investment. As in the case of saving incentives, particular forms of capital are often favored. Indeed, one of the dangers of investment policy in practice is its tendency to underrate the productivity of assets other than business equipment and structures. Assets such as business inventories and human capital are often neglected in the formation of tax policy. A bias in investment incentives toward certain types of capital may also have a specific policy justification. For example, a bias toward business capital may help to offset the tax advantage given to consumer durables (including owner-occupied homes) and household inventories under the existing income tax.

Four features of the tax system are manipulated to modify the incentives to save and invest. Although the difference between saving and investment incentives is not as sharp as is often supposed, we can categorize these four major tax features into two of each type of incentive:

- Investment incentives
    Accelerated depreciation of business investment in equipment and structures
    Investment tax credit
- Saving incentives
    Tax-sheltered retirement saving systems, including employer-sponsored pension plans, IRAs, and Keogh Plans
    Favored tax treatment of certain forms of returns to saving, including capital gains and life insurance

Another useful way to classify the features of the tax system that influence saving and investment is by the basic techniques involved. By analogy with the techniques employed to implement a consumption-type tax, I refer to as "consumption-rule incentives" either provisions that allow deduction or exclusion from the taxpayer's income of amounts saved or invested (or acceleration in time of otherwise allowable deductions), with subsequent taxation of any return flow upon realization (but no effort to tax accruing gain or earnings), or provisions that allow lighter-than-normal taxation of the return on amounts saved or invested. By the term "direct-grant incentives" I mean provisions that subsidize the purchase of assets or that supplement the return to investment in a way that is unrelated to the tax circumstances of the investor.

In the first group of consumption-rule incentives are the acceleration of depreciation allowances (an investment incentive) provided to the purchaser of qualifying assets, such as business equipment, and the deduction of contributions to an IRA (a saving incentive). In the second group are the deferral of tax on capital gains until realization, with exclusion of 60 percent of long-term capital gains and exclusion of all gains upon death of the asset owner, as well as the similar treatment of accumulation of life insurance wealth. The principal direct-grant incentive is the investment tax credit, which represents a subsidy to the purchaser of a qualifying asset in an amount that does not depend on the investor's tax rate (although it does depend on his having sufficient tax liability to claim the subsidy).

Consumption-rule incentives can be related directly to the choice between income and consumption as the principal basis for taxation. Recall that a consumption-type tax (levied at an unchanging rate over time) has the property of eliminating the tax on the return to saving. If the standard approach is taken, the saver is allowed to deduct amounts put aside; all subsequent return flows from the saved amount (including any recovery of principal) are then subject to tax. The effect of the standard approach is to make the government a partner in the saving activity, sharing both its costs and its benefits to an extent determined by the applicable tax rate. On the taxpayer's side, the pattern of outlays and receipts is the same as it would be with no tax at all (although both outlays and receipts are reduced in proportion). Under the prepayment approach, the other technique used in consumption-type taxes, the amounts put aside attract no deduction, but the subsequent return flows are exempt from tax.

Thus the first two methods of providing an incentive to save or invest involve the application of rules that deviate from good accrual-income tax principles in the direction of a consumption-based approach. Actually, if the tax system were systematically on a consumption basis, most of the rules that we think of as saving and investment incentives would be described as saving and investment *disincentives*. For example, under a consumption strategy, business outlays for equipment, structures, and inventories would be deducted immediately. Accelerated depreciation is an investment incentive only relative to the accrual-income-measurement rule that calls for deduction of the decline of asset values over time, rather than immediate deduction of cash outflows. The treatment of qualified pension saving, identified as a saving incentive, is exactly what would be called for in a consumption base and would hence not be regarded as a saving incentive under a consumption tax strategy.

Similarly, the deferral of taxation of capital gains and the exclusion of 60 percent of realized gain represent saving incentives only relative to accrual-income-measurement rules, which would require continual taxation of any accruing gain at full rates. Consumption tax rules, however, would imply no tax at all (not simply reduced tax) on the sale of an asset for which no deduction was taken at the time of acquisition.

Notice that in all these cases the degree of incentive is directly related to the applicable rate of tax. Neither an early deduction nor a reduced inclusion of returns is of any value to a taxpayer whose income tax rate is zero. This is characteristic of consumption-type saving and investment incentives. We know that in a consumption-based system the return to saving is not taxed, whereas the reward for working, inventing, and the like is taxed at graduated rates. The effect of partial and consistent implementation of consumption-rule incentives would be to shift the tax system toward a consumption base. It would proportionately reduce toward zero all tax rates on the return to saving, with a full consumption base being the limiting case.

The direct-grant approach, by contrast, provides the same degree of incentive independently of the tax rate applicable to the saver or investor. Unlike the consumption-rule incentives, the investment tax credit would be regarded as an investment incentive under either an accrual-income or a consumption tax strategy. One could imagine direct-grant saving incentives as well — for example, a bonus for deposits in a special savings account.

The difference between direct-grant and consumption-rule incentives would be largely cosmetic if it were not for the fact that different tax rates apply to different taxpayers. For example, there would be no difference between a tax credit of 10 percent on the purchase of an asset and an allowance of an extra 30 percent immediate write-off if all taxpayers were subject to a 33 percent rate of tax — the net reduction in the cost of the asset would be 10 percent in both cases. In our world of different tax rates, however, consistency of the rules applicable to saving and investment is very important. Although it poses design problems of its own, the direct-grant approach does not introduce the same sort of consistency problems that the consumption-rule approach does. For example, there is no inherent reason that interest should not be fully taxed on receipt and deducted on payment even though real assets are purchased subject to an investment tax credit. The effect of increasing the level of direct-grant incentive is to raise the after-tax return on the subsidized investment of all taxpayers relative to the before-tax return, but not to cause the after-tax returns to come closer to one another.

An example may help. Consider an investment in a machine that yields 10 percent per year before tax. A zero-bracket taxpayer receives 10 percent after tax as well; a 40 percent taxpayer receives 6 percent. Partial exclusion of the return from tax would represent a consumption-rule incentive. Fifty percent exclusion, for example, would provide the 40 percent taxpayer with an 8 percent yield after taxes (10 percent less 40 percent of 5 percent), whereas the return to the zero-bracket taxpayer would remain at 10 percent. In the limit, 100 percent exclusion would provide both taxpayers with the same return, namely, the before-tax rate of 10 percent. By contrast, if the government pays for 20 percent of the machine via a direct grant, the before-tax yield to both taxpayers is raised to 10 on 80, or 12.5 percent (2.5 percentage points in excess of the real underlying yield). This is also the after-tax return to the zero-bracket taxpayer, while the 40 percent taxpayer gets 7.5 percent (12.5 percent less 40 percent of 12.5 percent) — still 40 percent below the yield to the zero-bracket taxpayer. Whereas in the limit of the consumption-rule approach all taxpayers receive exactly the underlying return, raising the fraction of the investment paid for by direct grant further raises ⟨ the rewards to both types of taxpayer. At higher levels of the direct grant higher-bracket as well as low-bracket taxpayers obtain yields above that on the underlying asset. There is no natural limit, and no tendency for the after-tax returns to taxpayers in different brackets to converge.

Analysis of Incentives in a World without Inflation

Analyzing real-world saving and investment incentives is difficult because they usually apply to restricted classes of assets, function in an internationally open capital market, interact with rules that are grossly inadequate to deal with inflation, and are set in a system of multiple tax rates. Multiple rates are due not only to the graduated individual income tax rate schedule but also to the presence of tax-exempt or partially taxed holders of wealth (such as pension funds and life insurance companies) and corporations in very different tax situations. Nevertheless, by working through some examples, taking the complications one at a time, I hope to explain how the various saving and investment incentives work and to suggest guidelines for desirable tax policy.

One complication that cuts across all the others is inflation. I shall therefore begin by exploring how saving and investment incentives work in the absence of changes in the general price level. After working out the analysis with no inflation, I shall then explain how inflation changes the story.

Analysis of Investment Incentives in a Simple Case

To isolate clearly the way investment incentives work, suppose that in addition to no inflation there is no international financial market and just one form of real capital (call it equipment), which does not depreciate at all. Suppose the going rate of interest in the loan market is 10 percent and consider the equipment investment decision in the absence of taxes. The interest rate influences the investment that will take place because of the possibility of borrowing to purchase equipment, which is another example of arbitrage. What is being purchased is the flow of returns from the equipment, and what is being sold is a flow of interest payments on the borrowed money. Suppose that $100 worth of equipment yields more than $10 per year, say $12. Then $100 buys a flow of $12 per year. But a flow of $12 per year can be sold for $120 in the loan market; that is, by promising to deliver $12 per year, a borrower can obtain $120 now. In effect, the same thing is selling on two different markets at different prices. There is therefore an arbitrage surplus or profit to be made by buying future dollars cheap (via the equipment) and selling them dear (on the loan market).

Because the result of buying equipment with borrowed money generates a pure surplus for the investor (in this instance $20 per $100 of equipment purchased), the example describes a situation that cannot persist for long. Otherwise everyone could become a billionaire. A very powerful force is thus brought to bear. To make money in this situation, the investor does not need any personal wealth. If there is not to be an opportunity for pure profit from the arbitrage transaction, the yield on the equipment must be equal to the interest rate. Either the interest rate or the yield from buying equipment, or both, must change. If, for example, the interest rate remains at 10 percent, investment in equipment will continue to the point where the yield from owning equipment is driven down to 10 percent. The result, equality between market interest rate and rate of return on investment in equipment, is assured whether or not an individual who purchases a machine actually borrows for the purpose; it does not matter whether the equipment is "debt financed." It is enough that the potential to engage in such a transaction exists. In this way, market forces bring into equality all forms of return on saving and investing.

Adding an income tax to this story is fairly simple, provided that accrual income is properly measured. The yield from lending and the yield from owning equipment will then be taxed alike (economic depreciation is zero here). A person or corporation borrowing at 10 percent to buy $100 worth of equipment that yields 10 percent will have a gross income of $10 per year matched by an interest deduction of $10 per year. If there is a uniform 40 percent income tax, the after-tax interest rate in our example is 6 percent (10 percent less 40 percent of 10 percent), which is also the after-tax yield on the real investment in equipment. The tax thus reduces the return received by lenders, but the tendency toward equality between the market interest rate and the return on real investment is unaffected.

To consider now the effect of introducing consumption-type treatment of investment in the income tax, we must make yet a further simplifying assumption (which we shall subsequently relax), namely, that there is just one rate of tax applicable to all. For the example, suppose policymakers decide to encourage investment by permitting accelerated depreciation. Economic depreciation of the equipment is zero; another way of saying this is that depreciation allowances are postponed into the infinite future. The opposite extreme is to permit immediate expensing of the purchase of equipment — a clear case of acceleration.

The arbitrage operation is now changed a little from the previous situation because of the government's participation, which is why it may be referred to as tax arbitrage. An individual who now buys a machine for $100 obtains an income tax deduction of $100, saving $40 in tax liability. He therefore needs to borrow only $60 to obtain the machine without incurring any actual out-of-pocket expense. If the machine continues to yield $10 annually, the purchaser's annual taxable income will be $4 ($10 less $6 interest). So out of the $10.00 yield, he will pay $1.60 in tax plus $6.00 in interest, leaving $2.40 in pure surplus.

This, too, is a situation that cannot persist. The interest rate must rise or the investment in equipment must be pushed to the point that the yield is driven down, or, more likely, both. For example, the interest rate might settle down at 12 percent, and the before- and after-tax yield on equipment investment might stabilize at 7.2 percent. Then once again savers become indifferent between buying a machine, whose yield is effectively untaxed (because of the immediate write-off), and lending at the market interest rate of 12 percent and paying 40 percent in tax. Either way, the savers receive a rate of return of 7.2 percent.

Two of our simplifying assumptions — the universal tax rate of 40 percent and the choice of an asset that does not depreciate — make it easy to repeat the analysis for the case of a direct-grant incentive. An investment subsidy of 40 percent (whether or not administered in the form of a credit against tax due) will give rise to exactly the same effect as the immediate expensing: a $100 machine will cost the taxpayer only $60. The investment subsidy will thus also generate a shift in capital market equilibrium to an interest rate of 12 percent; the after-tax return to savers will be 7.2 percent, which will also equal the "social rate of return," that is, the rate of return net of subsidy on the underlying equipment investment.

Our simple example can be used to illustrate some features of investment incentives. First, such policies may indeed achieve an increase in the level of investment in real capital. They may also be expected to increase the interest rate, thereby increasing the yield to savers after the effect of the policy spreads through the economy.

Second, in the absence of international borrowing and lending, the division of the effect between capital formation and an increase in the interest rate depends on the responsiveness of the supply of savings to the rate of return. It is widely believed that private saving is rather insensitive to the rate of return on saving. In the extreme case, in which the demand for assets to hold is independent of the rate of return (that is, savings are completely *inelastic* with respect to changes in the interest rate), the entire effect of the policies in the example would have been to raise the interest rate. To restore the capital market to balance with no increase in the level of investment upon introduction of expensing or the 40 percent investment subsidy, an increase in the interest rate to $16\frac{2}{3}$ percent would have been required. At that point savers would have received a rate of return of 10 percent after taxes either in the loan market ($16\frac{2}{3}$ percent less 40 percent tax on $16\frac{2}{3}$ percent) or by purchasing equipment (10 percent effectively untaxed).

The same example also illustrates how the consumption-rule incentive — the immediate write-off of equipment — generates, for a given level of interest rate, a *larger* incentive at *higher* rates of tax. (As a review, try our pure arbitrage exercise with a tax rate of 50 percent instead of 40 percent.)[1] If the same tax rate applies to everyone, an increased tax rate also means a lower after-tax interest rate corresponding to a given before-tax interest rate. If real capital is the only form of net wealth (borrowing and lending cancel out in a closed economy), these two effects will just cancel each other. The effect of a higher tax rate is a higher interest rate, with no change in the level of investment.[2] If the interest rate did not rise, higher tax rates would tend to generate *higher* investment subsidies. Thus tax rate changes in the presence of consumption-rule incentives can have backward-seeming consequences.

The same essential point can be made in another way: with a uniform tax rate and no international capital flows, the outcome with consumption tax treatment (expensing) of all capital outlays and income tax treatment of interest (inclusion of receipts, deduction of payments) is actually the same as that which would obtain with consumption tax treatment throughout (no deduction or inclusion of interest). It is true that the interest rate on the market is higher in the case of taxation of interest than it would be without taxation of interest. (With no taxation of interest, the arbitrage argument will imply equality between the

1. The taxpayer now buys the machine with only $50 of borrowed money. The $10.00 annual yield less $5.00 annual interest implies a taxable income of $5.00 and a tax of $2.50; the net pure surplus is now up from $2.40 to $2.50 ($10.00 less $2.50 tax less $5.00 interest).

2. If we neglect the effect of the tax on other forms of income, we can see that the *only* effect of increasing the tax rate would be a sufficient increase in the interest rate to keep the after-tax level the same. Then the terms of saving and investing are exactly the same as they were before the tax change — by assumption, an equilibrium situation.

market interest rate and the return on investment in equipment.) But in the former case, for every inclusion of an interest payment in income subject to tax, there is a corresponding deduction at the same rate. The after-tax interest rate is the one relevant for individual decisions.

As I shall shortly confirm, this equivalence does *not* carry over to a world of international capital flows or to one in which different tax-payers have different marginal rates of income tax. Then to avoid undesirable portfolio effects, the depreciation rules must comport with the rules for taxing interest — in this case, no taxation of interest. With less-than-full expensing, partial taxation of interest receipts and partial deductibility of interest payments would be the appropriate rule.[3]

Consumption-Rule Incentives in More Complicated Cases

To account for some important complications, I shall first extend the analysis to a world with more than one kind of capital. Suppose, then, that there are two kinds of capital, equipment and inventories, but the consumption-rule incentive — immediate write-off — affects only equipment, with accrual-income principles continuing to apply to inventories. What happens then?

By the same reasoning applied to equipment, if inventories are accounted for according to accrual-income tax rules, investors will find it worthwhile to acquire additional inventories until the rate of return obtained just matches the rate of interest. We saw that introducing accelerated depreciation rules for equipment tended partly to increase the level of equipment investment and partly to increase the interest rate. The latter effect discourages investment in inventories. (In Chapter 9 I explained why the resulting difference between the before-tax yields on different kinds of assets causes a loss of productive efficiency.)

In the U.S. economy there are many kinds of assets that are subject to a variety of tax rules. In general, investment incentives apply to a fairly narrow subset of all assets, so the effect of increasing incentives — and this observation applies to both consumption-rule and direct-grant incentives — is partly to increase savings (by virtue of the higher after-tax interest rate) and partly to draw investment away from other sectors (for example, from owner-occupied housing to business fixed investment in the case of accelerated depreciation) and asset types (such as inventories).

3. There is no inclusion rate for intermediate degrees of write-off that provides precise consistency for all tax brackets. For details, see Bradford (1981).

The problem of consistency of the rules applied to different forms of investment becomes very clear when we relax the assumption that all taxpayers are subject to the same rate of tax. In fact, individuals are subject to tax rates ranging from zero to 50 percent on income earned directly, and their assets held indirectly by pension funds and insurance companies are subject to lesser rates, typically zero. Similarly, the tax rate on corporations ranges from zero to 46 percent. Complicating the picture further is the fact that the applicable tax rate may not be constant over time. For example, a corporation currently in a losing position is subject to a zero rate of tax, but it may anticipate having positive taxable income next year. Such situations may profoundly affect saving and investment incentives. To keep things manageable, however, I shall concentrate on how multiple rates alone (constant over time) affect the analysis.

The basic consequence of employing consumption-rule incentives in an income tax system with multiple rates is easily demonstrated by a case in which there are just two rates, zero and 40 percent. Recall that if immediate expensing of investment outlays is allowed, the market will tend to bring about equality between the rate of return on real capital and the after-tax rate of interest. Here, there are two tax rates to consider in determining the meaning of "after-tax." But the high rate of tax (in practice, the corporate tax rate) should tend to dominate this arbitrage situation.

Remember that the basic arbitrage argument involves borrowing to purchase a real asset. The relevant comparison is between the return on the real asset (after taking the tax consequences into account) and the after-tax rate of interest. The high-bracket investor will be able to make a profit as long as the after-tax return on the real asset exceeds the after-tax interest rate. The situation might settle down with the before-tax *and* after-tax yields (the same because of the immediate write-off) from investment in equipment of 7.2 percent, and with an interest rate (the before-tax but not the after-tax return on lending) of 12 percent. But the zero-bracket taxpayer can now make money by doing the opposite of the high-bracket taxpayer, namely, *selling* equipment (foregoing a return of 7.2 percent) and lending the proceeds at interest (which, by virtue of the zero tax rate, yields 12 percent). What prevents this profitable process from going on forever is the impracticability of selling more real assets than you own (note that you can sell more financial assets than you own — for example, by borrowing).

It is doubtful that many people recognize the implications of applying consumption-type rules to real investment while continuing to apply income-type rules to borrowing and lending. Accelerated-depreciation rules in a multiple-tax-rate system tend to drive the assets involved into the hands of the highest-bracket taxpayers and to induce low-bracket taxpayers (in particular, pension funds and life insurance companies) to hold their wealth in the form of nonpreferred assets and debt. This will tend to put moderate-income owners of normal businesses that employ tax-favored assets, such as apartment buildings and small manufacturing, at a competitive disadvantage compared with the same businesses in the hands of high-bracket individuals or corporations. The predictions of this simple theory are clearly borne out in practice. Rental real estate is an instance of the tendency of the rules to drive ownership into the hands of high-bracket taxpayers, an unfortunate outcome inasmuch as this asset seems ideally suited to owner-management by moderate-income individuals, including the elderly.

Extending the analysis now to allow for international capital flows is really a particular case of allowing for more than one type of capital, discussed above. Thus we would expect the introduction of accelerated-depreciation rules applicable to domestic equipment only, as in the United States, to draw funds from other assets, including net claims on foreigners. With an internationally open capital market, increases in the interest rate will attract flows from abroad (or reduce outward flows). These funds will be drawn in part from additional worldwide saving and in part from reduced foreign capital formation. (This is what happened in the aftermath of the 1981 changes in the U.S. tax law.)

To understand the effect of an open economy on the economics of investment incentives, it is convenient to work with the extreme assumption that the United States is a small actor in the world capital market, so the interest rate is not affected at all by U.S. policies. In this extreme case, *none* of the effect of investment incentives will translate into higher interest rates; the *entire* effect will be to expand capital formation in the United States. The issue to be addressed by policymakers is whether this would be a welcome development.

It is often taken for granted that domestic investment is a good thing. Therefore it is salutary to remind ourselves that the basic economics of evaluating investment opportunities extends to the acquisition of claims on the rest of the world, and that a subsidy to domestic capital formation may well *not* be an attractive policy. Consider a simple numerical example. Suppose the effect of incentives to undertake investment in the United States is to drive the before-tax rate of return to 10 percent annually, whereas the interest rate (taken to represent the return obtainable on U.S. funds used to acquire claims on foreigners) is

15 percent. Then it would be possible with no loss in current consumption to reduce the domestic capital stock by $100, foregoing $10 of annual future consumption, and to purchase a claim on $15 extra annually from foreigners. With these figures, the alternative of foreign investment at the margin is equivalent to augmenting the shifted capital resources by 50 percent.

It is sometimes argued that the increment in U.S. domestic capital has a favorable effect on U.S. workers that justifies the differential subsidy. But this argument overlooks the need to finance the subsidy. If the extra cost of the subsidy comes out of the reward to savers, one must compare it with the alternative transfer to workers that could be obtained directly (through higher taxes); otherwise one must compare the extra wages with the cost. In either case the workers can generally be made better off by a policy that equates the return to the United States from domestic and foreign investment.[4]

Direct-Grant Incentives in More Complicated Cases

Most of the discussion above extends to direct-grant incentives as well, with two important differences. One I have already stressed. The problems that occur in a system with multiple rates of tax when consumption-rule incentives are employed do not arise with direct-grant incentives in their pure form.[5] Direct-grant incentives are simply payments for engaging in activities the government wishes to encourage, and they have no connection with the tax circumstances of the recipients of the subsidy payment.

It would be helpful if this point were better understood. Commentators are often dismayed that certain companies or individuals nearly wipe out their tax liability through the use of investment tax credits. If people recognized that the investment credit is a subsidy available to all and is a payment for services rendered, much like payment for pencils delivered by a supplier or for the work effort of civil servants, they might

---

4. Recall that it will often be possible to make a gain for the United States by shifting investment to domestic forms because of the saving in foreign taxes, which are credited against U.S. tax liability. But this gain must be carefully evaluated in the context of assessing the value to the United States of the foreign tax credit institution as a whole.

5. This assumes the subsidy is independent of the tax status of the investor. Actual provisions, such as the investment tax credit, usually are conditioned in some degree on tax status (for example, the credit is only available to offset tax liability), and so they retain some of the consistency problems.

also appreciate that the credited amount has little or nothing to do with the true tax burdens borne by the taxpayers immediately affected.

Because direct-grant incentives do not raise the same problems of consistency as do consumption-rule incentives, they avoid certain complications. Yet the second difference is a source of greater complication under direct-grant incentives, namely, the necessity of calibrating the incentive properly to the durability of the acquired asset. This problem is more one of practice than an inherent property of the direct-grant approach. To illustrate, suppose there are two types of equipment, one (type A) infinitely durable and the other (type B) short-lived. The first type does not depreciate at all. The second type lasts only one year; then it falls apart. If both types yield 10 percent annually, $100 spent on asset type A gives rise to an annual return flow of $10 forever, whereas the same amount spent on asset type B generates a return flow of $110 one year hence and nothing after that. Now suppose we want to subsidize investment generally. If we give a 50 percent subsidy to purchasers of either type of asset, we markedly change the relative return to the two types. A net (after-subsidy) outlay of $50 on type A buys $10 per year forever, for a private rate of return of 20 percent. The same outlay on type B buys a gross return of $110 the following year, but the machine disappears then; by spending $50 per year on type B, a net annual flow of $60 can be sustained forever, for a private rate of return of 110 percent. The subsidy thus results in an enormous shift in incentives in favor of the short-lived asset.

The reason such a shift is undesirable is that when the subsidy has been fully incorporated into production arrangements, there will be a sharp difference in the social rates of return (the before-tax rates of return) on investment in short-lived and long-lived equipment. This is, once again, the problem of inefficient allocation of investment. The remedy is to calibrate the amount of the subsidy to the durability of the asset. The approach adopted in U.S. practice in the case of the investment tax credit is to apply a higher rate on long-lived than on short-lived equipment. The actual calibration, however, is extremely crude. There is a much simpler way of providing a direct-grant subsidy that automatically gives a neutral stimulus to investments of different durabilities, extending even to inventories. What is required is an annual subsidy based on the *stock* of affected assets.

In our example of asset types A and B, an annual grant equal to 10 percent of the value of stocks would provide the purchaser of $100 worth of asset type A with $10 per year forever; the purchaser of $100 of asset type B would receive $10 in the first year, and nothing after that. For both types of asset the private rate of return would be increased by 10 percentage points. The relative advantage of the two types of asset would have been unaffected by the choice of subsidy rate. Put more technically, the market's tendency to produce the same private (after-tax) return on all assets would have been harnessed to generate the equality of social rates of return desired for efficient resource use.

The Achilles' heel of this method is the same as that of accrual-income measurement generally: the need for accurate estimates of the value of assets. An annual subsidy of the sort described would presumably be calculated from the adjusted basis of assets, that is, from their value after deducting the accumulation of depreciation allowances and making any allowable correction for inflation. The neutrality of the resulting rule would depend on the adequacy of the allowances and adjustments. But even quite inadequate estimates would be greatly superior to existing techniques of coordinating the direct-grant investment incentive to asset durability.

Consumption-Rule Saving Incentives

Investment incentives can be understood as rules making it profitable for taxpayers to shift their portfolios in favor of real assets and against interest-bearing assets. Saving incentives generally work much the same way except that the opportunity is created to profit by shifting from one form of financial asset to another. But the fact that the same natural limiting mechanism that obtains in the case of investment incentives (the limited number of real investment opportunities) is ineffective in the case of arbitrage among financial assets has profound implications for the design and effectiveness of saving incentives.

For some reason, the saving incentives found in U.S. law are of the consumption-rule variety. One major example is the set of special provisions applicable to capital gains, which (generally) results in a partial exclusion of the reward to saving. This important and controversial issue will be discussed separately later. For now, let us examine the principles underlying standard consumption-rule saving incentives. The IRA provides an excellent example. The standard consumption-base rules call for deduction of amounts saved, no taxation of the accruing yield from the total sum put aside, and full taxation of any amounts withdrawn from savings — exactly the rules applicable to an IRA.

Such savings incentives are subject to most of the same difficulties as consumption-rule investment incentives, but there is an important additional problem. In the case of investment incentives, there are limits to the amount of the subsidized asset that can be purchased — only so many apartment buildings, for example. In the case of saving incentives, typically there is no difference between the asset purchased and the liability that may be issued to finance the purchase. Thus, as many people have noticed, the rules do not inhibit individuals from reducing other forms of saving or from borrowing for purposes of making deposits to an IRA. These other forms of saving are not accorded consumption-type treatment. The result is an opportunity for pure arbitrage profit. Simply by changing the composition of his portfolio, but not its total value or even its risk characteristics, the taxpayer can save on taxes.[6]

For example, suppose an individual holds $1000 in a money-market fund yielding 10 percent, on which he pays income tax at a rate of 40 percent. By shifting $1000 into an IRA, he saves $400 in income taxes; if the $400 tax saving is retained in the money-market fund, the transaction will have no effect on his current consumption. One year later the money-market fund will show a balance of $440 and the IRA a balance of $1100 (assuming the IRA is also invested in the same money-market fund). The taxpayer now withdraws the entire balance of $1100 from the IRA, resulting in a tax liability of $440; to which must be added $16 in tax on the money-market interest of $40. He is left with $1084, a figure that should be compared with the $1060 ($1000 plus $100 interest less $40 tax on the interest) he would have if he had simply left the money in the money-market fund. The difference, $24, can be thought of as the tax saved on the interest on the $600 representing the taxpayer's share of the $1000 deposited to the IRA; the other $400 of the initial IRA balance was contributed by the government in reduced current tax liability.

That seems like a reasonable return for doing nothing but shifting balances around, and it would look much better yet if we were to repeat the calculations for a twenty-year postponement of tax instead of a one-year postponement. Why not do more of it? The first problem is that the individual may not have any more in the money-market fund. That problem can be overcome to a degree by borrowing. Because the IRA should provide good collateral for a loan, borrowing against it should be easy. If the (tax-deductible) interest rate on the loan were the same as that on the money-market fund, the calculations above would continue to apply. If the borrowing rate were less advantageous, the

---

6. The text describes a rational individual who calculates the consequences carefully. Perhaps equally likely is the individual who will see the current tax saving as a windfall and fail to anticipate the future tax increase implied by a current addition to tax-sheltered savings; see Galper and Toder (1984).

arbitrage profit from the operation would be lower but probably still attractive for a taxpayer at the 40 percent marginal rate.

In some cases the tax law attempts to impede such arbitrage. It is very difficult to draw up rules to prevent someone from transferring existing savings into an IRA or equivalent plan. It at least appears possible, however, to limit the use of borrowed funds for that purpose, either by prohibiting the pledging of IRA assets as collateral or through limiting the deductibility of interest on borrowing to acquire or hold a tax-preferred financial asset. Rules of either sort are hard to administer fairly, inasmuch as it is difficult to determine what the true purpose of borrowing is or to observe the true collateral on a loan.

The other technique used to limit the extent of pure tax arbitrage is to place a ceiling on the amount that may be deducted in a given period. In the case of IRAs the ceiling is currently $2000 for each earner ($2250 for a one-earner married couple); in the case of most other retirement saving schemes, the limit is related to the amount of earnings, sometimes with an absolute ceiling as well. To the extent that workers are able (through borrowing or offsetting changes in other forms of saving) to maintain the same level of consumption as they would in the absence of the saving incentives while still maximally exploiting the tax shelter, all that is accomplished is a reduced level of taxation. For individuals who are constrained by the ceiling, the price effect of the provision is nullified; for them, the incentive to save at the margin is the same as it would be in the absence of any special rule at all.

The IRA is, of course, but one of several retirement saving incentives. Much the most important is the provision for employer-sponsored pension saving. The fundamentals of the entire set of policies are rarely examined. I have mentioned the question of the degree to which it is actually possible to induce saving specifically for retirement purposes. Perhaps more curious is the fact that the strongest incentives are aimed at those who would presumably need them least in the absence of the income tax, namely, those with high marginal tax rates. Low-income individuals are not discouraged much by the tax on savings (because their tax rates are low), and they receive little encouragement from saving incentives that take the form of tax exemption. To extend the incentive to low-income workers, an elaborate system of "nondiscrimination" rules applies to employer-sponsored pensions, the effect of which is to make high-bracket employees pay something for their retirement tax advantage in the form of a subsidy to pensions for low-income workers. One might think it would make more sense to put all workers on a consumption-type basis and to provide a direct-grant subsidy (or

Social Security benefits) for low-income individuals. The existing system is an example of a complicated machine devised to do a simple job.

Capital Gains

The current rules for taxing capital gains constitute a saving incentive in the context of an accrual-type income tax. As in the case of accelerated depreciation, the special treatment of capital gains would be described as a saving *disincentive* in the context of a consumption approach. The deferral of tax and the exclusion of part of the gain for assets held a sufficient period have the effect of partially implementing the tax-prepayment approach to a consumption-type tax (under which the purchase of an asset is not deducted and the return flow is not taxed).

The same sorts of arbitrage arguments already described apply to capital gains. The forces generated by the power of compounding may be surprisingly strong when the relevant rates of return are at all significant. The advantage of deferral alone, quite apart from the reduced rate applicable to long-term gains, can be very large and remains so even at relatively modest tax rates. For example, suppose a taxpayer in the 25 percent bracket could borrow $1000 at 15 percent interest, using the proceeds to purchase an asset on which the yield is at the same level but in the form of an accruing capital gain rather than a flow of cash. Each year for twenty years the taxpayer borrows a little bit more, enough to cover the interest on the accumulating loan, less the saving due to the deduction of the interest paid from taxable income. At the end of twenty years he liquidates the capital gain asset and pays off the loan.

In this example, which assumes annual compounding, the taxpayer has undertaken no new saving but merely exchanged a liability for an asset, both having the same yield before taxes but different tax treatments. Because the interest is deductible currently, the balance in the loan account after twenty years will be $8433; the value of the capital gain asset will be $16,366. After paying a 25 percent tax on the gain of $15,366 and repaying the loan balance, the taxpayer is left with a surplus of $4092. Since no actual saving or investing was undertaken, this surplus represents the tax lost to the Treasury from the combination of transactions.

This looks like a nice return on doing nothing but reallocating the taxpayer's portfolio. Once again, the question is: Why not do it some more? The answer is in part the limited availability of underlying real assets that generate returns qualifying as capital gains under the tax rules. But one might think that capital gain assets could be created by clever taxpayers through repackaging of existing financial assets, and one would be right. For example, instead of issuing a bond that pays annual interest, a borrower might issue a bond that pays no interest at all but sells at a discount. The lender thus receives his return in the form of the difference between the buying and the selling prices of the bond, a difference that one might expect to qualify for capital gains treatment.

The process, however, is not quite as straightforward as might be supposed. In the first place, the example gives only one taxpayer's view of the transactions. If the asset is acquired from another taxpayer, who provides the loan to balance out the transaction, all tax effects would cancel each other if that other taxpayer were subject to the same marginal tax rate. To make money by reshuffling financial assets alone requires taxpayers in different tax circumstances. This first condition is, of course, fulfilled, especially in view of the huge holdings of tax-exempt pension savings plans.

In the second place, the taxpayers must deal with intricate rules designed to inhibit the recharacterization of the return on an asset from an accrual to a deferred-realization basis. For example, users of the "original issue discount" technique (the name for the transaction just described) have long been required to impute an annual flow of interest between lender and borrower for income tax purposes. The 1984 tax act's provisions relating to imputed interest represent the latest addition to the arsenal of protections against such conversion of what the tax jargon calls "ordinary income" to capital gains.

The net effect of the system of rules is to permit at a given time a certain balance between returns characterized as ordinary income and those characterized as capital gains. Much as the consumption-type investment incentives tend to diminish the rate of return on the favored assets and drive their ownership into the hands of more highly taxed taxpayers, so the types of financial assets qualifying for capital gains may be expected to have a lower before-tax return (adjusting for risk) than the fully taxable interest-paying assets and to be owned primarily by high-bracket taxpayers. The net effect is in part a reduction in tax on high-bracket and low-bracket taxpayers alike and a more or less strong effect on the composition of their portfolios.

Although the special rules regarding capital gains can be usefully studied as a general saving subsidy in the context of an accrual-income tax, they are also widely viewed as furthering other social objectives, in particular the encouragement of risk taking. We may well ask why there is an interest in encouraging individuals to accept risk. After all, we would probably not regard it as a good thing if the tax rules encouraged gambling. Instead, the policy debate concerns the good sort of risk taking, the inventive effort that leads to new products and processes. It is an interesting question whether the discouraging effect of taxes in this sphere is any worse than in others — such as the application of work effort. Whatever the merits of offering an incentive, we may inquire how the capital gains rules affect the calculus of private gain and loss in a risky world.

The capital gains rules offer particular advantages in connection with risky assets. The basic mechanism is the choice given the taxpayer of the timing of realization. In this case, for the rules to have an incentive effect there is no requirement that taxpayers on the two sides of a transaction have different marginal rates.

Suppose, for example, an investor can find two assets, both risky, neither expected to pay any cash dividend over the foreseeable future and having the further special property that whenever one unexpectedly rises in price by 1 percent the other falls in price by 1 percent. Technically, such assets are said to have returns that are "perfectly negatively correlated." (If droughts tend to make the value of farm land fall and that of beach property rise, the prices of these two assets will be negatively correlated. Matching long and short positions on a share of common stock will yield essentially perfectly negatively correlated returns.) Normally we would say it made little sense to buy equal dollar amounts of the two assets, because the investor would be certain of no gain at all from holding the package: any gain on one asset would be exactly offset by a loss on the other. Application of the standard capital gains calculation for tax purposes changes the story, however. Investors who buy equal-value amounts of the two securities could (by selling it) realize their losses on the asset that declines in value, and (by holding on to it) postpone realization of the gains on the asset that rises in value. If the proceeds of the sale of the asset that falls in price are applied to the purchase of a similar asset, the investors will maintain positions of no net risk, simply carrying forward equal values of the exactly matching assets. Along the way, though, they derive tax savings by reporting the capital losses on their tax returns. By appropriately rolling over similar transactions, an indefinite deferral of recognition of gain would be possible, including deferral to a taxpayer's death, at which point the tax on the winning side of the transaction would be forgiven altogether. Complex rules have been developed to inhibit such transactions (for example, such literally offsetting positions in financial instruments are, in effect, consolidated under the income tax rules and taxed at a special rate on an accrual basis). But portfolio diversification permits the tax-payer to obtain substantial advantages from a realize-the-losers, defer-the-gainers strategy.

This strategy becomes even more effective as a result of the differential between short-term and long-term capital gains rates. For example, a 50 percent–bracket taxpayer could take offsetting positions on a risky asset. Suppose it were to fall in value by $1.00 in six months. By realizing the losing position, the taxpayer would obtain a deduction of $1.00 (short-term loss), for a tax saving of $0.50. A day later he could realize the winning position, which would lead to extra taxable income of $0.40 (40 percent of the $1.00 long-term gain) and an extra tax of $0.20. The taxpayer comes out $0.30 ahead on the deal, having undertaken no net saving and borne virtually no risk (because of fully offsetting positions, apart from the one day separating the two realization transactions).

The makers of tax law have not been oblivious to such possibilities and have written inhibiting rules. Thus the rules require a degree of consolidation of long-term and short-term gains and losses within a year. To pursue this strategy, therefore, the taxpayer must time transactions carefully and alternate years of long-term gains and years of short-term losses. Also, the limitation on the deduction of capital losses (currently $3000) in any one year keeps in bounds the payoff to the realize-the-losers, defer-the-gainers strategy. Of course, it also limits the ability of the taxpayer who is not playing realization games, but has simply suffered a loss, to reflect his real circumstances in his tax return.

Because of all these complexities, it is difficult to reach a summary judgment about the effect that the capital gains rules have on the incentive to save in the context of income-type rules on borrowing and lending at interest. A reasonable conclusion would seem to be that the capital gains rules moderate the burden of the income tax on deferral of consumption. But the fact that interest income remains an alternative use of funds (either interest received from lending or interest paid on borrowing) for all taxpayers (meaning that the after-tax interest rate is always the relevant rate of return at the margin) introduces doubt about the conclusion.

The capital gains rules have often been credited with encouraging entrepreneurs in the emerging high-technology fields. Economic analysis supports this common view, although the mechanism is probably not very well understood, nor is it widely appreciated that what is involved is not so much light taxation of the return on investment in the risky new industry as it is light taxation of the returns to innovation or invention that would normally be classified as rewards to work effort ("labor income").

Here is how it works: Suppose an individual has a bright idea for a new computer software product that he thinks will have a tremendous market value once developed and appropriately converted to a marketable property (such as by establishment of a patent, copyright, or trademark). If he were to carry out the necessary steps, write the programs, obtain the patents, and so forth and then sell the valuable property to a major software publisher, which has a much greater capability to market the product, his sales proceeds would be taxed as ordinary income. To avoid this heavy tax he forms a corporation in which he is the sole shareholder and which pays him some nominal salary while he carries out the development effort. Once the effort is completed, he sells all his shares in the company he created to the major software publisher; but this time, because he has held the shares for more than six months, only 40 percent of the sales proceeds are included in his income.

Two aspects of this example deserve emphasis. First, the reward in question is to the individual for his ideas and creative effort, not for his investment of funds. (Typically, of course, money is needed too; the example purposely emphasizes the creative and entrepreneurial effort.) Second, the reason there is any special preference at all created by the capital gains rules is the accrual-income-tax ideal. The ultimate sales of software by the publisher *will* be taxed in full as ordinary income. If the entrepreneur were as well equipped as the major publisher to market the results of his own idea, he could obtain exactly the same preference — in fact, do somewhat better — by marketing it himself. That is because the income-measurement rules do not adequately capture the accrual of wealth that he or his company experiences at the moment it becomes clear that his idea is going to pay off. All that the capital gains preference accomplishes is to enable him to do almost as well by selling out as he could by retaining the property and developing it himself *if* he had the same marketing skills as the major publisher.

The Effects of Inflation

One of the most complicating factors involved in the interaction between taxes and saving and investment is inflation. In Chapter 3 we explored the way the taxation of interest is affected under inflationary conditions, which sharply increase the incentive for high-bracket taxpayers to borrow and may actually improve the real after-tax return to lending attained by low-bracket taxpayers. In that instance, it was assumed that the interest rate adjusts roughly 1 percentage point for each percentage point of anticipated inflation. Unfortunately, the adjustment of interest rates to inflation is neither so regular nor so predictable (see Summers, 1983).

It is beyond the scope of this book to investigate in depth the effect of inflation on saving and investing. (For an extended study, see Feldstein, 1983.) The issues, however, can be briefly addressed here. In the absence of taxes, we would expect anticipated inflation to have only minor implications for saving and investment. In the equipment investment example, substituting an anticipated 5 percent annual inflation rate for the assumption of a steady price level would imply as well that the investment would yield a return in terms of current dollars (the *nominal* return) that grows at 5 percent a year instead of a steady $10 per year indefinitely. Similarly, in a no-tax world we would expect that the interest rate would increase from 10 percent with no inflation to 15 percent with 5 percent inflation. As a little experimentation with figures should confirm, such a shift would not have any effect on incentives to save and invest and would leave no scope for arbitrage profit by buying machines and selling bonds.

As we know, however, taxation of nominal interest upsets the picture. But even the taxation of interest could be offset through a further adjustment in the rate of interest if all taxpayers were in the same tax bracket. For example, with a uniform 30 percent tax on interest, an adjustment of the rate of interest from 10 percent in the absence of inflation to just over 17 percent would neutralize the effect of 5 percent annual inflation. With such an adjustment, the lender obtains a nominal after-tax return of 12 percent (17 percent minus 30 percent of 17 percent) and an after-tax real return (adjusting for inflation) of 7 percent (12 percent minus 5 percent inflation). The borrower, similarly, pays a net-of-tax real interest rate of 7 percent. When various tax rates apply in the taxpayer population, no such uniform adjustment of interest rates can offset inflation in this way.

The rules that apply to real investment are also upset by inflation. The key features are the rules specifying depreciation allowances and the calculation of capital gains. Indexing both depreciation allowances and the capital gains basis would eliminate the bias created by inflation. If combined with correction of interest inclusion and deduction (no simple task), indexing could also, in principle, render insensitive to variation in the rate of inflation the real tax liabilities imposed on taxpayers in given real circumstances. But neither sort of correction has been a feature of U.S. tax law. Instead, lawmakers have sought to offset the effect of inflation by investment incentives.

Without any change in the rules for depreciation and capital gains, an increase in inflation clearly puts an extra tax on the return to investment. Our earlier capital equipment example is inappropriate here because that machine was assumed not to depreciate at all. Consider, instead, a machine whose output declines by just 10 percent a year. In other words, ten one-year-old machines are exactly as effective in production as nine new machines. The economic depreciation of such a machine follows a simple declining-balance path: in the absence of inflation the true depreciation allowances for a $100.00 machine would be $10.00 in the first year, $9.00 in the second, $8.10 in the third, and so on. Thus the person who spends $1000 on machines and then $100 per year ever after on replacement machines will be able to maintain the original level of capacity forever. If the $1000 worth of machines generates $200 in gross revenues, and if the taxpayer is allowed the $100 annual depreciation allowance on his collection of machines of various ages, taxpayers in all brackets will be indifferent between buying machines for $1000 and lending $1000 at 10 percent interest. Either way, the tradeoff between current and future dollars is figured on the basis of a real after-tax rate of return that ranges from 10 percent for the zero-bracket taxpayer down to 5 percent for the 50 percent taxpayer. An implication of these figures is that there is no possibility for arbitrage profit by borrowing to purchase machines.

Enter inflation at 5 percent per year, so that the same collection of machines produces a gross product that grows in nominal value at 5 percent annually ($210.00, $220.50, $231.50, and so on). Because the price of machines grows along with the output price, the outlay needed to maintain the collection of machines also grows at 5 percent a year ($105.00, $110.30, $115.80, and so on). But the tax law no longer allows a depreciation deduction to match the actual outlays required to offset the decline in value of the stock of machines over the year. Instead, the allowance is based on the historical cost of the asset. If the original investment program were followed, it is true that the depreciation allowances would slowly rise as (nominally) more expensive machines slowly replaced the older machines, but the current allowance would always lag behind the actual loss in value of the capital stock. Consequently, the taxpayer would appear to the tax collector to be more profitable than was actually the case, and a business that was originally providing a real after-tax return ranging from 10 percent (for the zero-bracket taxpayer) down to 5 percent (for the 50 percent taxpayer) would now provide a return ranging from 10 percent (for the zero-bracket taxpayer) down to 3.7 percent (for the 50 percent taxpayer). In effect, inflation has raised the high-bracket tax applicable to this form of real investment from 50 percent to 63 percent.

The situation gets more complicated when we consider other possible inflation rates and other types of capital that depreciate at a slower rate of perhaps 2 percent a year (as structures do, for example) or at a faster rate of perhaps 30 percent a year (as computers do). Table 10–1 shows the real rate of return received after taxes by a 50 percent–bracket investor in capital of various proportional rates of depreciation, at various rates of inflation, where the taxable income calculation is based on the true depreciation rate but applied to the historical purchase price of the asset. At high-enough rates of inflation, the effective tax on real investment by the taxpayer nominally in the 50 percent bracket actually exceeds 100 percent.

The main response to the problem illustrated in Table 10–1 has been to use accelerated depreciation as an inflation correction. For this particular instance, it is possible to adjust the depreciation allowances to

Table 10–1. Real after-tax return and effective tax rates on investment in capital of various durabilities at various inflation rates under historical cost depreciation (percent; effective tax rates in parentheses)

Declining-balance depreciation rate	Inflation rate		
	5	10	30
2	4.6 (54)	4.4 (56)	4.2 (58)
10	3.7 (63)	2.8 (72)	1.4 (86)
30	3.0 (70)	1.4 (86)	−2.9 (129)

Note: The investor's nominal tax bracket is 50 percent; the assumed before-tax rate of return is 10 percent. Entries show the annual rate of return after taxes and after taking inflation into account; effective tax rates, in parentheses, are the ratio of the difference between pretax and posttax returns to the pretax return. The calculations are based on continuous compounding.

offset the effect of steady inflation for a given tax bracket. Here depreciation for any asset can be described by a simple declining-balance rate: 2 percent annually (a long-lived asset), 10 percent, 30 percent, and so on. For 5 percent inflation, the effective tax rate will be restored to 50 percent for the 50 percent taxpayer by allowing instead double-declining-balance depreciation (4 percent, 20 percent, 60 percent, and so on). In this way an exact correction can be provided for very narrowly defined circumstances (for technical details, see Bradford, 1981). Unfortunately, the exact correction for one set of circumstances will be inappropriate for others. For example, other inflation rates will require a different set of allowances for the simple-declining-balance investment. Inflation at 10 percent would call for triple declining balance; inflation at 30 percent, sevenfold declining balance. Furthermore, different corrections would be necessary for different marginal tax rates, for patterns of depreciation other than simple declining balance, and for different assumptions about the true underlying real rate of return. For example, if the true real interest rate were 5 percent instead of the rather high 10 percent assumed in my figures, the corrective factors for 5 percent, 10 percent, and 30 percent inflation would be 3, 5, and 13, respectively.

The calculations done thus far indicate the way accelerated depreciation may be used, not as an extra incentive to invest, but merely to offset the effects of inflation. I have focused on the tradeoff between current and future dollars obtainable through the mechanism of acquiring real productive capital. But I have neglected the alternative method available to the taxpayer, namely, borrowing and lending, and have thus not yet taken into account the arbitrage possibilities stressed earlier. How are these possibilities affected by inflation?

The analytical dilemma is illustrated by a well-known argument in the tax policy context. It is often pointed out that, although high-bracket individuals (or corporations) do experience an increase in effective taxation on real investment when historical depreciation rules are applied in a time of inflation, they have the advantage of being able to borrow with deductible interest at rates that often work out to be negative after the tax saving is taken into account. The basic point is correct. As noted earlier, when the rate of interest reacts to the rate of inflation by increasing roughly one point for each point of inflation, the incentives for the high-bracket taxpayer to borrow increase markedly. It may well be that the high-bracket taxpayer can make a profit by the arbitrage between debt and real capital even when the yield from the real investment is badly mismeasured by such practices as historical cost depreciation. Indeed, the remarkable fact is that if the interest adjustment for inflation is exactly point for point, eliminating the opportunity for arbitrage profit requires a *reduction* from historical cost depreciation.

We can see this most easily in the case of an asset that does not depreciate at all (a railroad tunnel, perhaps). With an interest rate of 10 percent, for example, a $1000 investment in a railroad tunnel would have to yield $100 per year to eliminate the opportunity to make money by borrowing a 10 percent to buy the asset. Now suppose inflation sets in at 5 percent a year. The value of what is produced by the asset will also begin to grow at 5 percent a year in nominal terms, as will the price of tunnels. There continues to be no real depreciation on an investment in a tunnel because its real value stays constant over time. The 50 percent–bracket purchaser of a $1000 tunnel gets a stream of annual returns after taxes that is actually the same as before when measured in initial-period purchasing power, namely, $50 per year ($100 less $50 tax).

The real after-tax interest rate under our assumption, however, falls from 5 percent (10 percent less 5 percent tax) to 2.5 percent (15 percent less 7.5 percent tax less 5 percent per year loss in purchasing power of the dollars owed). There is thus pure arbitrage profit to be made by borrowing to purchase a tunnel. Eliminating the profit opportunity would require a *cut* in depreciation allowances, in this case from zero to a *negative* 5 percent (so that the after-tax return on the $1000 investment in a tunnel falls from $50 to $25: $100 in receipts less tax on the sum of the $100 in receipts and $50 "negative depreciation").

In fact, it can be shown that for assets that would fall in value according to a declining-balance pattern, eliminating the profitability of borrowing to finance the purchase of assets would require *subtracting* the rate of inflation from the declining-balance rate allowed for tax purposes, always provided the interest rate adjusts point for point to the rate of inflation (see Bradford, 1981). The picture emerges of a situation in which inflation creates a disincentive to save (because of the low or negative after-tax interest rate) and an incentive to undertake investment financed by borrowing.

We are hampered in reaching conclusions about the interaction of inflation and taxes by the lack of a satisfactory explanation for the observed relationship between interest rates and inflation rate. The coexistence of accelerated depreciation with an interest rate that adjusts less than one point for each point of inflation ought to have produced very strong incentives for the issue of debt to purchase real assets. The simplifications adopted here, which include neglect of the risk characteristics of investment projects and of debt instruments, no doubt have much to do with the fact that the observed movements, while large, were not extreme (in other countries, debt finance is even more widespread than it is in the United States). Regrettably we are thrown back on analytical descriptions such as those provided by Jorgenson and Sullivan (1981) and King and Fullerton (1983), which tell us that the tax system in its present form provides an extraordinary array of incentives for saving and investing that are sensitive to the type of real asset acquired, its mode of financing, the industrial sector within which it is used, and the characteristics of the ultimate savers, but that do not completely spell out the mechanism by which the effects of the often-inconsistent rules are brought into economic balance.

Reform of Saving and Investment Incentives

The following three themes relevant to reform of the treatment of saving and investment may seem like mere technicalities to the layperson. Yet I would argue that few design matters are more important to the long-run stability and satisfactory functioning of the tax system.

Coordinating the Treatment of Real Investment and Interest

The first theme is the need to coordinate the tax treatment of real investment and interest. As we know, accrual-income accounting calls for the use of economic depreciation, that is, depreciation allowances that track the value of assets over time. The depreciation deduction in a given year will ideally match the decline of an asset's value in that year (and if the asset actually increases in value, as so often happens with real estate, the accrual-income deduction would be negative). Corresponding to economic depreciation accounting for real assets is accrual accounting for capital gains, full taxation of inflation-corrected interest received, and full deduction of inflation-corrected interest paid. These rules correspond to full taxation of the return to saving and investing and give rise to neither distortion of investment allocation among assets of various types and durabilities nor distortion of saver portfolios. Even in the context of rules that imperfectly achieve taxation of such assets as consumer durables and owner-occupied homes, there is a good case for seeking neutrality among other elements of the wealth stock. The effective tax rate calculations of King and Fullerton (1984), mentioned earlier, provide a graphic reminder of the waste generated by failure to coordinate taxation of different forms of saving, and the high visibility of tax-sheltering activity reminds us of the cost in terms of political support and morale.

The consumption strategy provides another set of guideposts. The cash-flow accounting treatment of real investment — that is, immediate expensing of investment outlays in calculating income subject to tax — has frequently been endorsed. The degree of approximation of the combination of ACRS and investment credit provisions of existing law to the results that would obtain under a simple regime of expensing business outlays is taken by many observers as a sensible policy criterion. But there is rather little appreciation of the mischief that results from the combination of depreciation provisions appropriate for a consumption-type tax with interest provisions appropriate for an accrual-income tax. In the context of a graduated-rate system, extreme pressure on the way taxpayers hold their wealth and strong incentives to engage in the arbitrage transactions associated with tax shelters are the consequence.

Consistent accounting for real and financial transactions would contribute greatly to efficiency (as well as to simplicity and to the perceived equity of the tax system). Exemption of interest from tax (no inclusion and no deduction) corresponds to full write-off of real investment. Inconsistent treatment is a recipe for endless efforts to defeat the irresistible forces of tax arbitrage that would be better deployed to further, rather than oppose, effective use of resources. There is no theoretically pure partial treatment of interest income and expense to correspond to the sort of partial write-off of real investment embodied in rules such as ACRS. But there is little doubt that an approximation could be developed that would improve significantly upon the status quo.[7]

Making the System Inflation-Proof

The second theme is the need to make the rules impervious to changes in the rate of price inflation. The inflation correction required is not the adjustment of exemptions and income tax brackets that has now become a welcome feature of U.S. income tax law. The issue here is the measurement of the consequences of saving and investment. To avoid capricious effects of taxes on the allocation of investment requires that depreciation allowances and capital gain calculations be corrected for

7. The correct interest exclusion corresponding to a given partial rate of expensing of real assets depends on the applicable marginal tax rate; higher-bracket taxpayers require a larger exclusion to maintain the desired portfolio neutrality. For details, see Bradford (1981).

the change in the dollar measuring rod that occurs under inflation. Equally important, and more difficult, is correction of the taxation of interest payments and receipts. In an inflationary environment, part of what is normally labeled interest income is actually a repayment of principal and should therefore be neither deducted by the payer nor taxed to the payee under an accrual-income tax. Failure to make the needed correction in this element of the income-measurement system can result in strong distortional incentives.

Consumption-type taxes offer a significant advantage in dealing with inflation. Because outlays for equipment, structures, and inventories are immediately expensed at the time they are incurred, the tax allowance is measured in the same dollars as the real activity. Similarly, under consumption-type rules capital gains are either ignored (the tax-prepayment approach) or are accounted for on a cash-flow basis, which again provides for measurement of both the base and its tax consequences in current dollars. Much the same comment applies to interest. Interest-yielding assets and liabilities are dealt with on a cash-flow basis in the context of qualified accounts or cash-flow-type company tax rules; alternatively, interest payments and receipts are ignored in the tax calculation. In either case the results are automatically correctly adjusted for inflation.

Correctly Relating Investment Incentives to Asset Durability

The third theme in our discussion has been the desirability of correctly relating investment incentives to the durability of acquired assets. Under accrual-income accounting a deduction is made each year to allow for the loss in value of assets used during the year. In the nature of the case, the deductions will vary with the durability of assets, because (by definition) long-lived assets decline more slowly in value than do short-lived assets. If the allowances for tax purposes are not correctly related to those called for by accrual-income measurement, taxpayers are led to make inefficient choices of assets for use in production. The result is unnecessary waste.

Consumption-type rules call for immediate expensing of asset acquisition, a procedure that automatically provides the correct calibration of allowances to durability (including the allowances for inventory accumulation). Investment incentives, such as ACRS, that amount to a halfway point between accrual-income and consumption rules must deal with the problem of correlating allowances to durability. Although the most pressing needs are to coordinate investment rules with the treatment of interest paid and received and to adjust the system for inflation, an important further question is whether the investment allowances are sufficiently finely related to asset durability.

Direct-grant provisions, such as the investment tax credit, represent an alternative way to provide investment incentives. Since these provisions can be constructed, in effect, as simple subsidy programs, they do not necessarily raise the same problems of coordination of the real and financial aspects of saving and investment taxation. Investment-grant programs could even be added to a consumption-type tax system (which provides automatically for neutrality with respect to saving and investment but does not automatically provide a relative subsidy to domestic capital formation) if it is decided that special incentives for domestic investment are desirable. These rules do have to deal with the problem of relating the grant to the durability of the acquired asset. Existing provisions that give a reduced rate of credit to short-lived assets illustrate that basic approach, although the present degree of discrimination is very crude, and it neglects altogether the problem of subsidizing inventories.

A natural way to implement a set of investment incentives correctly calibrated for durability would be to pay an annual amount (whether it is in the form of a credit against tax is unimportant) equal to a simple percentage of the stock of capital recorded in the depreciation accounts. (In technical terms, the subsidy would be calculated as a percentage of the taxpayer's aggregate basis in depreciable assets.) If economic depreciation is the principle on which allowances are based, this approach will automatically provide for correct calibration of incentives to durability. By adding a similar set of accounts for inventories, it would be a simple matter to extend the same principle to that major piece of the domestic capital stock.

Much attention is given in policy discussions to the *front-loaded* character of both the investment credit and ACRS. The economic analysis of the investment decision in this book has stressed the present value of incentives over the life of an investment and has downplayed the importance of timing as such. The suggested policy, however, would shift the timing of the payment of the investment subsidy toward the future, a feature that makes it attractive to politicians (who seem to worry more about present budget deficits than about future ones) and unattractive to business advocates (who, for various reasons, favor subsidies that are paid early).

Tax Expenditures **11**

But I was thinking of a plan
  To dye one's whiskers green
And always use so large a fan
  That they could not be seen.

Lewis Carroll, *Through the Looking Glass*

WHEN the salaries of officers in the armed forces are raised, we note the consequence as an increase in annual expenditures in the federal budget. When, instead, officers are permitted to exclude the value of government-provided housing from income subject to tax, the consequence is a reduction in revenue in the budget, year after year. Although the revenue cost of tax-free housing would be considered at the time of enacting the tax statute, this annual tax revenue loss would not be recorded in the traditional budget framework.

The two policies are identical in their objective: both improve the officers' financial terms of employment. Since the two policies have the same objective, they should be analyzed in the same terms. We should not use one set of criteria for the case in which the policy leads to a recorded annual expenditure and another when the policy leads to an unrecorded diminution in revenue from the tax system. This simple proposition motivates the concept of tax expenditure, the revenue foregone from the presence rather than the absence of specific provisions in the structure of tax rules. The tax expenditure figure is intended to be comparable to the measure of cost we would normally associate with a spending program.

The tax expenditure concept was introduced to U.S. tax policy discourse by Stanley S. Surrey, who was assistant secretary of the Treasury for tax policy in the Kennedy and Johnson administrations (see Surrey, 1973). To many people the idea that *not* taxing something is equivalent to spending smacks unpleasantly of the presumption that everything belongs to the state. But it would hardly be possible to make sensible decisions about tax provisions without regard to their revenue consequences. To make the cost of achieving some objective through the use of tax provisions comparable to the cost of alternative methods that require direct budgetary outlays is not itself to express a judgment about the desirability of the policy. Nor does it necessarily imply a position on the merits of provisions to recognize that their effects are comparable to those that might be attained through spending programs.

A tax expenditure figure is nothing more than a revenue estimate and therefore should not be controversial. Assembling an official list of tax expenditures, however, almost inevitably does court controversy. The Congressional Budget Act of 1974 mandated an annual accounting for just such a list of tax expenditures, to be submitted with the annual budgets prepared by the president.[1] The Budget Act specified that a tax provision should be included on the list if it represents a "special exclusion, exemption, or deduction from gross income" or "provides a special credit, a preferential rate of tax, or a deferral of liability." Implicit in the tax expenditure list, therefore, is a distinction between provisions of the tax code that are "special" and those that are not. There is naturally a temptation to take the small additional step of presuming that the part of the tax law that is not special is the embodiment of "good" tax policy.[2]

An interesting example of the resulting tension is the Reagan administration's shift in the basis for specifying the part of the tax law that is nonspecial. In the tax expenditure tables prepared in the early years (and in those prepared currently by the Joint Committee on Taxation of the Congress and the Congressional Budget Office), the collection of nonspecial rules was known as the "normal" income tax. (For unspecified reasons, deviations from a reference standard in the case of other taxes are not included in the tax expenditure budget.) Roughly speaking, the normal income tax is a broad-based hybrid income tax, including a classical corporation income tax and not including inflation corrections. For example, under the normal income tax, depreciation allowances for equipment are derived from historical asset costs using the "guideline lives" specified in the Asset Depreciation Range (ADR) system, which was a part of the actual income tax law until 1981.

Among the changes wrought by the Economic Recovery Tax Act of 1981 was the wholesale revision of depreciation rules known as the

1. Tax expenditures are detailed in a special analysis (in recent years, Special Analysis G) in the federal budget.
2. For a good discussion of the controversial quality of tax expenditure accounting, see Fiekowsky (1980) and his citations of Surrey (1969), Bittker (1969), Surrey and Hellmuth (1969), and Wagner (1979). See also Surrey and McDaniel (1985).

ACRS. The Reagan administration took the position in its budget materials that since the ACRS schedules had been specified by statute as the generally applicable rule for determining depreciation allowances, tax expenditures should be defined relative to that standard rather than to a standard defined in previous law. The administration also argued that various other deviations of the normal tax law from existing practice, such as the current taxation of the income of foreign subsidiaries of U.S. firms (rather than deferral of U.S. taxation until repatriation of the earnings), could not be justified on an objective basis. Accordingly, the Reagan tax expenditure lists define tax expenditures relative to a somewhat different standard, called the "reference" income tax. In doing so, the administration emphasized the function of tax expenditure analysis in a budgetary framework and rejected any normative connotation of the reference tax.

Treasury's practice in this case is in line with Fiekowsky's (1980, p. 215) suggestion of the following two-part test to determine whether a tax provision can usefully be analyzed as a spending program. (The test need not be confined to income tax provisions; it would apply as well to other general revenue sources.)

1. In the absence of the particular provision, does the existing tax law provide a general rule by which the results of a transaction would determine the transactor's tax liability?

2. If the answer to that question is yes, is it possible to formulate an expenditure program administrable by a cognizant government agency that would achieve the same objective at equal, higher, or lower budgetary cost?

Reasonable as these guidelines may seem, the differences in practices of the executive and legislative branches show that there can be disagreements about both parts.

Strictly speaking, it ought not to be a matter of great moment which framework one uses, provided one is explicit about the basis of comparison. In practice, though, it clearly does matter whether the tax expenditure list includes a revenue estimate for a particular provision. There is an inevitable presumption that reducing tax expenditures is desirable, that the nonspecial law expresses the set of tax rules one would wish to have if it were not for the introduction of some nontax objective into the system. The provisions identified as tax expenditures are prima facie candidates for elimination either outright or by replacement by expenditure programs. The implicit objective of reform is to whittle the tax system down to the part that does not constitute a special exception.

A good argument can be made for exactly the reverse perspective on tax expenditures. Tax reform in this view consists of changing the tax rule structure that is to be regarded as the point of reference — for example, to a more consistent accrual-income basis or to a consumption basis. Changing special rules is not tax reform; it is expenditure reform. That the particular programs in question are run through the tax system may affect their visibility in the budget and the legislative process by which they are enacted, but it does not affect the criteria by which they should be evaluated.

A tax expenditure list can be interpreted only in the light of the *basic* structure of taxation, to which specified provisions are regarded as exceptions. (Because it seems to have less of a normative quality than the term "normal tax structure," I propose to adopt the Treasury's term "reference tax structure" for the nonspecial rules.) Changes in the reference tax, including the applicable rate structure, change tax expenditures.

Here is a simple example: The 1985 federal budget figures show a fiscal year tax expenditure of $65 million to subsidize exploration and development for nonmineral fuels. This figure represents the estimated loss in tax revenue due to allowing firms to expense (write off in the current year) certain outlays for the indicated purpose, rather than obliging them to capitalize such outlays (write them off over a period of years), as would be required under the reference tax rules. If Congress were to change the basic rate of tax applicable to corporations from 46 percent to 35 percent, thereby changing the reference tax structure, the tax expenditure figure would also change. In this case, because the expenditure is essentially proportional to the corporate tax rate, the figure would decline by about 24 percent, from $65 million to about $50 million.

Other differences would obtain if we were to examine how revenues would be affected if particular provisions were brought into line with quite different structures. For example, we might look at the revenue effect of bringing the rules in each case into line with a structure based on inflation-corrected accrual income, with no double taxation of dividends. Or we might ask how the provisions stack up against a cash-flow type of tax base. In the latter case, the rule allowing expensing of the cost of exploration and development of nonfuel minerals would be part of the reference structure. The tax expenditure would be zero instead of $65 million. The tax expenditure in fiscal year 1985 attributed to accelerated depreciation of machinery and equipment would be changed from $24 billion (relative to the normal tax structure) or zero (relative to the Treasury's reference tax structure) to a *negative* amount.

These observations on the relative quality of tax expenditure figures express a point that will be made again in the Appendix: the distinction between the expenditure and revenue sides of the budget is, to a degree, arbitrary. Expenditure programs raise the same incidence and incentive issues that tax programs do. Furthermore, as a matter of accounting, just about any payment made by the government could be implemented as a tax credit, thereby converting an expenditure to reduced taxes. And it would be easy in principle to add a spending program that gives everyone obligated to pay income taxes an annual grant of $1000 while raising the level of the tax by the same amount, implying no real change but raising both spending and taxes on the books. The earned-income credit provides a good example. As a "refundable" tax credit, it sometimes results in a net payment by the Treasury to the taxpayer. In such cases current budgeting practice records an expenditure. To the extent of the taxpayer's liability in its absence, however, the credit leads to a reduction in tax receipts that would not be separately identified in the budget except by inclusion each year in the special analysis of tax expenditures. Thus it is clear that considerable care must be exercised in using tax expenditure figures in policy analysis.

An Extended Example: State and Local Bond Interest

To develop various issues in tax expenditure analysis, I shall use as an example the exclusion from taxable income of interest received on state and local bonds. This exclusion represents an exception to the general principle in the current tax law that interest received is included. By virtue of this provision, state and local governments are able to borrow at lower rates of interest than would apply if their obligations were taxable. Thereby Congress provides a subsidy to borrowing by state and local governments.

The exempt-interest provisions have the classic characteristics of a tax expenditure. Historically the rules emerged as a consequence of the general constitutional principle that the federal government should not tax the state governments. When the income tax was levied at low rates on a small number of individuals and companies, the special treatment of state and local bond interest was merely a quaint feature of the U.S. tax system. As the rates of tax rose, so did the stakes of all of those who took advantage of the exemption, both lenders and borrowers. The blanket exemption has long since been hedged around by regulations, limiting the debt to which exemption applies in various ways, essentially in recognition of the extraordinarily powerful economic forces that conflict with the apparently simple constitutional principle.

Today the exemption of interest on state and local debt has developed into a very complex economic and political system. The distributional and incentive effects of this system are poorly understood, and judgments about it are based on simple partial models, if not outright myth. As the economic analysis below suggests, it is most unlikely that anyone would design a system on purpose the way the exempt-interest provisions work in practice.

The system is nonetheless very durable. For example, one might argue that a matching-grant program would be a natural way to implement a subsidy on state and local borrowing. Under such a provision, state and local governments would be entitled to some specified payment from the U.S. Treasury for each dollar paid in interest on qualifying bonds. In 1978 the administration proposed just such a direct expenditure alternative, called the "taxable bond option." Strongly opposed by governors and mayors, who feared the change would lead to increased federal regulation and ultimately put in jeopardy their borrowing subsidy, the proposal died in Congress.

Given that the tax exemption is an alternative to a spending program that would serve substantially the same objective, several questions are then raised: What is the budgetary cost of the existing provision compared with the budgetary cost of alternatives that might be enacted as spending programs? What is the economic effect of the existing tax subsidy? What are the policy reasons for preferring the existing approach to spending-side alternatives?

Measuring the Tax Subsidy

To illustrate how to calculate the extent of the tax expenditure in such a case, imagine that there is a single tax rate of 30 percent for everyone. Suppose that the going rate of interest on taxable bonds is 14 percent. Then we would predict that tax-exempt bonds of equivalent riskiness would pay interest at the rate of 9.8 percent. With these figures, a 30 percent taxpayer will be indifferent between holding the taxable or the tax-exempt bond. In the former case he receives 14 percent interest less 30 percent of 14 percent in tax, which works out to 9.8 percent; in the latter case he receives the 9.8 percent directly and incurs no extra tax liability.

One approach to figuring the tax expenditure in this instance is to estimate how much additional tax would be paid by the holders of state and local bonds if the tax exemption were suddenly removed and nothing else changed. Thus, if exempt interest payments of $1 billion are made in the year on $10.2 billion of bonds, the estimated revenue effect of removing the exemption would be 30 percent of $1 billion, or $300 million. This figure, however, is undoubtedly an underestimate of either the budgetary cost of a substitute subsidy program or the extra tax revenue that would be generated if the tax exemption were removed.

An alternative subsidy program would have to provide the difference between $1 billion and the taxable interest payments that would be required for the state and local governments to maintain the same level of borrowing. Taxable interest of 14 percent on $10.2 billion amounts to $1428 million. The required subsidy is thus larger by $128 million than the figure reached by the method often employed. Does this mean that the tax provision provides the desired support to state and local governments at lower cost than the direct subsidy? The answer is no, because in the absence of the interest exemption, holders of the bonds would obtain a taxable yield of 14 percent on their assets, which would generate not $300 million, but $428 million in tax revenue. The revenue cost of the tax exemption is in this case equal to the spending required to provide the same subsidy.[3]

Matters are somewhat more complicated when there is more than one marginal tax rate. Suppose there are two rates, 30 percent and 50 percent. We might expect all tax-exempt bonds to be held by 50 percent–bracket taxpayers, and to find the tax-exempts yielding 7 percent when taxable bonds are yielding 14 percent. Then the analysis would go through as before except that the exempt interest on $10.2 billion of borrowing would be $714 million, and the tax expenditure estimated by the approach described above would also be $714 million.

But if the supply of tax-exempts exceeds the amount that 50 percent–bracket taxpayers wish to hold, so that the yield must rise to 9.8 percent to attract 30 percent taxpayers, the revenue effect of the exemption will be 7 percent (50 percent of 14 percent) of the value of tax-exempts held by 50 percent–bracket taxpayers, and 4.2 percent (30 percent of 14 percent) of the value of the tax-exempts held by 30 percent

3. The U.S. Treasury Department follows the procedure described in this paragraph. But Jon Hakken of the Treasury has pointed out to me that the $300 million figure is correct if the recipients of municipal bond interest pay the full extra tax that local governments must levy to cover the higher interest and deduct these extra payments of state and local tax on their federal tax returns.

taxpayers. If half the bonds are held by each of the taxpayer groups, the tax expenditure will be $571 million. This total, of course, exceeds the $428-million cost of the alternative spending-side subsidy needed to make up the difference between 9.8 percent and 14 percent for the entire sum borrowed.

In this instance, if the object of the exemption of state and local bond interest from tax is to provide a subsidy to state and local borrowing, the cost of that subsidy should be regarded as $571 million. This is a more costly method than the $428 million for the alternative of a straight interest-matching expenditure. But the tax provision also generates a transfer of $143 million to high-bracket taxpayers. (It is usual to regard transfers to high-bracket taxpayers as a bad thing, but obviously high-bracket taxpayers may not see it that way, nor would others who may think the reference tax system imposes too heavy a burden on savings.) In addition, the tax expenditure approach differs in legal, political, and administrative aspects from the spending-side alternative.

Economic Effects of the Tax Subsidy

In inquiring into the economic effects of a tax subsidy, it is necessary to specify the programs with which it is being compared. The usual context for the question is one in which policymakers propose to eliminate the provision, bringing the treatment of the transaction into conformity with whatever is accepted as the reference tax. In our example, the alternative policy might be simple elimination of the exempt status of state and local bonds, with no proposed spending-side replacement and with, instead, a general reduction in tax rates—the classic broaden-the-base, lower-the-rates case. Then the economic effects are compounded of the influence on the overall distribution of tax burdens and the impact on the targets of the subsidies, those who have a stake in state and local government finance.

Because it is often very difficult to determine the incidence of taxes, the best we may be able to do is to estimate the impact effects: Who pays how much more in taxes and who how much less? Which state and local governments pay how much more in interest? Who is going to have to finance the implied increase in required state and local revenue? These may be described as the income effects of the rule change. We learn a useful lesson from analyzing the income effects of eliminating tax-exempt interest in the case where all bond holders confront the same tax rate that would occur if all the bonds were held by those in the top bracket. Suppose the tax rate of all holders is 30 percent, so that the rate of return on tax-exempts will be 9.8 percent when the interest on taxable bonds is 14 percent. Then eliminating the tax exemption of state and local bond interest simply causes the yield from the bonds to rise to 14 percent; the after-tax return to the taxpayers who hold state and local bonds is not affected at all. This is because holders of the so-called tax-exempt bonds actually do bear a tax burden, equal to the differential between tax-exempt and taxable yields. Their burden goes directly to finance the subsidy to state and local borrowing, rather than indirectly via the U.S. Treasury, but the effect of the tax on their return is the same as if they sent in the money to the Internal Revenue Service. Therefore they are not hurt by the elimination of the interest exemption. (I am putting to one side capital losses to individuals who may own long-term tax-exempt bonds at the time of the rule change. Depending on the transition rules, they may experience windfall gains or losses.)

Table 11–1 represents a way of describing the distributional effect of the availability of tax-exempt bonds. The table, derived from Pechman (1983), is based on estimates of the amount of tax-exempt bond interest

Table 11–1. Conventional display of distributional effect of tax expenditure: the case of tax-exempt interest, 1985[a] (individual taxpayers classified by Adjusted Gross Income)

Adjusted Gross Income ($ thousands)	"Revenue change" due to tax-exempt interest ($ millions) (1)	Implied percentage change in liability (2)
3–5	8	[b]
5–10	86	[b]
10–15	164	1.3
15–20	180	1.0
20–25	160	0.7
25–50	886	0.8
50–100	992	1.4
100–200	672	2.3
200–500	488	2.7
500–1000	205	3.7
Over 1000	262	4.3

Source: Calculations based on Pechman (1983, table 4–12).

a. Entries show estimated change in tax liabilities for taxpayers in the indicated Adjusted Gross Income classes; only effects operating via the individual income tax are accounted for

b. Because liabilities in these classes may be negative, no percentage change in liabilities is shown.

received by individual taxpayers in a sample of tax returns. (Pechman does not explain how these estimates were prepared; in fact, we have very little information about individual ownership of tax-exempt bonds.) The amounts in column 1 show how much extra tax would have been collected from individuals for the 1985 tax year if their state and local bond interest had been added to the other income on their tax returns. Column 2 shows how much the tax saving would have amounted to as a percentage of the actual taxes paid. Overall, individuals would have paid $4.1 billion additional in 1985 if state and local bond interest were taxable. Furthermore, because the tax-exempt securities were relatively concentrated in the hands of high-bracket taxpayers, the table suggests that the effect of the provision was to reduce the progressivity of the tax.

I have already discussed why the indicated method produces an underestimate of the extra revenue that would be generated if the tax exemption were eliminated. In addition, it is clear from our example in which all taxpayers face the same marginal rate that the related method of describing the distributional consequences of the tax expenditure gives an inaccurate picture. In the example, the typical table would show taxpayers in the top bracket enjoying a total tax saving of $300 million (30 percent of the assumed total of $1 billion in tax-exempt interest). In actuality, as we have seen, the taxpayers in question obtain *no* benefit from the availability of the tax-exempt bonds; they get the same 9.8 percent interest whether the bonds are tax exempt or not.

The figures conventionally used to describe the distribution of tax expenditures by income category generally convey little about the actual value of the provisions to taxpayers. Taxpayers who use the provisions typically deliver something in return (in this case, loans at low interest rates). Market pressure will tend to eliminate any profit. In the illustration, all profit has been eliminated; the users of the special provision can in no sense be described as its beneficiaries. An analogy would be to describe the seller of a product to the government (pencils or weapons, for example) as the beneficiary of the gross amount received from the government. It would be nonsensical to attempt to draw distributional inferences from a table showing the amounts paid for such goods and services in relation to the income of the seller.

This is not to suggest that there are no interesting distributional issues raised by particular provisions of the tax law. Our example indicates an instance: the 50 percent taxpayers obtained an advantage in a market in which 30 percent taxpayers are the marginal purchasers of tax-exempt bonds. The usual figures, however, do not take into account the degree to which taxpayers are actually delivering something for the tax subsidy; hence they give a misleading impression of the provisions' effects.

To produce an estimate of the distributional effect of tax-exempt interest, we start with the information that, in the late 1970s, the yields on long-term tax-exempt bonds were approximately 70 percent of the yields on taxable bonds of comparable risk (see Gordon and Malkiel, 1981). We infer from this fact that taxpayers in marginal rate brackets above 30 percent were able to realize a net advantage from holding tax-exempts rather than taxable bonds. One distributional effect of allowing tax exemption or adopting a less rather than more stringent standard for defining the state and local obligations for which tax exemption will be allowed is therefore a moderation in the degree of progressivity of the income tax.

By working with the assumption of a tax-exempt yield at 70 percent of the yield on taxable bonds, we can make some rough adjustments to the figures in Table 11-1. These adjustments are presented in Table 11-2. In order to draw any conclusion about the effect of tax-exempt interest on the burden on individual taxpayers, we must know something about their marginal rate brackets. Since this information was not provided, I have simply tried to make a reasonable guess (Table 11-2, column 1) about the average marginal rate bracket of the taxpayers in each Adjusted Gross Income category.

Knowing the marginal rate bracket and the amount of tax saving estimated in the conventional way, we can estimate the amount of tax-exempt interest received in each group (column 2). Because the tax-exempt rate is assumed to be 70 percent of the taxable rate, we can then estimate the amount of taxable interest those taxpayers would have reported if the exempt bonds were not available (column 3). The difference between the two amounts (30 percent of the taxable interest) can be described as the tax implicitly paid by the holders of tax-exempts (column 4). If, instead, they had held taxable bonds, the tax would have been determined by multiplying the interest by the marginal rate in each group (column 5). Low-bracket taxpayers who for some reason choose to hold tax-exempt bonds pay more in implicit tax than the actual tax they would pay on taxable bonds. So tax-exempt bonds are shown in column 6 to be responsible for an increase in the tax burden on such individuals. Taxpayers in the 30 percent bracket break even; taxpayers in the top bracket save money.

The totals shown in Table 11-2 are also interesting. They indicate a total tax expenditure of $5863 million on the subsidy to state and local

Table 11-2. Estimating the distributional effect of tax expenditures: the case of tax-exempt interest, 1985

Adjusted Gross Income ($ thousands)	Assumed marginal rate (%) (1)	Implied tax-exempt interest[a] ($ millions) (2)	Alternative interest[b] ($ millions) (3)	Implicit tax[c] ($ millions) (4)	Tax on alternative interest[d] ($ millions) (5)	Tax change due to tax-exempts[e] ($ millions) (6)
3–5	10	82	117	35	12	23
5–10	15	574	820	246	123	123
10–15	20	820	1171	351	234	117
15–20	25	722	1031	309	258	52
20–25	30	533	761	228	228	0
25–50	35	2530	3615	1084	1265	−181
50–100	40	2481	3544	1063	1417	−354
100–200	50	1345	1921	576	961	−384
200–500	50	976	1394	418	697	−279
500–1000	50	410	586	176	293	−117
Over 1000	50	525	750	225	375	−150
Total				4713	5863	−1150

Source: Calculations based on Pechman (1983, table 4–12).

a. The amount of interest that, when taxed at the assumed marginal rate, would imply the revenue change shown in column 1 of Table 11–1.

b. Taxable interest that would be earned on the amounts invested in tax-exempts, assuming that tax-exempt interest rates are 30 percent below taxable interest rates.

c. Difference between the return before tax on taxable bonds and the return on tax-exempts (column 3 minus column 2).

d. Tax payable at the assumed marginal rate on the alternative interest return (column 1 times column 3).

e. Tax that would be paid on taxable interest less the tax implicitly paid by holding tax-exempts (column 5 minus column 4). A positive amount implies the taxpayers in that bracket are losing money by holding tax-exempts; a negative amount indicates a reduction in effective taxes.

Table 11-3. Differences between conventional and corrected distributional analysis:
the case of tax-exempt interest, 1985

Adjusted Gross Income ($ thousands)	"Revenue change" due to tax-exempt interest[a] ($ millions) (1)	Implied percentage change in liability[b] (2)	Corrected tax change due to tax-exempts	
			($ millions)[c] (3)	(%)[d] (4)
3-5	8	e	23	e
5-10	86	e	123	e
10-15	164	1.3	117	0.9
15-20	180	1.0	52	0.3
20-25	160	0.7	0	0.0
25-50	886	0.8	-181	-0.2
50-100	992	1.4	-354	-0.5
100-200	672	2.3	-384	-1.3
200-500	488	2.7	-279	-1.5
500-1000	205	3.7	-117	-2.1
Over 1000	262	4.3	-150	-2.5

Source: Calculations based on Pechman (1983, table 4-12).
a. Column 1 of Table 11-1.
b. Column 2 of Table 11-1.
c. Column 6 of Table 11-2.
d. Calculated from column 3 and liability totals implicit in Pechman (1983, table 4-12).
e. Because liabilities in these classes may be negative, no percentage change in liabilities is shown.

bonds. Of that total, an estimated $4713 million accrues to state and local governments in reduced borrowing costs. (Later in this chapter we look at who actually benefits from the reduced borrowing costs.) The remaining $1150 million represents the aggregate reduction in tax burdens. That total, however, consists of $1465 million in reductions for taxpayers above the 30 percent bracket and $315 million in increased taxes for those in lower brackets.

Table 11-3 summarizes the distributional information from Tables 11-1 and 11-2. Keep in mind that my calculations are built up from assumptions that may be reasonable but have not been confirmed with evidence. Furthermore, the original data from which I worked, the figures from Pechman's table, also rely on assumptions. (An obvious question: Why do all those low-bracket people hold tax-exempts? One hypothesis: the low-bracket holders are elderly individuals who acquired the bonds in a high-bracket period of their lives and have never gotten around to shifting their portfolios upon reaching low-bracket retirement years.) Any such statistics should be taken with a grain of salt.[4]

Historically the yield differential on short-term tax-exempts remained persistently close to the corporation income tax rate. The likely reason is that it is possible to engage in arbitrage with short-term tax-exempts with virtually no risk. Although individuals are limited in such arbitrage by the amount of their positive wealth (because interest paid on amounts borrowed to finance the holding of tax-exempt bonds may not be deducted from taxable income), banks were not so limited until 1983.[5] At least until that time, then, the corporate rate put a floor under the yield differential. For bonds with longer maturities, however, it is apparently difficult or impossible to arrange risk-free arbitrage — hence the limits on the amount of long-term instruments any taxpayer is willing to hold.

Currently issuers of long-term tax-exempts are having to provide higher yields relative to taxable bonds than in the past. Although it is not certain why this is so, it is true that the volume of tax-exempt bonds has grown as state and local governments, with the help of financial intermediaries, have developed increased financial sophistication. A larger volume of bonds tends to fill up the portfolios of higher-bracket taxpayers, forcing the sellers to make the bonds attractive to lower-bracket buyers. Perhaps also at work is the growth in opportunities for tax-exempt saving via pension funds, IRAs, and the like. In such portfolios, tax exemption is no advantage. Another possible explanation for the relative rise in tax-exempt yields is buyer uncertainty about the future of tax exemption. A perception by buyers that their interest may in the *future* become taxable amounts to an immediate reduction in its current exemption.

As our calculations indicate, whatever the impact of tax-exempt bonds on the effective burdens on high-bracket taxpayers, it is much smaller than the total revenue cost. The revenue cost is partly a reflection of the subsidy provided to state and local borrowing. Table 11-4 shows the breakdown of the tax expenditures aiding state and local government in 1983. The total of the tax expenditure estimates for

4. Ideally, one would carry out the analysis sketched here with due regard for the entire set of available assets, with their various special tax rules. For attempts, see *Blueprints*, chap. 5, and Galper and Toder (1984).

5. Under a provision introduced to the code by the Tax Equity and Financial Responsibility Act of 1982, banks may deduct only 80 percent of the interest paid in the years since 1982 on debt used to finance the holding of tax-exempts.

Table 11-4. Tax expenditures aiding state and local government, fiscal 1984 (millions of dollars)

Expenditure	Amount
Deductibility of—	
Property taxes on owner-occupied homes	8,050
Nonbusiness taxes other than on owner-occupied homes	18,140
Subtotal (neglecting interactions)[a]	26,190
Exclusion of interest on—	
Public-purpose state and local debt	11,800
IDBs[b] for certain energy facilities	190
IDBs for pollution control and sewage and waste disposal facilities	1,345
Small-issue IDBs	2,195
IDBs for airports, docks, and sports and convention facilities	485
Mass-commuting-vehicle IDBs	50
Owner-occupied mortgage-subsidy bonds	1,735
State and local debt for rental housing	715
State and local student loan bonds	230
Debt for private nonprofit educational facilities	140
Debt for private nonprofit health facilities	1,285
Debt for veterans' housing	265
Subtotal (neglecting interactions)[a]	20,435
Total (after interactions)	33,665

Source: Special Analysis H, *Budget of the United States Government for Fiscal Year 1985,* table H-2.

a. Because there are interactions among terms, the original table in the budget warns sternly against adding individual items to obtain a total. I have compromised and calculated subtotals only.

b. Industrial development bonds.

the exclusion of interest on state and local borrowing for various purposes *and* for the deductibility of state and local taxes is estimated in the federal budget at $33.7 billion for 1983. The budget does not give a separate total figure for the interest exemption. Adding together individual components yields subtotals of $26.2 billion for deductibility of taxes and $20.4 billion for the interest exclusion. Interactions among the items make the total (taking into account the interactions) less than the sum of the subtotals (excluding the interactions). Because the tax expenditure includes some transfer to high-bracket taxpayers, we may reasonably take $20 billion as a very high estimate of the total subsidy due to tax exemption. This figure may be compared with federal grants-in-aid to state and local governments of $86 billion and total state and local government receipts of $478 billion in 1983 (*Survey of Current Business,* 64 [September 1984], table 3.3).

Distributional and Incentive Effects of the Implicit Spending Program

Who benefits from this interest subsidy? Borrowing enables the citizens of a state or locality to postpone taxes. Borrowing by state and local governments thus substitutes for borrowing or dissaving by the taxpayers. It is a curious feature of the income tax that high-bracket taxpayers ought to want to do their own borrowing; their marginal tax rates are higher than the differential between the yields on tax-exempt and taxable bonds. High-bracket taxpayers will find it financially advantageous to pay their state and local taxes earlier rather than later with interest. There is thus perhaps a presumption that lower-income jurisdictions have more to gain from the interest exemption than do high-income jurisdictions.

For any income level, given a decision to borrow, the subsidy has the effect of reducing state and local taxes (relative to the situation with the same amount of borrowing and no tax exemption). The benefit should be thought of as distributed in the form of lower taxes than would otherwise prevail. It is obviously difficult to know how the increase in taxes required by eliminating tax exemption would be distributed. In conventional wisdom, state and local taxes tend to be regressive. Avoiding an increase in state and local taxes thus may be somewhat progressive.

A large fraction of state and local borrowing is used for special purposes, such as constructing sewage and waste disposal facilities. In recent years a substantial amount has financed industrial development and owner-occupied housing. Industrial development bonds, in particular, are used to finance capital investment on behalf of firms, typically as a way of attracting the firms to an area. The bidding in this form appears to be highly competitive; consequently we can presume that the benefits of the subsidy accrue in the form of higher profits to owners of firms, higher wages to their workers, and lower prices of their products.

Tax exemption not only has distributional effects but it also has incentive effects. State and local governments clearly have an incentive to borrow at tax-exempt rates and to lend at taxable rates. Specific provisions of the tax law attempt to prohibit such bald arbitrage transactions. Instead, state and local governments expand their investment activities within a more restricted set of available opportunities. Within that set, ordinary calculus of cost and profit would generate an excessive investment (because the citizens can obtain the yield in the form of services free of tax just as they obtain the services of owner-occupied houses free of tax), quite apart from the possibility of exempt-interest borrowing. Tying exempt-interest borrowing to specific types of state and local activities presumably further encourages them. Table 11–4 lists the major categories of state and local activities connected with tax-exempt financing. The point of subsidizing these activities is presumably partly to redistribute money to the citizens of jurisdictions that do meritorious things, and partly to encourage those governments to do more of those meritorious things than they otherwise would. Whether the use of exempt-interest borrowing is a particularly effective subsidy method is surprisingly little questioned.

Tax Expenditures and Tax Reform

Table 11–5 shows the major items of tax expenditure that have been distinguished in the federal budget, classified by the functional "national need" categories used for spending programs. By browsing through this table, the reader can obtain a fine overview of the U.S. income tax code.

The table includes data provided in the budget on tax expenditures according to the two standards I have discussed. Most expenditure figures are the same whether the provision is measured against the traditional normal income tax or against the Treasury's reference tax rules. Where there is a difference, the table distinguishes between amounts derived according to the "pre-1983 budget method" (uses the normal tax) and those derived according to the "1983 and 1984 budget method" (uses the reference tax). Notice that there are no negative entries; all the deviations accounted for from either the normal or the reference tax result in reduced revenues. This would not be the case if the standard of comparison were a consistent real income tax or an expenditure tax.

The table distinguishes between amounts of tax expenditure arising via the individual and corporation income taxes. I need hardly say that the distinction tells us little about who benefits from the tax provisions

Table 11-5. Tax expenditures: outlay equivalent estimates by function, fiscal 1985 (billions of dollars)[a]

Function	Corporations	Individuals	Total
National defense			
Exclusion of benefits and allowances to armed forces personnel	—	2,460	2,460
Exclusion of military disability pensions	—	125	125
Total (after interactions)	—	2,585	2,585
International affairs			
Exclusion of income earned abroad by U.S. citizens	—	2,215	2,215
Deferral of income from controlled foreign corporations:			
Pre-1983 budget method	1,045	—	1,045
1983 and 1984 budget method	0	—	0
Total (after interactions)	1,045	2,215	3,260
General science, space, and technology			
Expensing of research and development expenditures	575	30	605
Credit for increasing research activities	1,110	25	1,135
Total (after interactions)	1,855	60	1,915
Energy			
Expensing of exploration and development costs:			
Oil and gas	1,130	1,125	2,255
Other fuels	35	—	35
Excess of percentage over cost depletion:			
Oil and gas	440	1,125	1,565
Other fuels	455	20	475
Capital gains treatment of royalties on coal	75	245	320
Exclusion of interest on state and local industrial development bonds for certain energy facilities	85	90	175
Residential energy credits:			
Supply incentives	—	745	745
Conservation incentives	—	390	390

Table 11-5 (continued)

Function	Corporations	Individuals	Total
Alternative conservation and new-technology credits:			
Supply incentives	245	35	280
Conservation incentives	35	b	35
Alternative fuel production credit	45	—	45
Alcohol fuel credit	b	—	b
Energy credit for intercity buses	15	—	15
Total (after interactions)	1,820	2,680	4,500
Natural resources and environment			
Expensing of exploration and development costs, nonfuel minerals	65	—	65
Excess of percentage over cost depletion, nonfuel minerals	600	25	625
Exclusion of interest on state and local IDBs for pollution control and sewage and waste disposal facilities	625	710	1,335
Tax incentives for preservation of historic structures	160	310	470
Capital gains treatment of iron ore	20	20	40
Capital gains treatment of certain timber income	805	255	1,060
Investment credit and seven-year amortization for reforestation expenditures	45	10	55
Total (after interactions)	2,285	1,310	3,595
Agriculture			
Expensing of certain capital outlays	95	515	610
Capital gains treatment of certain income	65	720	785
Total (after interactions)	150	1,160	1,310
Commerce and housing credit			
Dividend exclusion	—	640	640
Net interest exclusion	—	2,730	2,730
Exclusion of interest on small-issue industrial development bonds	1,700	405	2,105
Exemption of credit union income	265	—	265

Table 11–5 *(continued)*

Function	Corporations	Individuals	Total
Excess bad-debt reserves of financial institutions	1,410	—	1,410
Exclusion of interest on life insurance savings	—	7,285	7,285
Deductibility of interest on consumer credit	—	10,920	10,920
Deductibility of mortgage interest on owner-occupied homes	—	25,330	25,330
Deductibility of property tax on owner-occupied homes	—	9,725	9,725
Exclusion of interest on state and local housing bonds for owner-occupied housing	450	1,195	1,645
Exclusion of interest on state and local debt for rental housing	420	660	1,080
Capital gains (other than agriculture, timber, iron ore, and coal)	2,155	25,290	27,445
Deferral of capital gains on home sales	—	2,550	2,550
Exclusion of capital gains on home sales for persons aged 55 and over	—	1,120	1,120
Carry-over basis of capital gains at death	—	6,845	6,845
Investment credit (other than ESOPs), rehabilitation of structures, energy property and reforestation expenditures	30,140	4,050	34,190
Accelerated depreciation on rental housing:			
Pre-1983 budget method	160	635	795
1983 and 1984 budget method	0	0	0
Accelerated depreciation of buildings other than rental housing:			
Pre-1983 budget method	220	195	415
1983 and 1984 budget method	0	0	0
Accelerated depreciation of machinery and equipment:			
Pre-1983 budget method	24,005	2,710	26,715
1983 and 1984 budget method	0	0	0
Amortization of start-up costs	45	355	400

Table 11–5 *(continued)*

Function	Corporations	Individuals	Total
Reinvestment of dividends in public utility stock	—	685	685
Reduced rates on the first $100,000 of corporate income:			
Pre-1983 budget method	11,045	—	11,045
1983 and 1984 budget method	0	—	0
Total (after interactions)	103,925	102,230	206,155
Transportation			
Deferral of tax on shipping companies	45	—	45
Exclusion of interest on state and local government bonds for mass-commuting vehicles	55	45	100
Deduction for motor carrier operating rights	70	5	75
Total (after interactions)	170	50	220
Community and regional development			
Five-year amortization for housing rehabilitation	40	45	85
Investment credit for rehabilitation of structures (other than historic)	255	215	470
Exclusion of interest on IDBs for airports, docks, and sports and convention facilities	215	235	450
Total (after interactions)	515	500	1,015
Education, training, employment, and social services			
Exclusion of scholarship and fellowship income:			
Pre-1983 budget method	—	625	625
1983 and 1984 budget method	—	0	0
Exclusion of interest on state and local student loan bonds	120	350	470
Exclusion of interest on state and local debt for private nonprofit educational facilities	80	120	200
Parental personal exemption for students aged 19 or over	—	1,025	1,025

Table 11–5 *(continued)*

Function	Corporations	Individuals	Total
Deductibility of charitable contributions (education)	420	825	1,245
Total education (after interactions)	620	2,975	3,595
Exclusion of employer-provided child care	—	90	90
Exclusion of employee meals and lodging (other than military)	—	885	885
Exclusion of contributions to prepaid legal services plans	—	60	60
Investment credit for ESOPs	3,640		3,640
Credit for child-care and dependent-care expenses	—	2,580	2,580
General jobs credit	b	—	b
Targeted jobs credit	970	50	1,020
Deduction for two-earner married couples	—	6,805	6,805
Total training and employment (after interactions)	4,610	9,610	14,220
Deductibility of charitable contributions, other than education and health	520	11,250	11,770
Deduction for certain adoption expenses	—	15	15
Total social services (after interactions)	520	11,265	11,785
Grand total (after interactions)	5,750	24,020	29,770
Health			
Exclusion of employer contributions for medical insurance premiums and medical care	—	28,235	28,235
Deductibility of medical expenses	—	3,440	3,440
Exclusion of interest on state and local debt for private nonprofit health facilities	705	1,085	1,790

Table 11–5 *(continued)*

Function	Corporations	Individuals	Total
Deductibility of charitable contributions (health)	260	1,645	1,905
Tax credit for orphan drug research	25	—	25
Total (after interactions)	990	34,750	35,740
Social Security and Medicare			
Exclusion of Social Security benefits:			
Disability insurance benefits	—	1,095	1,095
OASI benefits for retired workers	—	12,884	12,884
Benefits for dependents and survivors	—	3,770	3,770
Total (after interactions)	—	17,749	17,749
Income security			
Exclusion of railroad retirement system benefits	—	450	450
Exclusion of workmen's compensation benefits	—	2,225	2,225
Exclusion of public assistance benefits:			
Pre-1983 budget method	—	510	510
1983 and 1984 budget method	—	0	0
Exclusion of special benefits for disabled coal miners	—	155	155
Exclusion of untaxed unemployment insurance benefits	—	1,785	1,785
Net exclusion of pension contributions and earnings:			
Employer plans	—	80,725	80,725
Individual Retirement Accounts	—	14,170	14,170
Keogh Plans	—	2,645	2,645
Exclusion of other employee benefits:			
Premiums on group term life insurance	—	3,240	3,240
Premiums on accident and disability insurance	—	170	170
Income of trusts to finance supplementary unemployment benefits	—	20	20
Additional exemption for the blind	—	45	45
Additional exemption for the elderly	—	2,695	2,695

Table 11-5 *(continued)*

Function	Corporations	Individuals	Total
Tax credit for the elderly and disabled	—	205	205
Deductibility of casualty losses	—	575	575
Earned income credit[c]	—	280	280
Total (after interactions)	—	111,645	111,645
Veterans' benefits and services			
Exclusion of veterans' disability compensation	—	1,865	1,865
Exclusion of veterans' pensions	—	340	340
Exclusion of GI bill benefits	—	115	115
Exclusion of interest on state and local debt for veterans' housing	80	245	325
Total (after interactions)	80	2,565	2,645
General government			
Credits and deductions for political contributions	—	290	290
General-purpose fiscal assistance			
Exclusion of interest on public-purpose state and local debt	5,190	8,105	13,295
Deductibility of nonbusiness state and local taxes other than on owner-occupied homes	—	21,610	21,610
Tax credit for corporations receiving income from doing business in U.S. possessions	1,745	—	1,745
Total (after interactions)	6,935	29,715	36,650
Interest			
Deferral of interest on savings bonds	—	795	795
Total of after-interaction totals	*125,520*	*333,524*	*459,044*

Source: Appendix G, *Budget of the United States Government for Fiscal Year 1985,* table G-1.

a. Figures for provisions that have been repealed since submission of the budget (in particular, DISC and safe-harbor leasing) and programs with no revenues in 1985 have been dropped. Totals include only pre-1983 budget method amounts.

b. Amount is $2.5 million or less. All estimates have been rounded to the nearest $5 billion.

c. The figures in the table indicate the tax subsidy provided by the earned-income tax credit. The effect on outlays in fiscal 1985 is $1044 million.

in question, in spite of the common misuse of the figures to that effect. Nor do the estimates make any effort to determine how a change in the taxation of corporations would be reflected in the income tax liability of individuals.

The table includes the totals derived by the government for tax expenditures under the various national need headings. These entries are shown as being "after interactions," which means simply that the tendency of changes in one provision to affect the tax bracket of individual taxpayers and thus to affect the estimated revenue cost of other provisions has been taken into account. The "total of after-interaction totals" (shown at the bottom of the table) is not provided by the Treasury estimators; it is simply the sum of the other totals with no allowance for interactions. Because it does not allow for interactions, it does not represent a proper estimate of the total expenditure undertaken via the deviation of the actual from either normal or reference tax rules. But the comparison between the grand total of $459 billion and the outlay level of $926 billion proposed in the fiscal 1985 budget does perhaps suggest the influence of the tax rules on resource allocation.

Tax Expenditures Affected by Choice between Income and Consumption Tax Approaches

Because Table 11–5 is so detailed, it is difficult to get an overview of the items. One of the striking facts that emerges from an inspection of the entries, however, is how much of the total is accounted for by various subsidies to saving and investment. Although the size breakdown depends on the way the effects of the provisions have been displayed (the charitable deduction, for example, is spread among three entries under "Education, training, employment, and social services" and "Health"), it is notable that most of the large entries are associated with major tax features relating to saving and investment.

Here are some examples: Under "General science, space, and technology" are the provisions for expensing research and development and the credit for increasing research activities (combined total, nearly $2 billion); "Energy" includes expensing of exploration and development. "Commerce and housing credit" is credited with a number of the major special provisions relative to the normal, or reference, tax structure: the exclusion of interest on life insurance savings (over $7 billion), the exclusion of 60 percent of long-term capital gains (over $27 billion), exclusion or deferral of capital gains on homes (nearly $4 billion), write-up of asset basis upon death of the owner ($7 billion), and the investment tax credit ($34 billion). ACRS is also included under the "Commerce and housing" heading, with an estimated revenue cost of nearly $27 billion relative to the normal rules.

The same tax expenditure category contains the major items of interest deduction that are regarded as inconsistent with normal and reference rules. Allowing a deduction for interest on consumer credit is shown as having a revenue cost of $10 billion; the deduction of mortgage interest on owner-occupied homes, $25 billion. Although the general policy of allowing deductions for all interest is appropriate in an accrual-income system, these two interest deductions are sometimes regarded as roughly equivalent to the actual deviation from an income standard: exclusion of the return received in kind from owner-occupied housing and household durables.

The tax subsidy to state and local borrowing is scattered throughout the categories in Table 11–5. The federal government is shown as spending over $13 billion on "General-purpose fiscal assistance."

Huge entries in the table are associated with the existing rules affecting retirement savings. Under "Income security," the exclusion of pension contributions and earnings under employer plans, IRAs, and Keogh Plans is responsible for a revenue cost of over $97 billion.

Because so much of this book has been about the taxation of saving and investment, it is not necessary to rehash here the analysis of these provisions. To the extent that they are broadly directed toward encouraging saving and investment, their effects have already been discussed.

The approach one takes toward these items is strongly affected by the choice between income and consumption strategies. For example, the income strategy would imply taxing the return on retirement savings as it accrues, taxing capital gains on accrual, using economic depreciation, abandoning the investment tax credit, and so on. Under a consumption strategy, however, the existing treatment of retirement savings would be made more readily available, interest in general would be neither taxed nor deducted, capital gains would not be included, and investment would be expensed (the investment credit, although having the effect of reducing the tax on the return on saving, would not be a feature of the usual tax based on a consumption strategy).

These observations on general principles applicable to the major tax expenditure provisions should not distract attention from the important issue of uniformity with which investment and saving are treated. As repeatedly observed in this book, the hybrid character of the existing tax leads many provisions, which might make perfectly good sense in the context of a consistent consumption strategy, to generate costly inefficiencies — the problem of the "uneven playing field" for investment.

Tax Expenditure Choices Unrelated to the Income-versus-Consumption Strategy Choice

Most of the other major provisions for which revenue estimates are shown in Table 11–5 cut across the choice between income and consumption strategies. Among such provisions are exclusions of various receipts, such as benefits and allowances of armed forces personnel (over $2 billion), partial exclusion of Social Security retirement and disability insurance benefits ($14 billion), exclusion of workmen's compensation benefits ($2 billion), and partial exclusion of unemployment benefits ($2 billion).

Other examples are the deductions for state and local property taxes ($10 billion), sales and income taxes (almost $22 billion), and the provisions associated with individual health care, especially the exclusion of employer contributions for medical insurance premiums and medical care ($28 billion) and the itemized deduction of medical expenses (over $3 billion).

Most of these provisions can be regarded as aspects of the definition of consumption in the context of either an income or a consumption strategy. They therefore represent tax expenditures by virtue of their deviation from a particular broad conception of what the definition of consumption ought to be. The figures make clear that the details of that definition have very large implications for both the distribution of tax burdens and the allocation of resources. Viewing the choices as among implicit spending programs can be very helpful to the determination of tax policy.

12 The Goal of Tax Simplicity

If I understood it better, I could tell you exactly how I was being ripped off.

Taxpayer quoted in the *Wall Street Journal,* June 12, 1985

THE MAJOR tax-overhaul proposal made public by the Treasury Department in November 1984 was entitled "Tax Reform for Fairness, Simplicity, and Economic Growth." Its successor, six months later, was entitled "The President's Tax Proposals to the Congress for Fairness, Growth, and Simplicity." It is not clear whether great significance was to be attached to the changing order of the tax reformers' trinity of objectives — fairness, efficiency, and simplicity — in the two titles. However, truth in advertising would probably have called for leaving the third out of both titles altogether.

Of the three objectives, in tax legislation none has been more obviously honored in the breach than simplicity. It is sometimes said that it is utopian to look for a simple tax law. The law must function in a complex economy. The political system must accommodate interests that collide in complex ways. The government seeks to achieve complex objectives. All these factors work against simplicity. Simplicity is important, however, if for no other reason than that it serves the other two objectives. A law that can be understood (if at all) by only a tiny priesthood of lawyers and accountants is naturally subject to popular suspicion. By undermining popular support, complexity erodes the self-assessment on which economical compliance depends. Making taxpayers record and report information that is inherently difficult to audit places an often prohibitive tax on honesty. Furthermore, dealing with the law's arcane provisions requires rare talents that might be better applied to other tasks in the economic system.

Simplicity in taxation has various aspects, and often a change that simplifies in one way introduces greater complexity in another. We may distinguish three kinds of complexity: "compliance complexity" (referring to the problems faced by the taxpayer in keeping records, choosing forms, making necessary calculations, and so on); "transactional complexity" (referring to the problems faced by taxpayers in organizing their affairs so as to minimize their taxes within the framework of the rules); and "rule complexity" (referring to the problems of interpreting the written and unwritten rules). These three forms of complexity are related, but improving the law with respect to one form may make it worse with respect to the others. Moreover, an arrangement that enhances the simplicity of the system for one group of taxpayers may make it more complicated for others. For example, a rule that required employers to prepare the tax returns of their employees would simplify the compliance problem of the employees by shifting it to the employers.

Of particular importance is the tension between rule and transactional complexity. Transactional complexity arises basically because of the possibility that economically equivalent activities may have very different tax consequences, depending on the precise way the transactions are structured. For example, if the economic activity is putting aside some money now in order to have some extra money in the future, the tax consequences will depend importantly on whether the asset acquired generates a return flow that is considered capital gains rather than interest. Such distinctions make life complicated for the saver. They might be avoided by more complicated rules, such as full-fledged accrual accounting for all financial assets.

Rules with a high degree of economic consistency serve transactional simplicity, although they may impose costs in the form of compliance and rule complexity. Thus accrual income requires complex rules, particularly if the tax system is to be insulated from inflation. But the tension is not absolute, as the cash-flow accounting appropriate for consumption-type taxes shows. These taxes hold out the possibility of relatively simple rules for determining the tax base. In examining now some problems of complexity, I shall consider in each case whether adopting either a more consistent consumption approach or a more consistent income approach would be likely to help. Because the basic measurement issues have been discussed in detail earlier in the book, I shall not elaborate on the points here.[1]

1. For a discussion from the legal point of view of the simplification consequences of adopting comprehensive income-based or expenditure-based taxes, see the reports (1979 and 1982) of the American Bar Association's Committee on Tax Simplification.

Who Confronts Complexity?

Problems of the Average Taxpayer

Although the statutes and regulations fill thousands of all but unreadable pages, actual compliance with current law is, or at least would appear to be, simple for the majority of individual taxpayers. Taxpayers who do not claim itemized deductions and whose income is mainly from wages can very quickly and easily compute their taxes, most of which will have been withheld at source. They may be eligible for one of the two simple versions of the basic Form 1040, the so-called long form used for reporting individual income tax: a short form, 1040A, and a short short form, 1040EZ. The choice depends on just how simple their economic affairs are and whether they wish to claim certain credits or deductions. It is estimated that 62 percent of all individual-return filers in 1983 used the long form, 21 percent used the short form, and 17 percent used the short short form (Sunley, 1984).

For the average taxpayer, itemized deductions represent the main element of complexity in the law. Itemizers must use the long form. The fraction of individual tax returns including itemized deductions has varied over the years with the inflation-adjusted value of the zero-bracket amount (formerly the minimum standard deduction), which specifies the floor on the aggregate of personal deductions. Only

Table 12-1. Individual returns with itemized deductions, selected years

Year	Number of returns filed (millions)	Percentage with itemized deductions
1983[a]	90.4	36
1982[b]	95.3	35
1981	95.4	33
1980	93.9	31
1977	86.4	26
1975	82.2	32
1970	74.3	48
1965	67.6	41
1960	61.0	40

Source: U.S. Department of the Treasury, Internal Revenue Service, as presented in Sunley (1984).

a. Number of returns represents about 95 percent of 1983 returns to be filed.

b. Preliminary data.

amounts above the floor are subtracted from taxable income. Table 12–1 shows the number of individual income tax returns filed in selected years, together with the fraction of those returns that used itemized deductions. As the data indicate, the proportion of such returns has been drifting slowly upward in recent years from 30 percent of all returns filed. This means that "only" 30 million or so tax-filing units (individuals and married couples) have had to deal with the complexity of the law to the extent of filling out the schedule of itemized deductions. (Some unknown further number of taxpayers had to save the information required to itemize and to deal with the complexity of the rules to the extent of determining whether itemizing was worthwhile.)

Of course, itemized deductions are not the only complexity the average taxpayer may encounter in coping with the tax law. To begin with, the taxpayer must determine whether he is liable to tax at all. Then he must determine which form he should file and which of the several schedules that may comprise the form he chooses, including that for itemized deductions, applies to him. Whether or not he itemizes, he must determine which tax credits apply. Six of these have separate lines on Form 1040:

· Credit for the elderly (attach Schedules R and RP)

· Investment credit (attach Form 3468)

· Partial credit for political contributions

· Credit for child and dependent care expenses (attach Form 2441)

· Jobs credit (attach Form 5884)

· Residential energy credit (attach Form 5695)

The taxpayer may also be eligible for three other credits, which do not get separate lines on Form 1040:

· Alcohol fuel credit (attach Form 6478)

· Credit for fuel from nonconventional sources

· Credit for increasing research activities (attach Form 6765)

Even the short form requires the taxpayer to make a number of choices. For example, it includes lines for:

· Earned income credit

· Credit for child care expenses

· IRA contributions

· Two-earner deduction
· Taxable portion of unemployment compensation
· Presidential election campaign fund checkoff

It is perhaps not surprising that in 1983 paid preparers were called upon for help on 41 percent of individual tax returns, including 57 percent of the long forms (1040), 24 percent of the short forms (1040A), and even 4 percent of the short short forms (1040EZ).

These examples illustrate the sort of complexity that has been introduced to tax compliance by the use of the tax system to accomplish various social goals and by the effort to tailor tax burdens to individual circumstances. There is no doubt that adding various special functions to the tax return imposes costs on both citizens and the government. Yet the annual tax filing does offer distinct advantages as a mechanism for reaching a large fraction of the population in administering an array of public programs. Without this device, we might instead be confronted with a series of separate bureaucracies and procedures to implement programs such as subsidies for child and dependent care or matching grants for political contributions. Then there would surely be a clamor for the introduction of a streamlined, unified administration of federal subsidies to individuals. Perhaps we would view April 15 differently if we called it the "annual unified individual tax and subsidy" filing date.

Most of the complications discussed above cut across the choice between the income and consumption strategies of tax design. That is, they have little to do with the matter of how savings are taxed. Details of the list of credits and the like would have to change if a move were made toward consistent application of either strategy. For example, the investment credit would probably be omitted from either a pure accrual-income or any version of a consumption-type tax; the IRA deduction would be eliminated from an income tax but might be retained for a consumption-type tax. By and large, however, the policy choices bearing on these sources of complexity are unrelated to the choice between income and consumption approaches.

Problems of Taxpayers with More Complicated Economic Lives

Whereas the really mind-bending intricacy of the tax code affects the average person only indirectly, much as such a person is affected by the intricacy of banking regulations, some individual taxpayers do have to cope directly with tax complexity. The hardest problems have to do with financial affairs and directly owned businesses. Consider first, financial affairs. For the individual who engages in business — not directly but only indirectly as an employee, shareholder, or creditor — the complexities (in addition to those already mentioned) are typically those connected with the treatment of saving in the context of a hybrid system. Such taxpayers tend to be upper-income individuals, although certainly not uniformly so. Whether to buy bonds or stock or to invest in real estate, when to buy or sell financial assets, and whether to repay a mortgage are examples of decisions that have significant but not straightforward tax consequences Such questions as how a payment to or receipt from an insurance company or pension fund will be treated, whether interest payments are deductible, and so on may well require professional advice.

These matters are indeed much affected by the choice between income and consumption strategies. A good deal of the present complexity of the taxation of financial transactions has to do with the existing unhappy compromise between the two approaches, particularly the very different treatment of interest payment and expense and of real investment, which gives rise to the phenomenon known as sheltering. As the November 1984 Treasury proposals illustrate, however, the effort to implement a consistent accrual-income measurement system is virtually certain to involve complicated rules, particularly in view of the need to deal with the effects of inflation. Because consumption-type tax systems can rely on cash-flow accounting, they can avoid the most nettlesome problems altogether.

Business transactions introduce other issues. For an individual who conducts at least some business directly, or who has some expenses as an employee that are not reimbursed by her employer, one of the irritations in life is determining which outlays are eligible for deduction. For example, a part-time consultant who travels on business must keep track of the associated expenses and separate out those that are for purely personal purposes. Or consider a classic problem of tax administration: the office at home. Are all or any of the expenses deductible? Similar questions are confronted by individuals who spend money on activities directed toward improving the yield on their savings, such as subscriptions to financial journals. Home computers and automobiles used partly for business purposes are further examples.

The complexity involved in the tax treatment of such transactions is largely the result of the narrow line dividing expenses for purposes of earning a return and those for direct personal benefit. The necessary distinctions create headaches for taxpayer and tax collector alike. Unfortunately, there is no sure cure to this complexity problem. A highly conservative approach that imposes strict standards and insists on at least the appearance of accounting that can be objectively audited (such as keeping a diary of travel expenses), that proceeds from a presumption in questionable cases that outlays are for personal purposes, and that sets rule-of-thumb limits (such as a specified amount for meals while traveling) typically has a high cost in complexity of the written rules and of the records required for a narrow class of transactions, but may actually reduce complexity overall.

Decisions about matters such as whether to allow a deduction for a home office are often posed as equity issues. If one person uses a room at home for business purposes, while another earns his living working in an office provided by his employer, and both have the same receipts before taking into account the expenses due to the office at home, surely the person with the office at home has the lower income and should be taxed less. But in a competitive economy, if these two individuals are similarly productive, they will tend to command the same after-tax reward. If, in fact, the office is maintained at home purely for business purposes, disallowing a deduction will discourage its use, and the activity in question will tend to be carried out by employees working out of ordinary offices. If, on the other hand, the home office is actually just the study that would be maintained in any case, allowing a deduction will tend to encourage home-based provision of the service. Getting the rule wrong has an efficiency cost (too little or too much home-based production) but not an equity cost (tax burdens incorrectly related to individual endowments).

The many provisions introduced to the tax law in order to encourage specific business activities are a major source of complexity, particularly for business taxpayers. Congress has seen fit in many instances to provide special rules, usually involving a credit for investment, applicable to particular activities. Defining the activities eligible for the favorable provision can make for complex statutory language, with the complexity extending fully to the rulings, regulations, and litigation by which the statute is fleshed out. Depreciation, the investment credit, recapture, inventory accounting, and so on certainly represent areas of serious complexity in the law. The Accelerated Cost Recovery System, introduced in 1981, was billed as a simplifying measure. It did simplify life in one sense. The classification of assets into the various write-off categories is typically straightforward. There are no complex formulas to choose among and apply, and the potential for controversy on audit is reduced. But this simplicity has a cost in other forms of transactional complexity. Because the ability to take advantage of ACRS incentive features depends on the taxpayer's having a high enough tax rate, quite complicated tax-sheltering arrangements, such as limited partnerships, are made relatively more attractive by ACRS. (These arrangements, in turn, call forth complex rules to control perceived excesses.)

The provisions relating to the taxation of capital gains provide another instance of a compliance simplification that produces transactional and rule complexity. Realization accounting itself is generally regarded as a simplification relative to genuine accrual accounting. The special treatment of long-term capital gains, in turn, is a simple way to deal with the perceived excessive tax that would result from full taxation in the case of assets held for a long time (I do not address here the merits of the perception). Finally, the present policy of permitting the basis of an asset to be raised to its market value upon bequest, whereby any gain to that point escapes the income tax altogether, is defended as a simplifying step, avoiding difficult searches for the financial records of the deceased. This combination of features puts an enormous premium on correctly arranging transactions. It is sometimes said that one-half of the practice of a tax lawyer is finding ways to convert ordinary income into long-term capital gains, the other half being the conversion of long-term capital losses into ordinary losses.

The capital gains rules are consequently of the utmost importance, and they are generally credited with a high proportion of the law's bulk and complexity. The complexity is partly due to the need to draw limits around the conversion. In addition, the capital gains distinction provides a convenient handle for delivering political favors, and so it generates complicated special cases in the statute. One of my favorite examples of such special provisions concerns the limits of the application of long-term capital gains treatment to timber. According to the code:

If the taxpayer so elects on his return for a taxable year, the cutting of timber (for sale or for use in the taxpayer's trade or business) during such year by the taxpayer who owns, or has a contract right to cut, such timber . . . shall be considered as a sale or exchange or such timber cut during such year . . . For purposes of this subsection . . . the term "timber" includes evergreen trees which are more than 6 years old at the time severed from the roots and are sold for ornamental purposes.   (Internal Revenue Code Section 631)

It may not be immediately obvious to the reader that the last sentence brings Christmas trees into the charmed circle.

The problems of large companies (typically corporations) in complying with the law generally elicit little sympathy; they can "afford" the lawyers and accountants who can keep track of the complexity. Sympathy is, however, largely irrelevant. Companies as such do not bear the expense of dealing with the complexity, any more than they bear other costs of doing business. I have already discussed the incidence of taxes on corporations; dealing with complexity is just a form of tax on firms. One should keep in mind as well the cost created by complexity for those who must monitor the tax compliance of those large companies, and the losses to claimants on businesses and to the government that result from operating under the uncertainty created by incomprehensible rules.

There are undoubtedly some economies of scale in dealing with the tax law, however, and thus a complex tax system probably does penalize small companies. Small businesses, whether corporations, proprietorships, or partnerships, must deal with many of the same complexities that confront large corporations. Note, though, that some of the advantages of economies of scale are captured by firms that specialize in tax advice (that is, accounting and law firms). Much as a software company can invest substantial resources to develop a bookkeeping program that can be marketed to small businesses at a reasonable price, a specialized tax firm can sell advice to small businesses at a price well below what it would cost those businesses to develop the expertise themselves. Still, each business will typically have some highly specialized tax problems, and the larger companies will have the advantage of being able to spread a solution to those problems over a larger base.

Most provisions that are currently regarded as special, targeted exceptions to rules that would otherwise apply take the form of investment tax credits, extension of the use of tax-exempt bond financing, and accelerated write-off of investment. To the extent that these deviations from the rules that would apply in the absence of special provisions are designed as part of a general effort to alleviate the consequences of taxing the return to capital, one might expect them to be removed in connection with the adoption of a consistent consumption strategy. To the extent that they are in fact more narrowly targeted and not part of a more general pattern of counteracting investment disincentives, there is no reason to expect a clearer choice of tax strategy to affect the complexity caused by the special provisions.

Corporate taxpayers (who may be individual small-business owners) must deal with extra complexities of the law resulting from the division between individual and corporation income taxes. There is an unfortunate tendency for commentators to regard business and corporations as identical and, further, to equate corporations with the Fortune 500. The business tax complexity I have been discussing thus far applies to any business, corporation, partnership, or proprietorship. The corporation tax simply adds another layer of complexity for those businesses that are conducted in corporate form.

The complexity of corporate taxation is difficult to summarize. The essential problem of tax design is to develop a system of transaction-based rules (related to payment and receipt of dividends and interest, sales and purchases of financial and real assets, and so on) that works satisfactorily. The required system must implement the taxation of income at the level of the corporation that is called for by the classical (nonintegrated) approach theoretically underlying U.S. policy and must also provide the data called for to implement an accrual-income tax at the shareholder and creditor level. The problem would be daunting enough in the setting of a consistent system for measuring the real accrual income of individuals. In the context of income-measurement rules that are as beset with problems as those discussed earlier, particularly problems created by inflation, the provisions that concern transactions across the boundary between corporations and their owners come under special strain.

The basic rules are laid down in Subchapter C of the Internal Revenue Code. Subchapter C deals with such questions as when a payment is to be regarded as interest and when a sale transaction constitutes realization for purposes of capital gains. Additional rules bearing on the relation between corporate and individual taxpayers are contained in Subchapter G (concerning the use of retained corporate earnings to avoid shareholder-level income taxation). These parts of the tax law are extremely complicated and have been the subject of frequent reform-oriented scrutiny by legal specialists.

Because long-term business decisions are so dependent on the predictability of the tax treatment of the transactions involved, there is perhaps no clearer instance of a set of rules that ought not to be revised often. But a reading of the statute is recommended for a salutary lesson in the cost both of patching inconsistencies in the income-measurement system and of attempting detailed economic planning via the tax code. It is beyond the scope of this book to pursue this subject in the depth it deserves. However, it would be unfortunate if the costliness of the rules relating to corporations were forgotten in rethinking the income tax structure.

Many of the complexities of the existing rules relating to corporations can be understood as efforts to offset weaknesses in the rules applicable to individuals (weaknesses, that is, if these rules are understood as trying to measure accrual income). The realization basis for measuring capital gains and losses and the special treatment of long-term capital gains are the main culprits. Still, corporations present difficult challenges to income measurement even in the absence of a policy of double taxation of corporate income. By contrast, the cash-flow methods appropriate for implementing a consumption strategy at the individual level comport simply and well with either single or double taxation of corporations.

Graduated Rates and Complexity

To judge from much of the debate about flat taxes, many people appear to believe that the system of graduated tax rates is the main source of income tax complexity. There is a sense in which this perception may be correct, but it is almost certainly not because the calculation of tax, given the taxable income to which the rates are to apply, is a major challenge. (Throughout this section I use the term "income" loosely to mean the base of the individual and corporation income tax.)

Once the taxpayer has calculated his taxable income, it is a simple matter to determine tax liability. True, multiplication by a single rate, the same for all, would be about the simplest of all calculations. But looking the tax up in a table is a close second; and even for those who must refer to the full schedule of brackets and rates, the increased difficulty of computation could hardly qualify as a significant factor in determining how tax burdens should be shared.

The system of graduated rates, however, applied both to corporate and to individual taxpayers, is a source of complexity. Because rates differ from taxpayer to taxpayer, incentives exist to engage in complex transactions of the sort emphasized in the discussion of saving and investment incentives (Chapter 11). Furthermore, graduated rates inhibit the collection of tax *at source* (that is, at the level of the firm or agency where wages and salaries and other claims to the value generated originate). Thus, for example, because individual wage earners differ in the applicable marginal rate, it is not possible to match exactly the correct tax liability through application of a single tax rate to fringe benefits. Collection at source could be a rather powerful way to simplify life for many taxpayers.

Differences in rates among individuals also create incentives to carry out complex — and inconvenient and sometimes costly — transactions to move income from higher-bracket to lower-bracket family members.

Because the same taxpayer is subject to different tax rates in different years, graduated-rate schedules may also set up incentives to undertake complex transactions to move taxable income from one year to the next.

A decision thus needs to be made about the importance of graduated rates to the service of equity in the distribution of the tax burden. The most basic form of nongraduated system is, of course, the single flat rate that levies a tax on all taxpayers in simple proportion to whatever the chosen tax base may be. The next step up in complexity is the personal exemption, with perhaps a zero-bracket amount as well. A tax system with a single rate applied to taxable income in excess of such nontaxed amounts is still commonly considered flat even though it actually incorporates a simple graduation: first a zero-rate bracket and then a single top bracket.

Such a structure does give rise to a progressive tax distribution. For example, a tax at 25 percent on income in excess of $10,000 yields an average tax rate of zero for taxpayers with income up to $10,000. At that point there is a jump in the marginal rate from zero to 25 percent, but the average rate is still zero and rises only gradually with the level of income. At $20,000 the average rate is 12.5 percent (based on 25 percent of the excess of $20,000 over $10,000); at $40,000, 18.75 percent; at $100,000, 22.5 percent. The average rate tends toward 25 percent at the highest levels of income. But closely matching the degree of progressivity in the existing individual income tax (at least with the tax base definitions that have been seriously discussed) requires at least a "modified flat rate," that is, a graduated system with more than one bracket.

Clearly a straightforward argument can be made for graduated individual rates to influence the distribution of tax burdens, but the argument does not extend easily to the corporation tax. In this context, the corporation is a tax collector, with the burden of taxes falling in some ill-understood way among various individuals in the United States (and in other countries too). To the extent that the corporation tax is just an extra levy on a certain form of capital, it is very difficult to rationalize a graduated-rate structure at all (including, by the way, the zero rate applied to losses; economic efficiency would be served by a refundable tax). The main use of the graduated-corporate-rate schedule, however, is presumably made by closely held companies, and in such cases the profits of the company are likely to be as much a reward for innovation, effort, and entrepreneurship by the owner as a return on invested capital. In that context, and without integration of corporation and shareholder accounts, the graduated-rate structure (including the zero tax rate on losses) begins to make more sense.

Progressivity and its implied differences in average rates of tax among individuals give rise to some problems. A good example is the phenomenon in which the tax burdens of two individuals are affected either positively or negatively when they marry. Marriage must have tax consequences in any system that tries to combine the principle of progressivity (even that resulting from applying a flat rate to income beyond an exempt level) and the principle that married couples who have the same income should pay the same tax, regardless of the source of the income.

The inevitability of the marriage-tax problem when these two principles combine may be demonstrated as follows. If there is to be no marriage tax, two individuals who marry should not experience an increase in taxes. Because of progressivity, the tax-minimizing way to split a given income into two separately taxed portions will be an equal division. So, to satisfy the two principles and still ensure that no couple will experience a tax increase when they marry, the tax imposed on a married couple can be no more than twice that on a single individual with half as much as their joint income. But then marriage must imply a tax reduction for two individuals with *unequal* incomes.

If the taxes are adjusted so that there is a lesser marriage "subsidy," a positive tax on the marriage of two equal-earners must emerge. This proposition, again, is a matter of logic. But the quantitative importance of the tax consequences can be small or large. Low rates tend to generate smaller marriage taxes or subsidies. It is difficult to say much more than that in general. One must simply look at specific proposals and attempt to weigh the merits of the alternatives.

It is sometimes suggested that obliging all individuals to file separate tax returns would eliminate the marriage-tax problem and result in a gain in simplicity. Single filing obviates the marriage-tax problem by giving up the principle that couples with the same total income should pay the same tax. Once that principle is abandoned, there are many other possibilities (for example, the current law that permits a deduction for a portion of the labor market earnings of the lower-earning spouse in a two-worker couple). Whether single filing simplifies life depends very much on the techniques that are available to transfer income from one person to another.

Whatever the policy with respect to married couples, there remains the question of how to treat other members of a family group. If property income constitutes part of the base of the individual tax, there will be an incentive to shift the ownership of property to children in order to take advantage of "starting over" on the progressivity scale. Present income tax law makes no effort to discourage such shifting, although it does deny to dependent children the use of the zero-bracket amount (the old standard deduction) with respect to property income.

Present law does attempt, however, to prevent the shifting of income from property without shifting the full ownership. The result is a whole catalog of legal distinctions, including many that make little economic sense. It is a classic case in which good legal advice is essential because there is no reliable way of anticipating the tax law from the general principles involved. Furthermore, perhaps because there really is some merit to the idea of mitigating tax on savings accumulated on behalf of children (to pay for college education, for example), the tax law allows the transfer of income via trusts that satisfy special legal restrictions. When legislation in 1984 limited the use of interest-free loans between family members (the poor man's trust), legal specialists suggested that parents wanting to provide for college expenses consider use of a "spousal remainder trust."[2] The Treasury's November 1984 proposal and the follow-on administration proposal in May 1985 both made another assault on intrafamily income shifting, calling for a segregation of children's wealth received from parents from that received from other sources. The development of policy on this subject provides an excellent example of how the tax law becomes complicated.[3]

As long as the tax liabilities of family members are interrelated in a way that depends on the transactions they undertake, a certain amount of arbitrary and complex rule making seems inevitable. The choice between income and consumption strategies does not bear on the marriage-tax problem. But it does have a bearing on the problem of shifting property ownership to reduce taxes. In the senses discussed in earlier chapters, consumption-type taxes tend to exempt from tax the return to saving and investing. There is thus little incentive under such taxes to engage in transactions that shift the identity of the person doing the saving or investing, and so there is less at stake in the rules governing such transactions. Certain approaches to taxation, such as the Hall-Rabushka plan, would clearly eliminate the potential to affect tax liabil-

2. Normally, to avoid being taxed on the return from a sum of money set aside on behalf of another person, the donor must give up any claim to it for at least ten years. A spousal remainder trust allows the ten-year requirement to be skirted by providing that the amount placed in trust reverts not to the grantor, but to the grantor's spouse.

3. Ironically, because in some states payment of college expenses is coming to be considered a part of parents' legal obligation, it may be that trust devices will often fail in their main purpose of helping a family to accumulate funds for educational purposes.

ities by intrafamily transactions and would therefore remove rule, compliance, and transactional complexity from this source.

Proxy Taxes at Source

Uniform transaction taxes such as a VAT have the potential for simplifying the lives of most individuals. Such taxes have two sorts of simplification advantages. First, they may involve inherently simple base measurement rules, such as uniform cash-flow accounting. But, as experience in most countries confirms, policymakers usually insist on introducing special distinctions (as between sales of luxuries and sales of food) that exact a price in the complexity of the base. Second, a uniform transaction tax, which would typically be calculated and paid only by firms and other employers, can be administered with many fewer taxpaying units than is required for an individual tax. The number of taxpayers required to keep records and remit payment is much smaller than that required to tax each transaction at the household level.

The technique of such "entity-level" taxation could be employed more widely to achieve greater simplicity in the tax system. The design problem is to avoid undesired incentive and distribution effects. The potential use of entity-level taxation to substitute for individual-level taxation will be enhanced to the degree that the applicable marginal rate is similar across individuals.

Fringe benefits provide an illustration. It is sometimes possible to identify the market value of the benefits attributable to a particular individual; including such benefits in the tax base, if that were desired, would be no more difficult than including wages and salaries in the tax base. But many fringe benefits are difficult or impossible to assign accurately to particular employees — for example, subsidized meals in company cafeterias or athletic facilities provided by the firm. A natural and convenient way to tax income that occurs in such form would be to apply a uniform rate at the entity level — for example, by disallowing a deduction of all or some fraction of the amount involved from a tax levied on businesses. In addition to the usual policy arguments about the social virtues of fringe benefits, however, the entity-level tax is subject to the criticism that it would be applied at the wrong rate with respect to some employees. The logic of the argument is dubious (after all, a zero rate is clearly wrong for most or all employees), but its political effectiveness is evident.

Of particular interest is the potential for using entity-level taxation as a substitute for individual-level taxation of all sorts of income originating in businesses. This is the principle applied so effectively in the Hall-Rabushka Simple Flat Tax. For example, if, instead of allowing a deduction for interest paid and requiring taxation of interest received, the treatment was reversed (no deduction of interest paid and no taxation of interest received), the problems noted in connection with the proper measurement and taxation of interest would be eliminated, and individual tax compliance would be greatly simplified.

As in the fringe benefit case discussed above, because the tax rate applicable to the deducting entity is typically different from that applicable to the recipient under the existing tax system, the result of this alternative treatment of interest would be wrong to some degree. But applying a uniform tax to such types of income would permit such an enormous simplification of the system that serious consideration ought to be given to just how much the mismatch matters, particularly as marginal rate differences are reduced. I shall discuss this possibility further in the next two chapters.

TAX REFORM III

The Accrual-Income Strategy **13**

Now that the election is over, it may be possible to talk candidly about taxes without being considered a Bolshevik.

Herbert Stein, "After the Ball"

TAX REFORM is controversial for good reason. Fundamentally, what is at issue is the distribution of a burden. It is true that improvement of the tax system can enlarge the total economic pie, perhaps substantially. But reform almost always means increasing tax burdens for some individuals.

In Chapters 3–6 I described various pure forms of tax corresponding to consistent application of accrual-income and consumption strategies, and the illustrative reform programs discussed here aim for one or the other as their objective. This chapter and the next will give more attention to matters of transition and, especially, to matters of analysis: incentive effects, ease of administration, fairness, and the like. In my choice of illustrative reforms I also introduce my sense of what is conceivable politically, even if it is unlikely to occur.

In its November 1984 proposal the U.S. Treasury Department resolved the problem of describing a reform program based on the accrual-income strategy. The compromises that the Treasury felt compelled to make, and the fate of some of its more "radical" moves in pursuit of purity, will be part of my story. The consumption-strategy illustrations in Chapter 14 of this book lack such a political test, thus far, and my discussion must therefore be more speculative. As a preliminary to this discussion, I review the apparent shortcomings of the existing hybrid income tax and some of the constraints on changing it.

Consider first the matter of fairness. While there is obviously disagreement about how progressive the tax should be, there seems to be considerable agreement that the current system is lacking in horizontal equity, as it imposes different tax burdens on individuals who ought to be treated alike. For example, an individual who receives cash compensation from his employer pays more in tax than does one whose compensation has the same cash value but is received partly in the form of health benefits. An individual who receives interest payments on a municipal bond pays less in tax than one who receives the same amount of interest payments from a corporation. In the discussion of these sources of inequity in Chapters 7 and 8, however, a critical distinction was made between the nominal incidence of a tax (that is, the obligation to send a tax payment to the government) and the real incidence, consisting of the reduced purchasing power (or its equivalent) obtained by an individual as a consequence of the tax. Thus the individual who holds the tax-exempt bond bears some tax burden in the form of a lower before-tax interest rate than is available on taxable corporate bonds. It can be very difficult to sort out the real from the merely apparent in the description of the horizontal inequities of the existing tax system. Of course, even apparent inequities are a matter of concern in a democratic system, where what people believe about government policy affects their confidence in it and willingness to cooperate in it. Greater consistency in the treatment of various transactions may serve perceived equity, even if it is difficult to demonstrate clear gains in the fairness of the real distribution of burdens.

The hybrid character of the existing tax treatment of saving and investment (interest payments and receipts, dividends, capital gains, depreciation, depletion, investment tax credits, and the like) is an important source of trouble. For example, borrowers are allowed to deduct interest paid on amounts used to purchase assets on which the return is not fully taxed, including owner-occupied homes and business assets eligible for accelerated depreciation. This combination permits high-bracket taxpayers to shelter salary income, a practice perceived as inequitable even where there is no hint of irregularity in the legal sense. The portion of interest received that represents a compensation for inflation is subject to tax. Consequently the effective taxation of interest has frequently exceeded 100 percent in recent years. Correspondingly, the after-tax cost of borrowing has often been negative. Among the most contentious elements of the tax system is the treatment of capital gains. Substantial portions are excluded from the tax base by the rules relating to long-term gains, but the absence of any adjustment of an asset's basis for inflation means that taxes are often paid where there has been no gain at all. Each of these instances creates apparent inequity.

The taxation of corporations has also given rise to charges of inequity. Often a confusion about the interests of corporations as separate from the interests of shareholders, employees, creditors, and customers is at the heart of assertions that particular corporations, or corporations in general, do not pay their fair share. Still, this confusion is an element of popular perception about the economy that must be considered in the design of policy. Inconsistency in the income concept has contributed to the appearance of unfair differences in the tax liabilities of different corporations. More fundamental is the failure, discussed in Chapter 6, to coordinate the taxation of corporations with that of the individuals who have a claim on corporate income.

If the hybrid character of the existing tax deserves some of the blame for its real or apparent inequity, it deserves more of the blame for its complexity. The basic problem is the formidable difficulty of applying consistently the accrual-accounting techniques that would be necessary for implementation of an income tax. Practical income taxes must be based on transactions, and that has implied the complicated set of compromises that we call realization accounting. Arguably the simplest realization accounting system is cash-flow accounting, which provides the natural tool for implementing a consumption or consumed-income-base tax. The hybrid tax blends elements of accrual and cash-flow accounting, for example, in taxing interest receipts currently (and allowing current deductions for interest paid) but taxing capital gains only on realization. Such combinations give rise to complicated rules, complicated tax-planning problems for taxpayers, and complicated enforcement problems for the tax administration.

Complexity of tax law and practice creates the appearance and substance of inequity. It also gives rise to waste, that is, economic value lost to both taxpayer and tax collector. Some waste is unavoidable, for the simple reason that taxes must be levied on something, and they will inevitably discourage the taxed activity. In particular, some inefficiency is bound to be the price of an effort to impose a heavier burden on the well-off than on the less-well-off. But I doubt that the extent of the loss induced by taxes is widely appreciated. Furthermore, much of the inefficiency associated with the hybrid character of the taxation of saving and investment is unnecessary to achieve the other objectives of the tax system.

Not all the problems of the existing tax system are attributable to its hybrid character. Many provisions of the tax law, including such popular elements as the deductions for taxes and charitable contributions and the exclusion from employee income of various fringe benefits, can be viewed as policy choices about the definition of consumption. Viewed as tax expenditures, they are subsidies to particular activities, such as state and local government spending or charitable contributions. These provisions are often the targets of reformers; eliminating them, or even reducing marginal rates, is like cutting any subsidy and may need to be dealt with politically in similar terms.

Mention of politics brings us to the matter of constraints on reform. The tax policy debate as it appears in the press and in congressional testimony seems split between those who would radically reform the system and those who would, basically, tinker with it. There is merit to both positions. Those who argue for an immediate shift to very different rules, greatly broadening the tax base and greatly lowering the rates of tax, point to the historical failure of incremental reform. After all, "broaden the base and lower the rates" has been a reform theme almost since the income tax was instituted in 1913 and certainly since its evolution in World War II to a mass tax at significant rates. Advocates argue that only by offering a program that makes the advantages of reform — greater simplicity and lower rates — immediately available can the public be rallied to impose the costs that reform implies for those who would lose existing tax benefits. Moreover, eliminating many special preferences all at once increases the chance that the same taxpayer who loses from one change will gain from another.

Against this position, there is a "should" and a "will" case for gradualism, arguing that we should not make a major shift in tax policy overnight and that we are not likely to do so as a matter of political reality. The tax system impinges on our society in more ways than we generally realize. Perhaps most people are vaguely aware of the impact of tax rules on business life — the structure of industry and its mode of organization — and on the financial affairs of households, from life insurance and retirement savings to the holdings of residential real estate and art objects. But the list does not end there. The types of dwellings we inhabit, the character of our communities, the tasks we assign to state and local government, the nature of the arts and education, even our family mores, marriage, and divorce, all have been shaped by the federal income tax.

Princeton University President William G. Bowen put the point succinctly in testimony before the Senate Finance Committee (August 7, 1984):

[The existing tax] system, whatever its advantages and disadvantages might be in theory or in practice, has had pervasive effects on essentially all aspects of American life. Institutions, policies, and practices that seem to be a quite natural part of our society, and that are generally taken for granted, are in fact artifacts of the incentives — and disincentives — which that tax system has offered. Thus, in considering truly fundamental changes in the tax system, this

Committee is not simply evaluating technical problems of economics or finance. It is contemplating changes that almost certainly would have profound effects on the ways in which we serve national objectives.

There is a good case for moving gradually toward major changes in a system of rules that so greatly affects the society. Furthermore, the very fact that the tax system is so pervasive in its influence means that significant changes made abruptly will bring about major redistributions of wealth. For the most part these wealth effects are transitional; that is, they would not be part of the discussion of the distribution of tax burdens twenty years hence if we were to adopt the new rules today. But they are potentially large. That is why individual taxpayers and their representatives (such as the managers of firms) so fiercely defend their tax breaks. Well-informed tax reformers would want to find ways to eliminate the breaks without imposing heavy losses on those who currently depend on them.

That brings us to the "will" part of the argument for gradualism. It is often said that every feature of the existing law is there for a reason. No doubt this view is exaggerated. A reading of the tax law — to the extent that this is humanly possible — makes it hard to believe anyone constructed it on purpose. But political support for the main features of the law must be taken as a working hypothesis. Even though polls may register declining confidence in the income tax, what many people mean by reform is lower taxes, and few are prepared to give up their own tax preferences in the interest of a simple, low-rate system. Politicians typically report little serious constituent pressure for simplification or rationalization of the law (see, for example, Conable, 1983). A reform plan should be susceptible to incremental implementation.

Incremental implementation need not necessarily mean application of what has come to be called the cats-and-dogs approach to reform — the piecemeal closing of loopholes. There are various ways a phased transition to a redesigned system could be managed in order to mitigate the pain of transition. Furthermore, incremental implementation need not mean incremental adoption. Indeed, a good case can be made that predictability of the tax law has been one of the main casualties of the past decade's efforts at reform. An ideal reform would have the character of a preannounced series of changes in the rules. But because of the need to allow for ongoing political negotiation about serving some of the functions that are now the target of tax expenditures and for continuing adjustment to the inevitable unexpected reactions to new rules, the system should not require a rigidly fixed transition path.

In addition to a general preference for changes that permit gradual phasing in, there are more technical constraints that must be accommodated. Although by no means everyone agrees with me, I believe annual measurement of wealth must be considered out of the question as a practical matter. As I have repeatedly noted in this book, many of the peculiar features and pressures observed in the U.S. income tax can be traced to the difficulty of accounting consistently for various saving and investment transactions. The perennially vexing matter of the rules for taxing capital gains is a good illustration. Among the ways out of the inconsistencies, if not the complexity, of the existing system would be the adoption of thoroughgoing accrual-income accounting. This would mean annual estimation of the values of all assets and liabilities (not just of marketable securities). However, it is unlikely that actual rules will go very far in this direction. The tax base will continue to rely on realization accounting. That is, tax liabilities will be calculated (as they are now) on the basis of actual transactions — basically, buying and selling. Of course, this does not mean that what we have called cash-flow-type accounting will be used. Under cash-flow accounting, current tax liabilities are based entirely on current transactions. Under realization accounting, current liabilities may be based on past transactions, as in the recovery of basis in the calculation of capital gain or the allowance for depreciation of a past capital purchase.

If rigorous accrual-income accounting is impractical, I think that full-fledged personal cash-flow accounting (as described in Chapter 5) is probably too radically different from existing law to be acceptable. This approach would, for example, require all borrowing to be added to the individual's or firm's tax base and all lending or repayment to be subtracted. The procedure is unfamiliar and would complicate life for many taxpayers. I doubt that the political system is yet prepared to accept universal application of this principle. But taxpayers already deal with such cash-flow accounting for some savings as an option (for example, with respect to IRAs), and they should have no difficulty applying it uniformly to businesses. I also take for granted that corporations must be seen to pay taxes. Although corporations as such do not bear taxes, public perception that they do is so strong that substantial payments by corporations have to be taken as a given feature of the tax system. As discussed in Chapter 6, taxes at the corporate level can be designed to complement either accrual-income or consumption-type taxes at the individual level — either as withholding taxes or as extra taxes on the corporate form of organization.

The matter of gifts and inheritances deserves mention among the constraints as well. Some reform proposals would substitute inclusion of gifts and inheritances in income for the existing estate and gift tax. As of this writing this seems mainly a matter of academic interest. (For an extended study of American attitudes toward inheritance, see Hochschild, 1981). The question of what changes are possible in the taxation of gifts and inheritances, however, will affect views about desirable changes in income tax policy. For example, a number of commentators have expressed the opinion that rationalizing the income tax system along consumed-income lines would be desirable if inheritances were more heavily taxed, and undesirable otherwise.

Treasury I: Broad-Based Accrual-Income Tax

The Treasury's proposal of November 1984 (also known as "Treasury I" because it was put forth in anticipation of a revision in reaching the actual administration proposal, which was made public in May 1985) represents as close an approximation to a pure income tax as we are likely to see. It therefore provides an excellent framework for assessing the conversion of the income tax to a broad-based accrual-income standard. Table 13–1 reproduces the summary prepared by the Treasury Department, comparing the November 1984 proposal with current law, on the one hand, and with the administration's May 1985 proposal ("Reagan I"), on the other hand. I shall focus now on the first comparison. Relative to current law as of 1985, Treasury I moves the system toward the accrual-income ideal in the following major respects:

· Capital gains are taxed in full (with inflation adjustment of basis).[1]

· Depreciation allowances are refined to approximate the typical pattern of value decline for each asset class; the allowances are adjusted for inflation.

· The inflation-premium element of interest payments and receipts is excluded from tax by reducing the amount deducted or subject to tax by a percentage related to the inflation rate.

· Inventories are accounted for on an inflation-indexed FIFO basis.

---

1. The Treasury plan is silent on the question of changing the write-up of basis at the death of the asset owner.

Table 13-1. Comparison of highlights of current law, November 1984 Treasury proposal, and president's proposal

Tax category	Current law (1986)	November 1984 Treasury proposal	President's proposal
Individual tax rates	14 rate brackets from 11% to 50%, indexed	3 rate brackets 15%, 25%, and 35%, indexed	3 rate brackets 15%, 25%, and 35%, indexed
Exemptions			
Self, spouse	$1080, indexed	$2000, indexed	$2000, indexed
Dependents	$1080, indexed	$2000, indexed	$2000, indexed
Zero-bracket amount			
Single	$2480, indexed	$2800, indexed	$2900, indexed
Joint	$3670, indexed	$3800, indexed	$4000, indexed
Heads of household	$2480, indexed	$3500, indexed	$3600, indexed
Two-earner deduction	Yes	No	No
Earned-income credit	Yes ($550 maximum)	Yes, indexed	Increased and indexed ($726 maximum)
Child-care expenses	Tax credit	Deduction	Deduction
Fringe benefits			
Health insurance	Not taxed	Taxed above a cap	Limited amount taxed
Group-term life insurance, legal services, dependent care, education assistance	Not taxed	Taxed	Not taxed
Parsonage allowance	Not taxed	Taxed	Not taxed
Wage replacement			
Unemployment compensation	Taxed if AGI over $12,000 ($18,000 if married)	Taxed	Taxed

Workers' compensation	Not taxed	Taxed, but eligible for special credit for elderly and disabled	Taxed, but eligible for expanded and indexed credit for elderly and disabled
Veterans' disability benefits	Not taxed	Taxed	Not taxed
Itemized deductions			
State and local income tax	Deductible	Not deductible	Not deductible
Other state and local taxes	Deductible	Not deductible, unless incurred in income-producing activity	Not deductible, unless incurred in income-producing activity
Charitable contributions	Deductible by itemizers and nonitemizers	Deductible (above 2% of AGI) for itemizers, but no deduction for nonitemizers or for unrealized gains on contributed property	Deductible for itemizers, but no deduction for nonitemizers
Mortgage interest	Deductible	Deductible for principal residences	Deductible for principal residences
Other personal interest	Personal interest deductible; investment interest limited to $10,000 over investment income	Limited to $5000 over investment income for expanded definition of interest subject to limit	Limited to $5000 over investment income for expanded definition of interest subject to limit (with phase-in)
Medical expenses	Deductible (above 5% of AGI)	Deductible (above 5% of AGI)	Deductible (above 5% of AGI)
Tax abuses			
Entertainment expenses	Deductible	Not deductible	Not deductible

Table 13–1 (*continued*)

Tax category	Current law (1986)	November 1984 Treasury proposal	President's proposal
Business meals and travel expenses	Deductible	Deduction denied for meal costs above cap	Deduction denied for 50% of meal costs above cap
Income shifting to children and via trusts	Permissible	Curtailed	Curtailed, except for postdeath trusts
Retirement savings			
IRA	$2000	$2500	$2000
Spousal IRA	$250	$2500	$2000
Corporate pensions	Tax deferred	Tax deferred	Tax deferred
Social Security	Generally not taxed	Generally not taxed	Generally not taxed
Capital and business income			
Corporate tax rates	Graduated, up to 46%	33% flat rate	Graduated, up to 33%
Limited partnerships	Losses flow-through to partners	No loss flow-through	Current law
Dividend relief	$100/$200 exclusion	Exclusion repealed; 50% dividend-paid deduction	Exclusion repealed; 10% dividend-paid deduction
Depreciation	ACRS	Economic depreciation, indexed	Indexed, with investment incentive
Investment tax credit	6%–10%	No	No
Capital gains	60% excluded	Indexed, taxed as ordinary income	50% excluded (optional indexing in 1991)
Interest income/expense	Fully taxed/deductible	Indexed, partially excludable/nondeductible	Fully taxed/deductible

Inventory accounting			
LIFO conformity required	Yes	No	No
FIFO	Not indexed	Indexed	Indexed
Uniform production cost rules	No uniform rules	Uniform rules	Uniform rules
Installment sales	Deferral	No deferral if receivables pledged	Generally no deferral if receivables pledged
Bad-debt reserve deduction	Yes	No	No
Oil industry			
Percentage depletion	Yes	No; indexed cost depletion	Phased out with stripper exception
Expensing of intangible drilling costs	Yes	No	Yes
Windfall profits tax	Will phase out in 1991	Phase-out accelerated	Will phase out in 1991
Financial institutions			
Special bad-debt deduction	Yes	No	No
Deduction for interest to carry tax-exempts	Yes	No	No
Exemption of credit unions	Yes	No	No, except for small credit unions
Deferral for life insurance income and annuity income	Yes	No	No, except for existing policies

Table 13–1 (continued)

Tax category	Current law (1986)	November 1984 Treasury proposal	President's proposal
Exemption of certain insurance companies including fraternal organizations	Yes	No	Yes
Municipal bonds			
Public purpose	Tax exempt	Tax exempt	Tax exempt
Private purpose	Tax exempt	Taxable	Taxable
Rehabilitation and energy credits	Yes	No	No
Minimum tax on individuals and corporations	Yes	Not necessary	Retain and tighten

Source: *The President's Tax Proposals to the Congress for Fairness, Growth, and Simplicity,* May 1985, chart 18.

- The "inside buildup" on life insurance and annuity contracts is included in policyholder income subject to tax.[2]

- A partial integration of corporate and individual taxes is effected by allowing a deduction from corporate tax of one-half of dividends paid.

- Various transfer payments now wholly or partially excluded are subject to tax.

- A number of currently excluded fringe benefits are subject to tax.

- Personal deductions from taxable income are limited in various ways; in particular, the deduction for state and local taxes is eliminated entirely, and the deduction for charitable contributions is sharply cut back.

In addition, the proposal would eliminate a number of investment subsidy programs cleared through the income tax, including most notably the investment tax credit, both in general and in its many specific extensions. Important among the provisions that would be preserved is the earned-income credit, a wage subsidy for low earners with dependents.

Naturally, any practical plan oriented toward the accrual-income ideal will deviate from it many ways. The following are the more significant respects in which the Treasury plan deviates:

- It retains a separate "classical" tax on corporations, though with the partial integration already mentioned.

- It continues to apply realization rather than accrual-income accounting in a number of important instances, particularly with respect to capital gains (so that rules distinguishing capital gains from other income would still be required, and deduction of capital losses would still have to be limited).

- It preserves certain tax-sheltered retirement saving opportunities via employer-sponsored pension plans and an expanded version of the existing IRAs.

- It makes no effort to measure and tax the return from household durables, especially owner-occupied houses.

- It maintains current treatment of Social Security retirement benefits.

2. "Inside buildup" is the name given to the interest and other earnings on pension plans and the savings element of whole-life life insurance. Under current law it is partially or wholly exempt from tax until realized by the policyholder. In the case of life insurance, there is no income tax at the individual level at all if the value is realized by beneficiaries upon death of the policyholder.

It would be a mistake to concentrate too much on the specific rate structure of a proposal when attempting to understand its conceptual foundation, but we can get a rough idea of the base broadening involved in the Treasury plan from the rates estimated to be sufficient to maintain the existing level and roughly the existing distribution of tax liabilities. In the individual income tax, the rate structure starts from an exemption of $2000 for each taxpayer or dependent (compared with $1080 projected for 1986 under current law) and a zero-bracket amount of $2800 for single individuals ($2480 under present law) and $3800 for married couples filing joint returns ($3670 under present law). The graduated-rate structure has three positive rates: 15 percent, 25 percent, and 35 percent. The traditional family of four with no deductions and only wage and salary income would reach the tax threshold at $11,800, would pay 15 percent of income between $11,800 and $39,800, 25 percent on income between $39,800 and $71,800, and 35 percent on income above $71,800. Positive amounts of corporate income would be subject to tax at the rate of 33 percent, with no graduation. Although the plan does not make explicit the treatment of losses, presumably no refund would be made for negative amounts of income, while carry-over of losses would be allowed in both the corporation and the individual tax systems. The estimated net effect of all the proposed changes on revenue was a projected 6.5 percent reduction in receipts from the individual income tax over the fiscal-year 1986–1990 period, and a projected 30.4 percent increase in receipts from the corporation income tax.

Two recommended changes in the treatment of the family are worth noting. First are revisions in the rules relating to income shifting from parents to children. Treasury I would tax the "unearned" income of a child under fourteen derived from property given to the child by the parents, to the extent that it exceeds the child's personal exemption, at the parents' marginal tax rate. In addition, the proposal would tax the income set aside for children under certain widely used trust arrangements at the marginal rate of the trusts' creators, rather than at the rates of the beneficiaries.[3] Second is the repeal of the exclusion from tax of part of the earnings of the secondary worker of a two-earner married couple.

The Treasury plan provides transition rules designed to strike a compromise between minimizing arbitrary wealth gains and losses due to the reform and hastening the time when the new rules will be fully in

---

3. Note that neither of the problems addressed by these changes arises as a problem at all in a consumption-type tax.

effect. The mitigating techniques include grandfathering (for instance, as applied to existing depreciation allowances), delayed implementation (as applied to interest and capital gains indexing), and phased-in implementation (as applied to the new dividend deduction and to restrictions on the itemized deductions for state and local taxes and charitable contributions).

General Commentary on Treasury I

In comparison with other hybrid income tax reform proposals current in late 1984, the Treasury plan attracted most attention for differences in the treatment of itemized deductions, especially those for state and local taxes and for charitable contributions. Less obvious was the fundamental way the Treasury plan differed from all others then and since in taking on in full glory the problems of income measurement in a world with inflation. The coordinated provisions in question include indexing depreciation allowances, indexing inventory accounting, indexing the basis of capital gains, and indexing interest receipts and payments. Although some of these provisions have been considered separately, Treasury I takes the important step of putting them together; the provision for interest indexing, in particular, had not been seriously considered before in the United States. Another fundamental difference between the Treasury plan and most hybrid reform proposals is the treatment of corporations. In its recommended deduction of one-half of dividends paid from the base of the corporation income tax, Treasury I makes a move toward integration of individual and corporation taxes that was lacking in most other plans.

Considerable controversy was created by the substantial shift in liability from individual to corporate taxpayers implied by the Treasury proposal. As emphasized in Chapters 6 and 7, corporations should be viewed as collectors rather than bearers of taxes. The mere fact that the amount of tax paid by corporations increases or decreases does not in itself conclusively indicate a shift in the burden of taxes or an increase in the wedge established by the tax system between the rate of return generated by corporate investment and that received by the savers who finance that investment. I return to this issue below.

Among the deviations from the accrual-income standards is Treasury I's provision for increasing the allowed annual contribution to an IRA from the present limits of $2000 for the primary worker and $250 for a spouse who is not employed for pay, to $2500 for each spouse. For many people these limits would be sufficient to permit virtually all savings to be accumulated in tax-sheltered form. Although the proposed IRAs will be subject to more stringent limits than are currently in force, the Treasury plan can be said in a rough sense to continue or even reinforce the existing tendency to put the tax system on a consumed-income basis for individuals of modest means while shifting toward more consistent taxation of accrual income for individuals of greater means. Just how the IRA provisions would work and what their effects on both the incentive and the distributional characteristics of the system would be would continue to depend on the extent of the transfer of existing savings to tax-sheltered form and the related possibility of borrowing (at deductible interest) to finance contributions to an IRA. To the extent these possibilities are available, the modest-means taxpayer continues to face an income tax, and the IRA provisions amount to a lump-sum tax reduction for those clever enough to see it.

The inflation indexing of interest payments and receipts under the Treasury plan has been mentioned as an important innovation. Also of note is the proposed treatment of interest quite apart from inflation correction. The Treasury plan responded to overwhelming political pressure to retain the deduction of interest paid on a mortgage on an owner-occupied principal residence, but it otherwise limits the deduction of nonbusiness interest to $5000 plus cash flows constituting "passive investment income" (not defined, but presumably consisting of dividends, interest received, realized capital gains, and the like). As suggested in Chapter 3, such a limitation is not strictly required by fidelity to the accrual-income ideal (the interest deduction limit is usually justified as a substitute for taxing the implicit yield from household durables, especially owner-occupied housing). One could in any case anticipate considerable pressure on home mortgages as a source of borrowing favored both in being free of the limitation on interest deduction and in exclusion from the inflation-correction provisions (so that interest rates that include an effective repayment of principal are deductible in full under Treasury I).

Incidence

The Treasury plan claims to be generally distributionally neutral. The rates and exemptions were set to generate a percentage distribution of individual liabilities by income class that closely matches the percentage distribution of individual liabilities under the system it would replace. (A significant exception is the treatment of those at the lowest part of the income distribution among those now subject to tax. The exemptions in the Treasury plan would free many from income tax liability.) But no estimate is made of the effect on individual tax burdens of the plan's shift of tax liabilities to corporations to make up for an average 8.5 percent cut in individual tax liabilities. The shift of liabilities to corporations raises a host of interesting questions. For example, should one think about eliminating a tax subsidy to investment in a particular industry, say shipbuilding, as raising the tax on saving or as raising the price of ships?[4] The required incidence analysis is very much like that described in Chapter 7 for the traditional view of the corporation tax, and the effects of the change in rules in any particular instance depend on the relative responses of businesses in different industries as the system seeks a new balance. If the conventional wisdom that the corporation income tax is borne by owners of capital holds (see Chapter 7), the Treasury plan would represent an increase in progressivity over the existing system.

A major objective of the Treasury plan is to improve the horizontal equity of the system (see Chapter 8). Dozens of changes in the rules would shift tax burdens among individuals in apparently similar circumstances (for example, by eliminating or limiting itemized deductions, eliminating the two-earner deduction, repealing the partial exclusion of unemployment compensation, and curtailing business deductions for personal expenses), thereby bringing perceived tax burdens into closer alignment with perceived circumstances. We would expect some of these differences in the incidence of the system to be temporary, as individuals alter their behavior, and prices and wages adjust.

In spite of phased-transition rules, significant wealth effects from the imposition of the changed rules would be expected. Examples would be the effects on individuals taking most advantage of such provisions as exclusion of fringe benefits. To take a small instance, the plan would eliminate the exclusion of parsonage allowances. Over time, the loss to potential ministers would presumably be trivial, as the terms of employment would be adjusted to reflect the changed rules. But the immediate effect on an individual in an affected position would be a loss in wealth to the extent of, perhaps, two years' worth of tax benefits. The same analysis, amplified, applies to most of the proposed reform provisions. Perhaps most significant and interesting are the effects on those

---

4. It seems seldom noted that, although anything that makes an industry expand will call forth investment, subsidies to businesses in particular industries do not *have* to focus on investment.

holding claims on financial and business assets and liabilities. The story is, unfortunately, extremely complicated, and it is beyond the power of available techniques to sort it out with confidence. I can do little more than point out some of the instances of wealth effects.

As will be discussed below, one likely effect of the Treasury plan would be reduced interest rates. This shift would benefit those who have fixed long-term financial claims and would hurt those with fixed long-term liabilities. The plan would sharply increase the tax payable with respect to certain real assets (notably timber and other agricultural assets on which the return is now treated as long-term capital gain). Owners of such assets would suffer an immediate loss. Because of the lower tax rates, the plan would reduce the tax due on assets that have been deducted in the past. This applies to real assets that have benefited from accelerated-depreciation deductions (such as residential real estate) and from exclusion from income. In the latter class are the accumulated retirement funds of present employees. These funds have in many cases been excluded from salary income at a saving of 50 percent in tax and would now be taxed at 35 percent when received as retirement income.

Perhaps least understood is the likely gain to owners of existing real assets in the United States associated with a reduced incentive to acquire new assets here. This is just the reverse of the tendency to introduce an incentive, such as the investment tax credit, that applies only to new assets to cause a capital loss to owners of existing assets (which are unexpectedly subjected to competition from the more favorably treated new assets). To the extent that the Treasury plan increases the tax burden on new investment, it will tend to generate a transition gain for owners of existing capital.

Simplification

The Treasury plan would effect simplification for ordinary, average taxpayers by reducing the number of credits and itemized deductions and by raising the personal allowances. These steps would take many people off the tax-filing rolls and make many who would now be itemizers into nonitemizers. Apart from the new complications to deal with indexing of interest and capital gains, for most individual tax filers the law would be simpler. With respect to business and more sophisticated financial affairs, however, the rules would in many instances be more complex than at present. Indexing provisions, especially, would represent an increase in complexity, as would a number of more technical provisions relating to the time value of money (that is, improved approximation to true accrual accounting). However, as pointed out in Chapter 12, the move toward greater consistency of the tax treatment of transactions having similar economic effects (such as capital gains and interest receipts) reduces the premium on correct tax planning, thereby effecting transactional simplification.

Tax Distortions

Work Incentives. The Treasury plan's main emphasis is on reducing the influence of taxes on economic decisions. A major element of this effort is reduction in marginal rates. The Treasury estimates that the plan will reduce the average of marginal tax rates confronted by individuals (excluding the corporation tax) by 20 percent. The largest percentage reductions in marginal rates are projected for the highest brackets in the existing system (because that is where the base is most substantially broadened). As noted in Chapter 9, the payoff in efficiency to reductions in marginal rates tends to be proportional to the square of the rate in question, and so achieving the largest percentage reductions in marginal rates at the upper end of the rate structure appears very favorable for improving the incentive to work.

Because the marginal rate reductions are accomplished by broadening of the base, however, a certain caution is required in projecting the incentive effects as applied to particular activities, such as work effort. For example, some of the base broadening consists in making taxable forms of compensation that are free of tax in the existing system. The incentive to work of a hypothetical person currently in the 50 percent bracket would actually be diminished by a lowering of the marginal rate to 35 percent if 40 percent of his salary is currently tax exempt, while 100 percent is taxable under the reform. (If 40 percent of compensation is now untaxed, a dollar received implies just 30 cents in tax, for an effective marginal rate of 30 percent.) Much the same remark applies to base broadening via elimination of personal deductions. To the extent that the reward to working consists partly of taxable consumption and partly of tax-exempt activities (itemized deductions), simultaneous elimination of deductions and lowering of marginal rates may not significantly affect the incentive to work.

We can be more confident in predicting the effect of the proposal on the makeup of the compensation received by employees. The elimination of tax-exempt status for innumerable forms of fringe benefits would lead to a shift in compensation toward money wages and salaries;

individual workers would presumably buy some of the fringes for themselves, although removing the tax advantage would doubtless reduce the quantity.

Finally, the effect of the proposed treatment of capital gains under the Treasury plan on the incentives of entrepreneurs may be mentioned under the work-incentive heading, even though the subject may appear to belong under the heading of the taxation of saving and investment. As pointed out in Chapter 9, because the tax-accounting system cannot capture the accruing value of a new idea but must instead make tax liabilities await the realization of the payoff to the idea in the form of cash flows, the existing taxation of entrepreneurs is, in effect, on a consumption basis to the extent that the originator of the idea exploits it himself. If, however, the originator finds it advantageous to sell the idea to someone else to develop, or simply desires to diversify his portfolio by not having all of his wealth tied up in the enterprise that develops the idea, he can still obtain nearly the same advantages, owing to the light taxation of long-term capital gains. Because the Treasury proposal would subject long-term capital gains to full taxation (after correction of the basis for inflation), relative to existing law it would have a discouraging effect on entrepreneurship.

Incentives to Accumulate and Use Wealth. Full, uniform taxation of the return to saving is the critical identifying characteristic of accrual-income taxation. The Treasury plan would eliminate, at both the individual and the corporate level, most special saving and investment incentives; the important exceptions are owner-occupied housing and retirement savings. Table 13–2, taken from Fullerton (1985), presents an analysis of the effect of the major structural features of Treasury I, in comparison with 1985 law and the administration proposal of May 1985. The figures in the body of the table describe the "effective total marginal tax rate" on the return to investing in various assets. The "effective" part means that the tax-increasing or tax-decreasing effects of provisions such as depreciation allowances have been taken into account. The "total" part means that all taxes — state, local, and federal — including individual and corporation income taxes, have been taken into account. "Marginal" indicates that the rate applies to a forward-looking investment. The effective rate indicates the degree to which the specified after-tax return (here, a 5 percent real return) is lower than the before-tax return on a break-even investment. For example, according to Table 13–2, under current law and with an inflation rate of 4 percent per year, an investment by a corporation in a structure would have to earn just over an 8 percent real return per year to provide the savers who financed

Table 13–2. Effective marginal total tax rates on investment in various assets under 1985 law, Treasury I, and Reagan I (percent)

Tax rates	1985 law	Treasury I	Reagan I
Corporate sector tax rates			
Equipment	−18.3	40.2	24.5
Structures	37.9	45.6	36.3
Public utilities	29.5	43.5	29.7
Inventories	41.6	42.4	38.8
Land	44.9	44.8	41.9
Overall corporate tax rate	31.1	43.1	34.4
Noncorporate sector tax rates			
Equipment	−10.1	27.3	20.2
Structures	28.1	31.4	28.0
Public utilities	21.0	32.8	25.9
Residential structures	32.6	35.3	32.7
Inventories	30.5	28.9	28.7
Land	33.3	32.0	31.7
Residential land	38.2	37.3	37.1
Overall noncorporate tax rate	30.7	32.7	31.0
Owner-occupied housing tax rate	17.2	21.7	23.0
Overall tax rate	26.3	33.5	29.4
Standard deviation	1.71	1.17	0.93
Interest rate	13.2	11.1	12.3

Source: Fullerton (1985, table 5).

Note: Table assumes a 4 percent inflation rate and a 5 percent after-tax real discount rate. For details see Fullerton (1985).

the corporation (partly with debt, partly with new shares, partly with retained earnings) a real return of 5 percent per year: 8 percent less tax at an effective total marginal rate of 37.9 percent leaves 5 percent.

As Fullerton emphasizes, the specific figures are rather sensitive to such assumptions as the specification of the rate of inflation, the after-tax return to savers, and the details of financial markets. But the general picture, strikingly conveyed by Table 13–2, of the uneven taxation of the return to saving under current law is surely accurate. Note, for example, the negative effective rates of tax on investment in equipment, whether in corporate or noncorporate enterprises. Contrast this effective subsidy with an effective rate of over 40 percent applicable to corporate inventories. The consequence of Treasury I is both to raise the general level of taxation of the return to saving and to make it more uniform. The first may be seen in the figures for overall tax rates: up from 26.3 to 33.5 percent on all assets taken together, from 31.1 to 43.1 percent on corporate investment, from 30.7 to 32.7 on noncorporate investment, and from 17.2 to 21.7 percent on owner-occupied housing.[5] Greater uniformity within each sector is also apparent at a glance. Although the proposal widens the spread between corporate and noncorporate effective rates, the "standard deviation," shown at the bottom of the table, gives a statistical measure (the larger it is, the greater the degree of variation in the figures) indicating that the overall effect is also in the direction of uniformity.

Improved consistency of the taxation of saving would be expected to lead to improvement — perhaps substantial — in the productivity of the wealth owned by U.S. taxpayers and of the capital deployed in the United States.[6] Putting quantitative flesh on the extent of the gain requires a number of assumptions — for example, about the effect on worker productivity of adding capital in an industry. Work by Fullerton, together with colleagues Michael T. Allison and John H. Makin (1985), gives an idea of what might be at stake. For reasons of data availability, Allison, Fullerton, and Makin were obliged to analyze the effect of making Treasury I's major structural changes in the proposal — lower rates, depreciation changes, and so on — apply to 1973 law rather than to 1985 law. They estimated the increased value of production (reduced deadweight loss; see Chapter 9) due to improved allocation of capital to be equivalent, in terms of wealth, of $873 billion 1984 dollars, that is, equivalent to more than two years' worth of the total national output.[7] I mention these figures not because I consider them a particularly reliable measure of the efficiency effect of Treasury I. In fact, I have a number of

5. The positive rates on owner-occupied housing are due to state and local property taxes; the increase is due to the elimination of the state and local tax deduction under Treasury I.

6. Fullerton's analysis generates as a by-product a calculation of the interest rate consistent with his model of the capital market. It is notable that, holding fixed the after-tax real rate of return to savers, the Treasury proposals would lead to a significant downward pressure on interest rates.

7. I have inflated the Allison, Fullerton, and Makin figure to 1984 dollars by using the GNP deflator.

serious reservations. But the reservations concern details of the modeling, both of the economy and of the tax system, and not the general approach. I think the figures convey correctly the impression that large efficiency gains from tax revision are possible.

Apart from the transition gains and losses, the improved productivity achieved would be essentially free, an example of the potential of tax reform to increase the size of the economic pie. Unfortunately, transition gains and losses are not an insignificant matter, as was evident from the early reaction of industry to the Treasury plan. Making more similar the tax treatment of various investment categories brings with it shifts in industrial composition and consequent redistributions of wealth. Many of the more significant contentious transition effects would be associated not with the general structural changes analyzed by Fullerton, but with the elimination of various "special" features of the tax code — tax expenditures. As noted in Chapter 11, a preponderance of the tax expenditures set out in the annual publications of the Treasury Department and the Congress take the form of reductions in the effective tax rate on investment in favored activities or on favored forms of saving. The quantitative significance of these special features, which generally represent deviations from accrual-income accounting and are therefore eliminated under Treasury I, is brought home by their role in the estimated 30.4 percent increase in corporation income tax receipts that the reform would bring in over the fiscal-year 1986–1990 period. The cumulative effect of the following significant structural changes is, on balance, a small net corporate tax *decrease* over the period:

· Reduce the corporate rate

· Repeal investment tax credit

· Index capital gains and tax in full

· Replace ACRS with real economic depreciation

· Allow inflation-indexed FIFO accounting for inventories

· Index interest payments and receipts for inflation

· Permit deduction of 50 percent of dividends paid

All of the increase in corporation tax receipts is attributable to other features of Treasury I.

A good example of the sort of provision in question is the proposed change in the capital recovery rules applicable to the "intangible" (because they do not generate a tangible asset) expenses of drilling for oil and gas. Expenses incurred for this purpose, which presumably are made in the expectation of obtaining an asset of at least equal value, are nevertheless allowed as a write-off against income under current rules; such expenses would be capitalized and recovered over a period of years under the Treasury plan. Companies and individuals with substantial interests in oil and gas properties, or in the industries that serve the oil and gas recovery industry, were naturally not greatly comforted by the possibility that such rule changes might enhance the overall productivity of U.S. investment. I could cite many other instances.

As for the international allocation of capital, it seems likely that the overall effect of the proposed changes would be to discourage investment in the United States relative to the rest of the world. The reasoning is clear in the case of investment financed by borrowing from abroad. The proposed rules would approximate application of accrual-income principles to U.S. investment and the borrowing used to finance it. Existing rules — including ACRS, the investment tax credit, and the allowance as a deduction of all interest paid (including the inflation-premium element) — can be regarded as subsidizing investment in the United States. Thus the shift from the existing to the proposed rules would make investment in the United States relatively less attractive. As discussed in Chapter 10, determining whether such a shift in investment incentives is a good or bad thing is not a simple matter, particularly when one attempts to take into account the complex provisions relating to the taxation of international capital flows more generally. A natural reaction is to deplore the discouraging effect on domestic production. A broader view of policy, however, would try to evaluate the foregone productivity of U.S. wealth allocated abroad and the cost to U.S. taxpayers, including U.S. workers, of encouraging its allocation domestically. Whatever the analytical conclusion may be, the likely effect of the rules on domestic investment (probably somewhat discouraging) and on capital flows (probably reducing the net flow of capital to the United States, and thereby lowering the value of the dollar) are likely to be of considerable political interest.

The treatment of owner-occupied housing in the Treasury plan represents one of its more significant departures from the accrual-income standard. Although the proposal would discontinue the deduction for state and local property taxes, it would retain the other features of the law generally regarded as favoring owner-occupied housing. These are the exclusion from income of the service value of an owner-occupied house and the unlimited deductibility of mortgage interest (for general discussion of both these features of existing law, see Chapters 3, 9, and 10). Reducing the marginal rate of tax on saving in conventional form would in itself tend to moderate the existing bias in favor of owner-occupied housing. But because (1) the law would otherwise limit interest deductibility to an approximation of the inflation-corrected interest rate, and in the case of nonbusiness interest further limit deductions to $5000 plus investment income; (2) the likely effect of the law would be to lower interest rates generally; and (3) it would tend to increase the tax burden on domestic business investment — the proposal might well reinforce the existing bias in favor of owner-occupied housing relative to other forms of domestic investment.[8] Many observers regard the result to be an unfortunate waste of the potential productivity of U.S. savings, although those who advocate subsidies for owner-occupied housing obviously differ in their view of this aspect of the Treasury proposal.

A second major deviation of the proposal from the accrual-income standard is in the treatment of retirement savings. Although it would eliminate some opportunities for sheltered retirement savings, the Treasury plan would retain provisions similar to those in existing law that permit limited amounts to be put aside for retirement without being subject to current taxation, the two favored vehicles being employer-sponsored pensions and IRAs. Because the plans would be subject to limits, including the restriction that the saved amounts can be withdrawn without extra penalty only in retirement, it is very difficult to determine their likely effect on the overall incentive to accumulate savings. (An unfortunate aspect of the Treasury's continuation of the existing ad hoc approach to encouraging retirement savings is the certain requirement for exceedingly complex regulations along the lines of the current law.)

Definition of Consumption. The accrual-income standard demands full taxation of the return to saving. It does not, however, embody any particular definition of consumption. A major part of the revenue gain required to finance lower marginal rates in Treasury I comes from a broadened definition of consumption. I have mentioned an important instance, the inclusion of a much larger portion of the nonpension fringe benefits of employment, particularly the value of health insurance coverage in excess of specified minimum amounts. Limiting this benefit serves both to bring greater consistency to health outlays financed via the employer and self-financed benefits and to reduce an incentive to purchase insurance that is arguably excessive. A second major instance

8. For an analysis of the effect of the Treasury plan on both rental and owner-occupied housing, see Hendershott and Ling (1985); they conclude that the plan would strengthen the demand for owner-occupied housing and raise the level of rents by 20 percent.

is limiting the charitable deduction. Treasury I would limit contribution deductions to amounts in excess of 2 percent of income, with no "above the line" deduction, and would discontinue the policy of allowing deduction for the full market value of contributed property, even when that value had not been recognized for income tax purposes. A third very important instance is the elimination of the personal deduction for state and local taxes. The estimated individual income tax revenue gain from the three mentioned proposals — limit exclusion of health insurance, revise rules for charitable contributions, and repeal deduction for state and local taxes — accounted for nearly 40 percent of the total revenue cost of the lower tax rates and increased personal exemptions and zero-bracket amount over the fiscal-year 1986–1990 period. I cannot pursue in depth here any of these major departures in tax expenditures, but it is clear that they would have substantial implications for the incentives bearing on individuals and could be expected to have long-term consequences for the way certain social objectives are met and for the organization of local government.

Prospects and Promise of the Accrual-Income Reform Strategy

I referred to Table 13–1 in describing the changes from current law proposed in Treasury I. The table is equally interesting for its comparison between Treasury's November 1984 plan and Reagan I, the plan proposed by the administration to Congress in May 1985. It is instructive to go down the list of the measures cited earlier as representing a shift to an accrual-income standard:

· Capital gains: taxed on realization, with 50 percent exclusion of long-term gains, no indexing of basis (indexing as an option, starting in 1991)

· Depreciation: accelerated, indexing retained

· Interest: indexing dropped

· Inventory accounting: as in Treasury I

· Life insurance inside buildup: exempted for existing policies

· Corporate integration: dividend-paid deduction dropped from 50 percent to 10 percent

· Transfer payments: veterans' benefits excused

- Fringe benefits: token tax on health insurance *below* specified limits only
- Personal deductions: limits on charitable deductions relaxed

Obviously, the accrual-income standard has suffered defeat again. That does not mean that Reagan I is "inferior" to Treasury I. Even judged by the standard of uniformity of the tax on the return to saving, Reagan I is arguably superior to Treasury I (see Fullerton's figures in Table 13–2). What it does mean is that Reagan I will not eliminate the problems we have associated with a hybrid income approach, including notably the pressures associated with inflation. We need only recall the discussion in Chapter 3 on the remarkable consequences of failing to index interest payments and receipts in the hybrid system to be reminded of how great those pressures can be.

The accrual-income reform strategy seems unlikely to untangle the income tax. In Chapter 14 we shall consider whether the consumption approach offers any greater promise.

14 The Consumption Strategy

If I was you, I wouldn't start from here.

Advice of an Irishman to an American tourist seeking the best route to Dublin

Anonymous

WHEN I began work at the Treasury Department in 1975, I was a novice in the niceties of income definition. But I basically accepted the view that the accrual-income standard represented the best practical approach to setting consistent, fair tax policy, and I thought of expenditure and consumption taxes as academic ideas, desirable as methods of avoiding the discouragement of saving that is characteristic of income taxes, but not very practical and maybe not as fair as income taxes. The Treasury is a wonderful place to learn about taxation. The opportunity to direct the tax reform study culminating in *Blueprints for Basic Tax Reform* compounded the advantage of the Treasury setting. I acquired the knowledge of a native to the territory of the accrual-income standard. My advice to a visiting American who seeks a tax system that is fair and simple and that holds to a minimum the influence of taxes on private economic decisions: "If I was you, I wouldn't start from here." If the key to untangling the income tax, in the sense of understanding it, is a clear grasp of the concept of accrual income (and its components, consumption and saving), in my opinion the key to untangling the income tax, in the sense of actually straightening it out, is in following the consumption approach.

Most of the elements that led to my change of view are contained in this book. As I have stressed, there is no scientific answer to what is the best tax system. Others have considered the same arguments and have come out still favoring the accrual-income approach. Obviously, the Regan Treasury was largely unconvinced that following a systematic consumption approach would lead to a better tax system. Thus in summarizing the reasons for my preference, I am under no illusion that they will persuade all readers, nor, I hope, will I be misunderstood as representing the views of any others connected with this book.

I start with the practical. It is simply very difficult to design rules that can be administered by ordinary human beings and that will provide an acceptable degree of approximation to the accrual-income ideal. That is why the tax system requires continual patching — one year, tax straddles; another year, self-constructed assets; another year, installment sales; another year, discount bonds; and so on. The complexity generated by the taxation of capital gains on realization rather than on accrual is a classic instance. Commenting on the generally accepted impracticality of taxing gains on accrual, William Andrews (1983, p. 282) noted aptly:

A comprehensive income tax ideal with an immediate concession that taxation is not to be based on actual value is like a blueprint for constructing a building in which part of the foundation is required to be located in quicksand. If the terrain cannot be changed, the blueprint had better be amended.

If basing taxes on accrual income is a challenge in the best of stable-price times — recall from Chapter 3 the matters of integrating corporation and individual accounts, of providing proper depreciation allowances, and of measuring the return to investing in owner-occupied homes — in times of inflation the problems are much compounded. On the heels of Chapter 13's discussion of the indexing provisions in Treasury I, I should not have to elaborate the point. There are no technical solutions agreed upon among tax scholars for these various difficulties — simply more or less reasonable approximations. And the more technically sophisticated among the approximations (for example, the rules on installment sales) are very complicated.

By contrast, consumption-type taxes provide easy solutions to all these problems. The basic method of accounting — cash-flow — is inherently on a realization basis. The accounts automatically provide correction for inflation (because the proper figures on which to base taxes are always current cash flows). They avoid altogether the need for integrating corporation and individual tax accounts.

The consumption approach also promotes efficient resource use. I base this view less on the traditional argument that the consumption approach eliminates one of the distortions characteristic of an income tax — the distortion of the saving decision due to taxation of the return to saving — than on the extreme ease with which a uniform tax treatment can be applied to all types of assets. Depending on the details, the cash-flow accounting required for consumption-type taxation either leaves the government out of saving and investment transactions altogether (with the tax system sharing neither the cost nor the gains or losses) or it has the effect of making the government a full partner, sharing costs and payoffs in equal measure. Consequently assets of all types, including owner-occupied housing and other household durables, are given comparable treatment.[1] Allowing investment to flow to the point of highest yield would generate substantial gain to the economy. Consumption-type rules would also take tax issues out of most financial planning. Tax consequences would not be sensitive to the financial form of saving and investing transactions, whether for retirement or for any other purpose.

I do not mean to dismiss the gain that would result from the elimination of the wedge between the return on investment and that obtained by savers, or to neglect the likelihood that such a shift would result in greater accumulation of wealth, with the advantages that implies. By contrast with the gains from improved allocation of given amounts of savings, however, the extent of gains due to reducing the tax on saving in general are controversial. I regard those gains as likely to be large, but the case for basing taxes on consumption does not rest primarily on them.

The accrual-income approach, by nature, introduces a wedge between the return on investment and that received by the saver, as well as a wedge between the returns on saving considered attractive at the margin by different savers. (These are instances of consumer-producer and consumer-consumer distortions; see Chapter 9.) Equally important, I believe the great difficulty of measuring accrual income makes virtually inevitable the variety of effective tax rates that are actually applied to different assets. Practical rules designed to approximate accrual income are highly prone to imperfections leading to distortions of economic and financial affairs much beyond those implied by the concept as an ideal. The basic accounting involved in implementing the consumption approach is so simple that deviations from it would in most instances have to be on purpose.

The consumption approach is indeed simpler, solving with ease intractable problems in the existing hybrid and ideal accrual-income systems. And the consumption approach would indeed make it easy to write rules that hold to a minimum tax distortions in financial and business

---

1. In some instances it may matter which approach is taken to the tax treatment of a saving or investing transaction. We may feel it quite inappropriate that an individual should have the opportunity to strike it rich by drilling an oil well without sharing the venture with the government. I am obviously skimming over such important details in this short summary.

affairs. But we can think of an even easier and simpler tax — a flat per capita levy. Would it therefore be preferable to an accrual-income approach? Obviously not; the consumption approach can be taken seriously only if it competes with the accrual-income standard in fairness.

It has surprised me, as I have thought about the matter for a decade or so, to see how strong the equity case is for consumption-type rules. In economic theory people are conceived of as having certain "endowments" — of skills, of time that can be devoted to market work or other pursuits, perhaps of wealth received by transfer from another person or from an institution, and so on — that they then convert through exchange for other things they want. Thus a person sells his efforts as a carpenter and uses the proceeds to buy an automobile. Ideally, I think of the object of a good tax system as placing a relatively heavy burden not on those who make certain choices from their opportunities, but on those who have relatively good options for choice, that is, good endowments. Both accrual-income and consumption-type taxes, especially the progressive versions, do this to some degree. The difference between the two is in the treatment of saving. Between two individuals who are otherwise equivalently endowed, an accrual-income tax puts a relatively heavy burden on the one who saves more (or borrows less). In terms of the endowments–use-of-endowments distinction, the accrual-income approach puts an extra tax on one of the uses of endowment: the acquisition of future consumption via saving. Furthermore, thinking about saving as the purchase of future consumption reminds us that the future is multidimensional. There is next year, the year after that, and so on. An accrual-income tax, in effect, puts a geometrically increasing set of taxes on these different "commodities," these different uses of endowment. It is not at all clear why this rather odd collection of taxes should be regarded as a better way to share the burden of the public sector than a simpler tax more directly related to the underlying differences in endowment, and unrelated to at least this aspect of the uses of endowment. Neither an accrual-income tax nor one of the various consumption-type taxes is perfect, but it is hard to understand why the extra discrimination against savers that is added by an accrual-income tax is anything but a disadvantage in equity terms.

There are various explanations for the continuing dominance of the accrual-income standard. One, I suspect, is simply familiarity. We have long been accustomed to think of "income" as the fairest basis for taxation, even though we may not have thought much about what the term means. But I think there are two more compelling concerns. One relates to the possibility of undeserved gains and losses in transition, and the other relates to the use of an income tax as a substitute for the heavier taxation of gifts and bequests. I shall comment further on transition issues below. As for gifts and bequests, in my view the issue concerns relatively few individuals, and it is a mistake to allow the effort to deal indirectly with a problem we are apparently unwilling to tackle directly to dominate the design of the mass tax by which we fund a major part of our collective expenditure.

There are three plausible ways in which a consumption strategy of tax reform might be pursued. For simplicity, I call them Plans 1, 2, and 3. Each consists of a move to a consumption-type tax already described in Chapters 4 and 5. It remains here in some cases to fill in the details of transition and to engage in some of the same analysis as was carried out in Chapter 13 for the Treasury I accrual-income tax. Plan 1 implements the "phase-in of consumption-type rules to the existing income tax" of Chapter 5. Plan 2 introduces a VAT. Plan 3 would institute a two-tiered cash-flow tax (Chapter 5).

Plan 1: Consumption-Oriented Modification of the Income Tax Base

Plan 1 illustrates well the fallacy of the widespread view that shifting the tax system to a consumption basis would involve a radical departure from existing rules and practices. It is, of course, true that one can design a consumption-based tax that looks very different from the existing income tax. Many a consumption-type system would be described as a wholly new tax. But the fact that a consumption-based tax might look very different from the existing tax, and pose all the problems one would associate with the introduction of a new tax, does not mean that a consumption-type tax *has* to have these characteristics.

Because the existing system is a hybrid composed of consumption-type and accrual-income-type rules applicable to saving and investing, a shift to a full accrual-income system, along the lines of the Treasury proposal, involves changing a number of rules in one direction. A shift to a consumption-type tax would involve changing the rules in the other direction. The provisions in question relate to such transactions as receipt and payment of interest and dividends, capital gains, and investment outlays. For example, existing law provides for a special lower rate of tax on long-term capital gains. Consumption-type rules would ignore capital gains altogether unless the purchase of the asset in question had been deducted (for example, via an IRA). Accrual-income rules would tax all capital gains at full rates (and on accrual rather than on realization). Converting the hybrid tax to a closer approximation to an accrual-income tax thus implies changing the rules applicable to long-term capital gains toward full taxation on accrual. Converting the hybrid tax to a consumption-type tax implies changing the rules in the other direction (to ignoring capital gains). Either change might be regarded as major, but the second is not obviously more radical or more difficult than the first.

Plan 1 takes the major features of the existing system relating to the taxation of saving and investment and converts them to consumption-oriented rules. I describe the changes as applicable to existing law, although the same set of changes could be applied to the Treasury proposal to convert it to a consumption-type tax. The difference would be in the many base-broadening aspects of the Treasury plan that have nothing to do with the consumption – accrual-income dimension of policy choice. The basic structure of Plan 1 consists of a set of changes to convert the basis for taxing both individuals and corporations to a cash-flow measure of income, with tax-prepayment treatment of such financial saving and dissaving by individuals as is undertaken outside of IRA-like accounts. In addition, I have included a special tax on corporate distributions in Plan 1. The corporate distribution tax is conceived of primarily as an aspect of the transition from the existing system and is not essential to the structure of a conversion to a consistent consumption-type base.

Since they can be briefly stated, I repeat here the rule changes described in Chapter 5, which would apply to both individuals and corporations:

1. Phase out present restrictions (including age-related conditions) on deposits to and withdrawals from savings plans qualifying for tax-sheltered treatment, such as Keogh Plans and IRAs.

2. Phase out taxation of interest receipts, dividends, and capital gains, except as these are realized through withdrawals from tax-sheltered savings plans.

3. Accelerate depreciation deductions until full first-year write-off is the rule; similarly, move to immediate expensing of additions to inventory.

4. Allow borrowing from a tax-qualified plan, with the borrowed amounts immediately subject to tax, but all repayments of principal or interest fully deductible.

5. Phase out existing savings and investment incentives — in particular, the investment tax credit.

6. Phase out deductions for interest paid, except in the case of borrowing from a tax-qualified plan.

Among the transition effects of the proposed rules would be the forgiveness of taxes on dividends paid out of the accumulated earnings and profits of corporations, as well as out of the earnings and profits from already-committed investment. A proportional tax on the net distributions by corporations would be compatible with consumption-type rules at the individual level and would provide a possible way to moderate this windfall-gain aspect of the suggested basic plan (see Chapter 6 for discussion of details). The suggested additional rule is thus:

7. Introduce a proportional tax on all distributions by corporations with respect to equity shares (including not only dividends but also purchase of shares by a corporation from the public); net sale of equity to the public would qualify for subsidy at the same rate.

The provision for transition described here with the simple expression "phase out" or "phase in" is regrettably vague. Phased changes in depreciation rules, for example, can have strong effects on the incentives to alter the timing of investment. Thus some work would be necessary to design rules that would balance the desired moderation of transition incidence effects with undesired incentives. Details of the transition rules (treatment of "used assets" and sales from existing inventory) could have an important influence on the revenue effects of the plan as well, and, of course, the distribution tax suggested in rule 7 would affect the required revenue. It is at least possible, however, that rules 1–6 taken by themselves would have relatively little overall revenue cost. In particular, the changed taxation of interest would seem likely to lead to increased revenue, since interest deductions are at present concentrated in corporations and high-bracket taxpayers, while a large part of interest receipts flow to tax-exempt institutions, such as pension funds. Currently the taxation of capital gains is not a major source of revenue. Shifting to expensing from ACRS would presumably involve some net revenue cost, but eliminating the investment tax credit would generate revenue gains. Elimination of the taxation of dividends would cost revenue; the substitution of a uniform tax on corporate distributions could provide a possible compensating source that is reasonably compatible with the rest of the structure.

The plan demonstrates that one could convert the existing system to a consumption-type base while remaining within the general outlines of the present framework. Certainly it is arguable that the Treasury proposal, evidently regarded as feasible, is just as radical. Most of the steps involved in Plan 2 are quite similar to tax changes that have been enacted in the past, including acceleration of depreciation, alleviation of tax on capital gains, provision for tax-sheltered saving, and modification of the investment tax credit. The most extreme departure from existing practice is in the treatment of interest. Since the proposal would disallow deduction of interest paid, as well as eliminate the taxation of interest received, it can be described as providing for prepayment of tax at the business level. No doubt a particular sticking point would be the treatment of interest on existing obligations, particularly mortgage debt. A reasonably simple alternative rule might be adopted for mortgage debt, allowing the borrower to deduct the interest paid, but obliging the issuer to pay tax on the interest received at the full rate.

Assuming maintenance of existing rates, and depending on the rate applied in the supplemental tax on corporate distributions, it is possible that the system would be about as progressive as the existing one. The combination of no taxation of dividends, capital gains, and interest receipts with no deduction for interest paid would perhaps raise the liabilities of some well-to-do taxpayers. The extra tax on corporate distributions would disproportionately burden owners of existing corporate equity. Although equity ownership is widespread via institutions such as pension and mutual funds, presumably the distribution of ownership is skewed toward the well-to-do.

The data presented in connection with the Treasury's *Blueprints* Cash-Flow Tax provide another benchmark for the progressivity of the Plan 1 rules. That study concluded that modestly higher tax rates applied to a consumption base would match the progressivity of a comprehensive accrual-income system. For example, the rates under the *Blueprints* Comprehensive Income Tax for a married couple with two children ranged from 8 percent on income above $9800 to a top of 38 percent on incomes above $79,800. Under the *Blueprints* Cash-Flow Tax the rates ranged from 10 percent on "income" above $8225 to a top of 40 percent above $60,725. (The figures, expressed in 1984 dollars, are from *Blueprints,* 2nd ed., table 2.)

Even if the plan were phased in over several years, some transition incidence effects would remain. Allowing individuals who have accumulated savings in the past (apart from accumulations in retirement plans and the like, the nominal treatment of which would be unchanged by Plan 1) to obtain their future return free of tax appears to be a transfer to the well-to-do. But the rate of return they are likely to obtain will be lowered by the plan from current real (before-tax) interest levels. At present, wealthy individuals can assure themselves of at least the going rate of interest on tax-exempt bonds. When all bonds are tax exempt, their yield may not be much higher. If so there will be no new advantage for the well-to-do taxpayer with accumulated wealth. Furthermore, if the more favorable rules with respect to depreciation apply just to newly constructed assets, a transitional wealth loss to owners of existing assets is likely. This is because new assets would be eligible for the advantage of immediate write-off, whereas old assets would not. The resulting downward pressure on the value of existing assets is, in effect, a one-time tax on real assets, whether owned directly or in the form of corporate shares, that would be associated with the plan. This transition effect also tends to offset the advantage of tax-free future returns to those with accumulated assets. (The reverse effect, a windfall gain to holders of existing real assets, would be predicted for Treasury I's move in the opposite direction, toward an accrual-income tax.)

I shall not repeat here the favorable features of the cash-flow approach to taxation for the simplicity of the applicable rules, for the invariance of taxes to inflation, or for the efficiency of resource use. These were discussed in Chapters 10 and 12, in particular.

Plan 2: Value-Added Tax — the Universal Add-on

A VAT has the potential for substituting a very broad-based consumption-type tax for part of the income tax. Plan 2 would apply the revenue to reducing income tax rates, thereby reducing the taxation of savings and mitigating distortions due to anomalies in the income tax. In addition, to maintain a rough distributional neutrality of the reform, revenue would be applied to subsidizing payroll taxes of low-earning individuals.

Two large design problems are involved here: deciding what transactions are to be covered by the VAT and developing the mechanism for modifying its distributional effects. The two problems are not necessarily separate. For example, it is often suggested that goods with the character of necessities be dropped from a VAT to make it more progressive. I make a working assumption, however, that other tools (transfer programs plus the income tax) will be relied on to influence the distribution of burdens. Specifically, because our object is to look at policy changes intended to be revenue-neutral, I assume that the VAT is combined with reductions in income and payroll taxes. (To preserve the idea that the payroll taxes amount to premiums for social insurance, the plan would implement payroll tax cuts in the form of a subsidy by the Treasury of part or all of Social Security contributions made with respect to individual workers. Thus the effect of a payroll tax cut would be constructed out of an explicit subsidy for employer payroll tax outlays, paid for by a lesser income tax cut.)

Adjustments to payroll taxes can be rather precisely targeted to counteract the tax burden that a VAT would otherwise impose on those low-earning individuals who are not now subject to the income tax and who are therefore beyond the reach of adjustments to income tax rates. The alternative of an offset along the lines of the earned-income credit in the present income tax would involve more new administrative machinery. In particular, it would require low-earning individuals to file a form to claim the offset. The other broad groups of poor individuals are dependent on transfers. Protecting them presents less of a design problem. Government transfer programs either are indexed or could be indexed to counteract any tendency of a VAT to induce an increase in the general price level. Private transfers will not be systematically affected if the overall impact of the program is distributionally neutral.

In Plan 2 the VAT revenue would be applied to reduce income tax rates. Basically because a VAT would allow an indirect way to reduce tax expenditures, it should be possible to improve on selected incentives (for example, to exchange work for current consumption goods or current consumption for future consumption) across the board, much as Treasury I does by explicit elimination of tax expenditures. In effect, the VAT could be used to add a very broad-based element to the income tax.

I assume a VAT would be of the consumption type. The advantages in simplicity (no distinction between capital and current outlays, no depreciation allowances, no inflation adjustment problems, and so on), comparability with existing systems, and interest in encouraging private capital formation make this highly likely. But it would be possible to use a VAT to implement a flat-rate tax on income (including the return on investment). (I shall discuss this possibility in connection with Plan 3.) Specifying the VAT to be of the consumption type implies the use of cash-flow accounting with respect to all business purchases (whether for current use or for investment). As stressed in Chapter 4, however, a great many decisions must still be made about what is meant by consumption for tax purposes. Two inclusion issues cut across the matter of which commodities or services will be subject to a VAT: treatment of purchases by the federal government, on the one hand, and by state and local governments, on the other hand. Probably both would be excluded in a tax that would survive politically. Only the second — the treatment of state and local governments — really matters. The federal government pays any tax to itself anyway, although there are possibilities for misleading budget accounting (does one use before-tax or after-tax prices?), depending on the choice. Presumably the tax would be on a destination basis (rebated on exports and charged on imports). A last practical detail: it seems likely that the credit method would be employed to implement a VAT, partly for reasons of comparability with other systems, but mainly for the enforcement advantages potentially available through cross-checking of invoices whereby sellers record amounts subject to tax and buyers justify credits against tax.

Using Commerce Department figures for 1981, McLure (1983) estimates that the broadest concept of consumption (*excluding* government purchases) that might as a practical matter be included under a VAT would amount to 79.1 percent of personal consumption as reported in the national income accounts (main exclusions: housing services, part of medical care, and the value of services rendered by banks and insurance companies paid for by customers in the form of reduced interest receipts rather than explicitly billed). The much narrower base that might result from administrative problems and efforts to improve the distributive character of the tax (important additional exclusions: most food, all medical care, household utilities, legal and burial services) is put by McLure at 45.4 percent of personal-consumption expenditures. His calculations are reproduced in Table 14–1.[2] In recent years personal-consumption expenditures have been running at approximately 65 percent of GNP in the United States. This means it is reasonable to expect to be able to raise between 0.3 percent and 0.5 percent of GNP per percentage point of a flat VAT. For example, even on the narrower tax base, a 10 percent VAT would raise about 3 percent of GNP; on the broadened base, 5 percent of GNP.

Most actual systems exclude some types of consumption and apply different rates to different consumption classes. Both measures are

---

2. Note that it is assumed a VAT would not be charged on "consumption" undertaken via state and local government. Federal expenditures are also out of the base. This contrasts with the individual income tax base, which effectively includes a substantial portion of federal expenditure (the part financed by all but indirect business taxes and debt) and the part of state and local expenses not deducted on income tax returns.

Table 14-1. Estimated extent of consumption subject to VAT (1981 levels, billions of dollars)

	Personal consumption expenditures	Estimated tax base	
		Limited exemptions	Liberal exemptions
Food and tobacco	398.4	391.7[a]	121.1[b]
Clothing, accessories, and jewelry	136.4	136.3[c]	136.3[c]
Personal care	24.6	24.6	24.6
Housing	295.3	—	—
Household operation	256.5	249.4[d]	152.9[e]
Medical care expenses	194.6	194.6	—
Personal business	99.8	41.0[f]	20.7[g]
Transportation	260.8	260.8	256.3[h]
Recreation	117.2	117.2	111.2[i]
Private education and research	29.3	29.3	—
Religious and welfare activities	25.4	—	—
Foreign travel and other, net	5.2	13.7[j]	13.7[j]
Total personal consumption	1,843.2	1,457.6	836.8
Percentage of personal consumption	100.0%	79.1%	45.4%
Percentage of GNP national product	62.5%	49.3%	28.3%

Source: Derived by McLure (1983, p. 192) from U.S. Department of Commerce, Survey of Current Business, Washington, D.C.: Government Printing Office, July 1982, pp. 40–41.

a. Excludes food furnished to government and commercial employees and food produced and consumed on farms.

b. Includes only purchased meals, beverages, and tobacco products.

c. Excludes standard clothing issued to military personnel.

d. Excludes domestic services.

e. Excludes domestic services and household utilities (except telephone).

f. Excludes services furnished without payment by financial intermediaries except life insurance companies and expenses of handling life insurance.

g. Excludes items in note f and legal services and funeral and burial expenses.

h. Excludes bridge, tunnel, ferry, and road tolls; transit system fares; and commutation railway expenses.

i. Excludes admissions to legitimate theaters, opera, and entertainments of nonprofit institutions; clubs and fraternal organizations except insurance; and pari-mutuel net receipts.

j. Excludes foreign travel and expenditures abroad by U.S. residents, but includes expenditures in the United States by foreigners and personal remittances in kind to foreigners.

designed to make a proportional tax progressive. But for economic systems, such as that of the United States, that are well equipped with instruments for affecting the distribution of income or consumption, most commentators recommend applying a uniform rate to as broad a base as can be practically measured. A uniform rate on a broad base serves both the presumption in favor of neutrality among consumption categories and the clear administrative advantage of avoiding distinctions that raise compliance and enforcement costs. The dominant view of the participants at a Brookings conference on the European experience with VATs was summed up by Aaron (1982, pp. 4–5):

In highly developed industrial countries with well-articulated systems of transfers and income taxes, it is better to keep the VAT clean . . . and simple, and to take care of income redistribution questions with instruments other than the value added tax.

A VAT is flexible in the sense that it is compatible with other taxes. That is why I refer to it as the "universal add-on." For purposes of this analysis, however, I have suggested combining it with reductions in individual and corporate income tax rates and, to offset the regressivity of the tax, with reductions in the payroll taxes on low earners. The basic strategy of this package is to broaden the base, thereby reducing the distortions in the income tax (through lower rates). The particular target is reduction of the distortions due to the present inconsistent rules relating to saving and investment transactions. This is accomplished by using the revenue gained from the newly introduced consumption elements to finance general rate reduction in the income tax (rendering the rules less important). Depending on the details of the income tax cuts, it should be possible to achieve rough distributional neutrality. The base broadening would come primarily at the expense of tax expenditures in the current system. Because of this, it should be possible to produce a system that lowers marginal rates on both savings and labor in general, although, of course, it must correspondingly raise effective tax rates with respect to the currently favored transactions.

The transition to a VAT would presumably be handled by introducing it at a rate lower than the level ultimately anticipated, with the rate rising in stages over a period of years. The various offsetting features of the package — payment of part of the payroll tax from general revenue and reductions in income tax rates — would presumably be phased in in a similar way. Note that the same sort of incentive effects are raised by this process as those discussed in connection with Plan 1. For example, there will be an incentive for firms to postpone investment across the boundary of a rate increase: a write-off at 10 percent is worth more than a write-off at 5 percent.

One of the popular presumptions about a VAT is that its introduction must be inflationary. The economics of this view are, however, not clear. Suppose that tomorrow we begin collecting a 10 percent VAT on all sales by firms to households. At the same time, some combination of payroll and income tax cuts is introduced, so that the liabilities of households and firms are reduced by an amount roughly equal to the VAT revenues. What would be the likely effect? A natural first reaction is that the general level of output prices would have to rise by 10 percent in order for firms to cover not only their input costs but also the new tax liability. But there is an alternative possibility: the general level of input prices could fall by 10 percent. This result may seem less likely because we are so used to thinking about prices of either inputs or outputs as being "sticky downward." But note that the income and payroll tax cuts, taken by themselves, would have the effect of increasing take-home amounts. The process of adjustment might well lead to reductions in before-tax payments to input factors that leave after-tax payments much as they were before the policy change. In fact, we cannot be certain which of these two scenarios is more likely; presumably monetary policy matters, for example. The important point is that the difference between the two possibilities mentioned can be analyzed as the effect of a one-time 10 percent inflation. That is, the policy change under the assumption of an increase in output price level (and therefore with no reduction in primary input prices) can be broken down into the effect of the policy with no increase in output price level (and therefore with a reduction in primary input prices) followed by a general price inflation of 10 percent.

Assuming that the payroll-tax subsidy and income tax changes are such as to maintain the general degree of progressivity of the system, the incidence issues raised by Plan 2 are confined to transition wealth effects and to horizontal burden changes. With respect to the latter, because it shifts toward a consumption-type tax, the VAT plan would bring the system closer to treating equally those who have the same economic resources but different propensities to save. Also, because it has the effect of diminishing the various tax expenditure programs implicit in the income tax, Plan 2 would impose relatively greater burdens on those whose tax liability is reduced more than average by the various special provisions, a shift in burdens that is ultimately shared with those who benefit from the subsidized activities (for example, the beneficiaries of charitable contributions).

The transition incidence effects are of particular interest. It is often asserted that introduction of a VAT imposes a double tax on those with accumulated savings. They have paid taxes on the amounts set aside and on the interest they earned, and now they must pay taxes again on their purchases. My description of the situation shows that the story is somewhat more complicated, in that the effect of introducing the tax depends on an individual's portfolio. For example, an individual whose savings are held in the form of a portfolio of bonds timed to mature at the dates of planned consumption (a life insurance policy might have this property) would not observe any change in consumption possibilities if the general price level followed the path expected before the introduction of the tax. In general we can assume there is a portfolio best designed to cope with any given level of inflation. If the introduction of the tax would lead to a particular shift in the path of prices, an individual who correctly anticipated the effect would not be disadvantaged by the shift.

It is not my intention to suggest that the introduction of a VAT will lack wealth effects, but rather to point out that how those effects are shared is more complicated than a simple division between those who have accumulated wealth and those who have not. The basic wealth change predicted by theory is the reverse of the windfall gain to owners of capital described in connection with the Treasury plan. A windfall loss would be predicted in this case for the owners of existing capital assets, essentially because old assets would not enjoy the advantage of write-off against the new tax, although the return flow they produced would be subject to the tax. The windfall loss would be associated with ownership of the real assets (either directly or via share ownership), whereas any gains from ownership of financial claims (such as bonds) would be balanced by losses to the individuals on the other side of the transaction. This excludes the usual gain to the government from inflation. Purely inflationary effects ought to be dealt with as a separate matter, since they are subject to control through other instruments, such as monetary policy.

Much as in the case of the income tax, the simplicity aspects of a VAT can be divided into two categories. A VAT would be very simple for most individuals. Because the tax is incorporated in the prices paid for goods and services, it imposes no administrative burden on them whatsoever. Under a VAT the actual taxpayers — those who remit money to the Treasury — are firms, including individuals in their role as firms (for example, professionals or proprietors of small businesses). For them the simplicity of the tax depends importantly on its details. Provided that the base is uniform, calculation of liabilities can take advantage of straightforward cash-flow accounting with respect to purchases and sales of goods and services, with the added feature of complete exclusion of financial flows. This base is inherently much simpler than either the existing income tax base or an accrual-income base.

Enforcement of a VAT is generally believed to call for a great deal of specialized resources (beyond those required to enforce the income tax). The Treasury Department's November 1984 report cited estimates by the Internal Revenue Service that approximately 20,000 additional agents would be required to administer a VAT. As we have seen, however, in principle precisely the same sort of information is required for an income tax (including a consumed-income tax) as for a VAT. Essentially, what is required for both is a statement of the receipts of each business and a statement of outlays for business purposes. If the temptation to introduce new distinctions among goods sold is resisted, no monitoring is necessary for a uniform VAT that is not also required for an income tax.

For the consumption-type VAT (as for a consumption-type income tax — for example, Plan 1), there are in addition the great administrative advantages of cash-flow accounting, which eliminates judgments about value changes (or, alternatively, complex accounting rules, such as those determining depreciation allowances, that substitute for such judgments) and greatly extends the power of linked records of buyers and sellers. It is hard to see why such a tax would require any significant addition to the enforcement resources currently applied to the income tax.

The picture of the administrative situation changes, however, as soon as one introduces multiple rates, exclusions, and exemptions. Then, although a VAT retains its advantage of simplicity for the average individual, a very considerable new burden is introduced for the firms who must comply with the laws and for the tax collector who must monitor compliance. Now it becomes necessary to check not only totals but also the detailed composition of thousands of transactions. A major simplification advantage is thereby lost.

In Chapter 4 I discussed the claim that a VAT would provide an opportunity to impose tax burdens on those now escaping the income tax net. The basic problem under the income tax is unreported receipts from sales of goods or services, and exactly the same problem is confronted, with respect to the same transactions, under a VAT. But using the credit system, whereby the tax is assessed on gross sales receipts of each firm and a credit is allowed for tax paid on purchases, does have the advantage that a return must be filed by the final seller in order to claim a credit. Therefore firms now entirely outside the tax net would have an incentive to enter it; and when they did so they would be subject to monitoring. Furthermore, the linked accounting techniques — seller information checked against credits claimed by business purchasers — provides a potential enforcement advantage (which could be used in a consumed-income tax context as well). In any case, it is reported that introduction of a VAT improves compliance with the income tax.[3]

Yet it is hard to argue that adding a new tax, however simple, without removing another tax represents a gain in simplicity overall. It is possible that a VAT might be used to finance simplifying changes in the income tax (for example, by raising exemptions enough to drop some taxpayers from the rolls). Unfortunately, it is often taken for granted that a VAT would imply *adding* relatively poor taxpayers to the income tax to administer credits put in place to offset the regressivity of a VAT. (Plan 2 would deal with the problem through the device of offsets to payroll taxes for low earners.)

The main efficiency advantage of consumption-type taxes is their neutrality with respect to saving and investment choices. A well-designed VAT would have the sorts of helpful effects discussed earlier, especially in Chapters 9 and 10, including reduced distortion of the timing of consumption (the saving decision), consistent treatment of investments of different types, and insensitivity of the effect of taxes to the rate of inflation. I shall not review that discussion here. Because a VAT would not replace the income tax but would simply permit reduced reliance on it, the VAT would, of course, not have the same efficiency effects as a full shift to a consumption-type tax. There is, however, a presumption that disincentive effects increase with the square of the applicable tax rate. By permitting a general moderation in the income tax, a VAT would finance amelioration of its most serious distorting influences.

Proponents make strong claims for the favorable effect of a VAT on exports by U.S. businesses. This view is greatly exaggerated, if not totally false. The weakness of the argument is evident when one considers that in the long run the volume of exports from a country must be balanced by an equal volume of imports. The same arguments that are usually made to the effect that a VAT (rebated on exports and assessed

3. The source of this information is Vito Tanzi, director of the Fiscal Affairs Department of the International Monetary Fund.

on imports) will encourage exports also imply that it would discourage imports. But the two amounts must ultimately move in the same direction.

To illustrate the point, suppose imposition of a 10 percent VAT has the effect of raising the general price level by 10 percent. Then rebating the tax will leave the prices of U.S. goods that confront foreign purchasers exactly the same as they were before the tax and rebate. Similarly, the real situation of U.S. purchasers of foreign goods is unchanged. True, their prices are increased by the extent of the VAT, but so are the prices of all the domestic goods. If, alternatively, monetary policy succeeds in preventing any increase in the U.S. price level in response to introduction of a VAT, then a simple shift in the exchange rate between dollars and foreign currencies will produce exactly the same consequences. If a dollar costs nine francs on the foreign exchange market before the VAT, the effect of a rebatable VAT of 10 percent that (by assumption) has no effect on the before-rebate dollar price of a good will be totally offset by an increase in the price of a dollar to ten francs. The same exchange-rate change will similarly leave U.S. importers in their original position, so there is every reason to expect exactly such an adjustment. To the extent that price inflation is avoided upon introduction of a VAT, its principal effect will be to induce an appreciation in the dollar on foreign exchange markets.

Plan 3: A Two-Tiered Simplified Tax

The three packages considered to this point span a wide range of policy alternatives. Treasury I would totally revamp the income tax, individual and corporate. It confronts head-on the various political forces that made the tax code what it is today. Plan 1 provides a scheme for rationalizing the treatment of saving and investment along consumption lines without addressing many aspects of the tax system. Although it could equally be used to modify Treasury I, in itself Plan 1 deals with a limited (though very important) set of problems. Plan 2, a VAT, represents a kind of compromise with comprehensive reform. It would finance reduced dependence on the existing, arguably flawed system, but it does not offer the realistic possibility of replacing it altogether. Plan 3 is directed at the following objectives: (1) it should have the simplification advantages of a VAT; (2) it should be implementable as an add-on element of the existing income tax (and in that sense not be a new tax);

(3) it should be implementable on a small scale — that is, like a VAT, it should be possible to institute the plan at a low level as a permanent feature of the tax system, using the revenues to finance either deficit reduction or reduced reliance on the remainder of the income tax; and (4) unlike a VAT, it should have the potential to replace the existing income tax entirely on a phased-in basis.

Add-on taxes within the structure of the income tax are nothing new. The existing minimum tax on "preference income" provides an example. At the time of this writing, devices of a similar character are under active congressional consideration as deficit-reducing measures. The appeal of these provisions for this purpose over a simple increase in tax rates rests on the widespread dissatisfaction with the income tax. Raising tax rates is seen as exacerbating the problems. Yet the provisions typically apply to a narrow group of taxpayers, are complex and ad hoc, and lack the potential for expansion to a fuller program of income-tax reform. Plan 3 would introduce as an add-on tax a set of rules that are simple, that apply to all taxpayers, and that have the potential for expansion to replace the existing tax. Such a tax could be introduced at a low rate. At the same time, the existing tax would be cut, so that key marginal rates (such as those on the rewards for working and saving) could be reduced, even under a version designed to raise additional revenue.

For example, consider a plan that would provide an adequate system when phased in at rates of 15, 25, and 35 percent. The tax might be introduced with rates calculated systematically at 20 percent of those that will finally apply, at the same time cutting the liabilities under existing law by exactly 20 percent. Thus the initial effect would be an add-on tax at rates of 3, 5, and 7 percent, accompanied by a 20 percent cut in the bottom line of the income tax. Then, over a five-year period, the rates would be raised on the add-on tax by an extra 20 percent of the final target structure, with an additional 20 percent chopped off the existing tax each year. In the second year the rates would be 6, 10, and 14 percent, accompanied by a 40 percent cut in the income tax. Alternatively, the process might proceed in stages, with perhaps a phased transition to 50 percent of the final level, replacing 50 percent of the existing income tax, but with a decision about further phasing-in to await experience with the revised rules.

The main requirement of this strategy is that the add-on tax be *really* simple (so that the extra calculations can reasonably be imposed on taxpayers) and yet of a form that one is willing to see gradually replace the existing tax. The two-tiered cash-flow tax, discussed in Chapter 5, provides a structure of just this sort. The two-tiered cash-flow tax involves a coordinated pair of taxes, one at the business level and the other at the employee level. In this context the plan is modified slightly so as to make it fit into the existing split between individual and corporation taxpayers. The following changes would be made to the income tax:

1. An additional line would be provided on the individual income tax form on which to report "compensation," consisting of wages, salary, and pension receipts.

2. Individual proprietors and farmers would also have additional lines on Schedules C (for proprietors) and F (for farmers) of the individual income tax return on which to report total receipts from sales, total purchases from other businesses (including investment purchases), and compensation paid to employees (including employee-owners of the business). The difference between the receipts and outlays is "business income."

3. Partnership returns would provide for a calculation of business income in the same way (receipts from sales less employee compensation less purchases from other businesses); the net figure would be reported to partners for inclusion in Schedule E of individual tax returns.

4. Corporation returns would similarly provide for a calculation of business income.

Extra lines would be provided on individual tax returns for calculation of the extra compensation and business income taxes. Extra lines would be provided on corporation returns for calculation of the extra business income tax.

5. The last element of Plan 3 is a simple proportional reduction in the tax otherwise due under the income tax, the proportion related to the level of exemptions and rates provided for the extra compensation and business income taxes.

The rate structure would depend on the extent to which the plan is designed to replace the income tax. The original Hall-Rabushka (1983) Simple Flat-Tax proposal, after which the two-tiered cash-flow tax is patterned, claimed to be able to replace the existing individual and corporation income tax by imposing a rate of 19 percent on business income as just defined and on compensation in excess of the following personal allowances:

Married couple	$6200
Single person	3800
Single head of household	5600
Each dependent	750

The Hall-Rabushka calculations are based on optimistic assumptions about capturing elements of economic activity recorded in the national income and product accounts but not currently found on tax returns. Furthermore, the Hall-Rabushka base is extremely broad, with no allowance for itemized deductions or for financing the spending-side programs that might replace deductions. Finally, the original flat-tax proposal is probably less progressive than the existing system. (Hall and Rabushka, 1985, contest this view.) A guideline for the sort of rates that would allow for some of the more popular tax expenditures and that would be in line with the current degree of progressivity is provided by the structure of exemptions and rates of the Treasury I plan. A three-bracket structure with rates rising from 15 to 25 to 35 percent is plausible, designed to be comparable to the present system in progressivity and to raise the same revenue as the current income tax on individuals and corporations (the Hall-Rabushka analysis suggests that lower rates might suffice).

In this system the basic rate is the highest rather than the lowest one. Thus the 35 percent rate would apply to all business income, with no exempt amount; carry-over of losses (with interest) would be permitted, but there would be no interaction on individual tax returns between business income (on Schedule C, D, or E) and compensation. Compensation would be subject to tax at the graduated rates indicated, including any allowable exempt amounts, which would be related to family size.

During the phase-in period, or permanently if only a partial replacement of the income tax is intended, the applicable rate structure would simply be reduced in proportion. To replace 20 percent of the income tax would thus involve, for our illustrative structure, rates of 3, 5, and 7 percent, with the 7 percent rate applicable to all business income.

This scheme is economically equivalent to a VAT of the consumption type ("consumption type" because business outlays for capital purposes are expensed immediately, rather than capitalized and depreciated), together with a graduated earnings subsidy to offset any regressivity. But just as it seems to matter politically whether the employer or employee remits the payroll tax, it is likely that the two-tiered cash-flow tax would be very differently perceived from a VAT. Taken as a whole, even as a partial replacement of the income tax it offers some advantages over a VAT. First, it deals directly and simply with the regressivity problem by providing the graduation in the compensation tax component. Second, because its quality of being an income tax is, quite appropriately, stressed, it may be less vulnerable to erosion through exemption of favored commodities — no one ever seems to advocate that grocers be allowed to omit their receipts from sales of food from the calculation of income subject to tax, or that roofing companies not include payments from universities or local governments. Third, by splitting off the compensation portion of the base to be taxed at the employee level, the tax system remains visible to everyone, whereas a VAT is normally paid (not, of course, borne) by businesses alone. At the same time, such complexity as remains (and there does seem to be remarkably little) is only at the level of the firm.

Plan 3 describes a consumption-type tax. As such it offers the characteristic advantages of simplicity of cash-flow accounting and neutrality with respect to both amount and composition of wealth accumulation. But it also brings with it the controversial quality of a tax that exempts the normal return on that accumulation, also described as a zero tax on capital income. Just as a VAT can be designed as an accrual-income-type base, Plan 3 could be modified to provide a reasonable approximation to any *uniform* rate of tax on the return to investment. The modification in both instances is the same, namely, replacing the expensing of business capital outlays with a combination of expensing and economic depreciation (coupled with appropriate rules for accounting for inventory investment), adjusted to impose the desired uniform tax on the return to investment. Assuming economic depreciation were chosen, the fully phased-in system would impose a tax on the return to saving, paid at the business level, at the top marginal rate (the flat rate applied to businesses). By choosing any degree of expensing combined with economic depreciation of the remainder, the flat rate applied to savings could be reduced to any desired level, with a zero rate implied by full expensing.

For example, in the illustrative structure with a business tax rate of 35 percent, allowing businesses to write off one-half of their investment outlays while deducting the remaining amount over a period of years according to a schedule to approximate economic depreciation would impose an effective tax of 17.5 percent on the return to investment. Provided the tax is imposed only at the business level, thereby foregoing the attempt to graduate the tax on savings according to individual circumstances (the graduated-rate structure would continue to apply to compensation), much of the simplicity of the basic Plan 3 proposal could be retained.

Because of its similarity to a VAT, we need not devote further space to developing the transition-incidence, resource-allocation, and simplification effects of Plan 3. The discussion of Plan 2 covers the same ground. The ongoing incidence (vertical and horizontal equity) of the package would be similar to that of Plan 1.

Of the three examples of the consumption strategy of tax reform, Plan 3 — the two-tiered cash-flow tax as an add-on — seems to me the most promising approach. It would permit a gradual transition to a much improved tax system, simple, fair, and interfering minimally in economic decisions. But, of course, Plan 3 has not yet been subjected to White House approval, or tossed around in the Ways and Means Committee, or greeted with suspicion by governors and mayors. Awaiting a groundswell of support for Plan 3, we must do our best to understand the policies under current debate. I hope that readers of this book have found some help in developing opinions about tax policy based on sound economic reasoning and that they have enjoyed working through some of the analytical puzzles. Those who have persevered have, I suspect, acquired long-lived intellectual capital. For if events take their likely course, the income tax will be tangled for many a year to come.

Appendix / Bibliography / Index

Appendix. The Income Tax in Context

There are three kinds of lies — lies, damned lies, and statistics.

Attributed to both Benjamin Disraeli and Mark Twain

THIS APPENDIX brings together a variety of statistics that help put U.S. income tax policy into quantitative context. Because the numbers by which we describe the magnitudes of taxes are easily misinterpreted, I start with some basic matters of definition. We generally take for granted what taxes are — they are simply the devices by which governments extract money from the public — but there are actually several ways in which the government can accomplish the same things through tax and nontax means.[1] Here are some examples:

1. State governments typically impose taxes on alcoholic beverages. But some states put a ban on the private sale of alcoholic beverages and instead market them through state-owned-and-operated stores. Where one state has revenues from a tax, another has surplus from its liquor stores. Economically the two systems are essentially the same, but they have different labels.

2. Some of the many subsidy programs run by the federal government are identified as such and are treated as expenditure activities in the federal budget process. But many are operated through the tax system in the form of credits against tax liability or special deductions that have much the same effect. An example is the federal subsidy of 25 percent of expenditures to preserve and restore historic structures. This subsidy is paid not in cash directly, but in the indirect form of a credit against tax otherwise due. In addition, the taxpayer who makes qualifying investment outlays receives a further subsidy in the form of more favorable deductions for depreciation than are allowed on ordinary investments of a similar type. Substituting for such special tax rules an ordinary subsidy program that provided precisely the same incentive effects would result in an increase in expenditures and taxes on the books. The political process by which the program was enacted would also be different, and a different bureaucracy would implement it. But if the identical incentives were actually provided, such a relabeling would have no economically interesting consequences for anyone. (For a closer look at tax expenditures, see Chapter 11.)

1. For an excellent discussion of the arbitrary nature of conventional accounting for government activities, see Kotlikoff (1984). See also Eisner and Pieper (1984) and Boskin (forthcoming).

3. Many government activities are financed with no budgetary consequences whatever. These are programs implemented through regulation. For example, federal regulations require schools to provide facilities for handicapped people. In many instances the facilities would not be provided in the absence of federal rules. Such a regulatory program is economically equivalent to the appropriation of funds to pay for the special facilities, accompanied by taxes to cover the cost. (There are, of course, differences in administrative costs of the two methods.) The regulatory method generates no budgetary consequences; the appropriation and tax approach leads to higher recorded federal spending and taxes. Often the taxes implicit in regulatory programs are of a rather peculiar character. In the example just discussed, the implicit tax is levied on schools that are obliged to provide the mandated facilities. This is a most unusual form of taxation.

4. Some part of federal government activity is typically financed by borrowing. Debt finance differs from tax finance in that the resources are given up voluntarily by those who provide them. The government's claim on purchasing power is bought in that the providers are compensated with promises of future purchasing power. Debt finance thus can be taken as a commitment of future tax revenues; in this sense it is an indirect form of tax finance. We do not know who will pay this tax, however, nor does the current amount appear as tax revenue in the budget.

5. Expenditures themselves often take the form of commitments to future outlays that have no current budgetary consequence. The bond issued by the government when it borrows is a piece of paper promising to pay certain amounts in the future. The government sometimes makes such promises without issuing any pieces of paper. A striking instance is the large increase in retirement benefits under Social Security legislated in the 1970s. The increase might have been "funded," in which case either large tax receipts or large borrowing would have been shown in the budget. The actual choice was an "unfunded" increase, involving only implicit borrowing in the current budgetary periods. The result was a transfer of purchasing power to the government, and from the government to those who acquired new retirement income claims, financed by the indirect form of tax finance called borrowing, the borrowing itself being only implicit. To the detriment of our understanding of what is going on, neither the spending nor the borrowing in such a case shows up in the budgets of the years in which the implicit expenditure and taxation occur.

6. Inflation may give rise to another hidden tax or subsidy. People are interested in the real purchasing-power consequences of their saving and investment transactions. The lender of $100 will suffer a loss if there is an unexpected increase in the price level before the amount loaned is returned. The word "unexpected" is used advisedly. Inflation expected at the time of the execution of a loan is typically incorporated into its terms in the form of an interest rate sufficiently high for the borrower to compensate the lender for both the use of the funds and the loss in their real purchasing power. Because government has

the power to influence the course of inflation, it can, in effect, tax its creditors by allowing inflation in excess of that incorporated in the interest rate. This is equivalent to levying a tax on lenders and providing a subsidy to borrowers. As a large net borrower, the government gains from unexpected inflation. Conversely, an unexpected slowdown in inflation has the effect of a windfall subsidy to lenders and a tax on borrowers, and generates a loss for the government.

7. Although it is only inflation in excess of expectations that imposes a tax on those who lend to the government at interest, inflation is always a tax on the holders of the non-interest-bearing government debt called money. (These remarks concern only what might be called the direct effect of inflation. Inflation has, in addition, very strong indirect effects via the income tax, as discussed at length in this book.) The implicit taxes (positive and negative) effected by inflation represent genuine transfers of purchasing power to and from the government, often large ones, but they are not recorded in the usual accounting for taxes and spending.

At a fundamental level the object of the statistical measures assembled in the following tables is to describe all the ways the fiscal system modifies the economic opportunities of individuals. Whether the policy in question is implemented by issuing debt, by granting a tax credit, or by promulgating a regulation, its effects can ultimately be reduced to specific consequences for specific individuals. In principle we should be concerned with substance, not labels, be they taxes, expenditures, regulation, or borrowing. By the rules of accounting, fixing expenditures and taxes determines the policies labeled borrowing — a shortfall in any period must be made up through borrowing, and any surplus implies retiring debt. But as the examples have shown, the measures we use to describe the fiscal system — tax receipts, government borrowing, and the like — are very crude. In interpreting statistical data on taxes and spending, the warnings implied by the examples should be kept in mind.

The Domestic Economic Context

Tables A–1 through A–3 list the major revenue sources of federal, state, and local governments in the United States in calendar 1984, the most recent year for which a full set of figures was available at the time of this writing. The tables show the total sums raised both in dollars and, to give an idea of the magnitudes relative to the overall economy, as percentages of gross national product (GNP). Because the figures are on a national-income accounts basis, they differ in various technical details from those shown in federal, state, and local budgets, which are, in addition, usually shown on a fiscal-year rather than calendar-year basis. I have included in the tables the amounts currently borrowed as well, as a reminder that they are, in effect, deferred taxes.

Of the total amount raised by the federal government other than by borrowing, well over half (54 percent) was generated by the tax on individual and corporation income; about three-eighths (37 percent) was brought in by the

Table A-1. Federal government receipts, 1984 (includes debt issue)

Receipts	$ billions	% GNP[a]
Total receipts (including debt)	880.5	24.0
Deficit	175.8	4.8
Total receipts (excluding debt)	704.7	19.2
Personal tax and nontax receipts	315.0	8.6
Income taxes	308.4	8.4
Estate and gift taxes	5.9	0.2
Nontaxes	0.7	0.0
Corporate profits tax accruals	70.8	1.9
Indirect business tax and nontax accruals	55.5	1.5
Excise taxes	35.8	1.0
Customs duties	11.9	0.3
Nontaxes	7.8	0.2
Contributions for social insurance	263.4	7.2

Source: Survey of Current Business, LXV-5 (May 1985), tables 1.1, 3.2, and 3.3.
a. 1984 GNP: $3662.8 billion.

payroll taxes that finance Social Security, including Medicare and retirement benefits as well as unemployment compensation, with the rest (9 percent) raised mainly from the tax on estates and gifts, excise taxes, and customs duties.

For various reasons, including the fact that they operate in an environment of free migration of people and economic activity, state and local governments rely on a different mix of taxes. They make less use of income taxes (19 percent of receipts net of debt and grants in aid in 1984, counting the tax on corporate profits) and much less use of payroll taxes (Social Security taxes provided 10 percent of state and local revenue in 1984). Indirect business taxes are much more important. In 1984, sales taxes accounted for the largest share of state and local revenue (28 percent), followed by property taxes (23 percent), with an additional 7 percent raised from assorted other indirect business taxes. Miscellaneous other tax and nontax sources accounted for the remaining 13 percent.

The tables also describe the broad outlines of the U.S. fiscal structure in relation to the national economy. According to Table A-1, the federal government withdrew nearly one-quarter of GNP from the public in 1984, but only about 80 percent of that total was actually currently raised through taxes. (The figures are 24.0 percent of GNP in total receipts, 19.2 percent of GNP raised in taxes, and 4.8 percent of GNP borrowed.) The combination of individual and corporation income taxes transferred just over 10 percent of GNP to the federal government — an easy figure to remember, and one that relates rather uncomfortably to the federal budget deficits of roughly 5 percent per year foreseen for the indefinite future at the time of this writing.

The major role of state and local governments in the United States is not always appreciated. The two levels of government combined were responsible for 86 percent of all nondefense government purchases of goods and services (which totaled $525.9 billion) in 1984 (*Survey of Current Business,* 64 [October 1984], tables 3.2 and 3.3). Thus much the largest share of direct government services other than transfer payments and defense — notably education and infrastructure — is delivered at the state and local level. A national interest in these services may bear on such issues as the deductibility of state and local taxes under the federal income tax.

Table A–2 indicates that state and local governments were also important revenue raisers. Altogether, state and local personal income, sales, and property taxes raised $338.0 billion in 1984, exceeding the yield of the federal income tax. Taking account of their net retirement of debt during the year, altogether state and local governments withdrew 10.3 percent of GNP in 1984. Because they received funds transferred from the federal government amounting to 2.5 percent of GNP, state and local governments spent 12.9 percent of GNP, more than they raised in taxes and net borrowing (negative in 1984).

Taking all three levels of government together — federal, state, and local (Table A–3) — 34.3 percent of GNP was drawn into the governmental sector in 1984, including 3.4 percent of GNP in borrowed money and 31.0 percent of GNP from various tax and related sources. The federal income tax on individuals

Table A–2. State and local government receipts, 1984 (includes debt issue)

Receipts	$ billions	% GNP[a]
Total receipts (including debt)	470.7	12.9
Federal grants-in-aid	93.2	2.5
Deficit	−52.9	−1.4
Total receipts (excluding debt and grants-in-aid)	430.4	11.8
Personal tax and nontax receipts	120.3	3.3
Income taxes	64.5	1.8
Nontaxes	45.8	1.3
Other	10.0	0.3
Corporate profits tax accruals	19.1	0.5
Indirect business tax and nontax accruals	248.4	6.8
Sales taxes	119.4	3.3
Property taxes	98.3	2.7
Other	30.7	0.8
Contributions for social insurance	42.6	1.2

Source: Survey of Current Business, LXV–5 (May 1985), tables 1.1, 3.2, and 3.3.
a. 1984 GNP: $3662.8 billion.

Table A–3. Consolidated government receipts, 1984 (includes debt issue)

Receipts	$ billions	% GNP[a]
Consolidated receipts (including debt)	1258.0	34.3
Consolidated deficit	122.9	3.4
Consolidated receipts (excluding debt)	1135.1	31.0
Personal tax and nontax receipts	435.3	11.9
Income taxes	372.9	10.2
Other	62.4	1.7
Corporate profits tax accruals	89.9	2.5
Indirect business tax and nontax accruals	303.9	8.3
Federal excise	35.8	1.0
State and local sales	119.4	3.3
State and local property	98.3	2.7
Other	50.4	1.4
Contributions for social insurance	306.0	8.4
Federal grants-in-aid	−93.2	−2.5

Source: Survey of Current Business, LXV–5 (May 1985), tables 1.1, 3.2, and 3.3.
a. 1984 GNP: $3662.8 billion.

accounted for 25 percent of the total raised from the public and 27 percent of the entire amount raised other than by borrowing. The corresponding figures for the combined federal tax on individual and corporation income are 30 percent and 33 percent.

The Historical Context

The most remarkable feature of the history of public finance in the United States since the turn of the century is the extent of change.[2] Figure A–1 provides information about the revenue sources in the twentieth century of all levels of government combined (Table A–4 gives the underlying data for reference.) Figure A–2 (with Table A–5) shows the story on the spending side. A clear message conveyed by these graphs is that very substantial change in the government financial structure may occur over rather short time spans. There were, of course, great bursts of expenditure during wars. Because only widely separated years are provided in the statistical series for the early part of the century, the figures somewhat mute the effect of World War I on the level of both receipts and outlays. But the sharp hump of World War II is clearly visible.

2. In this review of the historical picture I have benefited particularly from the work of John F. Witte (1982) and from Pechman (1983, appendix A). See also Witte (1985).

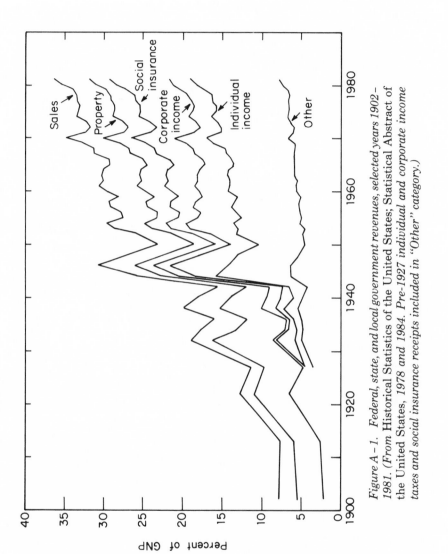

Figure A–1. Federal, state, and local government revenues, selected years 1902–1981. (From Historical Statistics of the United States; Statistical Abstract of the United States, 1978 and 1984. Pre-1927 individual and corporate income taxes and social insurance receipts included in "Other" category.)

Table A-4. Revenues of federal, state, and local government, selected fiscal years, 1902–1981 (percentage of GNP)

Fiscal year	Property	Sales	Corporate income	Individual income	Social insurance	All other	Total	GNP ($ billions)
1981	2.5	4.6	2.5	11.2	7.6	7.9	36.4	2954.1
1980	2.6	4.3	3.0	10.9	7.2	7.5	35.4	2631.7
1979	2.7	4.2	3.2	10.5	6.9	6.8	34.3	2417.8
1978	3.1	4.3	3.3	9.9	6.8	6.5	33.8	2163.9
1977	3.3	4.4	3.3	9.7	7.0	6.6	34.3	1918.3
1976	3.3	4.4	2.8	9.1	6.9	6.7	33.2	1718.0
1975	3.3	4.6	3.1	9.3	6.7	6.6	33.5	1549.2
1974	3.3	4.6	3.1	9.6	6.2	6.8	33.7	1434.2
1973	3.4	4.7	3.1	9.1	5.7	6.5	32.6	1326.4
1972	3.6	4.9	3.1	9.3	5.5	6.0	32.2	1185.9
1971	3.5	4.9	2.8	9.1	5.3	6.1	31.8	1077.6
1970	3.5	5.0	3.7	10.4	5.4	6.7	34.7	977.1
1969	3.3	4.8	4.3	10.3	5.0	5.9	33.6	930.3
1968	3.2	4.5	3.6	8.8	4.7	5.9	30.7	864.2
1967	3.3	4.6	4.6	8.5	4.9	6.0	31.8	793.9
1966	3.3	4.5	4.3	8.0	4.1	5.9	30.1	749.9
1965	3.3	4.8	4.0	7.7	3.9	5.9	29.6	684.9
1964	3.4	4.8	4.0	8.3	4.1	5.9	30.4	632.4
1963	3.4	4.9	3.9	8.6	3.9	5.9	30.5	590.5
1962	3.4	4.8	3.9	8.7	3.6	5.6	30.0	560.3
1961	3.5	4.8	4.3	8.5	3.8	5.7	30.5	520.1

1960	3.3	4.9	4.5	8.6	3.5	5.7	30.4	503.7
1959	3.1	4.5	3.8	8.0	3.0	5.2	27.5	483.7
1958	3.1	4.7	4.7	8.2	3.1	5.4	29.2	447.3
1957	2.9	4.7	5.0	8.5	2.8	5.4	29.3	441.1
1956	2.8	4.6	5.2	8.0	2.7	5.2	28.5	419.2
1955	2.7	4.3	4.7	7.5	2.4	5.1	26.7	398.0
1954	2.7	4.8	6.0	8.4	2.4	5.3	29.7	364.8
1953	2.6	4.7	6.0	8.5	2.3	4.6	28.7	364.6
1952	2.5	4.5	6.4	8.4	2.3	4.9	29.0	345.5
1950	2.6	4.6	3.9	5.8	1.9	4.6	23.4	284.8
1948	2.4	4.7	4.0	7.7	1.9	5.4	26.0	257.6
1946	2.4	4.8	5.9	8.0	2.1	6.4	29.5	208.5
1944	2.2	3.3	7.2	9.5	2.2	6.4	30.8	210.1
1942	2.9	3.7	3.2	2.2	1.7	4.3	18.0	157.9
1940	4.4	4.1	1.3	1.2	2.0	4.9	17.9	99.7
1938	5.2	4.5	1.8	1.8	1.9	5.5	20.6	84.7
1936	5.0	4.1	1.0	1.0	0.4	5.0	16.5	82.5
1934	6.3	4.4	0.7	0.7	0.4	4.9	17.4	65.1
1932	7.7	2.6	1.2	0.8	0.4	5.0	17.7	58.0
1927	5.0	1.6	1.4	1.0	0.2	3.5	12.8	94.9
1922	4.5	1.8	0.0	0.0	0.2	6.1	12.6	74.1
1913	3.4	1.7	0.1	0.0	0.0	2.4	7.5	39.6
1902	3.3	2.4	0.0	0.0	0.0	2.2	7.8	21.6

Sources: Historical Statistics of the United States and Statistical Abstract of the United States, 1978 and 1984.

Table A–5. Spending by federal, state, and local government, selected fiscal years, 1902–1981 (percentage of GNP)

Fiscal year	Education	Welfare	National defense	Social insurance	Interest	Other	Total	GNP ($ billions)
1981	5.3	2.5	5.9	6.6	3.3	13.9	37.6	2954.1
1980	5.5	2.5	5.7	6.1	2.9	13.8	36.4	2631.7
1979	5.4	2.4	5.3	5.7	2.6	13.0	34.4	2417.8
1978	5.5	2.5	5.3	5.8	2.4	13.0	34.4	2163.9
1977	5.8	2.6	5.5	6.2	2.3	13.3	35.6	1918.3
1976	6.2	2.6	5.7	6.2	2.3	13.4	36.4	1718.0
1975	6.1	2.5	6.1	5.7	2.2	13.5	36.2	1549.2
1974	5.7	2.2	6.0	4.8	2.1	12.6	33.3	1434.2
1973	5.6	2.0	6.3	4.6	1.9	12.5	32.9	1326.4
1972	5.9	2.0	6.7	4.4	1.9	12.6	33.5	1185.9
1971	5.9	1.9	7.5	4.3	2.0	12.6	34.3	1077.6
1970	5.7	1.8	8.6	4.0	1.9	12.1	34.1	977.1
1969	5.4	1.6	9.1	3.7	1.8	11.5	33.1	930.3
1968	5.0	1.3	9.7	3.5	1.7	11.5	32.7	864.2
1967	5.1	1.2	9.4	3.3	1.7	11.8	32.5	793.9
1966	4.6	0.9	8.1	2.9	1.6	11.8	30.0	749.9
1965	4.3	0.9	8.1	2.8	1.7	12.2	30.0	684.9
1964	4.3	0.9	9.1	2.9	1.7	12.1	31.1	632.4
1963	4.1	0.9	9.5	3.0	1.7	12.0	31.3	590.5
1962	4.1	0.9	9.8	3.0	1.6	12.0	31.5	560.3
1961	4.1	0.9	9.8	3.0	1.8	12.1	31.7	520.1

1960	3.9	0.9	9.7	2.7	1.9	11.1	30.0	503.7
1959	3.7	0.9	10.3	2.7	1.4	11.1	30.1	483.7
1958	3.8	0.9	10.6	2.5	1.6	10.8	30.2	447.3
1957	3.4	0.8	10.8	1.8	1.5	10.1	28.4	441.1
1956	3.4	0.8	10.4	1.6	1.5	10.0	27.6	419.2
1955	3.2	0.8	10.9	1.6	1.4	9.9	27.8	398.0
1954	3.1	0.9	13.5	1.3	1.5	10.2	30.5	364.8
1953	2.8	0.8	14.7	1.0	1.5	9.4	30.2	364.6
1952	2.8	0.8	13.9	0.9	1.4	9.1	28.9	345.5
1950	3.4	1.0	6.4	1.0	1.7	11.2	24.7	284.8
1948	3.0	0.8	6.2	0.5	1.8	9.0	21.4	257.6
1946	1.8	0.7	24.2	0.6	2.1	8.9	38.2	208.5
1944	1.3	0.5	40.7	0.1	1.3	8.4	52.3	210.1
1942	1.7	0.8	16.8	0.3	1.0	8.2	28.9	157.9
1940	2.8	1.3	1.6	0.5	1.6	12.6	20.5	99.7
1938	3.1	1.5	1.2	0.2	1.8	13.0	20.9	84.7
1936	2.9	1.2	1.1	0.0	1.8	13.3	20.3	82.5
1934	3.1	1.5	0.8	0.0	2.3	12.0	19.7	65.1
1932	4.0	0.8	1.2	0.0	2.3 *	13.1	21.4	58.0
1927	2.4	0.2	0.6	0.0	1.4	7.2	11.8	94.9
1922	2.3	0.2	1.2	0.0	1.8	7.0	12.5	74.1
1913	1.5	0.1	0.6	0.0	0.4	5.4	8.1	39.6
1902	1.2	0.2	0.8	0.0	0.4	5.1	7.7	21.6

Sources: Historical Statistics of the United States and Statistical Abstract of the United States, 1978 and 1984.

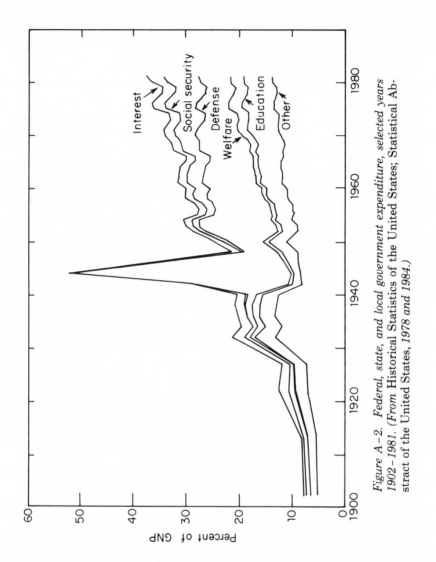

Figure A-2. Federal, state, and local government expenditure, selected years 1902–1981. (From Historical Statistics of the United States; Statistical Abstract of the United States, 1978 and 1984.)

Also notable is a long-term upward trend in the fraction of economic activity mediated by government. There is perhaps a correlation between the growth of defense expenditures and that of the income tax, and a more obvious connection between the growth of social spending and that of the payroll taxes. To judge naively from the pictures, the two world wars seem to have left lasting legacies in the form of an altered composition of both taxing and spending. World War II, in particular, is associated with a lasting change in the structure of taxes and transfers.

These events and trends show up more clearly in the figures relating to the federal government only. The spending spikes associated with the world wars cannot be missed in Figure A-3 (Table A-6), which displays the overall outlays, receipts, and budget deficits and surplus during this century. Figure A-4 (Table A-7) provides a closer look at the breakdown of federal revenue by major tax institution. Although obscured by lack of detail in the data, taxes on income emerged as major elements of the picture in financing U.S. efforts in World War I. Federal individual income taxation having been declared unconstitutional in 1895, the corporation income tax was introduced in 1909 as an "excise," pending ratification of the Sixteenth Amendment to the federal Constitution. Ratification was achieved in 1913, and in the same year an income tax was established, with rates of 1 percent on corporations and rates on individuals ranging from 1 percent to a high of 7 percent. The initial exempt levels of $3000 for single taxpayers and $4000 for married couples translate into roughly $34,000 and $45,000, respectively, in 1985 dollars, high enough that less than 2 percent of the population was affected by the individual income tax. During World War I rates on both individual and corporate income were sharply increased (with an "excess-profits" tax added to the corporate base), and the exempt-income levels were halved in the individual tax. The end of the war saw a marginal corporate rate of as much as 64 percent and a maximum marginal rate of 77 percent in the individual income tax (Witte, 1982, p. 7). While the years after World War I brought a lowering of rates again, the extraordinary revenue demands of World War II led to the full transformation of the individual income tax from one paid (at low rates) by a relatively small minority of citizens into a mass tax bearing (at fairly high rates) on almost everyone. The ratio of the number of income tax returns filed to the size of the labor force, which had declined from a peak of nearly 15 percent during World War I, reached nearly 90 percent by the end of World War II. Furthermore, many of those individuals now faced significant marginal rates of tax, with a top marginal rate of 94 percent applied to income over $200,000 (Witte, 1982, pp. 9-10). These developments in the income tax can be seen in revenue terms in the figures. Also noticeable is the parallel development of Social Security transfers and the expansion of payroll taxes. Naturally, this is not a coincidence, as Social Security taxes on payrolls have been motivated by a "pay-as-you-go" philosophy of finance.

Table A-8 provides a closer look at individual and corporation income taxes since World War II, as seen through the national-income accounts. The post-World War II experience can be roughly divided into three epochs: a period of stability in the income tax law through 1962; a period of rapid change after that,

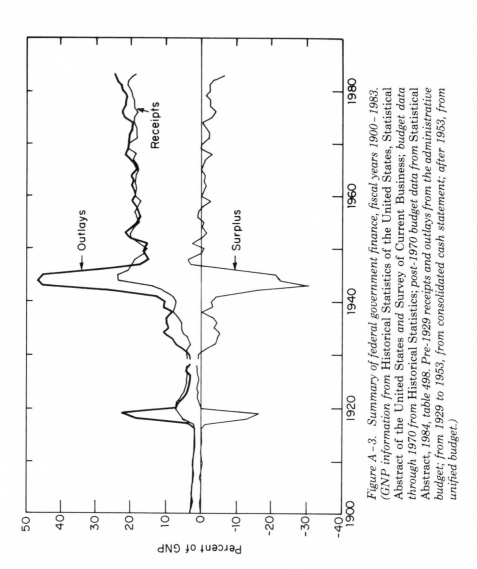

Figure A–3. Summary of federal government finance, fiscal years 1900–1983. (GNP information from Historical Statistics of the United States, Statistical Abstract of the United States and Survey of Current Business; budget data through 1970 from Historical Statistics; post-1970 budget data from Statistical Abstract, 1984, table 498. Pre-1929 receipts and outlays from the administrative budget; from 1929 to 1953, from consolidated cash statement; after 1953, from unified budget.)

Table A-6. Federal receipts and outlays, fiscal years 1900–1983 (percentage of GNP)

Fiscal year[b]	Consolidated cash and unified budget[a]			Administrative budget			
	Receipts (339)[c]	Outlays (340)[c]	Surplus (341)[c]	Receipts (335)[c]	Outlays (336)[c]	Surplus (337)[c]	FY GNP[d] ($ billions)
1983	18.4	24.8	−6.4	—	—	—	3246.9
1982	20.3	23.9	−3.6	—	—	—	3043.3
1981	20.9	22.9	−2.0	—	—	—	2873.5
1980	20.1	22.4	−2.3	—	—	—	2578.2
1979	19.7	20.9	−1.2	—	—	—	2354.3
1978	19.0	21.3	−2.3	—	—	—	2102.5
1977	19.0	21.4	−2.4	—	—	—	1868.2
1976	18.2	22.3	−4.1	—	—	—	1633.6
1975	18.7	21.7	−3.0	—	—	—	1491.7
1974	19.1	19.4	−0.3	—	—	—	1380.3
1973	18.4	19.6	−1.2	—	—	—	1256.2
1972	18.3	20.4	−2.1	—	—	—	1131.8
1971	18.2	20.5	−2.2	—	—	—	1027.4
1970	20.3	20.6	−0.3	—	—	—	953.7
1969	20.9	20.6	0.4	—	—	—	897.3
1968	18.4	21.6	−3.0	—	—	—	829.1
1967	19.4	20.5	−1.1	—	—	—	771.9
1966	18.2	18.8	−0.5	—	—	—	717.4
1965	17.7	18.0	−0.2	—	—	—	658.7
1964	18.4	19.4	−1.0	—	—	—	611.5
1963	18.5	19.3	−0.8	—	—	—	575.4
1962	18.5	19.8	−1.3	—	—	—	540.2
1961	18.4	19.1	−0.7	—	—	—	511.9
1960	18.7	18.7	0.1	—	—	—	493.7
1959	17.0	19.8	−2.8	—	—	—	465.5
1958	17.9	18.6	−0.7	—	—	—	444.2
1957	18.6	17.8	0.7	—	—	—	430.2
1956	18.2	17.3	1.0	—	—	—	408.6
1955	17.2	18.0	−0.8	—	—	—	381.4
1954	19.1	19.4	−0.3	—	—	—	364.7
1953	20.1	21.6	−1.5	—	—	—	355.1
1952	20.2	20.2	0.0	—	—	—	337.0
1951	17.4	14.9	2.5	—	—	—	306.6

Table A-6 *(continued)*

Fiscal year[b]	Consolidated cash and unified budget[a]			Administrative budget			
	Receipts (339)[c]	Outlays (340)[c]	Surplus (341)[c]	Receipts (335)[c]	Outlays (336)[c]	Surplus (337)[c]	FY GNP[d] ($ billions)
1950	15.1	15.9	−0.8	—	—	—	270.7
1949	16.2	15.8	0.4	—	—	—	257.1
1948	18.6	14.9	3.6	—	—	—	244.5
1947	19.8	16.8	3.0	—	—	—	219.9
1946	20.7	29.4	−8.7	—	—	—	210.2
1945	23.8	45.1	−21.3	—	—	—	211.0
1944	23.8	46.8	−23.0	—	—	—	200.9
1943	14.4	45.2	−30.8	—	—	—	174.8
1942	10.7	24.4	−13.7	—	—	—	141.2
1941	8.2	12.5	−4.3	—	—	—	112.1
1940	7.3	10.1	−2.8	—	—	—	95.1
1939	7.5	10.7	−3.3	5.7	10.1	−4.4	87.6
1938	8.0	8.2	−0.1	6.4	7.7	−1.3	87.6
1937	6.5	9.7	−3.2	5.7	8.9	−3.2	86.5
1936	5.4	9.8	−4.5	5.2	10.9	−5.7	77.4
1935	5.5	9.2	−3.5	5.4	9.5	−4.1	68.7
1934	5.1	10.8	−5.5	5.0	11.0	−6.0	60.4
1933	3.7	8.3	−4.6	3.5	8.1	−4.6	56.8
1932	3.0	7.2	−4.0	2.9	7.0	−4.1	66.9
1931	3.9	4.9	−1.2	3.7	4.3	−0.6	83.1
1930	4.1	3.2	0.9	4.2	3.4	0.8	96.8
1929	3.8	2.9	0.9	3.9	3.1	0.7	100.1
1928	—	—	—	4.1	3.1	1.0	95.5
1927	—	—	—	4.2	4.0	1.2	95.5
1926	—	—	—	4.0	3.1	0.9	95.1
1925	—	—	—	4.1	3.3	0.8	88.9
1924	—	—	—	4.6	3.4	1.1	84.9
1923	—	—	—	4.8	3.9	0.9	79.6
1922	—	—	—	5.6	4.6	1.0	71.9
1921	—	—	—	6.9	6.3	0.6	80.6
1920	—	—	—	7.6	7.2	0.3	87.8
1919	—	—	—	6.4	23.1	−16.7	80.2
1918	—	—	—	5.3	18.5	−13.2	68.4

Table A–6 *(continued)*

Fiscal year[b]	Consolidated cash and unified budget[a]			Administrative budget			
	Receipts (339)[c]	Outlays (340)[c]	Surplus (341)[c]	Receipts (335)[c]	Outlays (336)[c]	Surplus (337)[c]	FY GNP[d] ($ billions)
1917	—	—	—	2.0	3.6	−1.6	54.4
1916	—	—	—	1.7	1.6	0.1	44.2
1915	—	—	—	1.7	1.9	−0.2	39.3
1914	—	—	—	1.9	1.9	0.0	39.1
1913	—	—	—	1.8	1.8	0.0	39.5
1912	—	—	—	1.8	1.8	0.0	37.6
1911	—	—	—	2.0	1.9	0.0	35.6
1910	—	—	—	2.0	2.0	−0.1	34.4
1909	—	—	—	2.0	2.3	−0.3	30.6
1908	—	—	—	2.1	2.3	−0.2	29.1
1907	—	—	—	2.3	2.0	0.3	29.6
1906	—	—	—	2.2	2.1	0.1	26.9
1905	—	—	—	2.3	2.4	−0.1	24.0
1904	—	—	—	2.4	2.5	−0.2	22.9
1903	—	—	—	2.5	2.3	0.2	22.3
1902	—	—	—	2.7	2.3	0.4	21.2
1901	—	—	—	3.0	2.7	0.3	19.7
1900	—	—	—	3.1	2.9	0.3	18.1

Sources: GNP: *Historical Statistics of the United States, Statistical Abstract of the United States, 1984,* and *Survey of Current Business.* Budget data through 1970: *Historical Statistics;* budget data after 1970: 1984 *Statistical Abstract* (table 498).

a. Consolidated cash statement figures: 1929–1953; unified budget figures: 1954–1983.

b. Fiscal years end June 30 through 1976; thereafter September 30.

c. Series number in *Historical Statistics* and *Statistical Abstract.*

d. Fiscal year GNP by simple interpolation of calendar year data.

with the general trend toward higher marginal tax rates applying to a much larger fraction of the population than in the earlier period; and then a period of much greater political sensitivity to income tax rates beginning in 1981. The immediate postwar period, up until 1962, was notable for the relative stability of the tax law. There was just one tax cut after the war, before the revenue demands of the Korean War compelled increases again (Witte, 1982, p. 11). It is true that the Korean War was followed by a major recodification of federal tax law, which is still formally identified as the "Internal Revenue Code of 1954." The recodification brought with it a number of changes in the income tax,

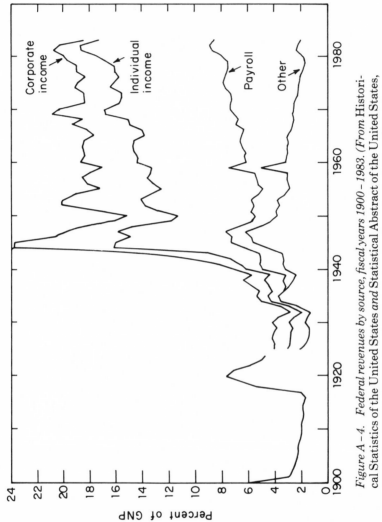

Figure A-4. Federal revenues by source, fiscal years 1900-1983. (From Histori-cal Statistics of the United States and Statistical Abstract of the United States, 1984. Pre-1925 individual and corporate income taxes included in "Other" cate-gory.)

Table A-7. Federal revenues, by source, fiscal years 1900–1983 (percentage of GNP)

Fiscal year	Individual income[a]	Corporate income[a]	Payroll	Estate and gift	Other	Total	FY GNP ($ billions)
1983	8.8	1.1	6.5	0.2	1.9	18.4	3246.9
1982	9.8	1.6	6.6	0.3	2.0	20.3	3043.3
1981	9.9	2.1	6.4	0.2	2.2	20.9	2873.5
1980	9.5	2.5	6.1	0.2	1.7	20.1	2578.2
1979	9.3	2.8	5.9	0.2	1.5	19.7	2354.3
1978	8.6	2.9	5.8	0.3	1.5	19.0	2102.5
1977	8.4	2.9	5.7	0.4	1.6	19.0	1868.2
1976	8.0	2.5	5.7	0.3	1.8	18.3	1633.6
1975	8.2	2.7	5.8	0.3	1.8	18.8	1491.7
1974	8.6	2.8	5.6	0.4	1.8	19.2	1380.3
1973	8.2	2.9	5.1	0.4	1.9	18.5	1256.2
1972	8.4	2.8	4.8	0.5	2.0	18.4	1131.8
1971	8.4	2.6	4.7	0.4	2.2	18.3	1027.4
1970	9.5	3.4	4.7	0.4	2.3	20.3	953.7
1969	9.7	4.1	4.4	0.4	2.3	20.9	897.3
1968	8.3	3.5	4.2	0.4	2.2	18.5	829.1
1967	8.0	4.4	4.3	0.4	2.3	19.4	771.9
1966	7.7	4.2	3.6	0.4	2.3	18.2	717.4
1965	7.4	3.9	3.4	0.4	2.7	17.7	658.7
1964	8.0	3.8	3.6	0.4	2.6	18.4	611.5
1963	8.3	3.8	3.4	0.4	2.7	18.5	575.4
1962	8.4	3.8	3.2	0.4	2.6	18.5	540.2
1961	8.1	4.1	3.2	0.4	2.7	18.4	511.9
1960	8.3	4.4	3.0	0.3	2.8	18.7	493.7
1959	5.8	3.7	2.5	0.3	4.7	17.0	465.5
1958	7.8	4.5	2.5	0.3	2.7	17.9	444.2
1957	8.3	4.9	2.3	0.3	2.8	18.6	430.2
1956	7.9	5.1	2.3	0.3	2.7	18.2	408.6
1955	7.5	4.7	2.1	0.2	2.6	17.2	381.4
1954	8.1	5.8	2.0	0.3	3.0	19.1	364.7
1953	8.4	6.0	1.9	0.2	3.6	20.1	355.1
1952	8.3	6.3	1.9	0.2	3.4	20.2	337.0
1951	7.0	4.6	1.9	0.2	3.7	17.4	306.6
1950	5.8	3.9	1.6	0.3	3.6	15.1	270.7
1949	6.0	4.4	1.5	0.3	4.0	16.2	257.1
1948	7.9	4.0	1.6	0.4	4.7	18.6	244.5

Table A–7 *(continued)*

Fiscal year	Individual income[a]	Corporate income[a]	Payroll	Estate and gift	Other	Total	FY GNP ($ billions)
1947	8.2	3.9	1.5	0.4	5.9	19.8	219.9
1946	7.7	5.8	1.5	0.3	5.4	20.7	210.2
1945	8.7	7.8	1.6	0.3	5.4	23.8	211.0
1944	10.0	7.6	1.7	0.3	4.2	23.8	200.9
1943	3.7	5.5	1.7	0.3	3.2	14.4	174.8
1942	2.3	3.4	1.7	0.3	3.0	10.7	141.2
1941	1.4	1.6	1.8	0.4	3.0	8.2	112.1
1940	1.2	1.0	1.8	0.4	2.9	7.2	95.1
1939	1.2	1.3	0.8	0.4	1.9	5.7	87.6
1938	1.5	1.5	0.8	0.5	2.1	6.4	87.6
1937	1.3	1.3	0.3	0.4	2.6	5.7	86.5
1936	0.9	1.0	0.0	0.5	2.8	5.2	77.4
1935	0.8	0.8	0.0	0.3	3.5	5.4	68.7
1934	0.7	0.7	0.0	0.2	3.5	5.0	60.4
1933	0.6	0.7	0.0	0.1	2.1	3.5	56.8
1932	0.6	0.9	0.0	0.1	1.2	2.9	66.9
1931	1.0	1.2	0.0	0.1	1.5	3.7	83.1
1930	1.2	1.3	0.0	0.1	1.6	4.2	96.8
1929	1.2	1.2	0.0	0.1	1.3	3.9	100.1
1928	1.4	1.4	0.0	0.1	1.3	4.1	95.5
1927	1.4	1.4	0.0	0.1	1.4	4.2	95.5
1926	1.2	1.2	0.0	0.1	1.6	4.0	95.1
1925	1.0	1.0	0.0	0.1	1.9	4.1	88.9
1924	0.0	0.0	0.0	0.1	4.4	4.6	84.9
1923	0.0	0.0	0.0	0.2	4.7	4.8	79.6
1922	0.0	0.0	0.0	0.2	5.4	5.6	71.9
1921	0.0	0.0	0.0	0.2	6.7	6.9	80.6
1920	0.0	0.0	0.0	0.1	7.5	7.6	87.8
1919	0.0	0.0	0.0	0.1	6.3	6.4	80.2
1918	0.0	0.0	0.0	0.1	5.3	5.3	68.4
1917	0.0	0.0	0.0	0.0	2.0	2.0	54.4
1916	0.0	0.0	0.0	0.0	1.7	1.7	44.2
1915	0.0	0.0	0.0	0.0	1.7	1.7	39.3
1914	0.0	0.0	0.0	0.0	1.9	1.9	39.1
1913	0.0	0.0	0.0	0.0	1.8	1.8	39.5
1912	0.0	0.0	0.0	0.0	1.8	1.8	37.6

Table A–7 *(continued)*

Fiscal year	Individual income[a]	Corporate income[a]	Payroll	Estate and gift	Other	Total	FY GNP ($ billions)
1911	0.0	0.0	0.0	0.0	2.0	2.0	35.6
1910	0.0	0.0	0.0	0.0	2.0	2.0	34.4
1909	0.0	0.0	0.0	0.0	2.0	2.0	30.6
1908	0.0	0.0	0.0	0.0	2.1	2.1	29.1
1907	0.0	0.0	0.0	0.0	2.3	2.3	29.6
1906	0.0	0.0	0.0	0.0	2.2	2.2	26.9
1905	0.0	0.0	0.0	0.0	2.3	2.3	24.0
1904	0.0	0.0	0.0	0.0	2.4	2.4	22.9
1903	0.0	0.0	0.0	0.0	2.5	2.5	22.3
1902	0.0	0.0	0.0	0.0	2.7	2.7	21.2
1901	0.0	0.0	0.0	0.0	3.0	3.0	19.7
1900	0.0	0.0	0.0	0.0	6.1	6.1	9.4

Sources: Historical Statistics of the United States and *Statistical Abstract of the United States,* 1984.
a. Pre-1925 corporate and individual income tax revenues are included in the "Other" category.

including the sanctioning of so-called accelerated methods of calculating depreciation allowances. But most of the changes could be described as "cleaning up" the system, and the rate structure, in particular, was left alone (Witte, 1982, p. 10). Rates under the individual income tax (ranging from 20 percent on the first $4000 of taxable income through 91 percent on taxable income over $400,000) were unchanged from 1954 through 1963; corporate rates were constant (30 percent on the first $25,000; 52 percent on income above $25,000) from 1952 through 1963. Personal exemptions were the same ($600 per taxpayer and dependent) from 1948 through 1969 (Pechman, 1983, Tables A–1, A–3, and A–6). Increases in the price level over the period eroded the real value of fixed money amounts somewhat, although inflation was modest by recent standards. In the eleven years from 1952 to 1963, the price level (measured by the GNP deflator) increased by a bit less than 25 percent.

We may note in passing the statistical record traced in Table A–8 over this period of income tax stability. Because of the progressivity of the rate structure, the ratio of individual income tax to GNP drifted upward from 1954 to 1963. Gross national product grew at an average annual rate of 5.0 percent over the nine-year period, during which individual income tax receipts grew at an average annual rate of 5.9 percent.[3] By contrast, the roughly proportional corpora-

3. A technical note for those who check calculations: these growth rates are obtained from a simple regression of the log of the variable in question against time.

Table A−8. Income taxes and corporate profit in relation to GNP, 1946−1984

Year	Individual income tax[a] ($ billions)	Individual tax as % GNP	Corporate income tax[a] ($ billions)	Corporate tax as % GNP	Pretax corporate profit ($ billions)	Corporate income as % GNP	Corporate tax as % profit	GNP ($ billions)
1946	16.3	7.8	8.6	4.1	16.6	7.9	52.1	209.8
1947	18.8	8.1	10.7	4.6	22.3	9.6	47.9	233.1
1948	18.1	7.0	11.8	4.5	29.4	11.3	39.9	259.5
1949	15.4	5.9	9.6	3.7	27.1	10.5	35.4	258.3
1950	17.4	6.1	17.2	6.0	33.9	11.9	50.5	286.5
1951	25.4	7.7	21.7	6.6	38.7	11.7	56.1	330.8
1952	30.1	8.7	18.6	5.3	36.1	10.4	51.5	348.0
1953	31.3	8.5	19.5	5.3	36.3	9.9	53.6	366.8
1954	28.0	7.6	16.9	4.6	35.2	9.6	47.9	366.8
1955	30.4	7.6	21.1	5.3	45.5	11.4	46.3	400.0
1956	33.8	8.0	20.9	5.0	43.7	10.4	47.9	421.7
1957	35.9	8.1	20.4	4.6	43.3	9.7	47.2	444.0
1958	35.4	7.9	18.0	4.0	38.5	8.6	46.7	449.7
1959	38.5	7.9	22.5	4.6	49.6	10.2	45.3	487.9
1960	41.8	8.3	21.4	4.2	47.6	9.4	45.0	506.5
1961	42.7	8.1	21.5	4.1	48.6	9.3	44.2	524.6
1962	46.5	8.2	22.5	4.0	56.6	10.0	39.7	565.0
1963	49.2	8.2	24.6	4.1	62.1	10.4	39.6	596.7
1964	46.0	7.2	26.1	4.1	69.2	10.8	37.8	637.7

1965	51.1	7.4	28.9	4.2	80.0	11.6	36.1	691.1
1966	58.6	7.8	31.4	4.2	85.1	11.3	36.9	756.0
1967	64.4	8.0	30.0	3.8	82.4	10.3	36.4	799.6
1968	76.5	8.8	36.1	4.1	89.1	10.2	40.5	873.4
1969	91.5	9.7	36.1	3.8	85.1	9.0	42.4	944.0
1970	88.8	8.9	30.6	3.1	71.4	7.2	42.9	992.7
1971	85.7	7.9	33.5	3.1	83.2	7.7	40.2	1077.6
1972	102.7	8.7	36.6	3.1	96.6	8.1	37.9	1185.9
1973	109.5	8.3	43.3	3.3	108.3	8.2	39.9	1326.4
1974	126.4	8.8	45.1	3.1	94.9	6.6	47.5	1434.2
1975	120.8	7.8	43.6	2.8	110.5	7.1	39.4	1549.2
1976	141.5	8.2	54.6	3.2	138.1	8.0	39.5	1718.0
1977	162.7	8.5	61.6	3.2	167.3	8.7	36.8	1918.3
1978	189.5	8.8	71.3	3.3	192.4	8.9	37.1	2163.9
1979	224.8	9.3	74.2	3.1	194.8	8.1	38.1	2417.8
1980	250.9	9.5	70.3	2.7	175.4	6.7	40.1	2631.7
1981	291.5	9.9	65.7	2.2	189.9	6.4	34.6	2957.8
1982	298.3	9.7	46.6	1.5	159.1	5.2	29.3	3069.3
1983	288.8	8.7	59.8	1.8	225.2	6.8	26.6	3304.8
1984	308.4	8.4	70.8	1.9	285.7	7.8	24.8	3662.8

Sources: U.S. Department of Commerce, Bureau of Economic Analysis, *National Income and Product Accounts of the U.S., 1929–1976,* tables 1.1, 1.11, and 3.2 (for 1929–1976); *Survey of Current Business,* July 1982 (for 1977–1978); July 1983 (for 1979); July 1984 (for 1980–1981); August 1984 (for 1982); and July 1985 (for 1983–1984).

a. Tax accruals on a national income and product accounts basis.

tion tax remained close to 44 percent of profits (both taxes and profits as measured in the national-income accounts) until 1962, when the investment tax credit was introduced. Four developments marked the period beginning about 1962 and culminating in 1981:

· Increased frequency of tax legislation

· Increased use of the tax system to encourage specific economic activities

· Severe distortion of the tax system by inflation

· An upward drift in the marginal rates applicable to "middle-class" taxpayers

These four developments are related to one another. First, the natural tendency of an unindexed progressive tax system to produce more than proportionate increase in revenue in response to growth of nominal income created a series of opportunities to cut taxes. The wartime evolution of the individual income tax into a mass tax at significant rates had sharply changed both the economics and the politics of federal taxation. Naturally, at high rates all the incentive effects of the tax were greatly magnified, and starting in 1962 policymakers sought, in particular, to diminish the tax burden on investment. Furthermore, high rates bearing even on "average" citizens raised the political payoff to achieving an exclusion or exemption on behalf of favored groups. Receiving compensation in the form of tax-free medical benefits rather than taxable cash came to have a strong attraction. All these tendencies were strongly reinforced by inflation, which created the need for tax reductions to offset revenue increases due to purely nominal increases in income. The legislative response was not to attempt a thoroughgoing correction of the measurement of income, together with indexing of the brackets and allowances. Instead, ad hoc measures were adopted that tended to narrow the base and exacerbate the system's instability and increasing complexity.

While it is difficult to draw conclusions from annual revenue statistics in the case of the corporation income tax (because current-year accruals depend so much on past decisions, and because corporate tax cuts often take the form of deferral rather than direct reduction), the path of corporation income tax accruals in Table A–8 does give an idea of the general effort undertaken by Congress to encourage investment.

Tables A–9 and A–10 summarize the evolution of the incentives operating on individuals in various relative income positions between 1965 and 1983. The substantial advance up to 1981 in both the ratio of taxes paid to income (the "average rate") and the tax applicable to the last dollar earned (the "marginal rate") for individuals, especially those at the median income level or above, is striking. It seems highly plausible that these rates were both cause (politically) and consequence (due to base narrowing) of the considerable expansion in tax expenditures. Witte (1982) has undertaken a careful classification of tax provisions reasonably regarded as tax expenditures and gives persuasive evidence that there was a very considerable expansion in their use during the post–World War II period and especially in the 1970s.

Table A–9. Effective (average) and marginal tax rates, federal individual income tax (single person, no dependents, selected income levels, 1960–1983)

Real income ($)	1960	1970[a]	1975	1979	1980	1982	1983
	Current income equivalent ($)[b]						
5,000	2,010	2,585	3,499	4,536	5,000	5,738	6,001
10,000	4,019	5,170	6,998	9,902	10,000	11,478	12,001
20,000	8,038	10,341	13,997	18,144	20,000	22,951	24,002
25,000	10,048	12,926	17,496	22,680	25,000	28,689	30,003
35,000	14,067	18,097	24,494	31,752	35,000	40,165	42,004
50,000	20,095	25,852	34,992	45,361	50,000	57,378	60,006
75,000	30,143	38,779	52,487	68,041	75,000	86,068	90,008
	Effective rates (%)						
5,000	12.0	7.5	4.0	3.9	5.0	5.7	5.7
10,000	15.5	13.8	11.4	10.9	11.8	11.5	10.8
20,000	19.3	17.0	16.7	17.9	19.2	19.0	17.4
25,000	21.0	18.7	19.0	20.9	21.9	21.3	19.6
35,000	24.4	21.1	23.2	24.9	26.3	25.6	23.7
50,000	29.6	24.8	27.7	30.0	32.1	31.0	28.5
75,000	36.7	30.2	34.4	37.5	39.1	35.7	34.0
	Marginal rates (%)						
5,000	20.0	16.8	16.0	16.0	16.0	16.0	15.0
10,000	22.0	21.5	21.0	19.0	21.0	19.0	19.0
20,000	30.0	25.6	22.7	30.0	34.0	31.0	28.0
25,000	34.0	27.7	31.0	34.0	39.0	35.0	32.0
35,000	43.0	31.8	38.0	44.0	44.0	44.0	40.0
50,000	50.0	41.0	45.0	55.0	55.0	50.0	50.0
75,000	62.0	51.2	60.0	63.0	63.0	50.0	50.0

Source: U.S. Treasury Department as reported in *Statistical Abstract of the United States,* 1984, table 527.

a. Rates for 1970 include tax surcharge.

b. Amount of adjusted gross income equivalent to adjusted gross income in 1980 dollars was calculated by using the NIPA personal consumption expenditure deflator (1972 = 100). The values of the deflators are as follows: 1960, 71.9; 1970, 92.5; 1975, 125.3; 1979, 162.3; 1980, 178.9; 1982, 205.3; and 1983, 214.7.

Table A–10. Effective (average) and marginal tax rates, federal individual income tax (married couple, two dependents,[a] selected income levels, 1960–1983)

Real income ($)[b]	1960	1970[c]	1975	1979	1980	1982	1983
	Effective rates (%)						
5,000	0.0	0.0	−10.0	−10.0	−10.0	−8.7	−8.7
10,000	6.1	5.8	1.2	1.4	3.7	4.6	4.7
20,000	12.2	11.4	10.2	10.3	11.3	11.6	10.9
25,000	13.7	12.9	12.1	12.8	14.0	14.2	13.4
35,000	16.1	15.3	16.1	17.4	18.8	18.6	17.4
50,000	19.0	18.3	20.5	22.8	24.2	24.0	22.3
75,000	23.6	23.3	26.8	29.4	31.2	30.2	27.8
	Marginal rates (%)						
5,000	0.0	0.0	−10.0	−10.0	0.0	0.0	12.5
10,000	20.0	16.8	26.0	26.5	16.0	14.0	15.0
20,000	22.0	19.5	18.5	21.0	24.0	22.0	19.0
25,000	22.0	22.6	22.0	24.0	28.0	29.0	26.0
35,000	26.0	25.6	28.0	32.0	37.0	39.0	35.0
50,000	30.0	32.8	39.0	43.0	44.0	44.0	40.0
75,000	43.0	43.0	50.0	54.0	54.0	49.0	44.0

Source: U.S. Treasury Department as reported in Statistical Abstract of the United States, 1984, table 527.

a. Only one spouse is assumed to work. The refundable earned-income credit is regarded as part of the income tax.

b. 1980 levels. For details of real income calculation, see Table A–9.

c. Rates for 1970 include tax surcharge.

The Economic Recovery Tax Act of 1981, which resulted from a Reagan administration initiative, was specifically designed to ameliorate the disincentives created by high marginal tax rates. The technique adopted was to cut individual tax rates and to reduce the burden of tax on saving and investment (including the part of the burden attributable to inflation) by providing more accelerated depreciation (the Accelerated Cost Recovery System) and expanding tax-favored saving instruments (for example, Individual Retirement Accounts). We can get a hint of the result of this legislation, including its revenue cost, in Tables A–8 through A–10. In an attempt to restore some of the revenue given up by the 1981 act, further legislation was passed in 1982 and 1984, which also took back a part of the investment-incentive effect of the 1981 law.

Table A–11. Taxes as a percentage of gross domestic product and of total tax revenues, selected countries, 1982[a]

Tax category	United States	France	Germany	Netherlands	Sweden	United Kingdom	Japan	Canada
As a percentage of GDP								
Total tax revenues	30.5	43.7	37.3	45.5	50.3	39.6	27.2	34.8
Individual income tax	11.5	5.6	10.8	10.9	20.5	11.2	6.9	12.4
Corporate income tax	2.1	2.2	1.9	3.1	1.7	3.8	5.4	2.8
Social Security taxes	8.4	19.8	13.5	18.9	15.3	8.0	8.3	3.9
Employee share[b]	4.2	6.2	6.3	10.9	0.6	3.1	4.1	1.4
Employer share	4.2	12.6	7.2	8.0	13.4	3.6	4.2	2.5
Property taxes	3.1	1.6	1.2	1.6	0.5	5.0	2.4	3.1
Sales and excise taxes	5.3	13.0	9.9	10.8	12.2	11.5	4.2	12.1
Other taxes	—	1.4	[c]	0.1	0.1	[c]	0.1	0.5
As a percentage of total taxes								
Total tax revenues	100.0	100.0	100.0	100.0	100.0	100.0	100.0	100.0
Individual income tax	37.8	12.9	28.9	23.9	40.8	28.4	25.3	35.6
Corporate income tax	7.0	5.1	5.1	6.8	3.3	9.6	19.7	8.2
Social Security taxes	27.7	45.4	36.2	41.6	30.5	20.2	30.4	11.3
Employee share[b]	13.8	14.4	16.8	24.0	1.1	7.9	15.0	4.1
Employer share	13.8	28.8	19.4	17.6	26.8	9.0	15.4	7.2
Property taxes	10.1	3.7	3.3	3.6	1.0	12.7	8.9	9.0
Sales and excise taxes	17.4	29.7	26.5	23.8	24.2	29.0	15.4	34.6
Other taxes	—	3.2	[c]	0.3	0.2	0.1	0.3	1.3

Source: Organization for Economic Development and Cooperation, *Revenue Statistics of Member Countries, 1965–1983,* Paris, 1984, as reproduced in U.S. Treasury Department (1984), vol. 1.
a. Includes all levels of government.
b. Includes taxes of self-employed.
c. Less than 0.1 percent.

Table A-12. Comparison of individual tax systems in selected countries

Tax category	United States (1984)	United States (proposed)	France	Germany	Netherlands	Sweden	United Kingdom (1986 projected)	Japan	Canada
Marginal tax rates (national)	11%–50%[a]	15%–35%[a]	5%–65%	22%–56%	16%–72%	6%–52%[b]	30%–60%	10.5%–70%[c]	6%–34%[d]
Average tax rate of median-income taxpayer in 1982[e]									
Single	13.8%	10.7%[g]	0.8%	15.9%	10.3%	30.0%	21.5%	9.6%	14.9%
Married[f]	7.0%	4.5%	—	9.2%	8.0%	27.0%	16.8%	1.4%	−0.4%
Indexing	Brackets; zero bracket amount and exemptions (1985)	Same	Brackets	No	Brackets	Brackets allowances; adjusted yearly	Brackets	No	Brackets; personal exemptions; certain deductions
Capital gains									
Occasional sales of portfolio securities	40% of net gain taxable	Taxable; basis indexed	Exempt	Exempt	Exempt	Under 2 years fully taxed; over 2 years 40% taxed	30% of gain above indexed exempt amount; basis indexed	Exempt	Generally 50% of net gain taxable; for certain investment plans, 12.5% of accrued indexed gain
Sale of principal residence	Deferred; $125,000 exemption if seller over age 55	Same	Exempt	Exempt if held more than 2 years	Exempt	Taxable with reliefs	Exempt	Exempt up to 30 million yen (approximately $125,000)	Exempt
Wealth tax	No	No	Yes	Yes	Yes	Yes	No	No	No
General sales tax	No[h]	No[h]	VAT[i]	VAT[i]	VAT[i]	VAT[i]	VAT[i]	No	Yes[j]

a. Does not include state taxes, which, where applicable, range from 0.5 to 16 percent. A few cities also impose income taxes at rates of 0.6 to 4.3 percent. These taxes are deductible from the federal tax base under existing law but not under the proposed broad-based tax.

b. Does not include local tax, estimated at 30 percent, which is deductible from the national tax base.

c. Does not include prefecture inhabitants' tax, which applies at 2 or 4 percent, and municipal inhabitants' tax at 2.5 to 14 percent; these taxes are not deductible from the national tax base.

d. Does not include surcharges for provincial income tax (48 percent in Ontario).

e. Compiled by the OECD from national statistics. Income taxes only; does not include Social Security taxes.

f. Married taxpayer, two children, one wage earner.

g. Since the 1982 data do not include the full effect of the tax cuts enacted in 1981, a better comparison between the two U.S. sets of rates may be obtained by noting that if the current law rules had continued in effect, in 1986 the average tax of the median-income taxpayer would have been 11.4 percent for a single taxpayer and 6.4 percent for a married taxpayer with two children.

h. However, most states impose sales taxes at the retail or manufacturers' level.

i. Value-added tax.

j. Imposed at the manufacturers' or importers' level. In addition, most provinces impose retail sales taxes.

Table A–13. Comparison of corporate income taxes in selected countries

Tax category	United States (1984)	United States (proposed)	France	Germany	Netherlands	Sweden	United Kingdom (1986 projected)	Japan	Canada
National tax rate	46[a]	33[a]	50	56[b]	43	32[c]	35	43.3/33.3[d]	46[e]
Dividend relief to shareholders									
Credit or reduced rate	No	Reduced rate[f]	Credit	Both	No	No	Credit	Both	Credit
Percentage of double tax relieved	0	50%	50%[g]	100%[h]	0	0	80%[i]	38%[j]	40%[k]
Indexing									
Depreciable assets	No	Yes	Occasional revaluation	No	Yes	No	No	No	No
Inventory	No[l]	Yes	Occasional revaluation	No[l]	No[l]	No	No	Yes[m]	Yes[n]
Liabilities	No	Interest[o]	No	No	No	No	No	No	No

Table A-13 (continued)

Tax category	United States (1984)	United States (proposed)	France	Germany	Netherlands	Sweden	United Kingdom (1986 projected)	Japan	Canada
Sample depreciation calculation equipment									
First year	14.24[p]		35%	30%	Negotiated	30%	25%	25%	50%
Years 1–3	55.1[p]		72.5%	65.7%	Negotiated	51%	57.8%	57.8%	100%
Write-off period	5 years		[q]	[q]	Negotiated	[q]	[q]	[q]	—
Investment credit	10%	No	No	No	12%	No	No	No	15.7%
Present value, depreciation, and credit, as percentage of investment expense[r]									
6% inflation	100%	76%	78%	75%	—	75%	71%	71%	129%*
4% inflation	103%	76%	81%	79%	—	79%	76%	76%	130%
Structures									
First year	9%		12.5%	2.5%	Negotiated	3%	4%	2.3%	5.0%
Years 1–3	26%		33.0%	7.5%	Negotiated	9%	11.5%	6.9%	14.3%
Write-off period	18 years		0	40 years	Negotiated	33 years	0	44 years	0
Investment credit	No	No	No	No	No	No	No	No	No
Present value, depreciation, and investment expense[p]									
6% inflation	54	42	56	25	—	30	29	23	33
4% inflation	59	42	61	30	—	36	33	28	38

Treatment of foreign
income and taxes[t]

Exemption	No	No	Generally[u]	No	Generally[u]	No	No	No	No
Credit	Overall	Per country	No	Per country	No	Per country	Per country and item	Overall	Per country
Deduction	Election[v]	Election[v]	Yes	Election[v]	Yes	Election[v]	Election[v]	Election[v]	Election[v]

a. State income taxes range from 0 to 12 percent. Some local income taxes also apply, typically at 1 or 2 percent, but at 9 percent in New York City. The state and local taxes are deductible from the federal tax base.

b. A 36 percent tax imposed on distributed profits is creditable to shareholders. There is also a local tax of about 15 percent, deductible from the national tax base.

c. There is a 30 percent local tax, deductible from the national tax base.

d. The lower rate applies on distributed profits. There are also a prefectural inhabitants' tax and a local inhabitants' tax (5 percent and 12.3 percent, respectively, of the national tax) and a prefectural enterprise tax of 12 percent of taxable income. Only the latter is deductible from the national tax base.

e. There are also provincial taxes of about 10 to 15 percent, of which 10 percentage points are credited against the federal tax. The federal tax shown is not reduced by that credit.

f. Corporations will be permitted to deduct a portion (50 percent when fully phased in) of the dividends they distribute out of taxed profits.

g. 25 percentage points of the corporate tax (= 50 percent of the dividend received) are added to the taxable income of the shareholder, who claims a refundable credit of the same amount.

h. The 36 percent tax on distributed profits (= 56.25 percent of the dividend received) is added to the taxable income of the shareholder, who claims a refundable credit of the same amount.

i. 27.86 percentage points of the corporate tax (= 42.85 percent of the dividend received) are added to the taxable income of the shareholder, who claims a refundable credit of the same amount.

j. The taxpayer claims a credit equal to 10 percent of the dividend received. The credit is not added to taxable income.

k. 18.36 percentage points of the corporate tax (= 34 percent of the dividend received) are added to the taxable income of the shareholder, who claims a nonrefundable credit of the same amount.

l. However, LIFO (last-in, first-out) valuation of inventories may be used. In the United States, if LIFO is used for tax purposes it must also be used for book purposes.

m. 2.5 percent of the book value of certain inventories and securities may be allocated to a special reserve fund against price rises, and LIFO may be used to value inventories.

n. An annual 3 percent inventory write-off is allowed.

o. Inflation premium excluded from interest receipts and payments.

p. Includes effect of basis adjustment for one-half of investment tax credit.

q. Declining balance ("open accounts") method used; write-off period not defined.

r. Assumes 4 percent real interest; considers equity investment only.

s. Investment credit translated into a deduction at a 46 percent corporate rate.

t. Statutory rules; may be modified in tax treaties. Similar rules apply with respect to foreign income and taxes of individuals.

u. Business income is generally exempt from tax; passive investment income is generally taxable with a deduction for foreign taxes paid.

v. Taxpayers may elect to deduct otherwise creditable foreign income taxes paid. In general, the election applies to all creditable foreign taxes paid or accrued that year.

Table A–14. Summary comparison of value-added taxes in selected countries

Tax category	France	Germany	Netherlands	Sweden	United Kingdom
Rates (%)					
Basic rate	18.6	14	19	23.46	15
Higher rates	33.3	—	—	—	—
Lower rates	7.0, 5.5	6.5	5	12.87, 3.95	—
Principal exemptions[a]					
Exports	Yes	Yes	Yes	Yes	Yes
Real property transfers	Some	Yes	Yes	Yes	Yes
Financial transactions	Most	Yes	Yes	Yes	Yes
Transfers of a business	—	Yes	Yes	Yes	Yes
Professional services	Many	—	—	—	—
Communications	—	—	Yes	—	—
Construction	—	—	—	—	Yes
Periodicals	—	—	—	Yes	—
Medicine	—	—	5%	Yes	Yes
Food	5.5%	6.5%	5%	—	Yes
Books	7.0%	6.5%	5%	—	Yes
Fuel	—	—	—	Yes	Yes
Transportation	7.0%	—	—	—	—

Source: U.S. Treasury Department (1984), vol. 1.

a. Some of the transactions classified as exempt may be taxable at a zero rate. The difference is that an exemption does not necessarily give rise to a refund of tax paid at prior stages, whereas a zero rate does carry a full credit. Exports, for example, are taxed at a zero rate with a refund of tax previously paid.

The International Context

Table A–11 presents an overview of the tax systems employed in a selection of major industrial economies. Since borrowing is not included, we cannot immediately discover from the table the full extent of the government draw on the public. Furthermore, as noted, many more or less arbitrary decisions are made in specifying what government intake and outlays are. But the figures no doubt correctly convey the impression that a significantly larger fraction of economic activity passes through government budgets in the European countries than in the United States, with Canada and the United States a step below, and Japan a step lower still. By and large the higher fraction of GNP raised in taxes in the European countries corresponds to higher levels of transfers to individuals. If we were to look at the spending side of the budgets, we would see a rough correspondence between the level of transfers and the combined levels of payroll and sales and excise taxes (including value-added taxes). Tables A–12 through A–14 provide for reference further information on the tax systems of the same eight countries and include in the comparison the features of the U.S. Treasury Department's November 1984 proposal.

Bibliography

Aaron, Henry A., ed. 1976. *Inflation and the Income Tax.* Washington, D.C.: Brookings Institution.

——1981. *The Value Added Tax: Lessons from Europe.* Washington, D.C.: Brookings Institution.

Aaron, Henry A., and Harvey Galper. 1984. "Reforming the Federal Tax System." In *Economic Choices, 1984,* ed. Alice M. Rivlin. Washington, D.C.: Brookings Institution.

——1985. *Assessing Tax Reform.* Washington, D.C.: Brookings Institution.

Allison, Michael T., Don Fullerton, and John H. Makin. 1985. "Tax Reform: A Study of Some Major Proposals." Working paper no. 2. Washington, D.C.: American Enterprise Institute.

American Bar Association, Committee on Simplification, Section of Taxation. 1979. "Evaluation of the Proposed Model Comprehensive Income Tax." *Tax Lawyer,* 32(3):563–686.

——1982. "Complexity and the Personal Consumption Tax." *Tax Lawyer,* 35(2):415–442.

American Law Institute. 1982. *Federal Tax Project, Subchapter C.* Philadelphia.

Andrews, William D. 1972. "Personal Deductions in an Ideal Income Tax." *Harvard Law Review,* 86(December):309–385.

——1974. "A Consumption-Type or Cash Flow Personal Income Tax." *Harvard Law Review,* 87(April):1113–88.

——1983. "The Achilles' Heel of the Comprehensive Income Tax." In Walker and Bloomfield (1983).

Atkinson, Anthony, and Nicholas Stern. 1974. "Pigou, Taxation and Public Goods." *Review of Economic Studies,* 41(January):119–128.

Auerbach, Alan J. 1982. "The New Economics of Accelerated Depreciation." *Boston College Law Review,* 30(September):1327–55.

——1983a. "Stockholder Tax Rates and Firm Attributes." *Journal of Public Economics,* 21(July):107–127.

——1983b. "Taxation, Corporate Financial Policy, and the Cost of Capital." *Journal of Economic Literature,* 21:905–940.

——1983c. "Corporate Taxation in the U.S." *Brookings Papers on Economic Activity.*

Auerbach, J. Alan, and Dale Jorgenson. 1980. "Inflation-Proof Depreciation of Assets." *Harvard Business Review,* September/October, pp. 113–118.

Auerbach, J. Alan, and Lawrence Kotlikoff. 1983. "Investment versus Savings Incentives: The Size of the Bang for the Buck and the Potential for Self-Financing Tax Cuts." In *The Economic Consequences of Government Deficits,* ed. L. H. Meyer. Boston: Kluer-Nijhoff.

Ballard, Charles L., John B. Shoven, and John Whalley. 1985. "General Equilibrium Computations of the Marginal Welfare Cost of Taxes in the United States." *American Economic Review,* 75(March):128–138.

Ballard, Charles L., Don Fullerton, John B. Shoven, and John Whalley. 1985. *An Equilibrium Model for Tax Policy Analysis.* Chicago: University of Chicago Press.

Bentz, Mary F. 1984. "Estate Tax Returns." *Statistics of Income Bulletin,* 4(Fall):1–12.

Bhagwati, Jagdish N. 1971. "The Generalized Theory of Distortions and Welfare." In *Trade, Balance of Payments, and Growth,* ed. J. N. Bhagwati et al. Amsterdam: North Holland.

Bittker, Boris. 1969. "Accounting for Federal Tax Subsidies in the National Budget." *National Tax Journal,* 22:244.

Black, Fischer. 1976. "The Dividend Puzzle." *Journal of Portfolio Management,* Winter.

Board of Governors of the Federal Reserve System. 1984. *Balance Sheets for the U.S. Economy, 1945–83.* Washington, D.C.

Boskin, Michael J. 1978. "Taxation, Saving, and the Rate of Interest." *Journal of Political Economy,* 86(April) pt. 2:3–27.

——Forthcoming. *The Real Federal Budget.* Cambridge, Mass.: Harvard University Press.

Boskin, Michael J., and Laurence J. Kotlikoff. 1985. "Public Debt and U.S. Saving: A New Test of the Neutrality Hypothesis." Mimeo. Cambridge, Mass.: National Bureau of Economic Research.

Bosworth, Barry P. 1984. *Tax Incentives and Economic Growth.* Washington, D.C.: Brookings Institution.

Bradford, David F. 1980a. "The Case for a Personal Consumption Tax." In *What Should Be Taxed: Income or Expenditure,* ed. Joseph A. Pechman. Washington, D.C.: Brookings Institution.

——1980b. "The Economics of Tax Policy towards Savings." In *The Government and Capital Formation,* ed. George M. von Furstenberg. Cambridge, Mass.: Ballinger.

——1981. "Issues in the Design of Savings and Investment Incentives." In Hulten (1981).

——1983. "The Choice between Income and Consumption Taxes." In Walker and Bloomfield (1983).

Bradford, David F., and Don Fullerton. 1981. "Pitfalls in the Construction and Use of Effective Tax Rates." In Hulten (1981).

Bradford, David F., and the U.S. Treasury Tax Policy Staff. 1984. *Blueprints for Basic Tax Reform,* 2nd ed. Washington, D.C.: Tax Analysts. (Orig. pub. as U.S. Treasury Department, 1977.)

Bradley, Bill. 1984. *The Fair Tax.* New York: Pocket Books.

Brennan, Geoffrey, and James M. Buchanan. 1980. *The Power to Tax: Analytical Foundations of a Fiscal Constitution.* Cambridge: Cambridge University Press.

Browning, Edgar. 1976. "The Marginal Cost of Public Funds." *Journal of Political Economy,* 74(April):283–298.

Browning, Edgar, and William Johnson. 1979. *The Distribution of the Tax Burden.* Washington, D.C.: American Enterprise Institute.

Buchanan, James. 1983. "The Flat Rate Tax and the Fiscal Appetite." In Walker and Bloomfield (1983).

Burton, David R. 1984. "Major Tax Reform Proposals at a Glance." *Tax Notes,* 23(June):1095–1100.

Conable, Barber B. 1983. "The Political Problems of Implementing a Comprehensive Income Tax." In Walker and Bloomfield (1983).

Conlin, Joseph R. 1984. *The Morrow Book of Quotations in American History.* New York: William Morrow.

Cox, Dennis. 1984. "Raising Revenue in the Underground Economy." *National Tax Journal,* 37(September):283–288.

Dixit, Avinash. 1984. "Tax Reform as Industrial Policy." Mimeo. Princeton, N.J.: Woodrow Wilson School, Princeton University.

Feld, Alan L. 1982. *Tax Policy and Corporate Concentration.* Lexington, Mass.: D. C. Heath.

Feldstein, Martin. 1976. "On the Theory of Tax Reform." *Journal of Public Economics,* 6(July/August):77–104.

——— 1983. *Inflation, Tax Rules, and Capital Formation.* Chicago: University of Chicago Press.

Feldstein, Martin, and Joel Slemrod. 1978. "Inflation and the Excess Taxation of Capital Gains on Corporate Stock." *National Tax Journal,* 31(June):107–118; reprinted in Feldstein (1983).

——— 1980. "Personal Taxation, Portfolio Choice and the Effect of the Corporation Income Tax." *Journal of Political Economy,* 88(5):854–866.

Fiekowsky, Seymour. 1980. "The Relation of Tax Expenditures to the Distribution of the 'Fiscal Burden.'" *Canadian Taxation,* 2(Winter):211–219.

Fullerton, Don. 1984. "Which Effective Tax Rate?" *National Tax Journal,* 37(March):23–41.

——— 1985. "The Indexation of Interest, Depreciation, and Capital Gains: A Model of Investment Incentives." Working paper no. 5. Washington, D.C.: American Enterprise Institute.

Galper, Harvey, and Eugene Steuerle. 1983. "Tax Incentives for Saving." *Brookings Review,* 2(Winter):16–23.

Galper, Harvey, and Eric Toder. 1984. "Transfer Elements in the Taxation of Income from Capital." In *Economic Transfers in the United States,* ed. Marilyn Moon. Chicago: University of Chicago Press.

Goode, Richard. 1977. "The Economic Definition of Income." In *Comprehensive Income Taxation,* ed. Joseph A. Pechman. Washington, D.C.: Brookings Institution.

Gordon, Roger H., and David F. Bradford. 1980. "Taxation and the Stock Market Valuation of Capital Gains and Dividends: Theory and Empirical Results." *Journal of Public Economics,* 14(October):109–136.

Gordon, Roger H., and Burton G. Malkiel. 1981. "Corporation Finance." In

How Taxes Affect Economic Behavior, ed. Henry A. Aaron and Joseph A. Pechman. Washington, D.C.: Brookings Institution.

Gravelle, Jane G. 1981. "The Social Cost of Nonneutral Taxation: Estimates for Nonresidential Capital." In Hulten (1981).

Greenwood, Daphne. 1983. "An Estimation of U.S. Family Wealth and Its Distribution from Microdata, 1973." *Review of Income and Wealth,* 29(March):23–44.

Guttman, George. 1983. "The Single-Rate Income Tax: Policy Questions and Technical Issues." *Tax Notes,* 21(November):539–557.

Haig, R. M. 1921. *The Federal Income Tax.* New York: Columbia University Press.

Hall, Robert E., and Alvin Rabushka. 1983. *Low Tax, Simple Tax, Flat Tax.* New York: McGraw-Hill.

———1985. *The Flat Tax.* Stanford, Calif.: Hoover Institution Press.

Harberger, Arnold. 1962. "The Incidence of the Corporation Income Tax." *Journal of Political Economy,* 70(June):215–240.

———1964. "Taxation, Resource Allocation, and Welfare." In *The Role of Direct and Indirect Taxes in the Federal Revenue System.* Princeton, N.J.: Princeton University Press.

Hendershott, Patrick H., and David C. Ling. 1984. "Trading and the Tax Shelter Value of Depreciable Real Estate." *National Tax Journal,* 37(June):213–223.

———1985. "The Treasury's Tax Reform Proposal and Housing." *Tax Notes,* 26(March):1041–46.

Henderson, Yolanda K. 1984. "Tax Reform: An Item for Any Industrial Policy Agenda." In *The Industrial Policy Debate,* ed. Chalmers Johnson. San Francisco: ICS Press.

Hochschild, Jennifer L. 1981. *What's Fair? American Beliefs about Distributive Justice.* Cambridge, Mass.: Harvard University Press.

Houseman, Jerry A. 1981. "Labor Supply." In *How Taxes Affect Labor Supply,* ed. Henry J. Aaron and Joseph A. Pechman. Washington, D.C.: Brookings Institution.

Hulten, Charles R., ed. 1981. *Depreciation, Inflation and the Taxation of Income from Capital.* Washington, D.C.: The Urban Institute.

Hulten, Charles R., and Frank C. Wykoff. 1981. "The Measurement of Economic Depreciation." In Hulten (1981).

Institute for Fiscal Studies. 1978. *The Structure and Reform of Direct Taxation: The Report of a Committee Chaired by Professor J. E. Meade.* London: George Allen and Unwin.

Jones, Nigel. 1981. "The Family, Inheritance, and the Intergenerational Transmission of Inequality." *Journal of Political Economy,* 86(October):928–958.

Jorgenson, Dale W., and Martin A. Sullivan. 1981. "Inflation and Corporate Capital Recovery." In Hulten (1981).

Jorgenson, Dale W., and Kun-Young Yun. 1984. "Tax Policy and Capital Allocation." Discussion paper no. 1107. Cambridge, Mass.: Harvard Institute of Economic Research, Harvard University.

Kaldor, Nicholas. 1955. *An Expenditure Tax.* London: George Allen and Unwin, 1955.

Kay, John A., and Mervyn A. King. 1983. *The British Tax System,* 3rd ed. Oxford: Oxford University Press.

King, Mervyn A. 1977. *Public Policy and the Corporation.* London: Chapman and Hall.

——1980. "Savings and Taxation." In *Public Policy and the Tax System,* ed. G. A. Hughes and G. M. Heal. London: George Allen and Unwin.

King, Mervyn A., and Don Fullerton. 1984. *The Taxation of Income from Capital: A Comparative Study of the United States, the United Kingdom, Sweden, and West Germany.* Chicago: University of Chicago Press.

Klein, William A. 1976. *Policy Analysis of the Federal Income Tax.* Mineola, N.Y.: Foundation Press.

Kotlikoff, Laurence J. 1983. "National Savings and Economic Policy: The Efficacy of Investment vs. Savings Incentives." *American Economic Review,* 73(May):82–87.

——1984. "Taxation and Savings: A Neoclassical Perspective." *Journal of Economic Literature,* 22(December):1576–1629.

Krueger, Anne O. 1974. "The Political Economy of the Rent-Seeking Society." *American Economic Review,* 64(June):291–303.

Lind, Robert, et al. 1982. *Discounting for Time and Risk in Energy Policy.* Washington, D.C.: Resources for the Future.

Lodin, Sven-Olof. 1978. *Progressive Expenditure Tax — An Alternative?* Report of the 1972 Government Commission on Taxation. Stockholm: LiberForlag. (Orig. pub. as *Progressivutgiftsskatt — ett alternativ?* Stockholm: Statens Offentliga Utredningar 1976:62.)

Manvel, Allen D. 1984. "Reported Income Sources by Income Level." *Tax Notes,* 22(January):340–341.

McLure, Charles E., Jr. 1983. "Value Added Tax: Has the Time Come?" In Walker and Bloomfield (1983).

Menchik, Paul L. 1980a. "The Importance of Material Inheritance: The Financial Link between Generations." In *Modeling the Distribution and Intergenerational Transmission of Wealth,* ed. James Smith. Chicago: University of Chicago Press.

——1980b. "Primogeniture, Equal Sharing, and the U.S. Distribution of Wealth." *Quarterly Journal of Economics,* 94(March):299–316.

Miller, Merton H. 1977. "Debt and Taxes." *Journal of Finance,* 32(May):261–275.

Miller, Merton H., and Myron Scholes. 1982. "Dividends and Taxes: Some Empirical Evidence." *Journal of Political Economy,* 90(December):1132–42.

Nicholas, Ted. 1984. *How to Form Your Own Corporation without a Lawyer for under $50.* Wilmington, Del.: Enterprise Publishing.

Park, Thae S. 1983. "Personal Income and Adjusted Gross Income, 1977–81." *Survey of Current Business,* 63(April):28–33.

Pechman, Joseph A. 1983. *Federal Tax Policy,* 4th ed. Washington, D.C.: Brookings Institution.

————1985. *Who Paid the Taxes, 1966–85?* Washington, D.C.: Brookings Institution.

Pechman, Joseph A., ed. 1977. *Comprehensive Income Taxation.* Washington, D.C.: Brookings Institution.

Poterba, James M., and Lawrence H. Summers. 1984. "The Economic Effects of Dividend Taxation." Working paper no. 1353. Cambridge, Mass.: National Bureau of Economic Research.

Ross, Stanford G. 1985. "A Perspective on International Tax Policy." *Tax Notes,* 26(February):701–713.

Shoven, John B., and Jeremy I. Bulow. 1975. "Inflation Accounting and Nonfinancial Corporate Profits: Physical Assets." *Brookings Papers on Economic Activity,* 3:557–611.

————1976. "Inflation Accounting and Nonfinancial Corporate Profits: Financial Assets and Liabilities." *Brookings Papers on Economic Activity,* 1:15–57.

Simons, H. C. 1938. *Personal Income Taxation.* Chicago: University of Chicago Press.

Slemrod, Joel, and Nikki Sorum. 1984. "The Compliance Cost of the U.S. Individual Income Tax System." *National Tax Journal,* 37(December):461–474.

Smith, James D. 1975. "White Wealth and Black People: The Distribution of Personal Wealth in Washington, D.C., in 1967." In *The Personal Distribution of Wealth,* ed. James D. Smith. New York: National Bureau of Economic Research.

Stein, Herbert. 1984. "After the Ball." *The AEI Economist,* December:1–8.

Steuerle, C. Eugene. 1985. *Taxes, Loans, and Inflation: How the Nation's Wealth Becomes Misallocated.* Washington, D.C.: Brookings Institution.

Stiglitz, Joseph E. 1983. "Some Aspects of the Taxation of Capital Gains." *Journal of Public Economics,* 21(July):257–294.

Stuart, Charles. 1984. "Welfare Costs per Dollar of Additional Tax Revenue in the United States." *American Economic Review,* 74(June):352–362.

Summers, Lawrence H. 1983. "The Non-adjustment of Nominal Interest Rates: A Study of the Fisher Effect." In *Macroeconomics: Prices and Quantities,* ed. J. Tobin. Washington, D.C.: Brookings Institution.

————1984. "The After-Tax Rate of Return Affects Private Savings." *American Economic Review,* 74(May):249–253.

Sunley, Emil M. 1984. "Statement on Tax Simplification." Testimony before the Ways and Means Committee of the U.S. House of Representatives, September 26.

Surrey, Stanley S. 1969. Speech to Money Marketeers, New York City, November 15; reprinted in *Annual Report of the Secretary of the Treasury for the Fiscal Year 1968,* Washington, D.C.: U.S. Government Printing Office, 1969.

————1973. *Pathways to Tax Reform: The Concept of Tax Expenditures.* Cambridge, Mass.: Harvard University Press.

Surrey, Stanley S., and W. F. Hellmuth. 1969. "The Tax Expenditure Budget — Response to Professor Bittker." *National Tax Journal,* 22:528.

Surrey, Stanley S., and Paul R. McDaniel. 1985. *Tax Expenditures.* Cambridge, Mass.: Harvard University Press.

Thorning, Margo. 1984. "Congressional Proposals for Fundamental Tax Reform. *Tax Notes,* 24(July):494–500.

U.S. Congress, Congressional Budget Office. 1983. *Revising the Individual Income Tax.* Washington, D.C.

——1984. *Reducing the Deficit: Spending and Revenue Options.* Washington, D.C.

——1985. *Revising the Corporate Income Tax.* Washington, D.C.

U.S. Government. 1984a. *Economic Report of the President and Annual Report of the Council of Economic Advisors.* Washington, D.C.: U.S. Government Printing Office.

——1984b. *Special Analyses, Budget of the United States Government, FY 1985.* Washington, D.C.: U.S. Government Printing Office.

——1985. *The President's Tax Proposals to the Congress for Fairness, Growth, and Simplicity.* Washington, D.C.: U.S. Government Printing Office.

U.S. House of Representatives. 1913. Committee report of the "Act of October 3, 1913" establishing the income tax, no. 5. 63rd Cong. 1st sess.; reprinted in IRS 1939-1, pt. 2, C.B.3.

U.S. Internal Revenue Service. 1984. *Statistics of Income Bulletin,* 4(Summer).

U.S. Senate, Committee on Finance. 1984. *Deficit Reduction Act of 1984,* vol. 3. Senate report 98–169. 19th Congress, 2nd Session.

U.S. Treasury Department. 1977. *Blueprints for Basic Tax Reform.* Washington, D.C.: U.S. Government Printing Office; reissued as Bradford et al. (1984).

——1984. *Tax Reform for Fairness, Simplicity, and Economic Growth,* vols. 1, 2, and 3. Washington, D.C.: U.S. Government Printing Office.

Walker, Charles E., and Mark A. Bloomfield, eds. 1983. *New Directions in Federal Tax Policy for the 1980's.* Cambridge, Mass.: Ballinger.

Warren, Alvin, and Alan J. Auerbach. 1982. "Transferability of Tax Incentives and the Fiction of Safe-Harbor Leasing." *Harvard Law Review,* 95(June):1752–86.

Witte, John F. 1982. "Incremental Theory and Income Tax Policy: The Problem of Too Much, Not Too Little, Change." Mimeo. Madison: Department of Political Science, University of Wisconsin.

——1985. *The Politics and Development of the Federal Income Tax.* Madison: University of Wisconsin Press.

Index

Aaron-Galper proposal, 10, 83, 89, 139
Ability-to-pay taxes, 150, 151
Accelerated Cost Recovery System
  (ACRS), 8, 52–53, 241, 272–273
Accelerated depreciation: as investment
  incentive, 210, 211; without inflation,
  215, 219; with inflation, 232–233, 234
Accounting: for income, 25–27; in
  current U.S. income tax system, 28–30;
  for gifts and bequests, 30–31; for
  value-added taxes, 61–64, 321, 327,
  328; with linked tax accounts, 65, 66,
  328; for saving and investment
  transactions, 290; for Treasury I plan,
  297; with consumption strategy, 313
Accretion-type tax, 32
Accrual income: defined, 19, 34n; in
  example of accounting for income, 26;
  in current U.S. tax system, 28–30
Accrual-income system: and tax reform,
  7–8, 9–10; tax form, 32–34; wages and
  salaries, 34–36; business expenses, 36;
  pensions and retirement plans, 36–37;
  gifts, inheritances, and bequests,
  37–38; interest, 38–46; dividends, 46;
  capital assets, 46–50, 193; trusts, 50;
  business receipts, expenses, and
  allowances, 50–54; allocated share of
  corporate earnings, 54–56; imputed income from durables, 56; itemized
  deductions, 56–57; vs. existing system,
  57–58; corporate taxation with,
  115–119, 127, 128, 129; tax equity with,
  157–167; distortion of labor supply
  choices, 184–185; fringe benefits, 186;
  saving vs. investing, 187–188; and
  portfolio distortions, 201–202; human
  capital, 205–206; tax expenditures,
  263–265; complexity, 271, 279–280;
  transition to, 285–311; reasons for
  dominance, 315–316
Add-on tax: corporation, 117–119, 129;
  universal, 320–329; two tiered, 329–334
Arbitrage. *See* Tax arbitrage

Asset Depreciation Range (ADR) system,
  240
Assets, 22–23; depreciable, 51–53;
  intangible, 112; prices, 143–145; foreign, 191–192, 195–197, 219–220, 308;
  influence of taxes, 202; durability, 221,
  237–238. *See also* Capital assets;
  Consumer durables
Auerbach-Jorgenson method, 53

Bank demand deposits, 86–87
Bankruptcy, 198–199
Bank services, 79–80
Base-broadening approach, 8–9
Basis, of capital assets sold, 46–50
Benefits, employee. *See* Fringe benefits
Benefit taxes, 150
Bequests, 20–21; in current income tax
  system, 29–30; accounting for, 30–31;
  in accrual-income tax system, 37–38,
  316; in value-added tax system, 71; in
  retail sales tax system, 74; in Simple
  Flat Tax system, 79, 81; in personal
  cash-flow tax system, 89; in *Blueprints*
  Cash-Flow Tax system, 97n; tax equity
  problems with, 157–160; distribution
  of, 169–173; tax reform for, 291
Blueprints for Basic Tax Reform, 9–10,
  89–94, 95–98
Bond option, taxable, 244
Bonds: tax-exempt vs. taxable, 38, 40,
  243–255; inflation and, 45
Borrowing: in accrual income system,
  41–42; in consumption-type rules, 98,
  317, 318; effect of tax-exempt bonds,
  254–255
Budget deficits, wealth effect, 192
Business: effect on individual income,
  50–54; tax complexity, 271–272,
  274–275
Business expenses: employee, 34–36;
  capital, 50–54
Business income, 331
Business tax, 76–77